Multimedia Introduction to Programming Using Java

ProgramLive CD-ROM included

Multimedia Introduction to Programming Using Java

ProgramLive CD-ROM Included

David Gries
Paul Gries

With 420 Illustrations

David Gries
Department of Computer Science
Cornell University
Ithaca, NY 14853-7501
USA
gries@cs.cornell.edu

Paul Gries
Department of Computer Science
University of Toronto
Toronto, Ontario M5S 3G4
Canada
pgries@cs.toronto.edu

CD-ROM: Courtesy *DataDescription.*
DataDescription, Inc.
840 Hanshaw Rd., Suite 9
Ithaca, NY 14850

ISBN 0-387-22681-8   Printed on acid-free paper.

Printed in the United States of America.   (MP)

9 8 7 6 5 4 3 2 1   SPIN 11019312

springeronline.com

To the women in our lives:
Anne
Elaine
Petra
Susan
Sage

Preface

This text is an introduction to programming using the Java programming language. It differs from most other such texts in several ways.

The livetext ProgramLive

Accompanying the text is a CD, which is itself a complete multimedia text on programming in Java. This CD acts like a book: you can turn the pages, look at the table of contents, the glossary, the index, and so forth. And because it is computerized, you can get to a particular page from the table of contents or the index with a click of your mouse.

Each page of the CD contains recorded lectures with synchronized animation. These lectures teach, using narration and animation, in a way that is impossible in a paper text. For example, students can watch execution of a method call, seeing the frame for the call being drawn and later erased. They can see the step by step development of a method body using step-wise refinement. They can see what abstraction means in a program, as they read a loop body in terms of an English statement and an increment of a counter, then have everything disappear from view except the English statement, and see its implementation.

An instructor can show some of these animated lectures in class —you would be amazed at how much energy that saves. Moreover, these lectures are repeatable: students can watch them at home.

The CD also contains all the programs that are used in this text, as well as material for over 35 guided closed-lab sessions.

Thus, this multimedia CD is a significant step forward in the kinds of materials that we give our students. It has been used successfully in a self-paced (no-lecture) and in a distance-learning course.

Activity 1-1.2

In this paper text, the lefthand margin contains many references to the CD (like the one on the left of this paragraph), emphasizing the places where the student might learn better by listening to (and watching) an animated lecture.

Using DrJava or BlueJ

This text makes a second departure from the norm. Typically in a course, students have several assignments that call for writing and testing Java programs. But students do not practice much outside of those assignments, so they do not become fluent in Java by the end of the semester. The emergence of DrJava, a new IDE from Rice University, can change this mode of operation. DrJava contains an "Interactions pane", where one can type any expression or statement and have it evaluated or executed immediately, *without having to have a full Java program*. There is no need for a class and no need for a method `main` with a `String[]` parameter. There is no more need for magic! Beginning students can use the Interactions pane to practice; until they write a full class, there is no need to compile. For example, after a lecture on `int` and **double** expressions, they can practice with such expressions and gain a real understanding of integer division, the remainder operation, and casting. Also, after a first lecture on creating an object and referencing its components, they can practice doing just that, without having to have a full program. Self-help exercises after many sections of this text are designed to get the students to practice with Java more frequently. Studying should involve doing as well as reading.

We have found DrJava to be so useful that we use it almost every day in lecture (with a projector that displays the computer monitor on a screen). It has radically changed our lecture style. We can use it to demonstrate the points mentioned above and much more, such as step-wise refinement.

This preface is not meant to convince you that DrJava is the One True Way. It *is* effective, but other IDEs may provide a similar experience, although, so far we have found them to be less polished and less intuitive. The excellent BlueJ, for example, has an expression evaluator, but at the time of this writing it does not allow variables to be declared and used in later expressions.

DrJava is free. Appendix I explains how to download and use it. Even if you prefer that your students use a more conventional IDE for writing regular programs, DrJava provides a wonderful practice environment, and something like it should be used for the first month of the term.

Objects as manilla folders in filing cabinets

This text differs also in its introduction to classes and objects. A class is viewed as a drawer of a filing cabinet filled with manilla folders, which represent the instances or objects of the class. Each manilla folder has a distinct name on its tab, and it is this name that is stored in variables of the class-type. This approach allows us to dispense with the terms "reference" and "pointer" at the beginning (we introduce them later), for which students have no concrete analogy, and makes the introduction of classes, objects, and variables much easier.

Some reviewers have asked us to use UML diagrams instead of manilla folders. We cannot do that because UML diagrams and manilla folders are used for entirely different purposes. UML diagrams are used when designing or analyzing a program, for example, to show relations between classes. Manilla folders are used when executing statements by hand. For example, evaluating a new-expression requires drawing a new manilla folder that represents the new object. The manilla folder has a "tab", which contains the name of (or reference to) the object. No such animal exists in the UML world.

This file-cabinet–manilla-folder analogy, together with DrJava, allows us to comfortably introduce the creation and manipulation of objects as early as the second lecture (after a lecture on expressions), and students can begin practicing immediately, creating objects themselves on the computer and interacting with them. This occurs before they see a class definition!

Also, with this analogy, we are able to discuss a general *inside-out* rule that is used in some manner in almost all programming languages: a construct (such as a method body) can reference variables and methods defined not only in that construct but in any surrounding construct (such as a class definition). This inside-out rule makes it easy to discuss issues of scope in various contexts.

Finally, the analogy extends easily to the discussion of nested classes (both static classes and inner classes), and we are able to show how a "flattened view" of an inner class is similar to how Java implements nested classes. We have not seen a text that does this so easily. Of course, the material on nested classes is beyond the first course, but the fact that we can (and do) treat this material is some indication of the appropriateness of this analogy.

The pace of the text

Some reviewers of this text felt that the first chapter has a great deal of material and is fast-paced. Yes, there is a lot of material, but our experience is that students can handle it. We believe this is due to a combination of factors:

1. The use of DrJava in the classroom to demo concepts and Java features.
2. The self-review exercises in almost each section of the first chapter (and often in later chapters). Practice is needed to gain ease and fluency.
3. Weekly mandatory closed labs, where the students are guided in using DrJava. (The CD contains over 35 guided labs.)
4. The file-drawer–manilla-folder analogy, which provides the students with a concrete idea of what an object is.

An execution model

The text has another difference from most texts. We introduce a "model of memory", which includes not only drawing objects but also executing method calls, including pushing a frame on a call stack and popping the frame when the method call is finished. We have several assignments in which the students have to execute method calls by hand, and they may be asked to do the same on tests. Without such a model of memory, the whole idea of a method remains vague, and nested method calls such as f(g()) are, to some students, bewildering. With the model of memory, students have a more concrete understanding, and we have found that a later explanation of how recursive calls work is trivial.

Knowing that some instructors will not want to introduce it, we have structured the text so that the sections on the model can be skipped.

Prerequisite structure of this text

Different instructors have different ideas on when to teach what in introductory programming (using Java). Some teach procedural programming first; others do object-oriented programming first. Some teach for-loops early; others wait until classes and subclasses are finished. Some teach class Vector early so that students can write programs that deal with collections of objects; others never mention Vector. Some teach file I/O; others do not.

This textbook is organized to allow for such variation. Chapters 1 and 2 give basic introductions to expressions, types, assignment, if-statements and for-loops, methods and method calls, and classes and subclasses (not in the order listed) and are prerequisites for the rest of the text. The following prerequisite chart (for part of the text) shows the order in which material can be taught after (or at the same time as) the first two chapters.

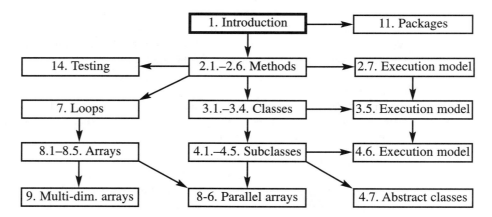

The short chapter on packages is needed to explain the import statement; we do not expect students to write their own packages.

Testing should be integrated throughout the course. However, for organizational purposes, it is best to have a separate chapter on testing and debugging, which the instructor and student can refer to from time to time. It is up to the instructor just how and when to cover this topic.

The three sections on the "execution model" are separate enough so that they can be skipped, should an instructor choose to do so.

The prerequisite diagram shown above gives the overall, gross structure. But different teachers emphasize different topics within that structure. The following diagram shows when various topics can be introduced.

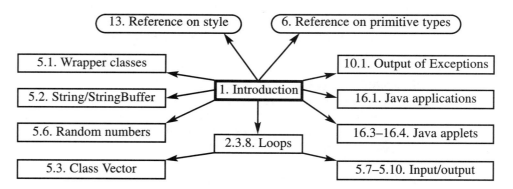

Much of the material in Chaps. 6 (primitive types) and 13 (programming style) appears in different places throughout the text; these chapters provide more thorough explanations and serve as references. They do not have exercises.

We provide several alternatives for I/O. Section 5.7 discusses a class, JLiveRead, that we have written to provide methods for reading integers, strings, etc, from the keyboard (i.e. Java console). We no longer use this class, preferring in the beginning to use either the DrJava interactions pane or our GUI JLive-Window for input.

JLiveWindow, discussed in Sec. 5.8, provides a number of **int**, **double**, and String fields and a "ready button". When the button is pressed, a certain method is called, and this method can be changed to do whatever you want. This GUI is great for providing simple input and for testing methods.

If you prefer to show your students the basics of reading from the keyboard and read/writing files, including appending to a file, using the classes of package java.io, use Secs. 5.9 and 5.10.

Various issues of style take several paragraphs or even a page to discuss. To place these discussions in the text would dilute the material. For example, placing a discussion of the various ways to indent an if-statement in the section that introduces the if-statement would distract from the topic at hand. We get around this problem by placing all discussions of style in Chap. 13 and placing references to the pertinent style material in the left margin, as in this paragraph.

Section 10.1 can be read at any time to help students understand the output resulting from thrown Exceptions and Errors.

Because we use DrJava or BlueJ, there is no need to introduce method main until well into the semester. Section 16.1 summarizes what one has to know about method main, and an instructor can choose to introduce it whenever they want. Similarly, sections in Chap. 16 on applets can be studied at any time.

The other topics in the diagram are discussed in terms of particular Java classes, and they can be studied after Chap. 1. We have suggested studying class Vector and I/O after a brief introduction to loops because using these classes in an interesting way usually requires loops.

Several topics covered in this text are not usually included in a first course: recursion, interfaces, nested classes (including anonymous classes), and the GUI packages in Java. We show in the diagram below when these topics can be taught. (The section on interfaces requires loops because one of the major uses of interfaces is in classes Enumeration and Iterator.)

> **Style Note**
> Chap. 13
> Introduction to
> style issues

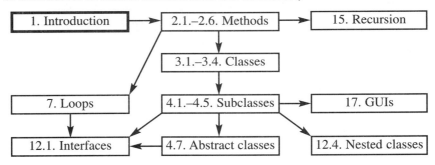

Acknowledgements

The computer science departments at Cornell, Toronto, and UGA have been extremely supportive of our work. We thank the introductory programming classes —and their instructor— who have used drafts of this book and the CD over the years.

The people at Data Description are great! Matt Clark wrote the software to produce the first livetext, *ActivStats*. As we wrote the CD *ProgramLive*, he responded quickly to our calls for changes and additions to fit our needs. John Sammis, the business manager, has been our constant companion and "encour-ager" for several years. Paul Vellemen, the author of *ActivStats*, was instrumental in getting us started on *ProgramLive*. And a cadre of other people at Data Description have been supporting the project in many ways, like producing the icons for each activity, cleaning audio files, synching animations to audios, and translating the CD from its Macintosh author-base to the Windows environment. The amount of work to be done to produce a livetext continues to amaze us.

We want to thank reviewers of the text, who helped tremendously.

Ann Kostant, Wayne Wheeler, and the rest of our Springer-Verlag contacts-deserve special mention for their great advice and for getting this book published in near-record time. Laurie Buck did an excellent job of as copy editor for this book, again in record time.

Last —and certainly not least— we thank our wives, Elaine Gries and Petra Hall, for all they have put up with over the years. They has been supportive in countless way and patient in many more during the long, drawn-out months and years of this project.

David Gries
Paul Gries

Contents

Part I

Basic Object-Oriented Programming

Part I introduces the basics of programming in an object-oriented language.

Chapter 0 provides an introduction to computers and programming.

Chapter 1 introduces *expressions* and how Java evaluates them. The reader already knows a lot about expressions and has to see only how one writes expressions in Java and and how they are evaluated by Java. Practice with expressions is the key to a quick understanding and obtaining fluency with Java expressions.

Thereafter, the notions of a variable, the declaration of a variable, and an assignment to a variable are explained. Again, practice with the concepts is key to a quick understanding

Chapter 1 also explains object-oriented concepts —what an object is and how a class definition is a template for a collection of objects with the same format. The first class definition one sees extends, or customizes, a class to fit one's needs. Our experience is that this is the easiest way to get across the concepts.

Finally, Chap. 1 introduces the notion of a method as a recipe for getting something done (a procedure) or calculating a value (a function).

Chapter 2 is a thorough, in-depth discussion of methods. It includes a discussion of the if-statement and a short introduction to the for-loop. Also included is a discussion of *stepwise refinement*, an idealized notion of how one goes about developing a method.

Chapter 3 then covers classes thoroughly, repeating some of the material of section 1 and going into more detail, while Chap. 4 covers subclasses.

Chapter 5 looks at some of the classes in the Java API (Application Programmer Interface) —like the wrapper classes, classes String and Vector, classes for formatting numbers and for generating random numbers, and classes for doing input/output (I/O). These are written so that the instructor can introduce them at almost any point, once Chap. 1 has been covered.

Chapter 6 provides a reference for the primitive types of Java.

Chapter **0**

Computers and Programming

OBJECTIVES

- Look at the organization of computers.
- Discuss computer software and compiling and executing programs.
- Introduce the programming language Java.

INTRODUCTION

Computers do not speak English. Instead, they have a rather peculiar communication system involving electric signals carried through silicon, etched using acids and electric current. Despite this rather alien and complex nature, humans still manage to create incredibly useful *virtual* tools using computers. (A hammer is real. A spreadsheet is virtual. You will not be able to pick up and hold anything that you learn how to build during your introductory programming course or, in fact, during your entire career as a programmer.)

A *program* is a set of instructions for a computer to follow. Over half a century ago, the first computer programs were created rather tediously, by plugging wires into sockets in intricate patterns. Flashing lights were used to indicate results. In the first programming courses, students would write a program on "paper tape" or "punch cards" and then submit the tape or deck of cards for processing. A few hours later, or even more, they would see the results of running the program and get their tape or cards back. Today, programs are created using a keyboard, or even automatically generated using drawing tools, and executed immediately. In a few seconds, you see the results. What a difference!

To understand how to build computers, engineering students go back to basics and think about the patterns of the wires. You do not have to go back that far, but, as beginning programmers, you will benefit from an understanding of hardware organization and of how programs and other files are stored and managed. Therefore, in the first section of this chapter, we discuss this topic. The rest of this chapter outlines what a program is and how instructions in a Java program are executed by the computer.

The livetext ProgramLive

This text is accompanied by a CD, which is totally different from CDs that accompany other texts. This CD, our original livetext *ProgramLive*, has on it a multi-media version of this text. It has "lesson pages", which are like the pages of a book. But each page contains several recorded mini-lectures with synchronized animation —there are over 250 such lectures. You can learn from these lectures, or *activities* as they are called, far better than you can from the static paper that you are now reading because the CD uses time, color, animation, and a recorded voice to enhance the presentation. The CD also contains a hypertext index and a glossary that is unmatched in any paper programming text, including this one.

In the left margin of the pages of this paper text, occasionally you will see an oval with an activity number in it, or a rectangular box, like the one in the left margin of the previous paragraph. The oval and rectangle point out material in the livetext that may be of interest to you. Often, it explains the same material, but in a more interesting and lively way. Make the CD an integral part of your learning experience.

> **Tip:** The first lesson in the livetext (the accompanying CD) explains how to use the CD. You will miss a lot if you do not read it.

0.1   Computer organization

Twenty years ago, the internet did not exist, and most new computer science students had never used a computer. Back then, typical programming texts began with instructions on how to use a computer: how to turn it on, how to open a file, how to save, how to make a backup copy. No longer. Today, most students in most of the world are quite comfortable navigating the web.

Still, most students have never opened up a computer or really thought about what is inside. In this section, we describe the major pieces and how information is stored.

We can view a personal computing system as consisting of the items shown in Fig. 0.1, which can be classified as follows:

1. The Central Processing Unit, or CPU. This is the core of the computer.
2. Memory. Contains data that the computer is processing. This data is lost when the computer is turned off.
3. Hard drive. Long-term data is kept here. The data is generally not lost when the computer is turned off.
4. Peripheral units: a keyboard, monitor, mouse, printers, scanners, CD/DVD units, cameras, small storage devices like floppy disks and zip disks, and more.
5. Ethernet and wireless connections to the internet and networks.

This view of a computer has not changed much in the past 40 years, although our ability to connect peripherals and the speed and flexibility of the connections has changed tremendously. For example, just ten years ago it was necessary to shut down a computer in order to attach most peripheral devices like hard drives and network connections. Wireless and ethernet were not available to consumers. Today we use USB (Universal Serial Bus) and firewire (spearheaded by Apple) to connect most peripherals, and we can just "plug and play".

The CPU

The central processing unit, or CPU, is perhaps the hardest part of the organization to understand. Its main purpose is to continually fetch instructions from memory and execute them. An instruction might be an addition, a subtraction, a test for one value being less than another, a command to store a value in a particular part of memory, a command to write a value onto the hard disk, and so on. CPUs have various *registers* in which to store temporary values.

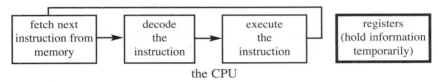

the CPU

A CPU is usually on a small *chip*, a piece of silicon with wiring on it and with a metal housing and connectors to the outside. The chip in your computer might contain several million electrical elements, called *transistors*, all wired together.

Some computers have two CPUs, which share the load of executing instructions. Also, most chips these days speed performance by carrying out several instructions at a time. Almost all computers have a graphics card, which provides an interface to the monitor and does much of the processing needed to make the monitor function quickly and smoothly. There is also a *cache*, where data that is used frequently is stored so that it does not have to be fetched from memory or the hard disk every time it is required. Such features complicate the logic of the CPU tremendously.

Activity 1-1.2

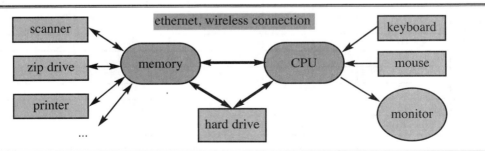

Figure 0.1:   Simplified view of a computer system

Memory

There are generally two kinds of memory. ROM, or *read-only memory*, contains data that can only be read. For example, the set of instructions that the computer executes when it starts up, or *boots*, is in ROM. RAM, or *random-access memory*, can be written as well as read. Memory is physically designed to provide extremely fast access to it, while access to a hard disk is much slower. Fast access to RAM is important because the CPU is constantly reading and writing RAM as it executes instructions. Because electricity maintains the data in RAM, the contents of RAM is destroyed when the computer is turned off.

Computers store information, such as words, numbers, sounds, and pictures, as a series of 1s and 0s, or *bits* (*binary digits*) because it is physically easy to build devices that represent 1 or 0. A device is on or off, is magnetized or not, has current running through it or not, allows light through it or not, and so on.

Humans normally write integers in the *decimal* number system. We have ten digits at our disposal, and we count like this: 0, 1, 2, 3, 4, 5, 6, 7, 8, 9. After all ten digits are used up we need two digits to keep counting, and ten is written as a 1 followed by a 0: 10. Similarly, after 99 comes 100.

In computer memory, integers (and all other data) are stored using the *binary* number system, in which only two digits are used: 0 and 1. Counting in binary follows the same algorithm as in the decimal number system, but with fewer digits. First, we count through all the digits: 0, 1. Because there are no more digits, the next number, two, is represented by 10. So the decimal number 2 is the same as the binary number 10. They are just different representations of what we call "two". In the binary system, after 10 comes 11, and then 100 ("four").

decimal	octal	hexadecimal	binary	power of 2
0	0	0	0	
1	1	1	1	2^0
2	2	2	10	2^1
3	3	3	11	
4	4	4	100	2^2
5	5	5	101	
6	6	6	110	
7	7	7	111	
8	10	8	1000	2^3
9	11	9	1001	
10	12	A	1010	
11	13	B	1011	
16	20	10	10000	2^4
20	24	14	10100	
64	80	40	1000000	2^6

Figure 0.2: Decimal, octal, hexadecimal, and binary numbers

Fig. 0.2 shows some integer values in the decimal system; the *octal* system, which uses eight digits; the *hexadecimal* system, which uses sixteen digits (0 .. 9, A .. F); and the binary system. As can be seen, the decimal integer 20 is written as 24 in octal, 14 in hexadecimal, and 10100 in binary. You will encounter hexadecimal numbers during your programming career and occasionally see octal numbers. A *hex dump*, for example, is a low-level printout of computer memory. Because 16 is a power of 2, binary numbers can be translated easily into hexadecimal, which is easier to read and interpret than binary.

Computer memory consists of a sequence of *bytes*, each of which consists of eight bits. As shown in Fig. 0.3, the first byte is numbered 0, the second 1, the third 2, and so on. This number is called the *address* of the byte, and bytes are often called *memory locations*.

Early computers had at most a few thousand bytes, and memory was expensive, on the order of a penny a bit. A megabyte is 2^{20} = 1,048,576 bytes, so at the 1950 price of a penny a bit, 512 megabytes of RAM would cost over $83,000! A gigabyte is 1024 megabytes. These days, 512 megabytes ("half a gig") of RAM, which costs only a few hundred dollars, is considered a good amount of RAM in a new computer. But in three years, it will probably not be enough to run the latest operating systems and applications well, especially the latest 3D immersive games and complex movie and photo editing software.

Because there are only eight bits in a byte, the largest integer that can be put in a byte is 11111111, or $2^8 - 1 = 255$. To deal with larger integers, several contiguous bytes are used. For example, suppose we use four bytes to store an integer; that is 32 bits. Since the sign of an integer has to be represented too, the range of integers that can be stored in the four bytes is $-2^{31}..2^{31}-1$.

Figure 0.4 describes some basic facts about binary numbers.

Storage devices

Most desktop and laptop computers come with an internal hard disk, and it is easy to attach external hard disks for extra storage, backup storage, and mobile storage —floppy disks (which are becoming extinct), zip drives, memory sticks, and so forth. A pretty good desktop at the time of this writing comes with an 80 gigabyte hard drive, 512 megabytes of memory, and any number of other external drives, depending on the buyer's choice. This is quite in contrast to the early

byte 0	10100101
byte 1	01001000
byte 2	11111111
byte 3	00000001
.	.
.	.
.	.

Figure 0.3: Bytes in memory

1. A binary number that consists of a 1 followed by 0s is a power of two. For example, binary 10000 = 2^4 = sixteen.
2. A binary number that consists entirely of 1s is 1 less than a power of two. For example, binary 111 = $2^3 - 1$ = seven.
3. To double the value of a binary number, append a 0. For example, 1010 is ten, and 10100 is twenty.

Figure 0.4: Binary number tidbits

1980s: Macintosh desktop computers in 1983 came with no internal hard drive, memory of about 256,000 bytes (1/4 megabyte!), and only a 3/4 megabyte floppy disk drive. (We sometimes wonder how anyone ever got any work done with such low-powered hardware.)

All storage devices use the same system of storing data that memory does: a sequence of bytes. But the way these bytes are stored, physically, differ from device to device.

0.2   Computer software

Computers are almost as common as microwave ovens and DVD players. People use computers for many common tasks: word processing, maintaining checkbook records, surfing the internet, and playing games. They use computers, often without knowing it, when they use an ATM, pay a bill by credit card, make a telephone call, and even drive their car (at least the newer cars). Most people, however, do not know how a computer works or how it is told what to do. They use computers only for services provided by *applications* written by others. Microsoft Word, Apple's iTunes, the browser that you use to surf the internet, the mailer you use to send and receive email, the thing that downloads an MP3 file, and the thing that plays the MP3 file —all these are examples of applications.

A program is simply a set of instructions to be carried out or executed by a computer, much like a cooking recipe is a set of instructions for a chef (or you) to carry out. A program is written in a notation called a *programming language*. The language could be C, C++, Java, Python, ML, Scheme, Fortran, or one of hundreds of other programming languages that have been developed since the advent of computers in the 1940s. The task of a programmer is to program, i.e. to write a programs. In this text and accompanying CD, you will learn how to program (i.e. write programs) in the Java language, one of the newer and more popular programming languages.

An *application* is a collection of programs that together accomplish some task, like the collection of programs that make up Microsoft word or the Norton utility to service your hard disk.

Compiling and executing a program

Programming languages are designed for humans to write and read. Programs, sometimes called *source programs,* cannot be executed immediately by a computer because they are not in the language of the computer itself, called the *machine language*.

Consider the expression x+y*z, which can appear in almost any programming language. The machine language version of this expression could consist of detailed instructions that do the following (remember: a register is a place in the CPU to hold a value).

1. load the value y from memory into register 1
2. load the value z from memory into register 2
3. multiply registers 1 and 2, putting the result in register 1
4. load the value of x from memory into register 2
5. add registers 2 and 1, putting the result in register 2

Of course, these instructions need to be represented as binary (or hexadecimal) numbers. Writing in the machine language, or a symbolic version of it called an *assembly* language, can be tedious and error-prone, and that is why "high-level" languages like Java have been developed.

So how does a Java program get executed? First, a software program called a *compiler* translates the Java program into an equivalent machine language program. Then, the machine language program is executed. The compiler makes sure that the program is *syntactically correct*, i.e. it follows the grammar rules of the programming language, including punctuation. If not, the compiler does not translate the program. When attempting to compile a program, we often get *compile-time error messages*, telling us what is syntactically wrong with the source program. We then have to fix these syntactic errors and try to compile again. We guarantee that you will see many of these error messages!

Deep thought: a compiler must have been written to compile the first compiler. How?

Now that you know a little bit about programming languages, we give you a perspective on the field of programming by presenting a brief history.

Early programming languages

During the early 1950s, when commercial computers first became widely available (to companies, not to individuals, because the computers cost millions of dollars), the main programming languages used were assembly languages. It took a *long* time to write, test, and debug an assembly-language program; consequently, programs had very little functionality, meaning they did not do much by today's standards. Not much emphasis was placed on how to write programs, i.e. on the programming task. Instead, maintaining the massive, expensive computer was the focus of most effort! Input to these computers was either by "IBM punch cards" or paper tape, which had to be prepared on other machines; there were no simple keyboards and mice attached to these computers! Generally, one gave the program to the systems group, who inputted it to the computer, ran it, and gave you back the program and the output —perhaps several hours later.

In the middle 1950s, the programming language Fortran I was developed and a compiler was written for it by IBM under the direction of John Backus (it took over 30 man-years to produce!). Fortran had the essential components of most *procedural* programming languages today: assignment statement, conditional statement, for-loop, variables, arrays, and subroutines (procedures and functions). It was the first widely used procedural language. Backus and his colleagues worked extremely hard to make the compiler and the machine-language programs that it produced very efficient because most programmers those days felt that they were far more competent in producing an efficient program (in assembly language) than any compiler could be. If Fortran was not efficient, they felt, no one would use it. Nevertheless, Fortran caught on quickly because *writing* in Fortran was so much quicker and less error prone than writing in an assembly language.

The year 1960 saw the emergence of three more languages: Lisp, a *functional* language (emphasizing expression evaluation and function calls, not assignment statements), developed by John McCarthy at MIT; Algol 60, a procedural language, which was developed by an international committee consisting mainly of Americans and Europeans (Backus and McCarthy were on it); and COBOL (standing for COmmon Business-Oriented Language), which was developed under the auspices of the U.S. Department of Defense, with help from computer manufactures and universities. Also, at about this time, research into the development of compilers for programming languages became one of the hot topics in computer science.

The 1960s saw the development of many more languages, many based on these four. But these four languages grew in use more than any other: Fortran in industry; Algol 60 in academia; Lisp mainly in the field of artificial intelligence in computer science departments; and COBOL in data processing activities within industry.

The software crisis

The problem throughout the 1960s was that the appetite for more functionality in programs outgrew the capability of the programmers to produce them. There was relatively little research on programming itself, so there was little progress on *how* to design, develop, test, and debug programs. As project teams and their proposed products grew in size, more and more projects failed to meet their deadlines, went way over their budgets, or were disbanded as failures. People talked of the *software crisis*.

As an illustration of the problem, clients reported hundreds of errors *each month* with one operating system, and fixing these errors inevitably introduced more errors. Imagine how many people had to be employed simply to process error reports, find the source of errors, fix them, and disperse the changes to customers. (There was no internet at the time, so communicating software changes to clients was not easy.)

Here were some of the issues that faced programming teams. How does one write program parts that can easily be reused? How does one design a large programming system? How does one manage a programming team consisting of ten or more (sometimes hundreds of) people? How is a large programming system to be tested and debugged as pieces of it are completed? How does one control the different versions of parts of the system, as pieces are created, tested, debugged, and changed? When a large system is finally given to customers, how is it to be *maintained* — changes have to be made due to error reports, to requests for new functionality, and to changes in hardware and operating systems; and these changes have to be tested, debugged, and finally sent to customers.

Compounding the problem of dealing with large programming systems was the fact that there was no systematic methodology for specifying and writing even *small* programs. If people could not write small programs effectively and correctly, how could they be expected to write large ones effectively and correctly?

In 1968, a conference was held in Garmisch, Germany, sponsored by NATO and chaired by F.L. Bauer of Munich. It was attended by the best computin peo-ple from academia and industry. For the first time programmers, researchers, and managers publically admitted that they did not know what they were doing when it came to designing and implementing programs. The term *software engineering* was mentioned, practically for the first time, and, in fact, the conference became known as the *NATO Conference on Software Engineering*. (Since then, *software engineering* has come to mean: the study and use of systematic and effective processes and technologies for supporting software design, development, and maintenance activities.)

There were glimmerings of hope; some people talked about preliminary research on correctness of programs, programming methodology, and software engineering issues. But the important point was the realization, by everyone, that programming and software engineering were not easy activities and that research needed to be done to understand how to do them better. This conference was the impetus for the great push forward in the 1970s on understanding these issues.

Structured programming

The early 1970s saw the emergence of work on *stepwise refinement*, or *top-down programming*, by Nicklaus Wirth and others (see Sec.2.5). This basic idea is that one should start with a specification of a program, written in English, mathematics, or a mixture of the two, and transform it through a series of small steps into a program. The idea has been put forth in other fields as well, as Sec. 2.5 shows.

A second, major, step forward was the work on *structured programming*, by Edsger W. Dijkstra. The term concerned reliance on program structures like the assignment statement, the conditional statement, the loop, and the subroutine (now called function, procedure, or method) call in designing programs, eschew-ing something called the *goto statement*, which was a mainstay of programming at the time. In fact, in 1968, Dijkstra's short article on the harmfulness of the goto statement in the *Communications of the ACM* caused an uproar in computer sci-ence circles, with several people rushing to defend the goto statement. But Dijkstra was right, and today, the goto statement does not even exist in the pro-gramming language Java.

Dijkstra's use of the phrase *structured programming* was meant to encom-pass not only the restriction to the kinds of statements discussed above but also a way of thinking about programming, of developing programs. The programming process itself was to be structured, not only the resulting programs. His work encompassed step-wise refinement, and it ultimately led to the next topic to be discussed, correctness concerns and the formal development of programs.

Correctness concerns

Until the 1970s, work on programming languages and programs was aimed mainly at how to *execute* programs (or have a computer execute them), not on how to *understand* programs. In 1967, Bob Floyd wrote a paper, *Assigning meanings to programs*, which gave the first inklings of how one could actually prove, mathematically speaking, that a program was correct. Tony Hoare picked up on Floyd's work and wrote a paper (1969), *An axiomatic basis for computer programming*, which provided the first definition of a programming language that was in terms of how a program could be proved correct, rather in terms of how it could be executed. This work was the foundation for a great deal of work on mathematical theories of program correctness in the 1970s and 1980s. The basic ideas found their way into programming texts as early as 1973, when Conway and Gries provided in their text, *An Introduction to Programming using PL/I*, a full account of understanding loops in terms of loop invariants.

However, at this point, the major idea was to take an existing program and try to prove it correct, and this was extremely difficult. Far better would be to develop a program and its proof hand-in-hand, with the proof ideas leading the way, but the field did not know how to do this. In the mid 1970s, Edsger W. Dijkstra published a paper and a book, *A Discipline of Programming*, which indeed showed us how a program and its proof could be developed hand-in-hand. The field of formal development of programs had emerged, and it was quite active throughout the 1980s and 1990s. The basics of this field appear in streamlined form in Appendix IV, complementing our presentation of loops and loop invariants in Chap. 7.

Object-oriented programming

Throughout the 1960s and 1970s, the main feature for structuring programs was the *subroutine*, or method (procedure or function), as it is now called in object-oriented programming. Like a cooking recipe, a subroutine is simply a set of instructions that can be invoked or called to perform some service. Until it is invoked, or called, it does not do anything. Books on cooking are organized in the same way that programs were organized; simply as a collection of subroutines, or recipes. There were attempts to add more structure, but the basic organization was still the recipe book.

The object-oriented (OO) approach provided a new structuring mechanism, the class (and subclass), with its principles of inheritance, instantiation, overriding, and polymorphism. The OO approach gave us a new way to think about constructing programs, and it actually provided a wholly new and useful mechanism for reusing program parts.

Actually, the first OO languages, Simula I and Simula 67, were developed by Ole-Johan Dahl and Kristen Nygaard in the 1960s, but the ideas espoused in them simply did not catch on. The field was not ready for them.

In the 1970s, Alan Kay's group at Xerox PARC used the ideas in Simula as a platform for their development of Smalltalk, an object-oriented language that got quite a bit of publicity. And in the 1980s, Bjarne Stroustrup started his development of C++ as an object-oriented version of the programming language C, and Bertrand Meyer created the Eiffel programming language. Object-oriented programming had arrived as a useful tool.

Object-oriented programming is a complement to procedural programming. Procedural programming consists of writing programs using assignment statements, conditional statements, loops, and subroutine calls. Object-oriented programming provides a new way of structure of programs that, ultimately, still contain the procedural aspects within their subroutines (or methods, as they are called in OO programming).

The programming language Java

Java is a relatively new OO programming language. Its roots are in a language called Oak, developed under the direction of James Gosling at Sun Microsystems in 1991 as part of the Green project; but it was introduced to the world as Java in 1995. Java is based on C, but it has several significant advantages.

First, Java is a relatively simple but powerful, well-designed, object-oriented language. With Java, one can begin teaching object-oriented concepts in the first week; with C++, this usually happens only in the second semester.

Second, the inventors of Java showed how Java programs could be embedded in browsers as *applets*, and, by 1996, both Netscape and Microsoft browsers supported applets. This meant that anyone who looked at your website could run your applet.

Third, the Java language comes with a machine language into which compilers have to compile Java programs. Called the Java Virtual Machine (JVM) language, it defines precisely what the machine language equivalent of a Java

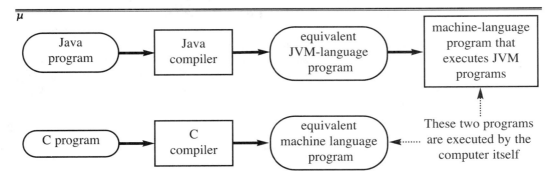

Figure 0.5: The process of compiling and running Java programs and C programs

program is. This provides an unheard-of measure of portability. A Java program runs the same on a Macintosh, a PC, Linux, Sun's Solaris —on any computer that implements a Java compiler and the JVM correctly. This is not the case, for example, with programs written in C, C++, and Fortran. Why? Because these programs interact directly with hardware, so on different hardware (i.e. on different kinds of computers), they may do different things. Java programs instead interact with a JVM (which in turn interacts with hardware), so any operating system that has a JVM can run any Java program.

The introduction of the Java Virtual Machine did have a drawback: programs ran slower in Java than in, say, C. Figure 0.5 explains this. At the bottom, you see that a C program is compiled into the language of the machine on which the compiler is running, and the resulting program is then executed by the machine. A Java program, on the other hand, is compiled into the JVM, and then another machine-language program has to execute the resulting JVM program. This makes executing (or *interpreting*) a program up to ten times slower.

However, we are often quite willing to pay the price of slower programs because in return we have a portable and simpler language. In fact, we do not even notice the change in speed on many programs. Further, if a particular part of a program *has* to be faster, we can program it in C (or another suitable language).

Fourth, the language is *safe*. As an example of what this means, if a Java program stores an integer somewhere, it is guaranteed that it will be used only as an integer (and not, for example, as a string of characters). This safety has ramifications that cannot be completely explained at this point, but here are two examples. In some languages (e.g. C and C++), managing memory correctly is very difficult; in Java, safety allows Java to handle memory management, so the programmer is freed from that task. Secondly, because of safety (and other factors), a browser can run a Java program called an *applet* on your computer with the assurance that it cannot store things on your computer, so it cannot destroy files or wreak havoc in other ways.

Fifth, the object-oriented nature of Java allows the language itself to be relatively small. Various parts that are usually part of a non-object-oriented language are instead written as Java *classes* that accompany every JVM. Literally thousands of Java programs, written as classes, come in an *Application Programming Interface* (API), which your Java programs can use. For example, all input and output (I/O) such as reading to or writing from a file, reading from the keyboard, and drawing on the monitor are defined in classes that accompany the language. I/O is not part of the language itself. But you do have to learn how to use these prewritten classes.

Chapter 1

Object-Oriented
Introduction to Java

OBJECTIVES

- Learn about expressions and types **int**, **double**, **boolean**, and String.
- Learn about declarations of variables and assignments to them.
- Learn the basics of object-oriented programming.
- Learn how to use classes from the Java API.
- Learn the importance of good style.

INTRODUCTION

The first section of this chapter deals with the evaluation of expressions in Java. Here is an example of an expression: 3 + 5. Java expressions differ slightly in some respects from the math expressions you have seen. We hope that you will immediately get on your computer, practice writing expressions, and see how the computer evaluates them. *Practicing on the computer with each topic will give you a fluency in Java programming that is otherwise hard to come by.* Appendix I outlines how you can do this on your own computer.

The second section introduce the concept of a *variable*, which can be viewed simply as a box into which a value can be stored, and how variables are used in Java.

The major part of this chapter is an introduction to object-oriented programming in Java, which will give you an understanding of the *class* as a fundamental mechanism for organizing and structuring programs. Interestingly enough, the concept of classes was not even taught twenty years ago; today, we do not know what we would do without it.

You will soon see that good programming style is important. Consistently using a simple style that lets you see the structure of your program gives you a chance to write correct programs. Not following a good style almost always leads to chaos in your program and a consequent waste of time trying to write it, understand it, and get it correct.

> **Expression evaluation.** Appendix I shows you how to evaluate expressions in a number of Java platforms. Currently, for the purpose of evaluating expressions, the IDEs DrJava and BlueJ offer the best support, although others plan to add support this year. DrJava and BlueJ are free, and they are easy to download and install. Whatever IDE your course is using, you can use one of these IDEs on your own in order to learn.

1.1. Types and expressions

Tip: Use lesson 6 as a reference for expressions and the types discussed in this section.

In this section, we introduce you to basic Java expressions. Here are examples:

```
2 - 5
3
(1 + 2 + 3 + 4 + 5 + 6 + 7 + 8 + 9 + 10) * 2
2147483647 + 1
```

These expressions are like mathematical expressions that you have seen and used before. You can use integer constants like 42, called integer *literals* in Java, and you can use the operations defined in Fig. 1.1. Also, you can use parentheses to help indicate the order in which operations are to be performed, as in (3 + 4) * 2. If you do not use parentheses, operations are carried out using conventional mathematical *precedences*:

- Unary – and + have highest precedence, so –5 + 6 has the value 1.
- Multiplication, division, and remainder come next, and sequences of them are carried out from left to right. So, 4 + 3 * 6 / 2 * 3 is 4 + 18 / 2 * 3, which is 4 + 9 * 3, which is 4 + 27, which is 31.
- Addition and subtraction have lowest precedence, and sequences of them are carried out from left to right. So 4 – 3 – 4 * 2 is 4 – 3 – 8, which is 1 – 8, which is –7.

Operator	Operation	Example	Result
unary +	no effect	+6	6
binary +	addition	5 + 6	11
unary –	negation	–(4 + 5)	–9
binary –	subtraction	4 – 5	–1
*	multiplication	4 * 5	20
/	division	8 / 2	4
%	remainder	13 % 3	1 (13/3 = 4 with remainder 1)

Figure 1.1: Basic integer operators in Java

> **Gaining fluency**. You will gain *fluency* in Java only by *doing*. As you read about expressions and assignment, have your IDE (Interactive Development Environment) running on your computer and practice typing in expressions and evaluating them. Experiment, experiment! Often! For example, evaluate 5 / 2 and see what you get. Type in `Integer.MAX_VALUE` and `Integer.MAXVALUE + 2` and see what they are. Try calling the mathematical functions with various arguments.

There is a major difference between conventional mathematical expressions and Java expressions. In mathematics, an expression may have any value. It might get big, but so what? But when using a programming language like Java, the values of expressions are stored in a computer, which is a finite, physical device. There is a tension among the sizes of the values of the expressions, the space the values occupy, and the speed with which the values can be operated on. Allowing expressions to have *any* value may cause values to take too much space and operations to take too long.

Java uses the concept of a *type* to let you declare the range of values that you want to work with and the operations you want to use. We define *type*:

A *type* is a set of values together with a set of operations on them.

In mathematics, we use the word *integer* for the type consisting of the integer literals {..., –3, –2, –1, 0, 1, 2, ...} together with these basic integer operations: negation, addition, subtraction, multiplication, and division.

1.1.1 Type int

In Java, type **int** consists of the integers in the range $-2^{31}..2^{31}-1$ (by which we mean the set of values $\{-2^{31}, -2^{31} + 1, ..., -1, 0, 1, ... 2^{31} - 1\}$). The value 2^{31} is 2 multiplied by itself 31 times, or 2147483648.

The usual operations of type **int** are: negation, addition, subtraction, multiplication, division, and remainder. (Unary + is also available, but it is rarely used.) *All* **int** *operations have* **int** *results.*

The smallest and largest values of type **int** are difficult to remember, so Java gives you a notation for accessing them:

    `Integer.MIN_VALUE`: smallest **int** value: –2147483648.
    `Integer.MAX_VALUE`: largest **int** type: 2147483647.

To see this, type this expression into Java and see what value it gives you:

    `Integer.MAX_VALUE`

Overflow

If a value of an **int** expression gets outside the range of type **int**, *overflow* occurs. When overflow occurs, the value is changed back into one that is in the range of type **int**. For example, 2147483647 + 2 in mathematics evaluates to

2147483649, but in Java it evaluates to –2147483647!

Integer.MAX_VALUE + 2   overflow occurs!

In your first programs, overflow will not be an issue. Just be aware that expressions in Java yield a value that is determined by the type of the expression, and if you try to produce a number outside the range of that type, overflow occurs and your answers are probably not correct.

Integer division

Division, as in 7 / 2, yields a value of type **int**. Hence, the value of 7 / 2 cannot be 3.5. Instead, the value is truncated toward 0 to produce an **int**:

7 / 2   has the value 3
–7 / 2   has the value –3

This will seem strange at first, but you will get used to it. Just remember that, because Java expressions are defined in the context of being evaluated on a computer, within Java programs (and indeed most programming languages), the rules are slightly different from conventional mathematics.

Finding out more about type int and its relation to other Java types

This section is a brief introduction to type **int**. It does not discuss its relation to other types that deal with integers. This introduction should satisfy your needs for weeks to come. However, at some point you should investigate such "integral types". Chapter 6 contains a complete discussion of such types and should be used as a reference.

1.1.2   Type double

Lesson page 6-3

Numbers written with a decimal point are of type **double**. Here are examples:

5.   4.3   .00000001

Java uses *scientific notation* to make **double** numbers like the rightmost one on the line above easier to read. The rightmost number can be written as:

1E–8

Tip: See the ProgramLive glossary for a definition of scientific notation.

Here, E stands for "exponent", and the integer following it indicates how many places to move the decimal point —in this case, 8 decimal places to the left. The corresponding mathematical *scientific notation* would be $1*10^{-8}$. As another example, 0.05E6 is equal to 50000: the E6 indicates to move the decimal point 6 places to the right.

Think about **double** values as approximations to the "real numbers". They are approximations because the number of digits that can be used is finite, while a real number can have an infinite number of digits. For example, the fraction 1/3 is 0.33333..., where the dots ... represent an infinite number of 3s. But in type **double**:

    1.0 / 3.0 is 0.3333333333333333

A **double** number such as 1.564E15 has two parts: the *mantissa*, which is the part before the E, and the *exponent*, which is the part after the E.

1. In the number 1.564E15, the mantissa is 1.564. Mantissas can have about 16 digits of accuracy. So, if you write 3.14159265358979324, it will be rounded off to 3.141592653589793.
2. In the number 1.564E15, the exponent is 15. The maximum exponent is 308. So if you write 1E309, Java will tell you that the exponent is too large. If you write 1E308*10, Java will evaluate this to Infinity, and any values that are created using it as an operand are garbage.

Java has notations for referencing the smallest positive **double** value and the largest positive **double** value. They are:

    Double.MIN_VALUE   (which is 4.9E-324)
    Double.MAX_VALUE   (which is 1.7976931348623157E308)

The basic operations on **double** values are:

unary –	(negation, as in -(40E5 + 5.0))
unary +	(non-negation, as in +5.1)
+	(addition, as in 5.0 + 6.0)
–	(subtraction, as in 4.2 – 5.1)
*	(multiplication, as in 4.0 * 6.2)
/	(division, as in 4.5 / 3.1)
%	(remainder: 5.1 % 2.0, which is 1.0999999999999996)

> Lesson 6-4 discusses the fact that **double** operations are approximations.

The last operation illustrates an important point with regard to double operations: often, they give only approximations to the real result. One would think that 2 goes into 5.1 twice, with a remainder of 1.1. However, a *roundoff error* occurs because there is only a finite amount of space for each number. Computer arithmetic give only an approximation to the answer: 1.0999999999999996.

The **double** operators have the same precedence as the corresponding **int** operators.

1.1.3   Casting between int and double

> Lesson pages 6-2 and 6-3 discuss casting from one type to another.

If the operands of an operation (one of +, – , *, /, %) are of type **int**, the operation is an **int** operation and produces an **int**. Thus, 10 / 4 evaluates to the **int** value 2. If the operands are of type **double**, the operation is a **double** operation and produces a **double**. So, 5.0 * 2.2 evaluates to the **double** value 11.0.

If one operand of the operation is an **int** and the other is a **double**, the **int** value is converted to a **double** value and a **double** operation is performed. For example, the expression 2 + 3 + 4 * 5.2 is evaluated as follows:

1. **int** expression 2 + 3 is evaluated to yield the expression 5 + 4 * 5.2.
2. 4 is converted to the **double** value 4.0, and 4.0 * 5.2 is evaluated to yield the expression 5 + 20.8.
3. 5 is converted to the **double** value 5.0 and the addition is performed to yield the value 25.8.

This conversion of value from type **int** to type **double** happens automatically; you do not have to worry about it. But, if you want, you can explicitly request such a conversion, or *cast* as it is called in Java, by preceding the value to be converted by the cast (**double**). (This "type cast" is actually another operator!) Here is an example:

5 / (**double**) 2

is evaluated as follows:

1. The value 2 is cast to type **double**, yielding the expression 5 / 2.0.
2. The value 5 is converted to **double**, yielding the expression 5.0 / 2.0.
3. **double** division is performed, yielding the **double** value 2.5.

Order of operations is important: to evaluate (**double**) (5 / 2) do the division in **int** arithmetic, yielding 2, and then cast 2 to **double** to yield 2.0.

You can also cast **double** values to type **int**, using (**int**). In the expression below, all operations are performed in **double** arithmetic, and then the result is cast to an **int**:

(**int**) ((3.5 + 4.6) / 21.2)

When casting to an **int**, the value is truncated toward zero, so (**int**) 3.9 evaluates to 3 and (**int**) –3.9 evaluates to –3. Casts from **double** to **int** are not performed automatically because they can lose information.

We say that type **int** is *narrower* than type **double** and type **double** is *wider* than type **int** because every **int** value is a **double** but not the other way around. A cast from **int** to **double** is called a *widening cast*, and a cast from **double** to **int** is called a *narrowing cast*. Java performs widening casts implicitly, when required, but narrowing casts must be explicitly given in order to be performed.

1.1.4   Type boolean and arithmetic relations

Lesson
page 6-6

Another type that you will use frequently is **boolean** (named after George Boole, a nineteenth-century mathematician who was one of the parents of logic). Type **boolean** has only two values: **true** and **false**.

In Java, there are three operations on **boolean** values. We describe them assuming that b1 and b2 are **boolean** expressions (their precedences are given later):

- Negation, or *not*:   !b1
  Expression !b1 evaluates to **true** if b1 is **false** and **false** otherwise.

- Conjunction, or *and*: b1 && b2

  Expression b1 && b2 evaluates to **true** if both b1 and b2 are **true** and evaluates to **false** otherwise. Operands b1 and b2 are called *conjuncts*.

- Disjunction, or *or*: b1 || b2

  Expression b1 || b2 evaluates to **true** if either b1 or b2 (or both) is **true** and to **false** otherwise. Operands b1 and b2 are called *disjuncts*.

For example, we evaluate the expression **true** && !(**false** || **false**):

1. **false** || **false** evaluates to **false**,
   so the expression becomes **true** && !**false**.
2. !**false** evaluates to **true**,
   so the expression becomes **true** && **true**.
3. **true** && **true** evaluates to **true**.

You are not likely to use operations !, &&, and || very much in the beginning. However, we need type **boolean** in order to talk about arithmetic *relations*, which yield **boolean** values. Assuming that e1 and e2 are both **int** or **double** expressions, we can use the following arithmetic relations:

e1 < e2	**true** if e1 is less than e2 and **false** otherwise.
e1 > e2	**true** if e1 is greater than e2 and **false** otherwise.
e1 <= e2	**true** if e1 is at most e2 and **false** otherwise.
e1 >= e2	**true** if e1 is at least e2 and **false** otherwise.
e1 == e2	**true** if e1 and e2 are equal and **false** otherwise.
e1 != e2	**true** if e1 and e2 are different and **false** otherwise.

For example, the expression 5 + 3 < 9 evaluates to **true**, and 5 + 3 < 8 evaluates to **false**. The operators <, >, <=, >=, ==, and != are called *relational operators*.

Be careful with equality: The phrase 5 = 6 is not a Java expression! Java uses the sign == for an equality test, rather than =, and uses = in another way, which we describe in Sec. 1.2. For example, 6 == 6 evaluates to **true** and 5 == 6 evaluates to **false**. This breaking of mathematical convention is unfortunate. For hundreds of years, ever since Robert Recorde introduced the sign = for equality in the 1600s, that convention has been in use. To have programming languages break with that tradition is a travesty.

Operator	Operation	Example	Result
!	*not*, or *negation*	! true	false
&&	*and*, or *conjunction*	true && false	false
||	*or*, or *disjunction*	true || false	true

Figure 1.2: Basic boolean operators in Java

Equality (==) and inequality (!=) can be used with operands of type **boolean**. For example, **true** == **true** evaluates to **true** and **true** != **true** evaluates to **false**.

Type **boolean** is covered in detail in Sec. 6.7. Look especially at the material on the marks of a **boolean** tyro at the end of Sec. 6.7.

1.1.5   Type String

Lesson
page 5-3

Type String is different from the previous three types we introduced, in a way that will be explained in Section 1.3.4. For the moment, we need just to be able to write some String values and *catenate* them together.

The expression

        "This is a String"

consists of a String *literal*: a sequence of characters enclosed in double-quote marks ". The value of a String literal is simply the sequence of characters. You can *catenate* two String values to yield the sequence of characters in the first String followed by the sequence of characters in the second String using operator +. Thus, the expression

        "First part" + " Second part"

has the value "First part Second part".

Operator + is *overloaded*; it is used for addition of two **int**s, for addition of two **double**s, and for catenation of two Strings.

If one operand of + is a String and the other is not, the other one is converted to a String before the catenation takes place. Thus, the expression

        "123" + 61

has the value "12361". Be careful when you use this feature. The two expressions

        "one" + 5 + 2   and   "one" + (5 + 2)

have different values. (Type these expressions into your IDE and evaluate them.) In the first one, the catenation of "one" and 5 yields "one5", and the catenation of this value with 2 yields "one52". In the second expression, because of the parentheses, the integer addition is done first and then the conversion to a String is performed, with the result "one7".

How does one get the double-quote character itself in a String? By preceding it by the escape character '\'. For example, the literal "a\"b" consists of three characters: a, ", and b. But this means that the backslash cannot be used to represent itself. Instead, use \\ to represent the backslash. For example, the literal "a\\b" consists of three characters: a, \, and b.

1.1.6   Precedences of operators

We have seen arithmetic operators, boolean operators, and relational operators. They can all be used in one expression, so we need to know their precedences. The following table gives the precedences, with the highest precedence operators first and the lowest ones last. For completeness, we include two operators that we have not yet explained: ++ and --.

> Unary operators: `+` `-` `++` `--` `!` `typecast`
> Binary arithmetic operators: `*` `/` `%`
> Binary arithmetic operators: `+` `-`
> Arithmetic relations: `<` `>` `<=` `>=`
> Equality relations: `==` `!=`
> Logical and: `&&`
> Logical or: `||`

Here are some examples of the use of precedences to eliminate parentheses.

> `(3 + 5) > (4 - 6)` can be written as `3 + 5 > 4 - 6`,
>   because + and - have higher precedence than >.

> **(true** `&&` `(3<5))` `==` `(4>5)` is the same as **true** `&&` `3<5` `==` `4>5`.

1.1.7   Function calls

Functions and function calls (or function invocations) are common in mathematics. For example, the square root function is used frequently. The *function call* `sqrt(25.0)` yields the square root of `25.0`, which is `5.0`. Here, `sqrt` is the *name* of the function and `25.0` is the *argument* of the function call. Java allows function calls as well, although Java names for the mathematical functions are a bit longer than those in mathematics.

In Java, functions are defined in *classes*. The Java class `Math` contains definitions of many mathematical functions. Other examples of classes are `Date`, which contains functions related to dates, and `File`, which contains functions related to the file system on your computer.

Here is a Java function call to obtain the square root of `37.0`:

```
Math.sqrt(37.0)
```

The prefix "`Math.`" is needed to indicate where the function resides: in class `Math`.

Some of the function names in class `Math` are *overloaded*, which means that the same name is used for two or more different functions. The type of the argument is used to distinguish between them. Functions with the same name generally do the same thing but on arguments of different types. Also, the type of the result depends on the types of the arguments. For example, we have:

```
        Math.abs(-5)        = absolute value of -5:    int value 5
        Math.abs(-5.0)      = absolute value of -5.0: double value 5.0
```

Here is a partial list of functions in class Math:

```
        Math.abs(a)         = absolute value of argument a.
        Math.sqrt(a)        = square root of argument a.
        Math.sin(a)         = sine of argument a.
        Math.min(a, b)      = smaller of arguments a and b.
        Math.max(a, b)      = larger of arguments a and b.
        Math.floor(a)       = largest integer that is not larger than a.
                              For example, Math.floor(3.9) = 3.0.
        Math.ceil(a)        = smallest integer that is not smaller than a.
                              For example, Math.ceil(-3.9) = -3.0.
```

If you want the floor of a **double** value as an **int**, then you have to cast it:

```
(int) Math.floor(3.9)      is the int 3.
```

1.1.8   Self-review exercises

These exercises will help you gain fluency with expressions in Java. Do not restrict your experiments to these exercises. Make up your own. If you are not sure what something does, study the material again, but also try it out. The more practice you get, the more fluent you will be and the easier the later material will seem to be.

SR1. Type the following **int** expressions into your IDE and see what their values are:

```
5 + 2                    5 + 2 * 5               (5 + 2) * 5
4 - 3 - 3                4 - (3 - 3)             -4 - --4 - -4
6 / 2                    6 / 3                   6 / 4
6 % 2                    6 % 3                   6 % 4
-6 % 4                   6 % -4                  -6 % -4
Integer.MIN_VALUE        Integer.MIN_VALUE - 1
                         Integer.MIN_VALUE + 1
Integer.MAX_VALUE        Integer.MAX_VALUE - 1
                         Integer.MAX_VALUE + 1
```

SR2. Evaluate the following **double** expressions:

```
5.0 + 2.0                1 + 1.99                (5 + 2.1) * 5
4.0 - 3 - 3              4.0 - (3 - 3)           -4.0 - -4 - -4
6.0 / 2                  6.0 / 3                 6.0 / 4
6.0 % 2.1                6.0 % 3                 6.1 % 4
-6.0 % 4                 6 % -4.0                -6.1 % -4
Double.MIN_VALUE         Double.MIN_VALUE - 1
```

```
                              Double.MIN_VALUE + 1
      Double.MAX_VALUE        Double.MAX_VALUE - 1
                              Double.MAX_VALUE + 1
```

SR3. Evaluate the following expressions to become familiar with casting between **int** and **double** and the precedence of the casting operators.

5 + 2.0	7 / (**double**) 4	2 * (7 % 4)
5.0 + 2	(**double**) 7 / 4	2 * (**double**) (7 % 4)
(7 / 4) * 5	(**double**) (7 / 4)	2 * ((**double**) 7 % 4)
(7 / 4.0) * 5		2 * (7 % (**double**) 4)
(**int**) 5	(**int**) (**double**) 4	
(**int**) 5.3	(**int**) (**double**) 4.3	
(**int**) 5.9	(**double**) (**int**) 4.3	
(**int**) −5.3	(**int**) (**int**) 4.3	
(**int**) −5.9	(**double**) (**double**) 4	

SR4. Type the following expressions into your IDE and see what their values are to become familiar type **boolean**.

true	**true** && **false**	**true** || **false**
false	**true** && **true**	**true** || **true**
!**true**	**false** && **false**	**false** || **false**
!**false**	!!**true**	
true && **false** && **true**		**true** || **false** || **true**
true && !**false** && **true**		**true** || **true** && **false**
true || **false** && **true**		**true** && **true** || **false**
true || (**false** && **true**)		**true** && (**true** || **false**)
(**true** || **false**) && **true**		(**true** && **true**) || **false**
true || **true** && **false**		

SR5. Type the following expressions into your IDE and see what their values are to become familiar with **Strings**.

```
"Truth " + "is" + "best"
("Truth " + "is") + "best"
"Truth " + ("is" + "best")
56 + "" + 56
```

SR6. Type the following expressions into your IDE and see what their values are to become familiar with precedences of operators.

"" + 4 / 2	("" + 4) / 2	"" + (4 / 2)
"" + 4 + 2	"" + (4 + 2)	("" + 4) + 2
4 + 2 + ""	4 + (2 + "")	
4 + 2 < 6	4 + 2 < 4 + 3	
4 < 3 == 3 < 4	4 < 3 == **true** || **false**	
4 <= 4 && 2 < 4	4 < 3 != **true** && **false**	

$$3 >= 4 \;||\; 4 >= 3 \qquad\qquad \mathbf{true} \;\&\&\; \mathbf{false} \;||\; \mathbf{true}$$
$$-3 < 3 \;||\; 3 > -3 \qquad\qquad \mathbf{true} \;\&\&\; (\mathbf{false} \;||\; \mathbf{true})$$

SR7. Reread Sec. 1.1.7 on function calls. Remember that, in a function call like `Math.abs(25 * -4)`, the expression `25 * -4` is called the *argument* of the function call. Have Java evaluate some calls to the functions in class `Math`. Experiment with expressions that have two or more calls, for example `Math.min(25, 4)` + `Math.max(25, 4)`.

1.2   Variables, declarations, assignments

In mathematics, a *variable* is a name together with an associated value. In programming, we use the same notion of a variable, and we draw a variable as a named box with the value in the box. Below is an **int** variable called `quantity` whose value is 4.

quantity | 4 |

In Java, a variable may be associated with different values at different times, but the values must all be of the same type. For example, `quantity` may be associated only with values of type **int**. When it is important to note what the type of a variable is, we place the type to the right of the box. Below is the same variable, `quantity`, and a second variable `price`, which is of type **double**.

quantity | 4 | int   price | 3.99 | double

In Java, a variable must be *declared* before it can be used. Below are Java *declarations* for variables `quantity` and `price`. Note that each declaration consists of three things: a type, the name of the variable, and a semicolon.

```
int quantity;
double price;
```

In any particular context, a variable can be declared only once. For example,

---

Variable names, identifiers, and keywords. A variable name, like `quantity`, is an *identifier*. In Java, identifiers are writen as a sequence of letters, digits, $, and _, but the first is not a digit. Java programmers do not use $ and tend not to use _ except in one situation, which you will see later. Java programmers follow certain conventions for identifiers, which we will explain from time to time. They are summarized in Sec. 13.1.1.

Identifiers are case sensitive: `truth` and `Truth` are different.

Keywords (e.g. **int** and **double**) may not be used as identifiers. To see the list of keywords, look up *keyword* in the glossary of the ProgramLive CD. In most IDEs, keywords are shown in their own distinct color, so you should not have trouble distinguishing keywords from identifiers.

Comments in Java. On this page, you see some text preceded with "//". Such text is called a *comment*. We write comments in a Java program to help us understand the program. Comments are ignored by Java.

A comment that begins with // ends at the end of the line; it is called a *single-line comment*. A comment can also have the form /* ... */; it can be a *multi-line comment*. The comment may span many lines.

---

we could not write this (try it in your IDE!):

```
int quantity;
int quantity;        // This declaration is illegal
```

To place a value in a variable, use an *assignment statement*. Here are examples:

```
quantity= 8;
price= 3.99;
```

Execution of the first assignment statement evaluates the expression, 8, and stores its value in variable quantity. The second assignment statement is executed similarly, and quantity and price now look like this:

quantity $\boxed{8}$ int   price $\boxed{3.99}$ double

Any **int** expression may appear in place of expressions 8 and 3.99 in the first assignment statement. For example, we can write this assignment statement (which has the same result as the first assignment statement above):

```
quantity= 4 + 4;
```

There is one restriction: the type of the variable in an assignment statement has to be the same as or wider than the type of the expression. For example, the first assignment statement below is legal but the second one is illegal because type **int** is narrower than type **double**. If the type of the variable is wider than the type of the expression, the value of the expression is cast to the type of the

---

The assignment sign =. In the 1600s, Robert Recorde introduced the sign = to stand for equality, and after many years, the world universally adopted that convention. In the late 1960s, the programming language C decided that = would be used for assignment and == for equality, because programmers wrote more assignment statements than equality relations. This change has caused more confusion and wasted time than perhaps any other notational convention. Beginning programmers often ask why we write x = x + 1; —how could x and x + 1 be equal?

We write the assignment in the form

```
x= x + 1;
```

with no blank before the =, so that it does not look symmetric and is less liable to be mistaken for an equality test.

Java syntax: Variable declaration

type variable ;

Example: **double** price;

Purpose: To declare that variable *variable* is needed and that it can hold values of type *type*. By *variable*, we mean the name of the variable.

Java syntax: Assignment statement

variable= *expression* ;

Additionally: The type of the *variable* is the same as or wider than the type of the *expression*.

Example: price= 8.99;

Purpose: To assign a value to a variable. To execute the assignment, evaluate the *expression* and store its value in the *variable*.

---

variable before the assignment is performed.

```
price= 4;         // legal: double is wider than int
quantity= 5.0;    // illegal: int is narrower than double
```

Expressions with variables

We can write expressions not only with literals (for example, 4, 6.2, and **true**), but with variables. Here is one such expression: price + 4.0. When an expression with a variable is evaluated, the value currently associated with the variable is used. For example, if quantity has the value 8 and price has the value 3.99, the value of the expression

```
quantity * price
```

is 31.92. If the value of a variable changes, later evaluation of the same expression yields a different value.

Below, we show a sequence of assignments to **int** variables v1 and v2. As each assignment is executed, one after the other, the new values of the variables are as shown in the comments to the right of the assignment. The values are the numbers that appear after the colons.

```
v1= 5;              // v1:   5      v2:   ?
v2= 3;              // v1:   5      v2:   3
v1= v1 + 1;         // v1:   6      v2:   3
v1= v1 + 2 + v1;    // v1:  14      v2:   3
v2= v1;             // v1:  14      v2:  14
v1= v2 + v1 + 1;    // v1:  29      v2:  14
```

Lesson page 13-2 discusses naming conventions in detail.

In mathematics, short variable names like x and y are common. In computer programs, longer names tend to be used in order to give some indication of their meaning, like price and taxIsIncluded. There is a tension between using short names, in order to keep a program compact, and long names, in order to provide more understanding. Our conventions for names are discussed in Sec. 13.1, and we recommend that you read the beginning of that section now.

The following convention is followed by Java programmers: a variable name starts with a lowercase letter. If the name contains several words, the first letter of each word, except the first, is capitalized, e.g. `numberOfApples`.

Initializing declarations

You can combine the declaration and assignment statement

```
int price;
price= 5;
```

into an *initializing declaration*:

```
int price= 5;
```

1.2.1   Self-review exercises

In these exercises, you get practice with the assignment statement and using variables in expressions. DrJava provides an easy way to get this practice (by far the easiest that we are aware of, in fact), but it can be done in other IDEs as well.

SR1. Type in this assignment statement and expression. What does Java say? What does that tell you about the initial value of a variable?

```
int rooms;
rooms
```

SR2. Type in these two declarations. What does Java say? What do you infer from this?

```
int temperature= 20;
int temperature= temperature + 1;
```

SR3. Type this declaration into Java:

```
int windChill= 5;
```

What assignment statement will add 10 to variable `windChill`? Type the assignment into Java and have Java evaluate the expression `windChill` to see whether you were right; the new value of `windChill` should be 15. In the same way, write assignments (and execute and test whether they worked) to double the value of `windChill`, to set the value of `windChill` to –10, and to square it.

SR4. Type this declaration and assignment into Java:

```
int daysOfRain= 45;
daysOfRain= daysOfRain / 2;
```

and then see what value `daysOfRain` has. Now try the same assignment statement again, but this time use the literal 2.0 instead of 2:

```
daysOfRain= daysOfRain / 2.0;
```

What happens? Can you fix it by putting in a suitable type cast? Try to change the order of operations by applying the cast to the whole expression, using parentheses.

SR5. Invent some declarations and assignments yourself so that you become thoroughly familiar with how they work. Include attempts to declare a variable several times, assignments where you have to cast, and expressions that contain calls to functions. (It is fun to see what happens when you intentionally do things wrong. Do not worry; you will not break anything.) Use all the types we have introduced: **int**, **double**, **boolean**, and String.

1.3   Classes and objects

1.3.1   The class as a file drawer of folders

Thus far, you have seen mostly primitive types: **int**, **boolean**, **double**, and so on. But Java is *object-oriented*. In this section, we show you what that means: what objects are and how they are created and used. Objects contain both data (using variables) and instructions (using methods), much like manila folders contain data and instructions in an office filing system. In fact, the similarities are strong, and we use the analogy throughout this text.

An office typically has filing cabinets (see Fig. 1.3). Each drawer of a filing cabinet contains manila folders. For example, each folder in a Patient file drawer might contain data for a different patient (patient name, billing information, and so on). Often, all the manila folders in a filing cabinet drawer have the same kind of data. For example, in a doctor's office, Patient folders are not usually in the same drawer as folders containing information related to building maintenance.

The tab of each manila folder has a unique name. To generate unique names easily, you can use the sequence a0, a1, ..., a9, b0, b1, ...b9, c0, c1, ... We will use these names to uniquely identify which particular object a variable refers to. (In the computer, the name is a memory address chosen by the operating system. When tracing by hand, it can be any unique name.)

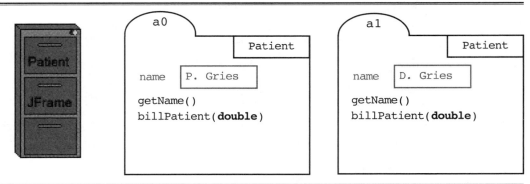

Figure 1.3:   Two folders of class Patient

In Java, each file drawer is called a *class*, and each manila folder in the class is called an *object* of the class, or an *instance* of the class. So, we use the terms *class* and *drawer* interchangeably, and we use the terms *folder*, *object*, and *instance* interchangeably. In Java, all the folders in a drawer contain the same kind of information.

Figure 1.3 shows a file cabinet and two folders of class `Patient`. The folders are named `a0` and `a1`. Each folder contains a box in its upper right corner that identifies the class, or file drawer, where it belongs. We follow this convention throughout this text.

A folder generally contains *fields* where data is entered. In the two folders in Fig. 1.3, we have drawn a field named `name`, which contains the name of the patient. There may be many more fields (birth date, billing address, medical history, and so on); in the interests of saving space, we show only `name`.

In a medical office, different people would handle a manila folder for a patient in different ways. A secretary would fill out the non-medical fields such as name and birth date. A doctor would make entries in the medical history when talking to the patient. An accountant would handle the folder when billing the patient. And so on. When processing the folder on a computer, we mimic these processes by calling *methods* that reside in the folders. For example, in Fig. 1.3, in each folder we have shown a method `getName`, which is used to retrieve the name of the patient. This method is like a mathematical *function* because it gives us a value. We have also shown a method `billPatient`. We call this method a *procedure*, not a function. Method `billPatient` does not give us a value back; instead, calling `billPatient` with a **double** value bills the patient that amount.

The methods that appear in each folder are called *instance methods* because they appear in each instance of the class.

As a rule, it is considered unsafe to directly reference the fields of a folder (both professional software engineers and your instructor will yell at you if you make a habit of it), and that is why field `name` is grayed out in the two folders in Fig. 1.3. Instead, as we will soon see, we use the instance methods to retrieve or change the values in the fields.

1.3.2 Packages and the import statement

Java comes with over 2000 predefined classes. They are used for all sorts of things. There are classes whose objects represent files on your computer, windows on your screen, dates, menus that can be placed in windows on your screen, lists of items, and so on. Because there are so many classes, Java organizes them in *packages*. You can find out all you need to know about packages by reading (the very short) Chap. 11.

One such package is `javax.swing`, which contains classes that are used in applications that use GUIs (Graphical User Interfaces). Think of `javax.swing` as a room that contains file cabinets full of classes that deal with GUIs. One class in this package is `JFrame`, whose folders represent windows on your monitor, or computer screen. The full name of the class is `javax.swing.JFrame`. Here is how we declare a variable of this class:

```
javax.swing.JFrame window;
```

Including the long package name can get pretty awkward. Working with classes from package `javax.swing.text.html.parser`, for example, is cumbersome! Java provides a way to shorten this; the *import statement* allows us to dispense with the package name and use only the class name.

If we use this import statement:

```
import javax.swing.JFrame;
```

we can declare a `JFrame` variable like this:

```
JFrame window;
```

Frequently, we want to use many classes from a package. Rather than write a separate import statement for each class, we can use the *wildcard* character, "`*`" to refer to all classes in the package:

```
import javax.swing.*;
```

Finding specifications of classes and methods in them

To use a class such as `javax.swing.JFrame`, you have to know what methods appear in the folders and what those methods do. The descriptions (or *specifications*) of all the predefined packages, classes, and methods are collectively called the *Application Programming Interface*, or *API*. The specifications tell you what the classes are for and what their methods do.

The latest version of the Java API specifications can be found on the world wide web at this url:

```
http://java.sun.com/api/index.html
```

Appendix II explains how to use the API specs. You will access this site often during your course on Java (and throughout your career as a Java programmer).

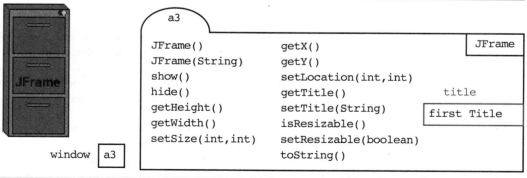

Figure 1.4:   An object of class `javax.swing.JFrame`

Java syntax: new-expression

new *class-name* (*arguments*)

Example: new JFrame("title 1")

Purpose: Create a new folder of class *class-name*, initialize its fields using the call *class-name*(*arguments*), and yield the name of the new folder as the value of the new-expression.

1.3.3 Objects of class JFrame

Class javax.swing.JFrame is a good class to study first because you will be able to use it and see immediately the effects of calling methods of one of its manila folders. An instance of JFrame is associated with a window on your computer monitor. To create an object of class JFrame, use this assignment:

JFrame window= **new** JFrame("first JFrame");

Figure. 1.4 shows three things. On the left is the filing cabinet with a drawer for class JFrame. To the right is the object, drawn like a manila folder, that is created by execution of the above assignment; this object belongs in JFrame's file drawer. The name on the tab of the folder, a3, is arbitrary but different from the names of all other folders. Finally, Fig. 1.4 contains a variable window, with the name a3 as its value. We describe the process that created the picture.

First, the *new-expression* is evaluated:

new JFrame("first JFrame")

Evaluating this new-expression is a three-step process:

1. Create a new folder of class JFrame and give it a name.
2. Execute the call JFrame("first JFrame"), which causes the *argument* to be stored somewhere in the folder. This String will be the title on the window.
3. Yield the name of the folder as the value of the new-expression.

Take a look near the top left of the folder in Fig. 1.4. It contains "JFrame (String)", which indicates that method JFrame is in the folder and, when this method is called, it has to have an argument that is a String. This is the method that is called in step 2 above.

Second, once the new-expression yields its value, a3, the assignment statement stores that value in variable window.

The contents of folder a3

We investigate the contents of folder a3 in Fig. 1.4. It has method JFrame(String), as discussed above, several other instance methods, and an instance variable title.

> **Monitors and pixels**. The word *pixel*, a shortening of *picture element*, is the smallest rectangle that your monitor can draw. The upper left corner of your monitor is called pixel
>
> Activity 1-5.5 explains pixels and talks about the resolution of a monitor.
>
> `(0, 0)`. In a pixel `(x,y)`, `x` is called the x-coordinate and `y` the y-coordinate. Value `x` measures the distance from the left of the window and `y` measures the distance from the top of the window, both in pixels.
>
> The position of each window on your monitor is given by the pixel (x, y) of its top left corner. The height and width of a window are also given in pixels.

Remember our brief discussion about how you should only rarely directly access instance variables? In fact, there are ways to limit access to instance variables and methods that you write, and you will learn about them later when you learn how to write your own classes. Folder `a3` shows variable `title`, but it is grayed out, and we cannot access it directly because the programmers who wrote class `JFrame` have limited our access to it. (In fact, we do not know the real name of this variable or precisely how the title is stored in it!) We display this variable only to make sure that you know this is the folder for the given url. This discussion perhaps seems a tad silly right now, but *information hiding* is a vital strategy when writing large programs.

In the folder are some instance-method names followed by parentheses; some have a type inside them, which indicate the type that an argument of a call on the method must have. These are only a few of the methods that are in each instance of class `JFrame`.

The instance methods are used to access and manipulate parts of the `JFrame`. Of course, the name of a method is not enough for us to know precisely what it does. For that, we have to look in the Java API specs — Appendix II tells you how to do this. Here, we briefly discuss some of the methods.

When a manila folder of class JFrame is first created, the associated window does not appear on your monitor. It is hidden. Execution of the procedure call

```
window.show();
```

causes the window to appear on your monitor, probably in the upper left corner, and quite small. You can drag its lower right corner to make it bigger, and the window will be like the right picture in Fig. 1.5.

In the call `window.show()`, "window" indicates that we are dealing with the manila folder whose name is in variable `window`. The "`.`" is used to indicate that

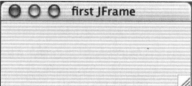

Figure 1.5:   Two instances of `JFrame` — windows on your monitor

<table>
<tr><td>

Java syntax: instance-function call

variable . name (*arguments*)

Example: `w.getTitle()`

Purpose: To call the function *name* that occurs in the folder whose name is in variable *variable*. A function call is an expression and does not end in a semicolon.

</td><td>

Java syntax: instance-procedure call

variable . name (*arguments*);

Example: `w.setTitle("Peace");`

Purpose: To call the procedure *name* that occurs in the folder whose name is in variable *variable*. A procedure call ends in a semicolon.

</td></tr>
</table>

a reference to a component of the folder follows; the phrase "show" is a reference to procedure show within that folder; and the parentheses indicate the (empty) list of arguments. In general, in order to access a component (variable or method) of a folder, use the form

<variable that contains the name of the folder> . <component-name>

We summarize how you can create and show on your monitor a window that is associated with a JFrame. Just type the following three lines into the Interactions pane of DrJava, and the window will appear in the upper left corner:

```
import javax.swing.*;
JFrame window;
window= new JFrame("first Title");
window.show();
```

The first line says that the classes in package `javax.swing` may be used. The second line declares variable `window`. The fourth line creates a manila folder of class `JFrame` and stores its name in `window`. The fourth line shows the window on the monitor.

Getter and setter methods

A folder of class `JFrame` contains lots of information about the window with which it is associated. One can generally get this information using calls on certain functions that appear in each folder of the class. In Java parlance, these are called *getter* methods because they *get* a value from the folder. For example, below, we show a few function calls and the results of their evaluation:

function call	value
`window.getTitle()`	title of the window
`window.getHeight()`	height of the window, in "pixels"
`window.getWidth()`	width of the window, in "pixels"

Thus, a getter method is a function that retrieves a value from an object.

A *setter method* is a procedure that sets (or changes) a value in an object. For example, you can change the title of the window to "another title" by executing the procedure call:

```
window.setTitle("another title");
```

We give the specifications of some of the method of class JFrame in Fig. 1.6.

We encourage you to experiment with class JFrame in your IDE. Create a JFrame and assign its name to a variable such as window. Then, practice using the methods of Fig. 1.6. For example, you can find out the width of window window by evaluating the call window.getWidth() and set the position of the window to (200, 300) by having this statement executed:

```
window.setLocation(200, 300);
```

As a more complex example, we develop statements that will change the height of window window to its width, thus making the window a square. To do this, we do two things:

1. Obtain the width of the window and store it in variable jfWidth;
2. Change the height of the window to jfWidth.

When determining how to perform a programming task, it helps to write it down in English as a sequence of steps to be performed, as above. Then, we can figure out how to write each of the steps in Java. Separating *what* to do from *how* to do it is an example of *separation of concerns*, which is an important strategy in any problem-solving task. Use it consciously to focus on one thing at a time.

We are also using a methodology called *stepwise refinement*. The development consists of a series of steps. At each step, we "refine" part of the task into more detailed steps, some of them in English and some of them in Java, until the whole task has been written in Java. We discuss stepwise refinement in Sec. 2.5.

We return to the task of refining the two steps given above into Java. To see how to obtain the width of the window (step 1), we look through the list of methods described in Fig. 1.6. There it is: method getWidth will do the trick. So, we can write a statement:

window.show();	Show window window.
window.hide();	Hide window window.
window.getHeight()	= height of window window, in pixels
window.getWidth()	= width of window window, in pixels
window.setSize(w,h);	Set width and height of window window to w and h
window.getX()	= x-coordinate of top left corner of window window
window.getY()	= y-coordinate of top left corner of window window
window.setLocation(x,y);	Set x- and y-coordinates of top left corner of window to x, y
window.getTitle()	= the title of window window (in the title bar)
window.setTitle(s);	Set the title of window window to s (a String).
window.isResizable()	= "window window can be resized by dragging it"
window.setResizable(b);	If b is **true** (**false**) make window resizable (not resizable).

Figure 1.6:   Calls on some methods in an instance window of a JFrame

```
int jfWidth= window.getWidth();
```

We now look in Fig. 1.6 for a method that will change the height of the window. The only one that looks appropriate is method `setSize`. But this requires us to give as arguments both the width and the height. So, we use the statement:

```
window.setSize(jfWidth, jfWidth);
```

Combining the steps

We can eliminate the need for variable `jfWidth` by putting function calls as arguments to method `setLocation`. Thus, instead of using the two statements shown above, use the following single statement:

```
window.setSize(window.getWidth(), window.getWidth());
```

Note that the arguments are evaluated before the call `setSize(…)` is executed.

Primitive values versus class values

Consider variables `x1`, `x2`, `u1`, and `u2` that are initialized as follows:

```
int x1= 5;
int x2= 5;
JFrame u1= new JFrame("peace");
JFrame u2= new JFrame("peace");
```

Variables `x1` and `x2` contain the same value: 5. Variables `u1` and `u2`, on the other hand, contain the names of objects, as shown in Fig. 1.7. Thus, there is a fundamental difference between values of primitive types (like **int**) and values of class types (like `JFrame`). This difference has several ramifications in programming, one of which has to do with testing for equality, which we now discuss.

About equality ==

The expression

```
x1 == x2
```

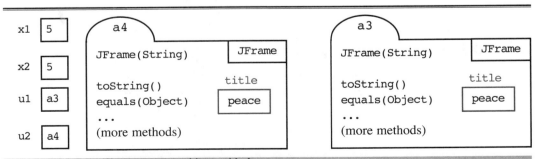

Figure 1.7: Two different `JFrame` objects with the same content

yields true because x1 and x2 contain the same value. However, variables u1 and u2 contain different values. Indeed, there are two different objects, a3 and a4, whose contents happen to be the same. In this situation, an equality test

    u1 == u2

evaluates to **false** even though the two folders contain the same thing. This is because the test is comparing the values in u1 and u2 (which are the folder names a3 and a4), not the contents of the folders.

The value null

If we declare a variable u3 like this,

    JFrame u3= **null;**

then u3 initially contains the value **null**, which means that u3 does not contain the name of an object. In this situation, executing u3.getTitle() will cause an error message to appear and execution to stop. (Try it!) So, before you try to access components of u3, assign a value to the variable, using a new-expression or perhaps an assignment like u3 = u1; (which copies the name from u1 into u3).

The three kinds of methods

We have already discussed two kinds of methods. Calls to *functions* are expressions and produce values. Calls to *procedures* are statements and do not produce values; instead, they perform some task, like billing a patient or storing a value in some variable.

The third kind of method is the *constructor*, whose only purpose is to assign initial values to fields of a folder when the folder is created. The name of a constructor is always the name of the class, and a constructor can be called only in a new-expression.

Above, we used the new-expression

    new JFrame("first Title")

to create a new folder of class JFrame and call method JFrame(String) to initialize the folder with the value of the argument "first Title". Method JFrame is a constructor.

1.3.4   Objects of class String

Now that we know about objects, we can state that a String is a class and String value is the name of an object. After declaring a variable of type String and assigning a value to it, as in

    String s1= "xyz";

variable s1 looks like this:

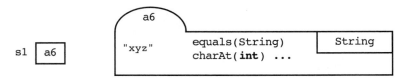

Variable s1 contains the name of a folder of class String, and the folder contains not only the string of characters but also many methods that are useful in manipulating those characters. These methods are discussed in detail in Sec. 5.2.

Here is an important point: testing two String variables s1 and s2 using

s1 == s2

does not test whether they represent the same string of characters. Instead, it tests whether s1 and s2 contain the same folder name, just like when two variables of class JFrame are compared. To test whether the strings of characters in the folders named by s1 and s2 are the same, use the test s1.equals(s2).

Equality is discussed in detail in Sec. 3.2.4.

1.3.5   Key concepts

• **Class**. A *class* is a file drawer of folders. Each folder in a drawer has the same *components*.

• **Instances and objects.** The terms *folder*, *instance*, and *object* are used interchangeably.

• **Components: fields and methods**. The possible components of an *object* are *fields*, which are variables and, thus, contain values, and *methods*, which are called to perform tasks.

• **Procedures, functions, constructors**. There are three kinds of method. A call to a *function* produces a value. A call to a *procedure* performs some task but does not produce a value. A call to a *constructor* initializes some or all fields of a newly created object. A method call can have *arguments*, which are expressions. The values of the arguments are used in some fashion when the method is called; the specification of the method explains how they are used.

• **New-expression**. Evaluation of a new-expression **new** *class-name* (*arguments*) creates a new object of the class, initializes its fields by calling constructor *class-name*, and yields as its value the name of the newly created object.

• **Class as a type**. A class name may be used as a type, and a variable declared with that type can contain the name of a folder of that type. For example, variable w of type JFrame can contain the name of a folder that goes in JFrame's file drawer.

• **Null**. The value **null** represents the absence of the name of an instance. If a variable u contains **null**, then attempting to access a component using u. *component-name* gives an error message.

1.3.6   Self-review exercises

This section introduced many new concepts, and it is important that you digest them at this point because the rest of the text builds on them. One way to gain understanding is to use an IDE to practice using the new concepts.

SR1. In your IDE (probably DrJava), create some folders of class JFrame, make them appear on your monitor (by calling method show), and drag the windows to different positions and give them different sizes. Now, experiment with calling the methods of Fig. 1.6 in these folders.

SR2. In this exercise, you will study class Date, which is in package java.util. Execute these statements in your IDE:

```
import java.util.*;
Date d= new Date();
```

Evaluate d to see what value it has. You see the date and time at which the new Date folder was created. Have your IDE evaluate this function call: d.getTime(). The value printed is the number of milliseconds since 1 January 1970, 00:00:00 GMT (Greenwich Mean Time) until the time given by variable d. That is a lot of milliseconds!

Class Date has methods that allow you to get and set the various parts of a date and time. Most of these are *deprecated* (literally, lessened in value) because there are now better (often more complex) ways to achieve their functionality. The API specification for class Date tells you about this. These methods make great examples, though, so we still use them. We list some of the methods below; their names should be enough for you to understand what they do.

getYear()	getMonth()	getDay()
setYear(**int**)	setMonth(**int**)	setDay(**int**)
getHours()	getMinutes()	getSeconds()
setHours(**int**)	setMinutes(**int**)	setSeconds(**int**)

They come in set/get pairs. Often, a property has both a *setter* and a *getter* method. Sometimes a property is read-only, in which case no setter method is provided.

The argument for setYear is a bit peculiar. Before you begin setting anything using setYear, first evaluate d.getYear() and then read the Java specifications for setYear and getYear.

There are at least two ways to find out whether setHours and getHours use 12-hour (AM/PM) or 24-hour time. What are they?

SR3. In this exercise, you will study class `Point` and practice reading the API. Class `Point` is in package `java.awt`, so type this import statement into Java:

> **import** `java.awt.*;`

Now open this url in your browser:

> `http://java.sun.com/api/index.html`

In the upper-left frame in the window, click on "`java.awt`". In the lower-left frame, scroll down and select "`Point`". In the right frame you will see a description of class `Point`. Notice that it says that an instance of class `Point` is a point representing a location in (x, y) coordinate space, specified in integer precision, by which they mean type **int**. Scroll down until you see "Field Summary", "Constructor Summary", and "Method Summary". These show you the components of every object of class `Point`. On a piece of paper, draw one folder (instance) of class `Point`, putting in it all the components. Do not forget to draw x and y as variables, and for each method, include the types of its parameters.

Create two instances of class `Point`:

> `Point p1= new Point();`
> `Point p2= new Point(5, 6);`

Class `Point` lets you access the fields x and y. See what their values are in p1 and p2. For example, evaluate p2.x.

In the `Point` webpage, the summary for x does not say what its initial value is. To find out what value x has when you do

> `new Point()`

click on "`Point()`" in the Constructor Summary. See whether the information that comes up tells you. Then use the back button to get back to the Constructor Summary.

Now look through the Method summaries. Type in some method calls and see what happens. For example, try, one after the other, these method calls:

> `p2.getX()`
> `p2.translate(5, 6);`
> `p2.getX()`

See what function `toString` gives you by typing in `p2.toString()`.
Experiment until you are familiar with `Point` and its methods.

1.4   Customizing a class to suit our needs

1.4.1   A subclass definition

Suppose we want to change the title of a `JFrame` to contain its origin (the posi-

Style Note
13.2, 13.2.5
indentation
conventions
for classes

Java syntax: Subclass definition

```
public class subclass-name extends superclass-name {
    declaration of methods and fields
}
```

Purpose: To define a new file drawer, named *subclass-name*, and describe the contents of its manila folders (instances of the class). They have the methods and fields that are defined in superclass *superclass-name* as well as the methods and fields being defined in the subclass.

---

tion of its top-left corner). For example, if the origin is (5, 3), we want to set the title to "(5, 3)". From Fig. 1.6, we see that procedure setTitle sets the title. As we learned in Sec. 1.3, if we declare and initialize a JFrame variable jf, the following expression will produce the desired String:

```
"(" + jf.getX() + ", " + jf.getY() + ")"
```

Note that this is a catenation of three strings and two **int**s, and the two **int**s are obtained by calling getter methods getX and getY. Using this expression, we can set the title of the window like this:

```
jf.setTitle("(" + jf.getX() + ", " + jf.getY() + ")");
```

Try this statement in your IDE to make sure it works. Do not forget to import the classes of package javax.swing and call method show.

Customizing JFrame: your first class, your first method

Every time we drag the window associate with a JFrame jf to a different position, we want to fix the title in a simple manner. To do this, it would sure help to be able to execute a method call that does this:

```
jf.setTitleToOrigin();
```

JFrame does not have this method. However, we can produce a customized version by *extending* JFrame.

In the rest of this section, we define a new class called OurFrame (your first class definition!) that has all JFrame's methods and fields plus a new method, setTitleToOrigin. In particular, we want to be able to execute the following code, which should create an instance of OurFrame, show it, and set its title to its origin:

```
OurFrame ourWindow= new OurFrame();
ourWindow.show();
ourWindow.setTitleToOrigin();
```

OurFrame objects should behave just like JFrame objects, plus they should have method setTitleToOrigin. Below is the outline of the definition of class OurFrame, which must be placed in a file named OurFrame.java:

Java syntax: Procedure definition

public void *procedure-name* (*parameter-declarations*) {
    sequence of statements
}

Purpose: To define a procedure named *procedure-name*, declare its parameters, and give the sequence of statements to execute when the procedure is called. Each parameter declaration has the form *type variable*, and adjacent parameter declarations are separated by commas.

```
import javax.swing.*;
public class OurFrame extends JFrame {
    place here the declaration of method setTitleToOrigin

}
```

Style Note 13.1, 13.1.3 class names

Class OurFrame is called a *subclass* of JFrame, and JFrame is a *superclass* of OurFrame. OurFrame acts just like a JFrame in most ways, but it is customized to have additional behavior.

The first line of file OurFrame.java makes available to the file all the classes in package javax.swing. The rest of the lines define class OurFrame. Keyword **public** indicates that this class is accessible to all other classes. The clause **extends** JFrame says that an instance of this class has all the components —methods and variables— that a JFrame has.

We encourage you to type in this class (everything but the italicized words), compile it, and try using it just as you did JFrame. Method setTitleToOrigin has not yet been defined, so your new class will behave in every way like a JFrame.

We now add the declaration of method setTitleToOrigin within the curly braces { and }. Below is your first method declaration:

Style Note 13.2, 13.2.4 indentation conventions for methods

```
/** Set the title of this instance to contain the origin of the window */
public void setTitleToOrigin() {
    place here statements to set the title
}
```

Keyword **public** indicates that this method is accessible from anywhere. Keyword **void** indicates that the method being defined is a procedure. Within the curly braces we will place the statements that set the title to the origin. The curly braces, together with any statements in between, constitute the *body* of the method.

We encourage you to type this method into class OurFrame (everything but the italicized words). After compiling, you can now call ourWindow.setTitleToOrigin(); (although nothing will happen yet).

We now figure out how to set the title. We want to place something like this statement in the body of method setTitleToOrigin:

```
jf.setTitle("(" + jf.getX() + ", " + jf.getY() + ")");
```

But we cannot use the name `jf` because that variable name is not available in method `setTitleToOrigin`. We need something more general, which can refer to *this* instance, the object in which the method resides. Java uses the keyword **this** for this purpose. So we put this statement in the body of `setTitleToOrigin`:

```
this.setTitle("(" + this.getX() + ", " + this.getY() + ")");
```

Class `OurFrame` is in Fig. 1.8. Our sequence of statements now works!

```
OurFrame ourWindow= new OurFrame();
ourWindow.show();
ourWindow.setTitleToOrigin();
```

Compile class `ourFrame` in your IDE and then experiment with it. After executing the above statements, drag the window to a different place on your monitor and then execute the call to method `setTitleToOrigin` again.

The manila folder for an instance of class OurFrame

Earlier, we showed how to draw an instance of a class as a manila folder, with the name of the folder in the tab, the name of the class in a box in the upper right, and the methods and fields in the folder itself. Drawing a folder of class `OurFrame` is slightly different because it extends class `JFrame`. An `OurFrame` manila folder has to have all the methods and fields that a `JFrame` has plus those that are defined in `OurFrame`.

We show a manila folder of class `OurFrame` in Fig. 1.9. The folder has two partitions. The top partition shows all the methods and fields that an instance of superclass `JFrame` has. The bottom partition has the methods and fields that are defined in subclass `OurFrame`. Of course, all the methods in both partitions are available for use.

It is easy to remember how to draw such a folder. The superclass partition is at the top, and the subclass (*sub* means *under*) partition is underneath the superclass partition.

```
import javax.swing.*;

public class OurFrame extends JFrame {

    /** Set the title of this instance to contain the origin of the window */
    public void setTitleToOrigin() {
        this.setTitle("(" + this.getX() + ", " + this.getY() + ")");
    }
}
```

Figure 1.8:   Class `OurFrame`, which is placed in file `OurFrame.java`

1.4.2   Remembering data: adding variables to the subclass definition

Now assume that the user of subclass `OurFrame` wants to be able to retrieve the old value of the title. They have dragged the window to another spot and would like the ability to remember where it used to be. We can help them out by placing a field in `OurFrame` that gives the previous title. Variables are used to remember values, so we introduce a variable to remember the previous title:

```
public class OurFrame extends JFrame {

    /** class invariant: previousTitle is previous title (initially "")*/
    private String previousTitle;

}
```

Style Note
13.4
describing
variables

The declaration of field `previousTitle` differs from declarations you have seen because of the *access modifier* **private**, which indicates that the variable can be accessed only in this class itself. No other class will be able to refer to it directly. Instead, they must use the *setter* and *getter* methods for it, which get values and store values in fields. You see the variable grayed out in the folder of Fig. 1.11.

The comment that precedes the declaration of the field has the title "class invariant". A class invariant describes what the values of the fields should contain, and it is the duty of each method that is called to ensure that that description is true when the method is finished executing. We often write such a class invariant, and whenever we write a method, we make sure that the class invariant is true when the method is finished.

Every object of type `OurFrame` will have its own copy of `previousTitle`.

Take a look at procedure `setTitleToOrigin` in Fig. 1.10. It now contains two statements instead of one. The first statement evaluates the current title, using a call to function `getTitle`, and stores the current title in field `previousTitle`. The second statement then sets the title of the window, as before. When the method is called, the statements are executed one at a time, in the order in which they appear.

Figure 1.10 contains a getter method, named `getPreviousTitle`. This method is a *function*, not a procedure. We know this because the *return type* is

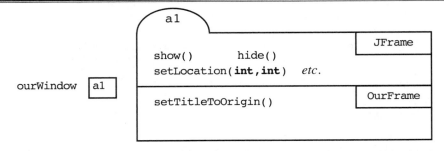

Figure 1.9:   A manila folder for instance ours of class `OurFrame`

class-type `String` instead of keyword **void**. This type defines the type of the variable that the function returns.

Functions are different from procedures in that they return a value. To state what a function returns, use a *return statement*, of the form

return *expression* ;

Execution of the return statement evaluates the *expression*, stops execution of the function body, and yields the value of the *expression* as the result of the function call. In `getPreviousTitle`, the *expression* is **this**.`previousTitle`, and its value is the value in that field.

Drawing a folder that contains a field

Figure 1.11 contains an instance of the revised class `OurFrame`. We have placed field `previousTitle` in it, as well as getter method `getPreviousTitle`. Field `previousTitle` is grayed out to indicate that it is **private**, so it cannot be referenced outside the class.

1.4.3   Self-review exercises

Hopefully, you have had your IDE open while you read Sec. 1.4 and have tried making `JFrames`. These exercises will give you more practice with `JFrames` and with writing customized window classes.

SR1. Type into Java this import statement:

import javax.swing.*;

```java
import javax.swing.*;
public class OurFrame extends JFrame {

    /** Class invariant: previousTitle contains the previous title (initially "") */
    private String previousTitle= "";

    /** Set the title of this instance to contain the origin of the window */
    public void setTitleToOrigin() {
        this.previousTitle= this.getTitle();
        this.setTitle("(" + this.getX() + ", " + this.getY() + ")");
    }

    /**= the previous title (empty "" if none) */
    public String getPreviousTitle() {
        return this.previousTitle;
    }
}
```

Figure 1.10:   Class `OurFrame`, revised to maintain the previous title

Create an instance of class `JFrame` and assign it to variable `myWindow`. (Read the beginning of Sec. 1.4 if you need help with this.) Now `show` the window, set the title to `"My Window"`, and evaluate `myWindow.getWidth()`.

Execute these statements:

```
JFrame myOtherWindow= myWindow;
myOtherWindow.setSize(444, 777);
```

Evaluate `myWindow.getWidth()` again. You changed `myOtherWindow`; why did `myWindow`'s width also change?

SR2. `myWindow.getWidth()` and `myWindow.getHeight()` get the width and height of the window. `myWindow.setSize(`*expression*$_1$`, `*expression*$_2$`);` sets the size of the window. Figure out a single Java statement that will swap the height and width of the window to which `myWindow` refers.

SR3. Write a custom `JFrame` class called `ResizerFrame` that has a single method `swapDimensions()` that sets the height to the width and the width to the height. (You can base it on the code in `OurFrame` in Fig. 1.10 a few pages back.) Compile it and then create an instance of `ResizerFrame` and assign it to a variable `rf`. Now call `rf.swapDimensions()` and make sure it works.

1.5   Static components

If a method does not access fields of a class or other instance methods, there is no need to place it in each folder of the class. An example of this is method `sum`, below, whose body references only parameters a, b, and c:

```
/** = sum of a, b, and c */
public static int sum(int a, int b, int c) {
    return a + b + c;
}
```

When writing such methods, we use keyword **static**. The presence of this keyword indicates that this component does *not* belong in each folder of the class. Instead, there is only *one* copy of the component, and it is stored right in the file

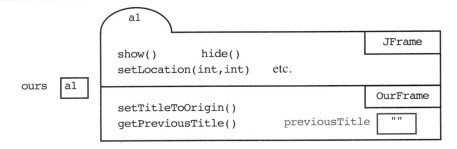

Figure 1.11:   Revised instance `ours` of class `OurFrame`, with field `previousTitle`

drawer for the class. Hence, a file drawer for a class can contain two kinds of things:

1. manila folders of the class,
2. components that are declared with keyword **static**.

Class Math, which is **public** and, therefore, accessible everywhere, contains many methods, and they are all **static** because there is no need to put them inside folders. Instead, file drawer Math simply contains a lot of static methods. It also contains two static fields, one of which is

```
Math.PI
```

which is a **double** value that approximates *pi*, the ratio of the circumference of a circle to its diameter.

Property **static** will be discussed in more detail later. Here, we just wanted to make you aware of it because you are sure to see the keyword **static** from time to time.

1.6   Graphics in a JFrame

We show you how to paint rectangles, circles, text, etc. in a JFrame. This process shows the usefulness and flexibility of working with classes and objects and extending (customizing) classes. Conceptually, there is nothing new in this section; it is just a matter of learning about some more predefined classes in the Java API and seeing how to use them. We keep this section short because the material is covered thoroughly and more easily in *ProgramLive*.

We will create another subclass of JFrame. The only thing we will do in an instance of the subclass is to draw in it —lines, rectangles, ovals, text, and the like, and in different colors.

Activity 1-5.6 also discusses JFrame's method paint.

Each instance of class JFrame contains a procedure paint, which is called every time your system has to redraw the associated window (for example, because it just became visible). This procedure does not do anything because its body has no statement in it. But if we define a subclass of JFrame, we can customize this procedure to draw pictures. We *override* procedure paint in JFrame with a new one in the subclass.

Figure 1.12 contains a subclass GraphicsFrame of JFrame that defines method paint. Here is the window that is shown by creating an instance of this subclass and showing it —we resized the window before taking a snapshot of it:

We investigate procedure paint in Fig. 1.12. First, your program never calls paint directly; instead, the system calls paint whenever it has to redraw the window —e.g. when the window is brought to the front or when it is moved. Second, procedure paint has a parameter g of class Graphics. The instance of class Graphics that is passed as an argument to paint contains the methods that draw in the window.

Look at the body of paint. The first statement calls procedure g.setColor, with argument Color.red. Class Color contains several constants, like Color.red, that represent various colors. Execution of this call sets the color of the pen so that anything drawn after this will be red. In the picture shown above, the part of the circle that is showing would be red on your monitor.

> Activity 1-5.5 explains pixels and talks about the resolution of a monitor.

The second procedure call draws an oval that will fit in the square whose upper left corner is pixel (0, 0) —given by the first two arguments— and whose width and height are both 40 (the second two arguments). Pixel (0, 0) is the origin of the window: its upper left corner. Half of the oval that was drawn is hidden by the title bar of the window.

We can change the origin by calling method g.translate. For example, execution of the following statement moves the origin to the right 20 pixels and down 30 pixels:

```
g.translate(20, 30);
```

Better yet, we can change the origin to the pixel right under the title bar by executing this procedure call —the two arguments yield the correct number of pixels to move:

```
g.translate(this.getInsets().left,
            this.getInsets().top);
```

If we insert this call as the first statement of method paint and create and show an instance of class GraphicsFrame, the window will look like this:

```
import javax.swing.*;
import java.awt.*;
public class GraphicsFrame extends JFrame {
    /** Draw a figure in the window accessed by g */
    public void paint(Graphics g) {
        g.setColor(Color.red);
        g.drawOval(0, 0, 40, 40);
    }
}
```

Figure 1.12: Subclass of JFrame with a method paint

Now, the upper-left corner of the rectangle that encloses the circle is just below the left part of the title bar.

Class `Graphics` has many methods for drawing. Methods exist for drawing a line, a rectangle, a filled rectangle (i.e. the whole rectangle and not just its border is painted), an oval, a filled oval, an arc of an oval, text, and more.

A footnote on lesson page 1.5 describes these methods and the Color contants.

Class `Color` contains a number of constants, like `Color.red`. It also contains methods for dealing directly with the RGB (Red-Green-Blue) coloring system, which is used for much of the image manipulation in computers.

It will help your progress with Java to type in a class like `GraphicsFrame` of Fig. 1.12 and to modify it to draw various lines, rectangles, and so on. You will not only become familiar with the methods of class `Graphics` but you will also gain fluency in the general task of writing method calls, using various expressions as arguments.

If you try to draw a figure like the one in the left margin, draw it first on a piece of paper, perhaps graph paper, and figure out roughly where each component goes.

1.7   Programming style and programming habits

You have now written, debugged, and run a few small programs, and you are beginning to have a feel for the programming process. The pieces of code you have written so far are quite small, of course. But by the end of this course you will have written programs that are perhaps several hundred lines long, and you may start to find it difficult to remember all the pieces that you have written and how they fit together. Several good programming habits will help you deal with this complexity.

There are two goals of these programming habits. First, the habits will make you a faster and better programmer. Second, other programmers will be able to read and understand your programs with a minimum of effort.

If you want to continue in computer science, these habits are even more important than they are for this introductory course. Second, third, and fourth-year programming courses often have you write thousands of lines of code

In the professional world, creating programs that are readable by others is even more important. Most programs live a long time and require *maintenance* —changes to adapt the code to new and different requirements, upgrades in other software, new hardware, and so forth. Frequently the author of the program will not be around when maintenance is required (having been promoted, moved to a different project, or fired), so other programmers *must* be able to read and understand the program.

Some programming habits concern syntactical measures, like indenting program parts properly and using certain conventions for names of variables, methods, and classes. Other habits concern describing code in comments so that the reader can understand how a program is designed.

It is important to practice good programming habits *all the time*. This will possibly be an uncomfortable part of learning to program, but it is the part that will help you the most in the long run.

From time to time, you will find short discussions on programming conventions and style in this text. These are summarized in Chap. 13, and we suggest that you skim that chapter now to get a sense of what it contains, and then return to it at regular intervals to make sure that you understand and are following our style conventions.

Exercises for Chapter 1

E1. Suppose d is of type **double**. For what values of x do the following expressions give the same result, and for what values do they give different results?

```
(int) d
(int) Math.round(d)
```

E2. Do the same as exercise 1 for these two expressions:

```
(int) d
(int) Math.ceil(d)
(int) Math.floor(d)
```

E3. Write and test a class DoubleFrame that customizes JFrame to have a method with this specification:

```
/** Double the width and height of this window */
public void doubleDimensions()
```

E4. Write and test a class SwitchFrame that customizes JFrame to have a method with this specification:

```
/** Switch the width and height of this window */
public void switchDimensions()
```

E5. Write and test a class DateFrame that customizes JFrame to have a method with the specification given below. Class Date has a special way of encoding the month and year; use whatever that class gives you for a month and year.

```
/**
 * Change this window as follows:
 *    Set the width to 150 + (the month of d)
 *    Set the height to 150 + (the year of d) % 200
 *    Set the title to d.toString()
 */
public void setByDate(Date d)
```

E6. Write and test a class `DoubleVisionFrame` that customizes `JFrame` to have two procedures, `createPartner()` and `resetPartner()`. The task of procedure `createPartner` in an instance of this class is to create and show another `JFrame` that is the same size as this one and whose origin is 20 pixels down and to the right of the origin of this one. Of course, if you drag either frame to another place or resize it, the other frame will not automatically follow. The task of procedure `resetPartner` is to again set the size of the partner frame to the size of the original one and to move it 20 pixels down and to the right of the original frame. **Hint:** you will need an instance variable (field) that will contain the name of the instance of the second `JFrame`.

E7. Write and test a class `StarFrame` that customizes a `JFrame` to have two procedures, `createStar()` and `resetStar()`. The task of procedure `createStar` in an instance of this class is to create and show four other `JFrames`; the width and height of each is 1/2 the width and height of this frame. The four frames form a four-pointed star around the original frame, each touching the original frame in one of its four corners. The task of procedure `resetPartner` is to reset the four frames so they have the size and position as stated for procedure `createStar`. **Hint:** you will need four instance variables (fields), one for each of the four new frames. Be sure to put comments near their declarations so that the reader can see which is which.

E8. Write and test a class `BullseyeFrame` that customizes a `JFrame` and has a method **public void** `paint(Graphics g)` that paints four filled circles with the same center, so that it looks like a bullseye. The inner circle should be filled with red and have a radius of 10; the next circle, black with a radius of 20; the next, white with a radius of 30; and the outer circle, black with a radius of 40. In which order should you paint the circles to get them to look right? Try from inner to outer; then try from outer to inner. Rather than using `g.drawOval`, you will need to find a method that draws a filled oval. Look online at the API for `java.awt.Graphics`, and look for an appropriate method that begins with "`fill`". See Appendix II for instructions on how to navigate the API.

E9. Below is a subclass of `JFrame` that paints a face in the frame. The mouth is placed 1/2 the radius of the face down from its center (10 + 20, 15 + 20) and is 1/2 the radius in length. The eyes are 1/3 of the radius of the face up and to the left and right of the center of face. The diameter of an eye is 1/6 of the radius of the face.

As a first step, type this class into your IDE and create and show an instance of it. Then, draw it on graph paper so that you can see where its parts are.

The problem with this class is that the numbers are all hard-coded. Rewrite the class so that it has the following fields, which are declared with initializing declarations: (x, y) gives the origin of the rectangle that contains the face, and r gives radius of the face. When making the change, declare the fields first and recompile. Then, change the constants in one statement at a time, testing after each one.

```java
import java.awt.*;
import javax.swing.*;
public class FaceFrame extends JFrame {

    /**
     * Draw a face in the rectangle whose origin is (10, 15) and whose
     * width and height are both 40.
     */
    public void paint(Graphics g) {
        g.translate(this.getInsets().left,
        this.getInsets().top);
        g.drawOval(10, 15, 40, 40);

        // Draw the mouth
        g.drawLine(10 + 20 - 5, 15 + 20 + 10,
                   10 + 20 + 5, 15 + 20 + 10);

        // Draw the left and right eyes, green
        g.setColor(Color.green);
        g.drawOval(10 + 20 - 6, 15 + 20 - 6, 3, 3);
        g.drawOval(10 + 20 + 6, 15 + 20 - 6, 3, 3);
    }
}
```

E10. Add to the class of the previous exercise a method moveFace(**int** originX, **int** originY, **int** radius) that changes the origin of the face and its radius. The last statement in the method body should be a call to repaint the frame: repaint();.

E11. In the previous exercise, look at a face with radius 60 so you can see it well. Notice that the eyes seem to be looking to the right. Why is that? Why aren't the eyes centered? Fix the eyes—but do not hack! That is, do not simply try many different things, hoping that one of them will fix the eyes. Instead, draw the face on paper, putting in the bounding boxes of all ovals that are drawn and labeling the various parts, distances, etc. If you do this carefully, you should be able to see the problem.

E12. Write (and test) a class that customizes JFrame with another method that paints a house, with a door, window, and roof.

E13. Write (and test) a class that maintains a time (hour and minute of the day). There should be a way for a use to indicate that they want 12-hour time (e.g. 8:20PM or 8:10AM) or 24-hour time (e.g. 20:20 or 8:10), and method `toString` should produce whatever is desired. The complete design of the class is up to you, but remember, fields should be private.

Chapter 2

Methods

OBJECTIVES

- Learn how to call methods based on their specifications.
- Learn how to design and write methods.
- Learn how to execute a method call, using a "model of memory".
- Study a methodology for writing method bodies called *stepwise refinement* or *top-down programming*.
- Learn how to conditionally execute a statement.
- Learn how to repeatedly execute a statement.

INTRODUCTION

Methods —functions, procedures, and constructors— were introduced in Sec. 1.3.3. In this chapter, we describe methods in depth, showing not only how to write them and to call, or invoke, them but also how they are executed by the computer. We will discuss two kinds of Java methods: *instance* methods and *static* methods.

2.1   Java methods are recipes

Cookbooks are filled with recipes. A recipe is a set of instructions for a cook to carry out. Java classes are like cookbooks, and Java methods are like recipes. Each method is a sequence of instructions for a computer to carry out.

Invoking a recipe or method

A recipe may require the use of another recipe. For example, a chocolate cake recipe may contain the instruction

Use White icing, page 250.

When a cook reaches that instruction when making chocolate cake, they pause, make the white icing, and then continue with the chocolate cake recipe. Similarly, Java methods can contain instructions to carry out other methods. In Java, an instruction that pauses the current method and executes another method is called a *method call* or *invocation*.

In Java, we say that a method is being *executed* while the computer (or you) is carrying it out.

Parameters

Rombauer and Becker's *Joy of Cooking* has a recipe for Chocolate Apricot Cake. This recipe merely says to make another recipe, for chocolate prune cake, but to substitute apricots for the prunes. Thus, the call of the prune cake recipe asks for a substitution of one ingredient for another:

> **Chocolate Apricot Cake**
> Follow the recipe for: Chocolate Prune Cake, but
> > Substitute for the prunes: 1 cup cooked pureed apricots.
> Omit the spices
>
> ...

This substitution of ingredients in recipes, with the substitution being indicated at the call on the recipe, is an important concept —much more so in programming than in cooking! We illustrate how the concept works in terms of recipes.

First, let's write a recipe for `Chocolate X Cake`, where `X` is a fruit to be named later. `X` is called a *parameter* of the recipe.

> **Chocolate (X) Cake**
> Sift: 1 1/2 cups cake flour
> Resift with: 1/2 t baking soda, ...
> Add: 1 cup `X`   // Note the use of parameter `X` here
>
> ...

To use this recipe to make a chocolate prune cake, we use the instruction

> Make `Chocolate (prunes) Cake`.

Executing this instruction results in following the `Chocolate (X) Cake` recipe with prunes substituted for `X`. We can use the same recipe to make an apricot cake as well:

> Make `Chocolate (apricots) Cake`.

The `Chocolate (X) Cake` recipe is a *parameterized* recipe, with `X` being the parameter. In the same way, methods in Java are parameterized sequences of instructions.

We recommend that you reread this section (Sec. 2.1) again in a week, especially if you are confused about parameters and method calls in Java.

2.2   The black-box view of a method

You know that a *method* is the programming equivalent of a recipe. We now see how methods are used in Java.

2.2.1   The anatomy of a method header

The definition of a method has three parts: specification, header, and body. Here, we describe the first two parts, which are used to understand a call on a method. When you call a method, we say that you are the *client* or *customer* of the method. Below is a method definition, with the contents of the body not shown:

```
/** Draw a line in graphics window from
    pixel (x1, y1) to (x2, y2) */
public void drawLine(int x1, int y1, int x2, int y2) {
    ...
}
```

The first part of a method declaration is a comment that describes what the method does. It is called a *specification*. As you can see from the specification given above, method drawLine draws a line in the graphics window.

The second part of a method declaration is the *method header*, which contains (in order) these items:

Style Note 13.1.2: method names

- **Modifiers**. In this header, the one modifier, **public**, indicates that every class can use this method. (You will see **private** methods later on.)
- **The return type**. Keyword **void** indicates that this method is a *procedure*, which is a method that does not return a value. For a *function*, the type of value the function returns replaces **void**.
- **The name of the method**, in this case, drawLine.
- **Declarations of the parameters** of the method, enclosed in parentheses and separated by commas. Each parameter declaration consists of a type and the name of the parameter (which is an identifier). In this case, all four parameters —x1, y1, x2, and y2— are of type **int**.

The *signature* of a method consists of the name of the method and the number and types of is parameters. We write the signature of drawLine as follows:

```
drawLine(int, int, int, int)
```

Style Note 13.1.1: parameter names

The idea of a parameter was discussed in Sec. 2.1 when relating methods to recipes. There, a parameter X was associated with a value —a bunch of prunes or apricots. Similarly, in Java, a value gets associated with the parameter when the method is called. The idea of a parameter may still seem foreign to you, so we recommend that you memorize the following definition:

Parameter: A parameter is a variable that is declared within the parentheses of a method header.

> **Java syntax: Typical procedure and function declarations**
> ```
> /** Comment describing what the procedure does */
> public void method-name ( parameter-declarations ) { … }
> ```
>
> Each *parameter-declaration* has the form *type identifier* (just like all variable declarations). Adjacent *parameter-declaration*s are separated by commas. There may be 0 parameter declarations. In a function declaration, keyword **void** is replaced by the type of value that the function calculates.

**Style Note
13.3.1:
method specs**

Above, we made a point of including the specification of a method as part of its definition. The specification is not needed for the program to compile and run; it is just a comment. But clients of your code need the specification to understand how to use the method. Get in the habit of always writing the specification of a method before you write the method body.

Here is some motivation: during your programming career you will come to rely heavily on the online Java API specifications. The online specifications were automatically extracted from the comments in the code and turned into HTML web pages using a tool called *Javadoc*; those comments were written by programmers. Without those comments the API classes would be useless. When you get a programming job you will have to write documentation: you will have no choice! Also, if you learn to comment now, it will serve you well: programmers who work with you will sing your praises.

Plus, you will get better grades.

In this chapter, we discuss mainly procedures and functions. A procedure call is a statement: it is *executed*. A function call is an expression, with a type, so it is *evaluated*. Throughout this chapter, we use the word *method* when discussing methods in general, and when we need to distinguish the two, we use *procedure* or *function*.

Here is an example of a specification and header of a function.

> **Ad hoc polymorphism.** *Polymorphism*, from a Greek word meaning *multiform*, means "capable of having or occurring in several distinct forms". When we write the calls `println(5)`, `println(b || c)`, and `println("xyz")`, it looks like *one* procedure `println` is able to handle arguments of many types, and if that were the case, this would be an instance of *parametric polymorphism*. Instead, in Java, one writes several different procedures with the same name but with different parameter types —the procedure name is *overloaded*. Java is able to distinguish which procedure to call based on the types of the arguments of the call. This is known as *ad hoc polymorphism*. We will see other types of polymorphism later on, for polymorphism is an important feature of OO languages.
>
> Polymorphism in programming languages was first discussed by Christopher Strachey in 1967, but the first major language that included polymorphism in a big way was Robin Milner's language ML, in 1976.

Java syntax: Procedure call (or procedure invocation)

procedure-name (*argument* , ..., *argument*) ;

Each *argument* is an expression whose type is the same as or narrower than the corresponding parameter of the procedure being called.

Example: `drawRect(5, 10, 20, 30);`

Purpose: We can view execution of a procedure call as doing what the specification of the procedure call says (with the parameters in the specification replaced by the arguments of the call).

```
/** = the larger of x and y */
public int larger(int x, int y) { … }
```

You can tell that this is a function because **of** the type **int** after **public**, which indicates the type of value that the function produces. The specification indicates that a call to the function evaluates to the larger of the two parameters x and y.

2.2.2   The procedure call

(Activity 2-1.4)

We now explain how the method specification and method header are used in writing a *method call*, or *method invocation*, as it is sometimes called.

```
/** Draw a line from pixel (x1, y1) to pixel (x2, y2). */
public void drawLine(int x1, int y1, int x2, int y2) {
    …
}
```

Suppose we want to use procedure `drawLine`, shown above, to draw a line in the graphics window from pixel (20, 20) to pixel (80, 40). Notice that if x1, y1, x2, and y2 in procedure `drawLine` are replaced with 20, 20, 80, and 40, the `drawLine` spec says that the procedure will do exactly what we want:

Draw a line from pixel (20, 20) to pixel (80, 40)

To write this statement in Java, we use a form of statement called the *procedure call*. Here is an example:

```
drawLine(20, 20, 80, 40);
```

This procedure call consists of:

- The name of the procedure, `drawLine`.
- A list of four integers, separated by commas and enclosed in parentheses; these are the *arguments* of the call.
- A semicolon.

A method call has one argument for each parameter of the method. The first argument corresponds to the first parameter, the second argument to the second parameter, and so on. The type of each argument must be the same as or narrower than the type of the corresponding parameter.

In our example, since each parameter of procedure `drawLine` is declared using keyword **int**, the corresponding arguments must be integer-valued.

Determining what execution of a procedure call does

Learn to rely entirely on the specification and header of the method to determine what a method call will do: simply copy the specification but replace each parameter in it by the value of the corresponding argument. The result is a statement that is equivalent to the call.

Here is an example. Consider this procedure:

```
/** Draw a rectangle with top-left corner at pixel (tx, ty) with
       height h and width w. */
public void drawRect(int tx, int ty, int w, int h) { … }
```

To figure out what the call

```
drawRect(20, 30, 25, 40);
```

does, make a copy of the specification and replace each parameter in that copy by the value of the corresponding argument:

> Draw a rectangle with top-left corner at pixel (20, 30) with
> height 40 and width 25.

The general form of a procedure call

A procedure call consists of:

- An identifier: the procedure name.
- Zero or more arguments, separated by commas and enclosed in parentheses.
- A semicolon.

There are several rules for the number and types of arguments:

- A method call has one argument for each parameter of the method.
- An argument is an expression, and its type must be the same as or narrower than the type of the corresponding parameter.
- If a method call has no arguments, the parentheses are still necessary.

Thus far, the arguments of method calls have just been integers, but any expression (of a suitable type) could be used. For example, the argument 40 could have been written as:

```
20 + 2 * 10
```

Writing a procedure call

Activity
2-2.6

Suppose you have to write a program segment to carry out some task, and you believe that a call to a certain method can be used for it. In such a situation, try to rewrite the task so that it is the same as the specification of the method, but with expressions instead of parameters. The call will then be easy to write.

For example, suppose we want to:

Draw a rectangle with top-left corner (20, 40) and
lower-right corner (40, 70).

Here is method drawRect again:

```
/** Draw a rectangle with top-left corner at pixel (tx, ty) with
       height h and width w. */
public void drawRect(int tx, int ty, int w, int h) { … }
```

The specification is not written in the same form as the desired task. So, we rewrite the task. The specification of drawRect uses the width and height of the rectangle, so we figure out the formulas for them and rewrite the task as:

Draw rectangle with top-left corner (20, 40),
height 70 + 1 − 40, and width 40 + 1 − 20.

Because this rewritten task has the same form as the specification of drawRect, we can easily write it in Java as the call

```
drawRect(20, 40, 40 + 1 − 20, 70 + 1 − 40);
```

Some programmers would look at the original task and immediately write the call

```
drawRect(20, 40, 21, 31);
```

They have saved two steps. They didn't rewrite the specification, and they calculated the width and height of the rectangle in their heads. You may do the same thing as long as you don't make a mistake!

As you will soon see, one of the hardest parts of programming is to find and correct mistakes. This process is called *debugging*. To debug, you run the program with various test cases, detect errors in the output, find the programming errors, and fix them. Often, more time is spent debugging than writing the program in the first place. Obviously, if you don't put mistakes in a program, debugging is much easier. You can approach this goal by developing a program in small steps that you know are correct, even if this approach seems to take more time.

Above, we took the small step of rewriting the task so that it looked similar to the specification of the method we wanted to call. We left to the computer the task of calculating the width and height from their formulas. Both of these choices helped eliminate potential errors.

> **Java syntax: Function call (or function invocation)**
>
> *function-name* (*argument* , ..., *argument*)
>
> Each *argument* is an expression; its type is the same as or narrower than the type of corresponding parameter of the function being called.
>
> **Example**: `larger(x * x + y, y * y + x)`
>
> **Purpose**: View evaluation of a function call as yielding the value given by the specification of the function (with the parameters replaced by the arguments of the call).

2.2.3   The function call

Activity 2-4.2

Writing a function call, or function invocation, is similar to writing a procedure call. The parameter declarations tell us the types of the arguments to use in the call, and the specification tells us what they are for. We give an example with a bit of an oddity: x and y are used as parameter names as well as names of the variables in the arguments. The process does not change: replace the parameter names with the values of the corresponding arguments.

Recall method `larger`, whose specification and header we gave earlier:

```
/** = the larger of x and y */
public int larger(int x, int y) { … }
```

Suppose we want to find the larger of two expressions:

the larger of x * x + y and y * y + x.

The specification of function `larger` has the same form as our desired value; it just has parameters x and y in place of the expressions x * x + y and y * y + x. Therefore, the desired value will be calculated by the function call

```
larger(x * x + y, y * y + x)
```

Note that a function call does not terminate in a semicolon, the way a procedure call does. A procedure call is a statement to be executed; a function call is an expression to be evaluated. For example, we could use a function call within another expression:

```
45 + larger(x * x + y, y * y + x)
```

2.2.4   Self-review exercises for calls

Below are the specifications of a few methods:

```
/** Print x, x², and x³ on a single line */
public static void print3(int x)
```

```
/** Print "true" if  x + y > z */
public static void print4(int x, int y, int z)
```

```
/** = the value of the statement "x + y is greater than z" */
public static boolean testLengths(int x, int y, int z)
```

```
/** = the value of the statement "s contains the letter e" */
public static boolean containsE(String s)
```

```
/** = the larger of x² and y² */
public static int larger2(int x, int y)
```

For each of the following calls, state what it does, using the specifications of the methods being called. For a procedure, the specification is a command to do something; for a function, it is the value of the expression.

SR1. `print3(3);`

SR2. `print4(3, 4, 5);`

SR3. `print4(a, a, b);`

SR4. `testLengths(b, b, b)`

SR5. `testLengths(b, c, c * c)`

SR6. `larger2(2, -3)`

SR7. `print3(larger2(4, -5));`

SR8. `print4(larger2(4, -5), 7, 9);`

Answers to self-review exercises

SR1. Print 3, 3^2, and 3^3 on a single line

SR2. Print "true" if 3 + 4 > 5

SR3. Print "true" if a + a > b

SR4. the value of the statement "b + b is greater than b"

SR5. the value of the statement "b + c is greater than c * c"

SR6. the larger of 2^2 and $(-3)^2$

SR7. Print z, z^2, and z^3 on a single line, where z is the larger of 4^2 and $(-5)^2$.

SR8. Print "true" if t + 7 > 9, where t is the larger of 4^2 and $(-5)^2$.

Java syntax: print procedure call	Java syntax: println procedure call
`System.out.print( ` *expression* ` );`	`System.out.println( ` *expression* ` );`
Example: `System.out.print(5);`	**Example**: `System.out.println(5);`
Execution: Place the value of the *expression* in the Java console (which is a window or pane that contains error messages and output from such `print` and `println` calls).	**Execution**: Place the value of the *expression* in the Java console and then start a new line (in the Java console).

2.3   Method bodies

You know about the caller's view of a method (as opposed to the writer's view), and you know how to understand a method call. In this section, we investigate the third part of a method definition, the method body, and discuss its execution.

2.3.1   The procedure body

Style Note
13.2, 13.2.4:
indentation
conventions

A procedure body is a sequence of statements enclosed in braces { }. Here is an example:

```
/** Print b, c, and b + c on separate lines. */
public static void print3(int b, int c) {
    System.out.println(b);
    System.out.println(c);
    System.out.println(b+c);
}
```

This procedure body contains three statements. Notice the indentation:

- The opening brace { appears on the same line as the header;
- The sequence of statements is indented; and
- The closing brace } appears indented exactly under the header.

This convention is used by many Java programmers. We use it throughout the text.

Note: Class `java.lang.System` has in it a `static` variable `out`, which refers to a `PrintStream` object. `PrintStream` objects deal with output and have a method `println`, which prints its argument, followed by a new-line character.
Execute this statement in your IDE:

```
System.out.println("Howdy");
```

Compiling and calling static methods

Every method needs to be inside a class, so in order to test `print3` we must write a class in which to place it. Over the next few pages, we will write several related methods, including `print3`. We will create a single class, `PrintExample`, to contain them. `PrintExample` has nothing to do with `JFrames` or `Dates` or any other API class that we have seen; rather, it exists only as an organizational tool. We do not want to customize an existing class, so we leave off the **extends** clause. We place the method inside the class as before:

```
public class PrintExample {

    /** Print b, c, and b + c on separate lines */
    public static void print3(int b, int c) {
        System.out.println(b);
        System.out.println(c);
        System.out.println(b+c);
    }
}
```

How do we call `print3` with, say, arguments –3 and 4? Much like we write `Math.max(-3, 4)` to call static method `max` in class `Math`. We write:

```
PrintExample.print3(-3, 4);
```

Before you continue, type class `PrintExample` into your IDE and have a call to `print3` executed.

Variable scope

The *scope* of a variable is the area of a program in which that variable can be used. The scope of a parameter is the method body. Thus, two different meth-

```
public class PrintExample {
    /** Print b, c, and b + c on separate lines */
    public static void print3(int b, int c) {
        System.out.println(b);
        System.out.println(c);
        System.out.println(b+c);
    }

    /** Print b + c */
    public static void printSum(int b, int c) {
        System.out.println(b + c);
    }

    /** Print  b + c and b + c * c */
    public static void printSums(int b, int c) {
        printSum(b, c);
        printSum(b, c * c);
    }
}
```

Figure 2.1: Class PrintExample, with three procedures

ods can use the same name for a parameter. For example, we can define the following procedure inside class `PrintExample` (place it either before or after method `print3`), even though it uses the same parameter names as `print3`:

```
/** Print b + c */
public static void printSum(int b, int c) {
    System.out.println(b + c);
}
```

Within the body of method `print3`, b refers to the parameter declared in the definition of `print3`; within the body of method `printSum`, b refers to the parameter declared in the definition of `printSum`. The variables are not related.

2.3.2   Executing a procedure call

We now discuss how a procedure call is executed. This is necessarily a high-level explanation. Later, we will give a lot more detail, giving a model that explains precisely how Java method calls work.

Suppose we have two variables, x and y, with values 20 and 5. We draw these variables as boxes, with the names to the left and the values inside:

x   20   y   5

In this situation, execution of the procedure call

```
PrintExample.print3(x, 2 * y);
```

proceeds as follows:

1. Draw the parameters of the method, as variables.
2. Evaluate the arguments of the call and store their values in the corresponding parameters of the procedure.
3. Execute the statements of the body of the procedure.
4. Erase the parameters of the method.

In this case, argument x corresponds to parameter b and argument 2 * y corresponds to parameter c. Therefore, the first and second steps result in this state:

In performing step three, the statements are executed one by one, beginning with the first. If a parameter name is used, the value of the parameter is used in its place. In this case, execution of the method body results in three values being printed on three separate lines: 20, 10, and 30. Finally, the parameters are erased.

It is important that you can execute a procedure call yourself, as just shown.

As you already know, a method body can contain calls on other methods. In fact, it is typical for one method to contain several calls on others. As an example, we write a method printSums, which contains two calls to method printSum. Class PrintExample, with all three methods discussed in this section, appears in Fig. 2.1.

Method printSums go inside class PrintExample. Because printSum and printSums are defined in the same class, procedure printSums can call printSum without having to write PrintExample.printSum(...);.

At times, you may want to execute parts of a program by hand. In doing so, there are two different ways that we might execute a call: by *stepping over* it and by *stepping into* it. Most IDE debuggers have these two possibilities, and it is essential that you understand the difference.

Stepping over a call

We describe what it means to *step over* a call. Suppose we are executing this call to procedure printSums:

```
PrintExample.printSums(20, 6);
```

We have assigned the arguments to the parameters, so that we have this situation:

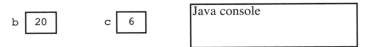

We are ready to execute the statements in the method body. The first statement is a function call printSum(b, c). We execute it by *stepping over* the call. To do this, we do what the specification of the procedure says to do: print the larger of b and c. So, we place 26 in the Java console, yielding this state:

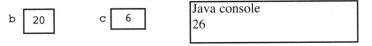

Thus, *stepping over a call* means simply to execute it as an indivisible action, doing what the specification says to do.

Stepping into a call

Now, the second statement is to be executed: printSum(b, c * c);. We execute this statement using the second method, *stepping into the call*. To do this, we go through the detailed steps mentioned earlier: assign the arguments of the call to the parameters of the method and then execute the method body. In this case, the parameter names are b and c. To avoid mixing up the parameters b and c for this new method call with those that already exist, we place them in boxes as shown below. Each box has in its upper left a subbox that contains the name of the method called.

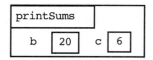 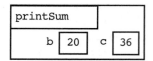 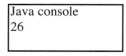

We have carried out the first step of assigning the arguments 20 and 36 to the parameters. Notice that there are 2 b's and 2 c's in the picture. These variables are independent of each other.

We now execute the statement in the body of procedure printSum, printing 56 in the Java console:

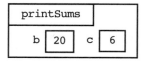 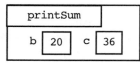

Execution of the call to printSum is finished, so we erase the box. We are now in this state:

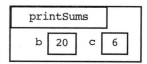 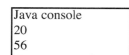

We summarize:

- **To step over a call**, execute it as an individual action, doing what the specification of the method does. The method being called is a black box into which we cannot look, and we rely only on its specification.
- **To step into a call**, (1) draw the parameters of the method, (2) assign the arguments of the call to the method, (3) execute the method body, and (4) erase the parameters of the method.

Suppose you are executing a program yourself, or you are using a debugger, presumably to find an error in the program. Which of these two ways you use to execute a call will depend on the situation. If you are 100% sure that a method is correct, you can step over a call to that method. However, if you believe an error may be in a particular method, step into calls to it.

2.3.3   Conditional statements and blocks

The body of a method is a sequence of statements, which are executed in the order in which they appear. So far, we have seen assignments and procedure calls as statements that can appear in a method body. We now introduce three more kinds of statement: the if-statement, the if-else-statement, and the block. The if-statement and if-else-statement are examples of *conditional statements*.

Java syntax: if-statement

if (*boolean-expression*)
    then-part

Example: `if (x < 0) {`
       `x= -x;`
    `}`

Then-part: any statement

Execution: Evaluate the *boolean-expression*. If it is **true**, execute the *then-part*.

Java syntax: if-else statement

if (*boolean-expression*)
    then-part
else
    else-part

then-part and else-part: each is a statement

Example: `if (x < y) {`
      `y= y - x;`
    `} else {`
      `x= x - y;`
    `}`

Execution: Evaluate the *boolean-expression*. If **true**, execute the *then-part*; otherwise, execute the *else-part*.

The if-statement

Style Note 13.2, 13.2.1: indenting if-statements

There are situations in which you would do something depending on whether some condition is true. For example, if it is cold, you would put your coat on, but not if it is warm.

In a Java program, a *conditional statement* is used for this purpose. As an example, the statement below tests whether x < 0, and if so, it executes the assignment x= −x;. But if x ≥ 0, the assignment is not executed.

    `if (x < 0) x= -x;`

An if-statement has this form:

    if (*condition*) *then-part*

where the condition is a **boolean** expression and the *then-part* is a statement.

To execute an if-statement, evaluate the condition; if it is **true**, execute the then-part. If the boolean expression is **false**, execution of the if-statement is finished.

The block

Suppose we want a statement that adds 2 to both x and y if x is larger than y. To do this, we write the then-part of the if-statement as a *block*: a sequence of statements enclosed in braces { and }. Here is the Java code for it:

```
//  Add 2 to both x and y if x > y
if (x > y) {
    x= x + 2;
    y= y + 2;
}
```

The braces { and } are used to aggregate the sequence of statements into a single statement. In the if-statement shown above, the then-part consists of this block:

```
        {
    x= x + 2;
    y= y + 2;
}
```

Notice the indentation: statements inside a block are indented. The opening brace is put on the same line as the condition. The closing brace appears on its own line, indented the same amount as the **if**. (A method body is a block, so it follows these conventions.)

We (and Sun Microsystems) strongly advocate using a block for the then-part even if there is only a single statement within the braces, as in this example:

```
if (x < y) {
    x= x + 2;
}
```

Why? Because often, after writing some Java code, we have to change it. Here is an example of a fairly common occurrence, even among professional programmers. We have written this statement, without braces:

```
if (x < y)
    x= x + 2;
```

and we want to change it so that the then-part adds 2 to y as well as to x. We are quite likely to simply append the new assignment, yielding:

```
if (x < y)
    x= x + 2;
    y= y + 2;
```

But this is not correct because the braces are missing, and it is actually equivalent to:

```
if (x < y)
    x= x + 2;
y= y + 2;
```

Thus, if we don't make the then-part a block right from the beginning, we are liable to make a mistake if we have to change the then-part later on.

Hereafter, we always include the braces.

The if-else statement

At times, we want to execute one thing if a condition is **true** and another if it is **false**. For this we use an if-else statement. Here is an example:

Style Note
13.2, 13.2.1:
indenting if-
statements

```
// Set z to the minimum of x and y
if (x < y) {
    z= x;
} else {
    z= y;
}
```

If the condition x < y is **true**, the then-part {z= x;} is executed; otherwise, the else-part {z= y;} is executed.

Here is the general form of an if-else statement:

> **if** (*condition*) *then-part*
> **else** *else-part*

where the *else-part* is a statement. To give a complete example, we write a procedure that prints the smaller of its two parameters.

```
/** Print the smaller of b and c */
public static void printSmaller(int b, int c) {
    if (b < c) {
        System.out.println(b);
    } else {
        System.out.println(c);
    }
}
```

2.3.4   Self-review exercises for ifs

In the exercises that ask you to write code, it is best that you actually type them into your Java IDE and test them to make sure that they work. We recommend starting a class Chapter2Exercises that will contain all the static methods you write for these self-review exercises.

SR1. Create a class called Chapter2Exercises that does not extend anything. Write a **public static void** method called sr1 that has an **int** parameter x. Inside method sr1, write a conditional statement that (1) adds 1 to x if x is negative and (2) prints the value of x. To test this method, try these calls:

```
Chapter2Exercises.sr1(-3);
Chapter2Exercises.sr1(3);
Chapter2Exercises.sr1(0);
```

SR2. What is a *block*?

SR3. Write a conditional statement that, if x is negative, sets x to 0 and adds 1 to y. The then-part will have to be a block. (If you write this conditional statement in a method, the method should have two parameters.)

SR4. Write a conditional that stores x in z and y in x if z is greater than 0.

SR5. Write a conditional statement to set z to the minimum of x + y and x − y.

SR6. In the following conditional statement, the else-part is written in English:

```
// Set d to the minimum of a, b, and c
if (a <= b && a <= c) {
    d= a;
} else { // the minimum is b or c
    Set d to the minimum of b and c
}
```

Replace the else-part by a Java statement to accomplish that task. You will end up with a *nested conditional statement*: a conditional statement that appears within another conditional statement.

SR7. In the following conditional statement, the then-part is written in English:

```
// Set d to the maximum of a, b, and c
if (a < b || a < c) {
    Set d to the maximum of b and c
} else { // the maximum is a
    d= a;
}
```

Replace the then-part by a Java statement to accomplish that task. You will end up with a *nested conditional statement*: a conditional statement that appears within another conditional statement.

SR8. Variables b, c, and d contain integers. Write a program segment that sets boolean variable t to the value of "b, c, and d are the lengths of the sides of a triangle". Three integers are the lengths of the sides of some triangle if and only if the sum of any two sides is at least the third side.

Answers to self-review exercises

For the answer to SR1, we provide class Chapter2Exercises and method sr1. For the rest, we provide only the conditional code.

SR1.
```
public class Chapter2Exercises {
    public static void sr1(int x) {
        if (x < 0) {
            x= x + 1;
        }
    }
}
```

SR2. A block is a sequence of statements delimited by (enclosed in) braces { and }. It *aggregates* the sequence of statements into a single statement.

SR3.
```
if (z > 0) {
    x= 0;
    y= y + 1;
}
```

SR4.
```
if (z > 0) {
    z= x;
    x= y;
}
```

SR5.
```
if (x + y <= x - y) { // you could write the condition as  y <= 0
    z= x + y;
} else {
    z= x - y;
}
```

SR6.
```
// Set d to the minimum of a, b, and c
if (a <= b && a <= c) {
    d= a;
} else if (b <= c) {
    d= b;
} else {
    d= c;
}
```

SR7.
```
// Set d to the maximum of a, b, and c
if (a < b || a < c) {
    if (b >= c) {
        d= b;
    } else {
        d= c;
    }
} else { // This else belongs with the first if, not the second.
    d= a;
}
```

SR8. There are several ways to write this program segment. The following one illustrates nested if-statements:

```
if (b + c < d) { t= false; }
else if (c + d < b) { t= false; }
else if (d + b < c) { t= false; }
else { t= true; }
```

Here is a neater solution:

```
t= (b + c >= d) && (c + d >= b) && (d + b >= c);
```

Java syntax: procedure return statement	Java syntax: function return statement
return ;	return *expression* ;
Example: `return;`	**Example**: `return b + c;`
Purpose: Terminate execution of a procedure call.	**Purpose**: Terminate execution of a function call and use the value of the *expression* as the value of the function call.

2.3.5   The return statement

When a procedure is called, the statements in the procedure body are executed one at a time, in the order in which they appear. However, it is occasionally advantageous to terminate execution of the body before the last statement has been executed. We use the return statement for this purpose. It has this form:

```
return;
```

Execution of a return statement terminates execution of the procedure body and, hence, of the procedure call. Once a return statement is executed, no more statements in the procedure body are executed.

Procedure `printSmallest` in Fig. 2.2 contains two return statements. Suppose the call `printSmallest(5, 6, 6);` is to be executed. Then, parameter b will be 5, c will be 6, and d will be 6. Therefore, the condition of the first if-statement will be **true**, b will be printed, and execution of the return statement will terminate execution of the procedure body and, hence, of the procedure call. The second if-statement and the last print statement are not executed.

Consider a call `printSmallest(6, 2, 5);`. In this case, parameter b will be 6, c will be 2, and d will be 5. Therefore, the condition of the first if-statement is

```
/** Print the smallest of b, c, and d */
public static void printSmallest(int b, int c, int d) {
    if (b <= c && b <= d) {
        System.out.println(b);
        return;
    }
    // { the smallest is c or d }
    if (c <= d) {
        System.out.println(c);
        return;
    }
    // { the smallest is d }
    System.out.println(d);
}
```

Figure 2.2:   A procedure with **return** statements

false, so execution of the first if-statement is finished. The condition of the second if-statement is **true**, so the value of c, or 2, will be printed, and execution of the return statement will terminate execution of the procedure body and, thus, of the procedure call.

Using an assertion to help the reader

The reader of a program can benefit from the insertion of comments at judiciously chosen places in the program to alert them to what is true about the variables at those places. For example, after the first if-statement in this body, it may help to indicate that b is not the smallest parameter. Such a description of the variables is called an *assertion* because we are asserting that it is true at a point of execution of the program. By convention, we enclose assertions in curly braces (note that the curly braces are not part of the assertion). The braces alert the reader to the fact that this comment is an assertion about the values of the variables, not a specification or command to do something.

Style Note
13.2, 13.2.2:
assertions

2.3.6   The function body

Activity
2-4.1

The procedure in Fig. 2.2 prints the smallest of its three parameters. In many programs, it may be useful to use the smallest of three values in a later calculation, rather than print it, and in these applications, procedure printSmallest is useless. Instead, we need a function that calculates the smallest of three values and returns it for later use. This function is given in Fig. 2.3.

A function must return a value. Therefore, execution of a function must terminate by executing a return statement of the form

> **return** *expression* **;**

where the type of the *expression* is the same as (or narrower than) the type of the result of the function. Execution of such a return statement terminates the func-

```
/** = smallest of b, c, and d. */
public static int smallest(int b, int c, int d) {
    if (b <= c && b <= d) {
        return b;
    }
    // {the smallest is c or d}
    if (c < d) {
        return c;
    }
    // {the smallest is d}
    return d;
}
```

Figure 2.3:   A function that returns the smallest of its parameters

tion body, and, thus, the function call, and yields the value of the *expression* as the result of the call.

Since execution of a function body must terminate with execution of a return statement, a return statement is usually the last statement in the function body. However, return statements may appear in other places as well, see e.g. Fig. 2.3.

Suppose the call smallest(2, 6, 6) is to be evaluated. Then, parameter b is 2, c is 6, and d is 6. Therefore, the condition of the first if-statement is true, and the then-part of that if-statement, **return** b; , is executed. This terminates execution of the function body and yields 2 as the value of the function call.

Executing a function call

Earlier, we gave a list of four steps for executing a procedure call. The only difference in executing a function call is that the value of the expression in the return statement whose execution terminates the call has to be returned as the value of the function. For purposes of completeness, we summarize here the steps in executing a function call:

1. Draw the parameters of the function, as variables.
2. Evaluate the arguments of the call and store their values in the corresponding parameters of the function.
3. Execute the statements of the body of the function.
4. To execute **return** e; , evaluate expression e, erase the parameters of the method, and use the value of e as the value of the function call.

2.3.7   Local variables

A *local variable* is a variable that is declared within a method body. The *scope* of a variable is the area of a program where it can be used. The scope of a local variable is the sequence of statements that follows its declaration, up until the end of the block in which it is declared. The declaration of a local variable has this form:

> *type variable-name* ;

Its initial value is unknown, and the variable cannot be referenced until a value has been stored in it. An initializing declaration of a local variable has this form:

```
/** Using g, draw a triangle that fits in the rectangle drawn by drawRect(x, y, w, h).
    One side is the base of the rectangle; the other two sides meet at pixel (x + w / 2, y). */
public void drawTriangle(Graphics g, int x, int y, int w, int h) {
    g.drawLine(x, y + h, x + w, y + h);
    g.drawLine(x, y + h, x + w / 2, y);
    g.drawLine(x + w, y + h, x + w / 2, y);
}
```

Figure 2.4:   Drawing a triangle

Java syntax: local variable declaration	**Java syntax: initializing declaration**
type variable ;	*type variable-name= expression* ;
Example: **int** temperature;	**Example**: **int** temperature= 50;
Purpose: Introduce a variable that can be used in the sequence of statements that follows the declaration.	**Purpose**: Introduce a variable that can be used in the sequence of statements that follows the declaration and give it an initial value.

Style Note 13.1.1: local-variable names

Style Note 13.4: describing variables

Activity 2-3.2

type variable-name= expression ;

Method drawTriangle of Fig. 2.4 draws a triangle in a graphics window g. Its body is not as easy to understand as it could be because of the many expressions, some of which are duplicated. For example, the expression y + h appears four times. Not only does this complicate the body, it is inefficient. We can make the body clearer and more efficient by using local variables.

Figure. 2.5 shows the same procedure as in Fig. 2.4, but with three local variables. While their declarations and initializations make the procedure look longer, the statements that do the work (the three calls to procedure drawLine) are easier to understand.

Note the use of a comment to describe what a local variable is being used for. The comment mentions not only the local variable but other variables as well. Variables are related to each other, and one often describes them together.

Quite often, a declaration of a variable is followed by an assignment that provides the variable with its initial value. It is possible —and usually advantageous— to combine the two into a single *initializing declaration*. For example, the three local variables in Fig. 2.5 were declared and initialized using these three initializing declarations:

```
int  y= y + h;        // (x, y1) is the left lower vertex
int  x1= x + w;       // (x1, y1) is the right lower vertex
int  x2= x + w / 2;   // (x2, y) is the top vertex
```

A variable can be declared only once, but it can be assigned many times. In

```
/** Using g, draw a triangle that fits in the rectangle drawn by drawRect(x, y, w, h).
    One side is the base of the rectangle; the other two sides meet at pixel (x + w / 2, y). */
public void drawTriangle(Graphics g, int x, int y, int w, int h) {
    int y1= y + h;        // (x, y1) is the left lower vertex
    int x1= x + w;        // (x1, y1) is the right lower vertex
    int x2= x + w / 2;  // (x2, y) is the top vertex
    g.drawLine(x, y1, x1, y1);
    g.drawLine(x, y1, x2, y);
    g.drawLine(x1, y1, x2, y);
}
```

Figure 2.5: Drawing a triangle using local variables

Java syntax: for-loop for processing a range of integers b..c

```
for (int i= b; i <= c; i= i + 1) {
    Process i;
}
```

Purpose: To perform the sequence of statements "Process b; Process b+1; ...; Process c;". Here, "Process i" can be any statement sequence that refers to variable i. Also, b and c can be any integer expressions such that b <= c + 1. If b = c + 1, then no integers are processed.

---

the following sequence, the second declaration is illegal, since variable b is declared in the first line. But the third line, the assignment to b, is legal.

```
int b= 45;      // A legal initializing declaration
int b= 61;      // An illegal declaration, since b is already declared
b= b + 2;       // A legal assignment
```

2.3.8 Processing a range of integers

This section need not be read at this time. It is presented here so that instructors who want to introduce loops early can do so. If you are not interested in studying loops at this point, skip this section.

At times, we want to write a program segment to process a range of integers. Here are some examples of tasks that we might want to perform:

- Add the squares of the integers in the range 1..100 (i.e. the integers 1, 2, ..., 100).
- Determine whether some integer in the range 2..n divides an integer k.
- Find the first integer in the range 100.. (i.e. the first integer ≥ 100) that is a power of 2 (i.e. can be written in the form 2^k for some k).
- Find the number of times the letter 'e' appears in String s (this requires processing the possible indices 1..(s.length-1) of s).

Program segments to process a range of integers are usually written using a *loop*, and often with what is called a *for-loop*. Chapter 7 covers loops in detail; here, we provide just enough information to allow you to write simple loops to process a range of integers.

Suppose you want to implement the following sequence of statements, which stores in **int** variable x the sum of the integers in the range 2..200. Here is one way to do it:

```
(1) x= 0;
    x= x + 2 * 2;
    x= x + 3 * 3;
    x= x + 4 * 4;
    ...
    x= x + 200 * 200;
```

200 lines is a lot to type. It would be nice to be able to paraphrase it like this:

For each number i in the range 2..200, add i*i to x.

Here is a for-loop (preceded by an initializing declaration of x) that does just that:

```
(2) int x= 0;
    for (int i= 2; i <= 200; i= i + 1) {
        x= x + i * i;
    }
```

Variable i is called the *loop counter*.

The constituents of this loop are:

- The part of the loop within the parentheses:

    - The initializing declaration of **int** variable i (initialized to 2);
    - A semicolon;
    - The loop-condition i <= 200. It can be any boolean expression;
    - A semicolon;
    - An assignment that adds 1 to loop counter i.

- The block after the parentheses (the opening brace { followed by the sequence of statements followed by the closing brace }) is called the *repetend* of the loop. *Repetend* means "the thing to be repeated".

Program segment (2) performs exactly the same task as program segment (1) above. It is just a shorthand version. Thus, sequence (2) executes x= 0; and then executes the statement

```
x= x + i * i;
```

with i containing 2, then with i containing 3, and so on up to i containing 200.

You can (and should) put that code in a method and step through it in your debugger.

As a second example, we write a loop that performs the following assignment:

```
x= 1 * 1 - 2 * 2 + 3 * 3 - 4 * 4 + ... + 21 * 21 - 22 * 22;
```

Here, the squares of odd integers are added and the squares of even integers are subtracted, so this assignment is equivalent to:

```
x= 0;
x= x + 1 * 1;
x= x - 2 * 2;
...
x= x + 20 * 20;
x= x - 21 * 21;
x= x + 22 * 22;
```

Thus, we write the following loop (with initialization):

```
x= 0;
for (int k= 1;  k <= 22;  k= k + 1) {
    if (k % 2 == 0) {
        x= x - k * k;
    } else {
        x= x + k * k;
    }
}
```

The general for-loop

We have shown the use of the for-loop to process a range of the integers. That should be enough for now, and the following may be skipped. The general for-loop is discussed in Chap. 7. However, for those who want to know a bit more at this point, we discuss the for-loop further here.

The general form of the for-loop is

> **for** (*initialization* ; *condition* ; *increment*) *repetend*

where

- The *initialization* is an assignment to the *control variable*, including, optionally, its declaration.
- The *condition* is a boolean expression.
- The *increment* is generally an assignment (without a semicolon) to the control variable.
- The *repetend* is any statement —usually a block.

Execution of the for-loop can be explained by the following flow chart

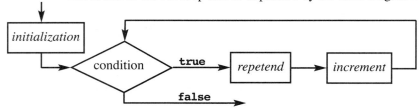

As an example, we write a loop (with initialization) that sums the even positive integers 2, 4, ... until the sum gets over 500.

```
/* Set x to the sum of the first even integers 2, 4, 6, ... such the sum
      > 500 but the sum of one less even integer is ≤ 500. */
x= 0;
for (int k= 2; x <= 500; k= k + 2) {
    x= x + k;
}
```

Here is another example. Assume n is at least 2. We write a loop segment that sets m to the largest divisor of n that is smaller than n. We do not declare n and m because we assume they are declared elsewhere. This loop is strange because its repetend does nothing. Everything is done in the test of the condition and the decrementing of m. Execute this loop by hand, using for n the value 5, so that you see how it works.

```
/* Precondition: n >= 2. Store in m the largest integer that is
      less than n and that divides n. */
for (m= n - 1; n % m != 0; m= m - 1} {
}
```

2.3.9   Self-review exercises for for-loops

After writing an exercise, test it on the computer. That is the best way to determine that your answer is correct. This usually requires you to calculate some of the answers by hand for small values of the variables in question. Most, but not all, of these loops require a statement that initializes a variable or two.

SR1. Write a for-loop to print the values in the range 4..24 on the Java console (use statement System.out.println(...);).

SR2. Assume n ≥ 2. Write a loop to store this value in x:

$$1*(n - 1) + 2 * (n - 2) + 3 * (n - 3) + ... + (n - 1) * (n - (n - 1))$$

SR3. Given n ≥ 1, write a loop that stores in **double** variable v the sum:

$$1 / 1 + 1 / 2 + 1 / 3 + ... + 1 / n$$

What happens to the sum as n gets large? What would happen if n < 1? (Try it!)

SR4. Given n ≥ 1, write a loop that stores in **double** variable v the sum:

$$1 / (1 * 1) + 1 / (2 * 2) + 1 / (3 * 3) + ... + 1 / (n * n)$$

Once you have tested your loop to make sure it is right, try it for increasingly large values of n. What value does the sum "converge" to as n gets larger?

SR5. Given n ≥ 2, write a loop to find the smallest integer that is greater than 1 and that divides n.

SR6. Given n ≥ 2, write a loop that sets boolean value b to the value of the sentence "no integer in the range 2..(n - 1) divides n". Make sure you test your answer for various values of n.

SR7. Given n ≥ 1, write a loop that stores in x the sum of the first n values of this sequence: 1, 2, –3, 4, 5, –6, 7, 8, –9, ...

2.4   Static versus non-static methods

The purpose of this section is to make clear, once more, the difference between static and non-static components of a class. This material is placed here for completeness, so that everything about methods is in this one Chap. 2. We assume that you know about class definitions and how to draw an instance (manila folder) of a class.

Below is a class that contains a static method called staticMethod and a static variable staticVar, as well as a non-static method called nonStatic-Method and variable nonStaticVar:

```
public class C {
    static int staticVar;
    int nonStaticVar;
    static void staticMethod(int x) {...}
    void nonStaticMethod(int y) {...}
}
```

The distinction between static and non-static components is simple: static components go directly into the file drawer for the class, while non-static components appear in each and every instance of the class. Figure 2.6 illustrates this, showing a filing cabinet with a drawer named C and, to its right, the contents of the drawer. Static components staticVar and staticMethod are in the drawer. The drawer also contains two instances of class C. (We would create them using new-expressions.) Note that both instances contain a field nonStaticVar and a method nonStaticMethod because these are defined to be non-static.

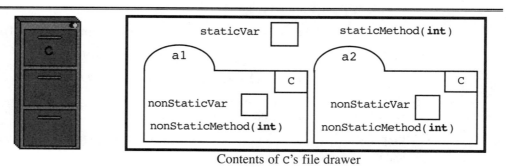

Contents of C's file drawer

Figure 2.6:   The file drawer for class C

Any static variable or static method can be referenced using the name of the class: `C.staticVar` and `C.staticMethod(5)`.

The non-static components cannot be referenced without having a variable that contains the name of an instance. Suppose a variable `cVar` contains the name `a1`. Then `a1`'s two components can be referenced using `cVar.nonStaticVar` and, say, `cVar.nonStaticMethod(5)`.

The inside-out rule

We consider the question of what, exactly, can be referenced from the body of method `nonStaticMethod` in instance `a1`. Almost all programming languages have a general inside-out rule that can be used to answer this question.

> **Inside-out rule:** Code in a construct can reference any of the names that are declared or defined in that construct, together with any names that appear in the enclosing construct(s) —unless the name is declared twice, in which case the closer one prevails.

Naturally, there may be restrictions on this general inside-out rule. For example, a local variable cannot be used in a statement that precedes its declaration, and the use of some of Java's access modifiers (**public**, **protected**, **private**, and the default) may give further restrictions. But this general inside-out rule is a good first step in understanding scope issues.

Here, we use the inside-out rule to determine what can be referenced from `a1.nonStaticMethod`'s method body, based on Fig. 2.5:

1. The parameter and any local variables of `a1.nonStaticMethod`.
2. Field `nonStaticVar` and method `nonStaticMethod` itself because they appear in an enclosing construct.
3. Static members `staticVar` and `staticMethod` because they appear in an enclosing construct.

By the inside-out rule, method `staticMethod` can reference only its parameters and local variables, static variable `staticVar`, and `staticMethod` itself. The inside-out rule does not let it reference components of instances `a1` and `a2`. We will apply the inside-out rule in other situations later on.

2.5   Stepwise refinement

See lesson 2-5 for a discussion of stepwise refinement.

You now have an understanding of the following kinds of statements: assignment statements, conditional statements (if- and if-else-statements), method calls, statements to read and write on the Java console, statements to read and display values in fields of a JLiveWindow GUI, and statements to draw in a graphics window. With this knowledge, we discuss the task of developing sequences of Java statements to solve some task. In an ideal setting, we use what is called *top-down programming*, or *stepwise refinement*.

2.5.1   Stepwise refinement: making coffee

This discussion is also presented in activity 2-5.1, using synchronized animation.

We introduce the notion of stepwise refinement with this problem:

> Get coffee in the morning.

This statement says *what* to do; we want to replace it by a sequence of instructions, or statements, that say *how* to do it.

So how do we get coffee? If no one in the house has made coffee yet, we have to make it. After that, we can pour coffee into a cup:

```
// Get coffee in the morning.
if (coffee not made) {
     Make coffee.
}

Pour coffee into cup.
```

Note that we made the original task into a *statement-comment*, and we have written its implementation underneath it. A *statement-comment* states *what* the corresponding code does; it is often a big help when reading the code.

Note also that we use Java notation where appropriate. Some people prefer to continue to write everything in stylized English —they call it *pseudocode*. We prefer using programming notation whenever it is reasonable, so that the final result is as close to being a program as possible.

We now work on refining the statement *Make coffee*. There are two choices: real or instant, so we insert an if-else statement with those two choices:

```
// Get coffee in the morning.
if (coffee not made) {
     // Make coffee.
     if (real coffee desired) {
          Brew coffee.
     } else {
          Make instant coffee.
     }
}

Pour coffee into cup.
```

We now have two statements that could be refined further: *Brew coffee* and *Make instantcoffee*. We can refine them in any order; they are independent. We also have a choice of notation. If we continue to make each statement into a statement-comment, the program becomes harder and harder to read. It exhibits too much nested structure. Another choice is to introduce a method for a task and to make an English statement into a procedure call. This allows the program to stay short and simple. So let us create two methods:

```
// Get coffee in the morning
if (coffee not made) {
    // Make coffee
    if (real coffee desired) {
        brewCoffee();
    } else {
        makeInstant();
    }
}
```

Pour coffee into cup.

```
/** Brew coffee. */
public void brewCoffee() { }

/** Make instant coffee. */
public void makeInstant() { }
```

Notice that we write the specification and header of the new procedures, but we leave their bodies empty. If one of them were a function, we would write a return statement that produced some value of the right type, simply so that we could compile the program, if we were writing and testing the program incrementally.

We can now work on either procedure; we decide to implement the body of procedure brewCoffee. To brew coffee, we grind coffee, put the coffee in the filter, put the filter in the coffee maker, add water, and turn the coffee maker on:

```
/** Brew coffee */
public void brewCoffee() {
    Grind coffee.
    Put coffee in filter.
    Put filter in coffee maker.
    Add water.
    Turn coffee maker on.
}
```

We stop the stepwise refinement of this program now, for the idea should be clear. (Much more detail could be added — e.g. how do we boil water?)

2.5.2 A summary of stepwise refinement

We summarize the ideas of stepwise refinement, or top-down programming. The development of the program consists of a series of steps.

1. Each step consists of replacing a statement that says *what* to do by a sequence of one or more statements that describe *how* to do it. The replacement is called the *implementation*, or refinement, of the statement.

There are many choices for what the implementation can be:

2. The implementation can be a single statement (e.g. an assignment statement or a conditional statement), a sequence of statements (some in English and some in the programming language), and so forth.

There is a choice of notation to use:

3. We prefer to use a mixture of English and Java, moving closer and closer to Java at each step, so that the final result *is* a Java program.

To this end:

4. We make heavy use of statement-comments.

5. We introduce methods and method calls in appropriate places, to keep the program appearance simple.

It is important to realize that:

6. At each step, the program that has been written so far is correct. However, some of the methods are not completely in Java. They contain English statements.

One point that we have not discussed yet is the introduction of variables:

7. If a step of a top-down design introduces variables, this may cause changes in several statements that have to refer to those variables. When variables are introduced, it is important to write program comments that describe the meanings of the variables.

Top-down design in other fields

Activity 2-5.2 discusses Poe's amazing essay. You *have* to see it. You can get the essay and the poem in footnotes.

We often think that what we are doing is new and exciting and all ours. This is true also of top-down design when it was first discussed in programming in the very early 1970s. However, top-down design is used in almost all fields, since it is about the most logical way one can think of to develop anything. In fact, even people in poetry have used it. Edgar Allen Poe, for example, wrote an essay on how he developed the poem *The Raven*. He did not use the term top-down design, but he sure used the concept! We urge you to put the *ProgramLive* CD in your computer and watch a discussion of his essay.

2.5.3 Top-down development of a Java task

Activity 2-5.3 does this better, using time and synched animation. Watch it!

We look at stepwise refinement in a real programming situation. In this development, we emphasize that we are not only doing stepwise refinement, we are also using incremental programming and incremental testing. At every step, we compile the program to make sure that it is syntactically correct and then do whatever testing we can. This is far better than writing the whole program and then trying to compile it and debug it. Waiting to compile until the program is done may mean seeing dozens (literally) of syntactic error messages, which can be overwhelming. Also, if we test only when we believe the program is finished, we have no idea how to go about it. Finished programs are possibly *thousands* of lines long. There will be too much to test all at once, too many places that might have errors. Programming, commenting, compiling, and testing incrementally lends a great deal of control —and will your preserve sanity at 3am the day your assignment is due.

Anglicizing integers

We write a function that anglicizes integers, producing their English equivalents. For example, for the integer 2001, our function produces the String "two thousand one". We start with a specification and a function heading:

```
/** = English equivalent of n, for 0 < n < 1,000,000 */
public static String anglicize(int n)
```

For small numbers like 2 and 5, the English equivalent is easy to get; the larger the number, the more work it takes to get its English equivalent. Because of this we investigate large numbers, just to see what the problems are. The value 1000 is a point of differentiation: if n ≥ 1000 the result has the word "thousand" in it; if n < 1000, it does not. Thus we can make an educated guess that the first step of the body of anglicize is to make this differentiation:

```
/** = English equivalent of n, for 0 < n < 1,000,000 */
public static String anglicize(int n) {
    if (n >= 1000) {
        return anglicized n (for 1000 <= n < 1000000);
    } else {
        return anglicized n (for n <= 1000);
    }
}
```

Refining the expression "anglicized n (for n > = 1000)"

Anglicizing an integer n in the range 1000 ≤ n < 1000000 requires breaking it into the parts n / 1000 and n % 1000, anglicizing the two parts, and placing " thousand " between them. For example, the English equivalent of 2121 is the word for 2121 / 1000 followed by " thousand " followed by the anglicization of 2121 % 1000. We can therefore write the then-part of the if-statement as

```
return (anglicized (n / 1000))
      + " thousand " + (anglicized (n % 1000))
```

This return statement calls for anglicizing two integers that are less than 1000, and the else-part also calls for anglicizing an integer that is less than 1000. Therefore, in three places we have to do essentially the same task. It makes sense to write a function, say `anglicizeHundreds`, to perform this service. We show this method, together with function `anglicize` but modified to call the new function, in Fig. 2.7.

In Fig. 2.7, function `anglicize` is finished, and we should test it before proceeding. But how do we do that? Look at function `anglicizeHundreds` in Fig. 2.7. We have "stubbed it in", by which we mean that we have fixed it to return something that allows us to test function `anglicize`. It does not produce the English words for n, but it does produce n. With this function, for the call `anglicize(2024)` we expect to get the value `"2 thousand 24"`. Writing `anglicizeHundreds` in this fashion allows us to test function `anglicize` thoroughly before proceeding.

In fact, if you test `anglicize` thoroughly, looking at "extreme" cases like n = 999, n = 1000, n = 1001, n = 999999, you will find an error. Calling `anglicize(1000)` yields the value `"1 thousand 0"`, and the 0 does not belong at the end. The problem is that we wrote `anglicizeHundreds` to handle an integer n in the range 0 < n < 1000, but it is called at least once with n = 0. We should change the specification on `anglicizeHundreds` so that it accepts integers in the range 0..1000 and also state expressly (in the specification) that the English equivalent of 0 is the empty `String` `""`.

In general, when programming and testing incrementally, compile often: every few lines. Test just as often: as soon as you have written the specification and header of a method, you can write a test for it. To facilitate testing, after writing the specification and header of a new method, write a body that is simple and short but that allows you to test the parts of the program that call it.

The development of function `anglicizeHundreds` proceeds along similar lines, so we do not show it. As you proceed, you will find the need for other functions, e.g. a function `teenName(n)` that produces the English equivalent of n in the range 10..19 and a function `tensName(n)` for n in the range 0..9.

A procedural approach

The above development focused on introducing more and more functions,

```java
/** = English equivalent of n, for 0 < n < 1,000,000 */
public static String anglicize(int n) {
    if (n >= 1000)
        { return anglicizeHundreds(n / 1000); +
               " thousand " + anglicizeHundreds(n % 1000);}
    else { return anglicizeHundreds(n % 1000); }
}

/** = English equivalent of n, for 0 < n < 1,000 */
public static String anglicizeHundreds(int n)
    { return "" + n; }
```

Figure 2.7: Function `anglicize` with stubbed-in function `anglicizeHundreds`

all of which are short and almost trivial. It could be called a *functional approach*, since there are no assignments and all the work is done using function calls (and the if- and return statements). It is an effective manner of programming, and entire programming languages (e.g. LISP and Scheme) have been built on it.

It is possible to use a *procedural approach* to solve this problem, ending up with a program that has fewer functions and whose main function contains some local variables that are being manipulated. We outline this approach here.

To set the stage, consider the following. When summing a list of values, we would initialize a variable x (say) to 0 and then, one by one, add values to x.

In the problem of anglicizing n, we can imagine initializing a String variable s to be the empty string "" and then, little by little, appending pieces of the English equivalent to s. In doing this, we let an integer variable k tell us what remains to be anglicized and appended to s.

Thus, we start out with this function:

Activity 2-5.4. The activity gives the complete development, in a way that is impossible on paper.

```
/** = English equivalent of n, for 0 < n < 1,000,000 */
public static String anglicize(int n) {
    // anglicize(n) = s + (the English equivalent of k)
    int k= n;        // the part of n left to translate
    String s= "";  // the translation so far

    Reduce k to 0, keeping the definition of s and k true;
    return s;
}
```

We cannot overemphasize the importance of the definition of s and k as:

```
anglicize(n)  = s + (the English equivalent of k)
```

In developing the method body, this definition will be the key. Note, for example, how the statement before the return statement refers to this definition. Assuming that the English equivalent of 0 is "", this is a correct description of the task. We can refine the statement to reduce k to 0 as follows. The first step, as it was in the functional approach, is to deal with the case when k ≥ 1000. We refine anglicize to deal with this case:

```
/** = English equivalent of n, for 0 < n < 1,000,000 */
public static String anglicize(int n) {
    // anglicize(n) = s + (the English equivalent of k)
    int k= n;        // the part of n left to translate
    String s= "";  // the translation so far

    // Handle the part that is ≥ 1000
    if (k >= 1000) {
        s= s + (English equivalent of k / 1000) + " thousand ";
        k= k % 1000;
    }
}
```

```
        // { k < 1000 }
        Reduce k to 0, keeping the definition of s and k true;
        return s;
    }
```

In making this refinement, we have made progress. The statement to reduce k can now assume that k < 1000. And, because of the way the statement to reduce k is written, the program is still correct.

To test what we have done so far, we can replace the expression "English equivalent of k / 1000" by (k / 1000). We should call the function several times, perhaps with several boundary-case arguments —999999, 2000, 1001, 1000, 999, and 1— and make sure we get the expected answers back. We can then proceed to refine "English equivalent of k / 1000".

We stop the development of this algorithm here because the main ideas have been illustrated. Activity 2-5.4 on the CD explains the development far better than can be done on paper.

Summary of the functional and procedural approaches

The functional approach emphasizes the use of function calls and de-emphasizes the use of local variables and assignment statements. The procedural approach makes heavy use of variables and assignments and creates far fewer functions. Which method you prefer is a matter of taste —and perhaps your previous programming experiences. If you prefer one over the other, make a conscious effort to practice the other so that you become adept at both approaches. Then, you can use whichever is more preferable in any given situation.

2.6 Assertions in programs

Style Note
13.2, 13.2.2
assertions

A program usually contains comments to help the reader understand it. Some comments explain what a program segment does. Other comments describe relationships between variables of the program. Here are two examples of the latter type of comment:

```
        // { x < y }
        // { n is the number of values read in so far }
```

In this section, we study such comments. We begin by studying the notion of a *relation*.

2.6.1 Relations about variables and values

Activity
1-6.1

A *relation* is simply a true-false statement about some variables. For example, the relation 2 < 3 is a true statement, which happens not to mention any variables at all, while the relation 2 = 3 is a false statement. The relation 2 < x concerns the single variable x; we cannot tell whether it is true or false until we know what value x is associated with. If x contains 7, the relation is true; if x contains 2, the relation is false. Here is a more complex relation concerning variables x, y, and z: x = y + z.

The relations given so far were in mathematical notation. Java boolean expressions are also relations, and relations can also be written in a natural language. For example, here are some relations, using **int** variables x, y, z and String variable s:

> Variable s contains the character 'g'
> The number of characters in s is 2*y
> The temperature in Ithaca got below x on 1 January 1999
> x is the number of values read in so far

The first relation concerns variable s. The second is a relation between variables s and y. The third is a relation about variable x. The fourth could be about a variable x in a particular Java program.

Note that the mathematical relation b = c is written in Java as b == c. When discussing a program, we rely on mathematical notation; when we have to write such a relation in Java, we have no recourse but to use the bad notation.

Simplifying relations

Some relations take this form:

> (0) If Bill has black hair, blackHair is true.

What is often meant is this:

> (1) If Bill has black hair, blackHair is true; else, blackHair is false.

But these two relations mean different things. The first does not say what value blackHair has if Bill has red hair, while the second says that if Bill has red hair, blackHair is false. Some might say that it is implicit in (0) that blackHair is false if Bill has red hair, but mathematical convention disagrees.

There is a much simpler alternative for the second relation. It is shorter and doesn't have any case analysis:

> (2) blackHair = "Bill has black hair"

We have placed quotes around the sub-relation to make clear that it is a unit. The quoted phrase is itself a relation; the equality says that blackHair is equal to the value of that relation.

Let us show why relations (1) and (2) mean the same thing. In the case that Bill does have black hair, (1) reduces to "blackHair is true", while (2) reduces to "blackHair = true". These two are equivalent, so in the case that Bill has black hair, (1) and (2) mean the same thing.

In the case that Bill does not have black hair, relation (1) reduces to "blackHair is **false**", while relation (2) reduces to "blackHair = **false**". Again, these two are equivalent, so in the case that Bill does not have black hair, (1) and

Activity 1-6.2

(2) mean the same thing.

Since (1) and (2) mean the same thing whether or not Bill has black hair, they mean the same thing.

It takes time to get used to writing relations using form (2) instead of (1). Do the self-help exercises at the end of this section to make the transition easier.

Examples

Here are more examples in which using the value of a relation provides a better alternative. This statement stores the value of relation x < y in variable v:

```
if (x < y) { b= true; }
else { b= false; }
```

Instead of this if-statement, you can use this assignment:

```
b= x < y;
```

Now consider this specification of a function:

Return **true** if x is less than y and **false** otherwise.

Instead, write more simply:

Return x < y.

A footnote on lesson page 1-6 has a hilarious example of ambiguity.

Here, the value of the relation x < y, which is written as a Java boolean expression, is to be returned.

One goal of the earlier part of this discussion is to make clear to you that English is ambiguous. Computer programs should never be ambiguous: when writing a specification of part of a program, be alert to any possible ambiguities and do your best to remove them. Your teammates will love you for it.

2.6.2   Assertions

Activity 1-6.3

Below, the assignment is preceded and followed by a comment:

```
// {x > 0}
x= x + 1;
// {x > 1}
```

Each comment is a relation enclosed in braces { and }. We call such a relation an *assertion* because we are asserting something about the state of execution whenever the place where the comment appears is reached. Here is how to read this code:

The code says nothing about what the statement does if x ≤ 0! It deals only with x > 0. And, if x is greater than 0 initially, when the statement terminates, x will be greater then 1.

Style Note
13.2, 13.2.2
indenting
assertions

An assertion that precedes a statement is called a *precondition* of the statement. An assertion that follows a statement is called a *postcondition* . Such a pre-condition-statement-postcondition triple has the following meaning:

Execution of the statement begun with the precondition true is guaranteed to terminate, and when it terminates, the postcondition will be true.

When you see a relation enclosed in braces within a comment, you should assume that the program author is asserting that that relation is true at that point. The earlier code ensures that the relation is true; the later code relies on it being true. In later sections, you will see hints from time to time about when and where to use such assertions.

2.7   A model of execution

We now show you precisely how a method call is executed. Learning this material, and being able to execute method calls yourself using our model of execution, will make writing programs much easier. You will *know* what is going on inside the computer. Further, from time to time you will want to execute a method call by hand in order to pinpoint a difficult-to-find error in your program.

This section requires knowledge of classes and our view of a class as a file drawer of manila folders.

2.7.1   Frames for method calls

Activity 4-3.3
gives a pictorial
description of
this complete
subsection.

Whenever a method is called, some memory is set aside to contain information related to the call: parameter values, the current statement being executed, and so on. This memory is called the *frame for the call*. Figure 2.8 shows the format of the frame that we use throughout this text. We discuss its components:

- **Method-name.** The method name appears in a box in the upper-left of the frame.

Figure 2.8:   Format of the frame for a method call

- **Program counter.** The program counter is the number of the next statement of the method body to execute. Initially, it is 1, and it is incremented each time a statement is executed.
- **Scope box.** The scope box is used to find a variable or method that is referenced in the method body. Its value depends on what kind of method this is:

  for a static method: The name of the class in which the method is defined.

  for an instance method: The name of the object in which the method resides.

  for a constructor: The name of the object that was just created.

- **Parameters.** Each parameter of the method appears as a variable. Parameters are drawn in the lower left of the frame for reasons that will become clear later.
- **Local variables.** Each local variable of the method appears in the frame.

As an example, consider this class:

```java
public class C {
    public void meth(int p) {
        double d;
        ...
    }
}
```

Suppose we execute these statements:

```java
C c= new C();
c.meth(5);
```

Execution of the first statement creates a new folder, stores its name in variable c, and calls procedure c.meth. Figure 2.9 shows variable c, the folder, and the frame for the method call c.meth just after the frame is created and the argument is stored in the parameter.

The call stack: the stack of frames for uncompleted method calls

A frame for a method call lasts as long as the method call is being executed. When the call is finished, the frame is erased. If the method is called again later, a new frame is created for it.

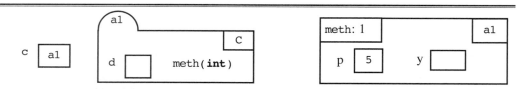

Figure 2.9:   The frame just after the argument has been assigned to parameter p

This fact explains why local variables do not retain their values from one call of a method to the next call of the same method: all the information about the first call is in a frame, and the frame is erased when the call is completed.

Suppose a call of method m1 is being executed so that a frame for the call exists. Suppose also that m1 calls m2. A frame for the call is created so that there are now two frames. If m2 now calls a method m3, there will be three frames.

Of the three frames, the frame for m3 will be erased first, then the frame for m2, and finally the frame for m1. This is because the call to m3 is the first to complete. The last frame to be created is the first to be erased, and the first frame to be created is the last to be erased.

The creation and destruction of frames follows a last-in-first-out, or LIFO discipline, and the frames may be maintained on what is called a *stack*.

A stack is a list of items with two operations for changing the list: *pushing an item* onto the stack (inserting a new item on its top) and *popping an item* from the top (removing the topmost item).

As an example of a stack, consider the stack of trays in a cafeteria. An employee will load a large number of trays onto the top of the stack; then, people take them off the top one at a time. The last one added by the employee is the first one removed by a customer.

We show how a stack is used to maintain the frames for a series of calls. Consider class X of Fig. 2.10, which contains two static methods. Assume that a call printLarger2(20, 6) is about to be executed and that the call appears in a method m. At this point, the stack of frames is as shown in the first (leftmost) diagram in Fig. 2.11. The second diagram in Fig. 2.11 shows the situation just after the frame for the call to printLarger has been created and the arguments have been assigned to the parameters.

The first statement in the body of printLarger2 is a call to procedure printLarger, so a frame for this call is created and pushed onto the stack of frames. The third diagram in Fig. 2.11 shows the situation after this frame has

```
public class X {

    /** Print the larger of b and c */
    public static void printLarger(int b, int c) {
        if (b >= c) { System.out.println(b); }
        else { System.out.println(c); }
    }

    /** Print larger of b and c and larger of b and c * c */
    public static void printLarger2(int b, int c) {
        printLarger(b, c);
        printLarger(b, c * c);
    }
}
```

Figure 2.10:   Class X with two **static** procedures

been created and the arguments have been stored in the parameters. When this
call is completed, the frame is erased, and the situation is as shown in the third
diagram again, but with the program counter changed to 2 to indicate that the
statement 2 of the method body is to be executed next.

The *active frame*, the frame for the call, whose body is being executed, is
always at the top of the stack. The frames below the top one are *inactive*.

Placing argument values on the call stack

Above, we simply said that the argument values are assigned to the parameters. But how is this done? The arguments are evaluated before the frame for the
call is created, and the calling side, the method body where the call is made,
knows nothing about how big the frame for the call will be.

Here is how it works. The argument values are pushed onto the call stack,
simply as values. When the frame is created, the locations containing these values become the parameters. Thus, the call stack itself acts as the communication
device for argument values.

Figure 2.12 illustrates this "parameter passing" mechanism. It shows the call
stack just before the first call to procedure printLarger2, after the arguments
have been placed on the call stack, and then again after the frame has been created. Notice that in the middle picture, the values are not yet named.

The return value of a function

The call stack is also used for communicating the value of a function to the
caller. When a statement **return** e; is executed, the active frame is popped from
the call stack and the value of e is pushed onto the call stack. At the place where
the function was called, the value is popped from the call stack and used as the
value of the function call.

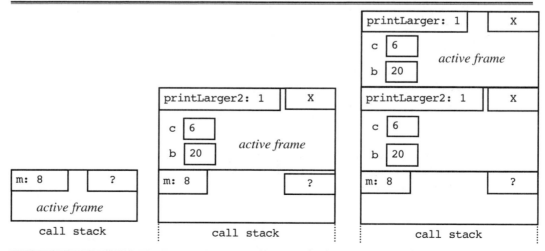

Figure 2.11   The call stack: the stack of frames for uncompleted calls

2.7.2   The steps in executing a method call

Now that we have shown the format of a frame for a method call, discussed the call stack of frames, and discussed the communication of argument and result values, we give the sequence of steps for executing a method call. It is wise to memorize them and practice doing them on 5-10 small examples..

1. Evaluate the arguments of the call and push them onto the call stack.

2. Draw a frame for the call at the top of the call stack; the frame includes the argument values at the top of the stack.

    2(a) Fill in the name of the method and set the program counter to 1.

    2(b) Fill in the scope box with the name of the entity in which the method appears: the name of a folder for a non-static method or constructor, and the name of the class for a static method.

    2(c) Draw all local variables of the method body in the frame.

    2(d) Label the argument values pushed onto the call stack in the first step with the names of the corresponding parameters.

3. Execute the method body. Whenever a name is referenced, look in the frame for it. If it is not there, look in the item given by the scope box of the frame.

4. Erase the frame —pop it from the stack. If the method is a function and the call is terminated by execution of a return statement **return** e; , push the value of e onto the call stack.

2.8   Key concepts

• **Method**. A *method* is a recipe for getting something done or producing a result. There are three kinds of methods in Java: *procedure*, *function*, and *constructor*. Constructors have to do with initializing objects and are covered fully in Chaps. 3 and 4.

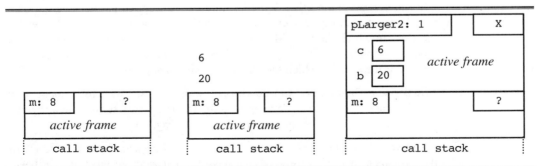

Figure 2.12   The call stack as a communication device for argument values

- **Parameter**. A method may have *parameters*, which are variables that are declared in the header of the method (within the parentheses and separated by commas).

- **Method body**. A method body consists of a sequence of statements. It may also contain declarations of *local variables* to simplify the body and make it more efficient.

- **Assertion**. An assertion is a relation that we place as a comment before or after a statement in a method body to assert that the relation is true at that point. Assertions help programmers understand method bodies.

- **Return statement in a function**. Execution of a function body must terminate by executing a statement `return` *expression*`;`; the value of the *expression* is the result of the function call.

- **Method call (or invocation)**. A method does nothing until is called, or invoked, just as a cooking recipe just sits there until someone looks at it and follows the instructions for cooking something. A *procedure call* is a statement; it is executed. A *function call* is an expression; it is evaluated. A *constructor call* is executed; it can appear only in a new-expression.

- **Argument**. Each method call can have *arguments*, which are expressions that appear within the parentheses of a call (and separated by commas).

- **Execution or evaluation of a method call**. Executing or evaluating a call consists of assigning the values of the arguments to the corresponding parameters and then executing the body of the called method. The process of executing the method body stops when there are no more statements to execute or until a return statement is executed.

- **Method specification**. The *specification* of a method gives constraints (pre-conditions) on the parameters of the method and explains precisely *what* it does (or what value it produces). The specification should generally be written before writing the method body. Someone wanting to write a call to the method should be able to do so using only the specification and header of the method.

- **Static versus non-static**. Method definitions (except constructor definitions) may have the modifier `static`. A *static method* is placed in the file drawer for the class in which the method definition appears. A *non-static method* is called an *instance method* because a copy of it is placed in each folder (or instance, or object) of the class in which the method definition appears.

- **Stepwise refinement or top-down programming**. Stepwise refinement is an idealized approach used to develop a method. The process starts with a specification and refines it, step by step, into the final program.

- **An execution model**. Our model of execution of a method call is in terms of the call stack of frames for calls that have been started but have not yet been-completed. Understanding this model is important for overall understanding, and you should practice executing method calls yourself, using this model. If you cannot do it, then it is likely that you do not understand some important details of how a program is executed!

2.9   Self-review exercises

SR1. What is the difference between a static method and a non-static method?

SR2. A function call is an _____; a procedure call is a _____.

SR3. Is the following a function call or a procedure call? `meth(4, 3);`

SR4. Is the following a function definition or a procedure definition?

```
public void method(int b) { … }
```

SR5. Define *parameter:* _____.

SR6. Define *argument:* _____.

SR7. To figure out what a procedure call `meth(a1, a2)` does, we _____.

SR8. The scope of a parameter is: _____.

SR9. The scope of a local variable is: _____.

SR10. A local variable keeps its value from one call of the method to the next (true or false).

SR11. A function call must terminate with a statement whose syntax is: _____.

SR12. Draw a frame for the call `C.meth(45, 6 + 2);` on method `meth` of the class shown below. Show the state just after the arguments have been assigned to the parameters but before the method body is executed.

```
public class C {

    public static void meth(int b, double c) {
        String s;
        ...
    }
}
```

Answers to Self-review exercises

SR1. A static method is placed in the file drawer for the class in which it is defined. A nonstatic method appears in every instance of the class in which it is defined.

SR2. A function call is an expression, so it has a value. A procedure call is a statement, so it does not have a value.

SR3. It must be a procedure call because it ends in a semicolon.

SR4. The presence of keyword **void** tells you that it is a procedure.

SR5. A parameter is a variable that is declared within the parentheses of a method definition (adjacent parameter declarations are separated by commas).

SR6. An argument is an expression that appears within the parentheses of a method call (adjacent arguments are separated by commas).

SR7. To figure out what a call meth(a1, a2) does, copy the specification of the method and replace all occurrences of the parameter names by the corresponding arguments.

SR8. The scope of a parameter —i.e. where it can be referenced— is the method body.

SR9. The scope of a local variable is the sequence of statements following its declaration (until the end of the block in which the local variable is declared).

SR10. False.

SR11. **return** *expression* ;

SR12.

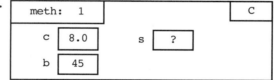

Exercises for Chapter 2

Each exercise below asks you to write a method and test it thoroughly. To do this, write a single class Functions and place all the functions and procedures in this class. Here is how you can test a method. Suppose you named the function of the first exercise average. Then, after writing the function and compiling class Functions, type this expression into DrJava's Interactions Pane:

```
Functions.average(3, 5, 7)
```

Make sure you specify your methods, with comments that precede the method definitions. If an exercise asks you to print values, label them suitably on the output. For example, for the above function call, print average: 5.0.

E1.   Write a function that returns the average of its three **double** arguments.

E2.   Write a procedure that prints the average of its three **double** arguments on the Java console.

E3.   Write a procedure that prints the sum, difference, and product of its two **double** parameters.

E4.   Write a function that returns "Hooray" if one of its three arguments is less than 10 and returns "Booo" otherwise.

E5.   Write a procedure that prints "Hooray" in the Java console if one of its three arguments is less than 10 and prints "Booo" otherwise.

E6.   Write a function that computes the area of a circle, given its radius r. The formula for the area is πr^2. You can get π using Math.PI.

E7.   Write a procedure that prints the area of a circle, given its radius r. The formula for the area is πr^2. You can get π using Math.PI.

E8. Write a function that, given the number of gallons of gas a tank can hold and the fuel efficiency of the car (miles per gallon), calculates how far the car can go on one tank of gas.

E9.   Write a procedure that, given the number of gallons of gas a tank can hold and the fuel efficiency of the car (miles per gallon), prints how far the car can go on one tank of gas.

E10. Write a procedure with three parameters that prints, on separate lines of the Java console, the smallest parameter, then the middle one, and finally the largest.

E11. Write a function that converts its parameter from miles to kilometers. One mile equals 1.60935 kilometers. Use type **double**.

E12. Write a procedure that converts its parameter from kilometers to miles and prints the result. One mile equals 1.60935 kilometers. Use type **double**.

E13. Write a function that converts its parameter from pounds to kilograms. One pound equals 0.45359237 kilograms. Use type **double**.

E14. Write a procedure that converts its parameter from pounds to kilograms and prints the result. One pound equals 0.45359237 kilograms. Use type **double**.

E15. Write a function that is given as parameters the number of hours, minutes, and seconds of a time on a particular day and yields the total number of seconds that the time represents.

E16. Write a function that is given an integer in the range 0..999999 and returns it as a String, with a comma separating the last three digits from the first ones. Of course, include the comma only if the number is at least 1000. For example, for argument 1546, the returned value is "1,546", and for argument 34, the returned value is "34".

E17. Write a procedure that is given a dollar amount and prints out how many quarters, dimes, nickels, and pennies it takes to make that amount. As many higher-valued coins as possible should be used. For example, for the amount $4.20, the program should print on one line:

```
16 quarters, 2 dimes, 0 nickels, and 0 pennies
```

E18. Write a function that is given the number of seconds from midnight and returns a String that contains the number of hours, minutes, and seconds from midnight that it represents, suitably annotated. For example, called with argument 3675, it yields "1 hour 1 minute 15 seconds".

E19. Write a procedure that is given the number of seconds from midnight and prints the number of hours, minutes, and seconds from midnight that it represents, suitably annotated. For example, called with argument 3675, this should be printed: 1 hour 1 minute 15 seconds.

E20. Write a function that is given a time in terms of hours, minutes, and seconds and returns the time in seconds only (as an integer). This is, in a sense, the inverse of the previous exercise. For example, for 1 hour, 1 minute and 15 seconds, return the integer 3676.

E21. Write a function that is given two times in military format and prints the hours and minutes between the two times. You may assume that the second parameter is the bigger of the two. For example, for the arguments (0352, 1900) —that is 3:52AM and 7:00P— the result is: 15 hours 8 minutes. To make things easier for you, try doing it by calling the function and procedure of the previous two exercises.

E22. Write a function with an **int** parameter whose value is in the range 0..15 and that returns a String of length 4 that depicts its binary equivalent. For example, for the number 7, the answer is the String "0111". Here is a hint. The rightmost bit is 7%2, and the first three bits are the binary representation of 7/2.

E23. Write a procedure with an **int** parameter whose value is in the range 0..15 and that prints its binary equivalent. For example, for the number 7, this should be printed: 0111. Here is a hint. The rightmost bit is 7%2, and the first three bits are the binary representation of 7/2.

E24. In Sec. 0.1, near Fig. 0.2, we outlined the relationship between the decimal, hexadecimal, octal, and binary numbers systems. Write a procedure that prints the first 7 natural numbers (0, 1, 2, ..., 8) in all four systems. The first line should contain 0 in all four systems; the second; 1 in all four systems; and so on. For descriptions of static methods to help you do this exercise, turn to lesson page 5-1 of the CD and click on the footnote for static methods of class Integer (near activity 3).

E25. Do the same as for the previous exercise, but print the decimal values 21, 22, 23, 24, 25 in each of the four number systems.

E26. Write a function that has three **int** parameters a, b, and c and returns the value of the statement "a, b, c are the lengths of the sides of a triangle". Three such values form the lengths of the sides of a triangle if and only if a ≤ b + c, b ≤ c + a, and c ≤ a + b.

E27. Write a procedure that has three **int** parameters a, b, and c and returns one of these strings: "equilateral" (meaning the sides have the same length), "isosceles" (only two sides are equal), "triangle" (no sides equal, but they form a triangle; see the previous exercise), or "not a triangle".

E28. Write a function that has as its parameters the lengths a, b, and c of a triangle and returns the area of the triangle. Let s be 1/2 the perimeter of the triangle. Then the area of the triangle is the square root of the expression s * (s – a) * (s – b) * (s – c).

E29. Write a procedure that has as its parameters the (two) lengths of the sides of a rectangle and prints: the area, the perimeter, and the length of the diagonal.

E30. Write a function with an **int** parameter n, with the precondition that 0≤n<1000, and returns the three digits of the number (with leading zeros if necessary) with a blank between adjacent digits. For example, for argument 43, the string "0 4 3" is returned.

E31. Write a function that is given the coordinates (x_1, y_1), (x_2, y_2) of two points and returns the distance between them: the square root of $(x_1 - x_2)^2 + (y_1 - y_2)^2$.

E32. Write a function that is given a letter in A..Z and returns the corresponding digit on the telephone. Here is the translation: 2:ABC, 3:DEF, 4:GHI, 5:KHL, 6:MNO, 7:PRS, 8:TUV, and 9:WXY. For Z, return –2, and for Q, return 1.

E33. Turn to lesson page 2-1 of the CD *ProgramLive* and click the Project icon. Do Project Dates, which asks you to write 5-6 functions that manipulate dates in various ways.

E34. Write an if-statement that swaps (exchanges) the values of **int** variables b and c, if necessary, so that the larger of the two is in c.

E35. Is it possible to write the body of procedure swap, shown below, so that it is consistent with its specification? For example, if you write a call swap(d, e);, is the larger of d and e guaranteed to be in e after the call? If you do not fully understand, do not guess. Instead, write the procedure body and then execute the call to it by hand, using the steps given in Sec. 2.7.2, and see what happens. Explain your answer.

```
/** Swap the larger of b and c, if necessary, to get the larger in c. */
public static void swap(int b, int c) {
    ?
}
```

E36. Consider class C shown below. Draw a frame for the call meth(42, 43), showing the state just after the arguments have been assigned to the parameters:

```
public class C {
    public static void meth(int c, int d) { … }
}
```

E37. Consider the class C shown below.

```
public class C {
    public static void meth(int c, int d) { … }
    public static void m() { … }
}
```

Let the active frame be as shown below, and assume that this call appears in method m: v.meth(45, 46);. Copy the active frame and folder a1 onto a piece of paper and view the frame as the top frame in the call stack. Then execute the method call, using the steps provided in Sect. 2.7.2 (omit the steps of executing the method body and erasing the call.)

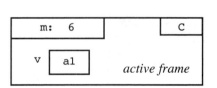

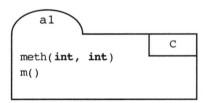

Chapter 3

Classes

OBJECTIVES

- Discuss the class definition as a template for its instances (folders).
- Discuss information hiding for fields, but show when public fields are useful.
- Show how the inside-out rule is used in Java.
- Define the constructor and show how it is used.
- Compare testing of folder names with testing of their contents.
- Show when to make a method or field static.
- Discuss object-oriented design.
- Look at a model of execution.

INTRODUCTION

Chapter 1 introduced classes. You saw the use of class JFrame and the creation and use of at least one subclass of class JFrame. In this chapter, we provide an in-depth discussion of classes, reviewing the concepts introduced in Chap. 1 and introducing the rest of the concepts needed to understand and use classes.

3.1   Class definitions

A similar class is discussed in activity 3-6.1

Figure 3.1 contains the definition of a class Employee. There are a few new things in this class, which we explain below.

An instance of this class represents a person in a company, with a name, the year they were hired, and a starting salary of $50,000. In a real program, an instance would contain more information —the person's address, social security number, and so on. We maintain only three pieces of information in an instance in order to keep the class manageable in this discussion.

```
/** An instance contains a person's name, year hired, and salary */
public class Employee {
    private String name;        // Employee's name
    private int start;          // Year hired
    private double salary= 50000;     // Salary

    /** Constructor: a person with name n, year hired d, salary 50,000 */
    public Employee(String n, int d) {
        name= n;
        start= d;
    }

    /** = name of this Employee */
    public String getName()
        { return name; }

    /** Set the name of this Employee to n */
    public void setName(String n)
        { name= n; }

    /** = year this Employee was hired */
    public int getStart()
        { return start; }

    /** Set the year this Employee was hired to y */
    public void setStart(int y)
        { start= y; }

    /** = Employee's total compensation (here, the salary) */
    public double getCompensation()
        { return salary; }

    /** Change this Employee's salary to d */
    public void changeSalary(double d)
        { salary= d; }

    /** = String representation of this Employee */
    public String toString() {
        return getName() + ", year " + getStart() +
                ", salary " + salary;
    }
}
```

Figure 3.1: Class Employee

Style Note
13.1, 13.1.3:
class name
conventions

Java syntax: Class definition

public class *class-name* {
   declarations of methods and fields
}

Purpose: To define a new file drawer, named *class-name*, and describe the contents of its manila folders (instances, or objects, of the class).

Note that the class definition does not include the clause "**extends** ...". This class does not explicitly *extend* another; it stands alone, by itself. The subclasses of JFrame that we wrote in Chap. 1 extended JFrame.

Style Note
13.1, 13.1.1:
field name
conventions

A class definition defines the contents of manila folders that are placed in its file drawer. Such a manila folder is called an *instance of the class*, or an *object of the class*. An instance of class Employee appears in Fig. 3.2, along with the file drawer in which the instance appears. Each instance of a class contains the following components:

1. The *fields*, or *instance variables*, of the class, which are the variables defined in it that do not have modifier **static**.
2. The *instance methods* of the class, which are the methods defined in it that do not have modifier **static**.

Initial values of fields

Activity
3-4.2

If a field is declared without an initializing assignment, the field has a default value, which depends on its type. Here are the default values:

byte:	(**byte**) 0	**float:**	0.0F
short:	(**short**) 0	**double:**	0.0D
int:	0	**boolean:**	false
long:	0L	**char:**	null character, '\u0000'
class-type:	**null**		

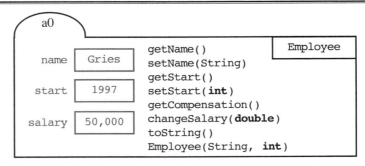

Figure 3.2:   An instance of class Employee

Placement of classes

A class named C (say) is placed in its own file, named `C.java`. Thus, class `Employee` is placed in file `Employee.java`. All the files that you use in a program should be placed in the same directory on your hard drive. It is a good practice to have a different directory for each program. Get in the habit of creating a new directory for the `.java` files whenever you start on a new Java project.

Importing predefined classes

A class C may need to reference classes that are predefined in *packages* (see Chap. 11) that come with the Java system. To be able to reference any class that is defined in a package, say package `java.util`, place the following *import statement* before the class definition in file `C.java`:

```
import java.util.*;
```

To import just one class of the package, say `Date`, use this import statement:

```
import java.util.Date;
```

Any number of import statements may be placed before the class definition in the file. The order in which they occur does not matter, and a class may be imported several times.

3.1.1   The principal of information hiding

The principle of information hiding is:

> **Principal of information hiding**. Do not give someone access to information that they do not need to know.

In some situations, information hiding is a bad principal. For example, some governments use it, with their own definition of "need", to suppress information and keep people in the dark, leading to corruption and even suppression of their people. To protect against this, some countries have passed "freedom of information" acts, which attempt to limit what can be kept from the public.

In programming, the principal of information hiding can be useful. Limiting what can be seen in a particular place can help the reader understand parts of the program better, and it can help make later changes in the program easier.

Java has several mechanisms to help in hiding information. The one that concerns us here is the use of *access modifiers* **public** or **private** in declarations of components of a class. The presence of **public** means that the component may be accessed from any part of the program that has access to the class. Modifier **private** restricts access to the class in which the declaration appears. In Fig. 3.1, the methods are public. The three fields are private, which is indicated in the instance of `Employee` in Fig. 3.2 by graying out the fields.

Generally, we make fields of a class private so that a user of an instance cannot access them directly. Instead, the user accesses using methods of the class, which are usually public. Making the fields private has two advantages:

1. We can change the implementation of the class without requiring the user to make changes. For example, suppose we decide to maintain the name of an employee in two fields, the employee's last name and first name, but still present the full name as a `String` to the user. We can do this by changing the fields and then changing the methods appropriately. The user would not know the difference.

2. We have control over how the field is used. For example, we can provide only the ability to read or *get* the value of the field, but not to change it.

Style Note
13.1, 13.1.2
method names

In general, it is the *behavior* of a class —as presented by its public methods— that is most important. Who cares how names and salaries are stored in fields? That is not important to a user of the class. What *is* important is how they can be obtained and how the salaries can be changed.

Later, we will see situations in which it makes sense to make fields public. Also, a method should be private if it is used only within the class and the user does not need to know of its existence.

Getter and setter methods

Access to the value of a private field can be granted using a *getter method*, which is a method that simply returns its value. Examples of getter methods in class `Employee` are methods `getName`, `getStart`, and `getCompensation`.

A good naming convention for a getter method is the name of the field, capitalized and preceded by "`get`". We used this convention for two getter methods. We did not use it for field `salary` because of the way method `getCompensation` is used later in Chap. 4. The term `getSalary` will be too narrow for its use.

In the same way, we write a *setter method* for a field, in order to change its value. Examples of setter methods in `Employee` are `setName` and `setStart`. The parameter of the method contains the value that is to be stored in the field.

Here is a good convention for naming a setter method: use the name of the field, capitalized and preceded by "`set`".

3.1.2   The inside-out rule

Keyword **this** used in a method refers to the instance in which the method appears; to reference a component named c (say) of that instance, we use the notation **this**.c. In Chap. 1, we made extensive use of keyword **this** when referring to components of the class within the class. For example, in Chap. 1, we would have written method `toString` of class `Employee` like this:

```
/** = a representation of this instance */
public String toString()
  { return this.getName() + ", this.year " + this.getStart();}
```

However, most programming languages, including Java, use a general *inside-out rule*, which in this instance makes the use of **this** unnecessary. Here is the general rule:

> **General inside-out rule**: In a subpart (e.g. a method) of a construct (e.g. a class), all the names that are declared or that can be referenced in the construct can be referenced in the subpart, unless the subpart redeclares them.

Here is the inside-out rule as it pertains to method bodies in Java:

> **Inside-out rule for non-static method bodies**: In a method body, all the components of the class in which the method is defined can be referenced, unless they are redeclared (e.g. as parameters).

This inside-out rule in Java lets us write method toString more simply as:

```
/** = a representation of this instance */
public String toString() {
   return getName() + ", year " + getStart();
}
```

because getName, year, and getStart are declared in class Employee.

We illustrate a case where the use of **this** is necessary. Consider writing method setName using name for the parameter instead of n:

```
/** Set the name of this Employee to name */
public void setName(String name)
   { this.name= name; }
```

Since the parameter is named name, name cannot be used directly to refer to field name. The assignment name= name; assigns to the parameter and not to the field. To assign to the field, write the assignment as: **this**.name= name;

Some programmers use the convention that in a setter method, the parameter name is the same as the field being set. When using this convention, the use of keyword **this** is needed to assign to the field.

3.1.3 Declaration of constructors

Activity
3-5.2

Chapter 2 contains an extensive treatment of procedures and functions. Here, we discuss the third kind of method, the *constructor*. There is one constructor in class Employee, which we give here:

```
/** Constructor: a person with name n, year hired d, salary 50,000 */
public Employee(String n, int d) {
      name= n;
      start= d;
}
```

Java syntax: constructor declaration
public *class-name* (*parameter-declarations*) {
   sequence of statements and declarations
}

Purpose: To define a constructor in class *class-name*, declare its parameters, and give the sequence of statements to execute when the constructor is called. Each parameter declaration has the form *type variable*, and adjacent parameter declarations are separated by commas. The purpose of a constructor call is to initialize the fields of a newly created folder.

Style Note
13.3.1
spec for a
constructor

A constructor is called when an instance is first created —we see how this is done in Sec. 3.2. The purpose of a constructor is to *initialize the fields of the newly created instance*. That is all. In the constructor shown above, field `name` is initialized to parameter `n` and field `start` to parameter `d`. Field `salary` need not be assigned because the initialization appears in its declaration.

How does one distinguish a constructor from a procedure or function? A procedure has keyword **void** just before the procedure name in its declaration. A function has the return type in this place. A constructor has neither. Furthermore, the constructor name must be the same as the class in which it is declared.

Note carefully the specification of the constructor. In this text, all constructor specifications have the form "Constructor: an instance with ...", where we state exactly what value each field is initialized to, mentioning the parameters where necessary. Please use this convention for your constructor specifications.

The default constructor

If no constructor is declared in a class `C` (say), Java declares this one for you (but it does not appear explicitly in the class definition):

```
/** Constructor: an instance with initialization as given in
    the field declarations */
public C() { }
```

Thus, if you can give the initial values of the fields in their declarations, there is no need to write a constructor.

If you do define a constructor in a class, the default constructor is not placed in the class by Java. So, if you want two constructors, one of which is the default, you have to explicitly define the constructor shown above in the class.

The use of several constructors

The constructor in class `Employee` has two parameters, the name and hire date. Most people for whom an instance will be created will be new hires, so the year will be the year in which the instance is created. To save users effort, we can write a second constructor that has only the name of the person, with the hire date being the current year. Such a constructor is presented below.

```
/** Constructor: person with name n, hired this year, salary 50,000 */
public Employee(String n) {
    name= n;
    start= (new Date()).getYear() + 1900;
}
```

(The year is obtained using an instance of class `Date` of package `java.util`, so we need to import classes of this package. First, an instance of `Date` is created; then its function `getYear` is called, which yields the number of years assuming 1900 as year 0; finally 1900 is added to this value.)

Writing more than one constructor takes time and effort, but it will save time and effort in using the class and is well worth it. Having several constructors can make the user's task easier.

Calling or invoking one constructor from another

Activity
3-5.4

Class `Employee` of Fig. 3.1 contains a constructor that initializes fields `name` and `start`. In the body of the second constructor, shown above, instead of initializing the fields directly, we would like to call the first constructor. At first glance, it would seem that we could replace the two statements in the body of the above function with one constructor call:

```
Employee(n, (new Date()).getYear() + 1900);
```

However, this is not the syntax that Java uses to call one constructor from another. The syntax uses keyword **this** instead of the constructor name:

```
this(n, (new Date()).getYear() + 1900);
```

Note that there is no period following keyword **this**.

Thus, we write the second constructor as follows:

```
/** Constructor: person with name n, hired this year,
    salary 50,000 */
public Employee(String n) {
    this(n, (new Date()).getYear() + 1900);
}
```

Only the first statement of a constructor body can call another constructor.

3.1.4   Function toString

Activity
3-7.2

A Java convention is to define instance function `toString()` in each class, as we did in class `Employee` of Fig. 3.1. The purpose of function `toString` is to create a `String` description of the instance in which the function appears. Generally, though not always, the result will contain the values of all the fields of the instance. In class `Employee`, `toString` yields a `String` that contains the name and year of hire, but not the salary.

Suppose you have an instance v of some class and method toString is defined in the class. To find out what the instance contains, simply type v into the DrJava Interactions pane; automatically, the value of the call v.toString() will be printed.

Here is another way in which toString is useful. Execution of

```
System.out.println(v.toString());
```

will print the description of instance v in the Java console. As another example, to assign a description of instance v to String variable s, use the assignment:

```
s= v.toString();
```

Implicit calls to toString

In certain situations, given the name v of a class instance, Java will automatically call method toString of the instance. For example, one can give v as the argument of a println or print statement, and the effect is as if the argument was v.toString():

```
System.out.println(v);
```

Consider attempting to assign the description of instance v to String s using this assignment:

```
s= b; // Syntactically incorrect
```

Activity 3-7.3 shows how a call to toString is evaluated, step by step.

Because of Java's typing rules for assignment, this statement is syntactically incorrect. Instead, write the assignment like this:

```
s= "" + b;
```

Since one operand of + is a String, the other operand is converted to a String using its method toString; then the catenation of "" with the converted value is assigned to s.

Make the toString description fit the problem

Activity 3-7.4

The form of the description produced by function toString should be in terms of the area with which the class is concerned. For example, consider a class Point whose instances are points in the xy plane. Then, toString should produce conventional notation for points, e.g. "(5,3)".

As another example, suppose that a class BowlingFrame contains the results of one frame of the American game of bowling. Function toString could produce the notation used for keeping score in that game, e.g. "X" for a strike, "8/" for a spare on which the first ball knocked down 8 pins, and "81" for a frame in which the first ball knocked down 8 pins and the second 1.

Take the time to write function toString so that it produces the description in the notation of the problem domain. It will make future testing and debugging easier.

3.1.5   Self-review exercises

SR1. A definition of a class `Circle` goes in a file named _____.

SR2. A class definition describes the contents of _____ .

SR3. The syntax of a class definition is: _____.

SR4. To import the classes of package `javax.swing`, place this statement before the class definition: _____.

SR5. State the principle of information hiding. What keyword is used to hide fields or instance methods of a class?

SR6. State the general inside-out rule in programming languages. How does it apply to method bodies?

SR7. A getter method is to used to _____.

SR8. A constructor is called to _____.

SR9. How do you write the constructor call `C(7, 60);` from another constructor in class `C`, and where do you put the call?

SR10. The purpose of function `toString` in a class `C` is to _____.

SR11. Obtain file `Employee.java` from the bottom of lesson page 3-3 of *ProgramLive*. Place it in a folder by itself. Open it in DrJava and compile it. In the Interactions pane, create an instance or two of the class and experiment with calls to its methods.

Type the second constructor for it, the one just before Sec. 3.1.4. Compile and experiment with creating instances using calls to this constructor.

SR12 Write a class that represents a point in the `(x,y)` plane. What fields does it have? Should they be private or public? What methods will it have? Type your class into DrJava and test all the methods.

Answer to Self-review exercises

SR1. `Circle.java`.

SR2. The folders (instances, or objects) of the class.

SR3. **public class** *class-name* {
            declarations of variables and methods
        }

SR4. Put this statement before the class definition: **import** `javax.swing.*;`

SR5. Make available to someone only what they need to know. Keyword **private** hides fields or instance methods of a class.

SR6. The general inside-out rule in programming languages says that a subpart of a construct can reference anything that is declared in or is accessible in the construct, unless the subpart redeclared it. A method body can reference names declared in the class in which the method is declared, unless the name is redeclared as a parameter of the method.

SR7. Retrieve a value from the instance.

SR8. Initialize fields of a newly created instance.

SR9. Make `this(7, 60);` the first statement of the constructor.

SR10. Yield a description of the fields of the object in which `toString` appears.

SR11. We do not answer this one here.

SR12. Class `Coordinate` will have two private fields, the x and y coordinates of a point. There will be a constructor with two parameters to initialize the fields, as well as getter and setter methods for them. Finally, there will be a `toString` function, which will produce a `String` that looks like this (depending on the coordinates): `"(5,2)"`.

3.2   Using classes

3.2.1   The class as a type

Activity
3-3.4

In the next subsection 3.2.2, we show how a program can create new folders (or instances) of class `Employee` and other classes. Generally, when a folder is created, its name (the label on the folder) is placed in a variable, just as an integer is placed in an `int` variable. To declare the variable that can contain the name of a folder, we use the name of the class as a type.

For example, the first declaration below declares x to be a variable that can contain an `int`, while the second declaration declares v to be a variable that can contain the name of an instance of class `Employee` (or, to abbreviate, the name of an `Employee`):

```
int x;
Employee v;
```

Suppose we assigned 4 to x and the name of the object in Fig. 3.2 to v (we show how to do this in the next subsection). Then, the variables look like this:

x | 4 | v | a0 |

It is important to realize that the name of the instance, and not the instance itself, is placed in v. The consequences of this are discussed in Sec. 3.2.4.

From the above, we see that class `Employee` can be viewed as a type. Since it is also a class, we sometimes talk of Employee as a *class-type*. And just as we say that x is of type `int`, we say that v is of type or class-type `Employee`.

Java syntax: New-expression

new *class-name* (*arguments*)

Purpose. Create a folder (instance, object).

Evaluation. Create a folder of class *class-name*, execute the constructor call *class-name(arguments)*, and yield the name of the new folder as the value.

The values of type `Employee` are the names of folders of class `Employee`.

When a variable of type `Employee` is first declared, it contains the value **null**, which means that it does not contain the name of a folder.

3.2.2   The new-expression

Activities
3-4.1, 3-5.2

The new-expression is used to create new folders, or instances, of a class. Consider this expression, where class `Employee` is given in Fig. 3.1:

```
new Employee("Gries", 1966)
```

Its evaluation is done in three steps:

1. Create a new folder of class `Employee` and place it in `Employee`'s file drawer. Its fields are initialized according to the declarations of the fields. The first part of the new-expression, "**new** `Employee`" tells us to do this.
2. Execute the constructor call `Employee("Gries", 1966);` where the constructor `Employee` that is called is the one in the newly created folder whose parameter types match the argument types of the call.
3. Yield as the value of the call the name of the new folder.

We evaluate the new-expression **new** `Employee("Gries", 1966)`. Step 1 is to create a new folder of class Employee; the folder is shown in the left of Fig. 3.3. The fields have initial values as given by their declarations in the class — default values are used if an initializing declaration is not used.

Step 2 is to execute the constructor call `Employee("Gries", 1966)`. We do this here by stepping over the call. According to the specification of the constructor, the first argument is stored in field `name` and the second in field `start`. We show the result on the right side of Fig. 3.3.

Step 3 is to yield the name `a0` as the result of the expression evaluation.

Here is some terminology. The manilla folder created by evaluating a new-expression is called an *instance* of the class, or an *object* of the class. Evaluating a new-expression *instantiates* the class by creating an instance of it.

Placement of a new-expression

The main use of the new-expression is on the righthand side of an assignment statement, for example, as in:

Java syntax: Referencing a field

expr . field-name

Example: (**new** Date()).x

Purpose: To reference field *field-name* of the folder whose name is given by the value of expression *expr*.

Java syntax: Calling an instance method

expr . method-name (arguments)

Example: (**new** Date()).getyear()

Purpose: To call instance method *method-name* that appears in the folder whose name is given by the value of expression *expr*. If the method is a procedure, the call needs a semicolon.

```
Employee e= new Employee("Hall", 2000);
```

If evaluation of the new-expression in this assignment created the folder that is on the right side of Fig. 3.3, the value a0 would be stored in e.

But an Employee new-expression can appear in many other places —wherever an expression of type Employee can appear. For example, the following statement creates an Employee and prints its description using its toString function; thereafter, the newly created folder cannot be referenced anymore:

```
System.out.println(new Employee("Gries", 1966));
```

This example may not seem so useful. Here is a more useful one. We would like to obtain the current year (or month, day, minute, etc.). We can do this by constructing a new instance of class Date (in package java.util), calling its function getYear, and adding 1900 to the result:

```
int year= (new Date()).getYear() + 1900;
```

In this example, a desired value is retrieved from the new Date folder, and the Date folder is never used again.

In this text, you will come across other cases where a new-expression is used in places other than the righthand side of an assignment. Get used to the fact that the new-expression is just that, a new kind of expression.

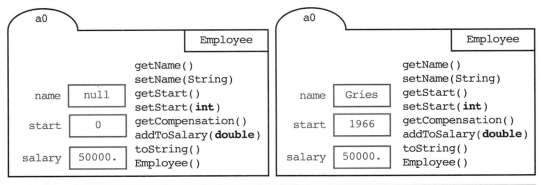

Figure 3.3: Evaluating a new-expression

3.2.3   Referencing components

You already know how to reference a component, but we repeat the information here for completeness. Suppose v contains the name of some folder of class Employee. Then we call a method like getStart that is in the folder using:

v.setStart(arguments);

Of course, the method must be public in order to do this outside the class.

Actually, v can be any expression whose value is a (suitable) folder; it need not be a variable. For example, above, we assigned the current year to variable year using this assignment statement:

int year= (new Date()).getYear() + 1900;

Here, **new** Date() creates a folder of class Date and yields the folder's name a3 (say); so we have a3.getYear(). This calls function getYear of folder a3.

In the same way, if expression e yields the name of a folder and the folder has a field name, then e.name refers to that field.

3.2.4   Equality testing and aliasing

Lesson page 3-7 discusses this topic.

Consider the following two statements:

Employee b= new Employee("Gries", 1966);
Employee c= new Employee("Gries", 1966);

These two statements store in variables b and c the names of two different folders, whose contents happens to be the same. The folders and variables after the assignments are shown in Fig. 3.4.

In this situation, the relation

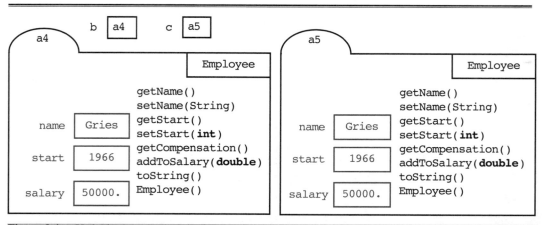

Figure 3.4:   Variables b and c and the folders whose names they contain

```
              b == c
```

evaluates to false. The contents of variables b and c are being compared, not the contents of the folders whose names they contain, and they contain different names.

To be able to compare the contents of the folders named by b and c, we define a boolean function equals in class Employee:

```
/** = "This Employee and e contain the same fields" */
public boolean equals(Employee e) {
    return this.name == e.name
        && this.start == e.start
        && this.salary == e.salary;
}
```

Later, in Sec. 4.3.2, when we have defined the subclass and class Object, we will revisit function equals and write it slightly differently.

Given the situation in Fig. 3.4, suppose we execute the assignment

```
              b= c;
```

Then, b and c both contain the name a5:

```
   b  | a5 |        c  | a5 |
```

and we can get the name of the person using b.getName() and c.getName() — we have two ways of referencing the components. This is called *aliasing* because variables b and c refer to the same object.

In the real world, aliasing often has negative connotations —crooks masquerade under several aliases to stay ahead of the law.

In object-oriented programming, aliasing is a natural occurrence. In terms of our model of file drawers and folders, it makes sense. Barbara (variable b), the person in charge of salaries for a company, might change a5's salary. Charles (variable c), an administrative aide, might later change the name of the person in folder a5 to fix a mistake.

You, the programmer, must be aware of this phenomenon of aliasing in order to design and develop correct programs.

3.2.5 Making fields public

Consider class Coordinates of Fig. 3.5, whose sole purpose is to aggregate the x-coordinate and y-coordinate of a point (x, y) in the plane. It has two fields, which are public, and only two methods, a constructor and function toString.

This class exists not so much for its behavior but simply as a way to collect two values in one place —in an instance. In fact, we could remove the two methods and still find the class useful. The class (or its instances) is similar to the language Pascal's *record* and the language C's *struct*.

There *are* times when we want a class simply to aggregate a few values, and we should not hesitate to construct a class with public fields if that suits the purpose. However, more usually, a class is developed for the *behavior* of its instances: the fields are private, and all interaction with an instance is through public methods. Classes URL, JFrame, Date, and Employee are examples of this; they represent the more popular case.

In Fig. 3.6, we show a use of class Coordinates. Field cent of class Circle contains the center of a circle. There are four methods, which give the usual properties of a circle: center, radius, diameter, and area. We have not used the convention for getter-method names in naming these methods. In this case, the more conventional names seem more appropriate. We leave the writing of a toString method for this class to you.

3.2.6 Self-review exercises

SR1. Write a declaration (with no initialization) of two variables: one of class-type String and another of class-type Employee.

SR2. Write down the three steps in evaluating a new-expression (it is important for future work that you memorize these three steps).

SR3. Below is a new-expression. Evaluate it. In executing the constructor call, *step over* the call, i.e. execute it as an indivisible action based on what the specification of the constructor says. See Fig.3.1. What is the value of the call?

```
new Employee("Clinton", 1996)
```

SR4. Figure 3.6 contains a class Circle. What is wrong with this expression?

```
/** An instance is a point (x, y) in the plane */
public class Coordinates {
    /** The point is (x, y) */
    public int x;
    public int y;

    /** Constructor: an instance for point (x,y) */
    public Coordinates(int x, int y) {
        this.x= x; this.y= y;
    }

    /** = the String "(x, y)" */
    public String toString() {
        return "(" + x + ", " + y + ")";
    }
}
```

Figure 3.5: Class Coordinates

new Circle()

SR5. Figure 3.5. contains a class Coordinates. Evaluate the expression shown below. When executing the constructor call or evaluating the call to function String, step over the calls, i.e. do the call as an indivisible action in terms of the specification of the method.

(**new** Coordinates(5, 6)).toString()

SR6. Consider these three assignment statements:

```
Coordinates x= new Coordinates(5, 6);
Coordinates y= new Coordinates(5, 6);
Coordinates z= y;
```

What is the value of the expression x == y? Of x == z? Of y == z? Of x == x?

Answers to Self-review exercises

SR1. String s; Employee emp;

SR2. (1) create a folder of class C, (2) execute the constructor call C(*args*);, and (3) yield the name of the new folder as the value.

```
/** An instance is a circle with a center and a radius */
public class Circle {
    /** The circle has center cent and radius rad */
    public Coordinates center;
    public int radius;

    /** Constructor: a circle with center (x, y) and radius r */
    public Circle (int x, int y, int r) {
        center= new Coordinates(x, y);
        radius= r;
    }

    /** = the center of the circle */
    public Coordinates center() { return center; }

    /** = the radius of the circle */
    public int radius() { return radius; }

    /** = the diameter of this circle */
    public int diameter() { return 2*radius; }

    /** = the area of this circle */
    public double area() { return Math.PI * radius * radius; }
}
```
Figure 3.6:   Class Circle

SR3. The folder looks like the one in Fig. 3.1, except that `name` has value `"Clinton"` and `start` has value `1996`. The value of the call is the name that you placed in the tab of the folder.

SR4. A constructor without parameters is not defined in class `Circle`. Two arguments are needed within the parentheses.

SR5. Evaluation creates this folder and yields the name a9:

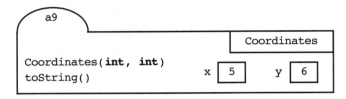

SR6. `false`, `false`, `true`, `true`.

3.3   Static components

Lesson pages 3-1 and 3-2 discuss static methods. Page 3-2 looks at class Math.

As you know, a component (variable or method) that is declared in a class may have the modifier **static**. Such a component is called a *static component*, or *class component*. During execution of a program, a static component is in the file drawer for the class in which it is defined. There is only one copy of the class component —it does *not* appear in instances of the class. One references a static variable v (or method m) in a class C using `C.v` (or `C.m(…)`).

We now discuss the reasons for making a component static.

3.3.1   Static variables

A variable that is declared with modifier **static** within a class is called a *static variable*, or *class variable*. Such a variable does not appear in each manila folder of the class; instead, there is only one copy of it, and it goes directly into the class file-drawer. We discuss two uses of class variables.

Constants

Style Note 13.1, 13.1.1 naming constants

A *constant* is a variable that is declared with modifier **final**. Such a declaration must be an initializing declaration, and no other assignments to it are allowed. The variable cannot be changed. An example is variable MAX_VALUE in class `Integer`:

```
public static final int MAX_VALUE= 2147483647;
```

The purpose of such a constant is to provide a mnemonic name for a value, making it easier for programmers to reference a value. Another example is the constant `Math.PI` (i.e. the constant PI in class Math), which is the closest **double** approximation to the value of π, the ratio of the circumference of a circle to its diameter.

A constant is usually made static because there is no need for more than one copy of it. Placing one copy of the variable in each instance of a class would waste space. Making it static means that there is exactly one copy, in the file drawer of the class. Further, it can be referenced even if no instance of the class has been created. Just use the class name followed by a period followed by the constant name, e.g. Math.PI.

Providing communication among instances of a class

A bank account generally has an account number. The bank gives each account a different, unique, number — it would reek havoc on the system to have two different accounts with the same number.

Consider designing a class BankAccount, each instance of which maintains one bank account, with an owner, account number, and balance. We need a way to assign a new account number to each instance as it is created. To do this, we use a static variable nextAccountNumber, which always contains the next account number to generate. We show how the account numbers are created in Fig. 3.7, which contains part of class BankAccount.

```java
/** An instance is a bank account */
public class BankAccount {
    /** The next account number to assign —numbers 1000..nextAccountNumber-1
        have already been assigned */
    private static int nextAccountNumber= 1000;

    private String person; // The account owner
    private int number; // The account number
    private double balance; // The balance in the account

    /** Constructor: an account for person p with initial balance b */
    public BankAccount(String p, double b) {
        person= p
        balance= b;
        number= nextAccountNumber;
        nextAccountNumber= nextAccountNumber + 1;
    }

    /** = the bank account number */
    public int getNumber() { return number; }

    /** = the number of accounts created thus far */
    public static int numberOfAccounts()
        { return nextAccountNumber - 1000; }
}
```

Figure 3.7:   Assigning bank account numbers (only three methods are shown)

Style Note
13.1, 13.1.1
naming static
variables

Static variable `nextAccountNumber` is initialized to 1000, the first account number to use. Look at the constructor. It assigns `nextAccountNumber` to field `number` and increments `nextAccountNumber`, thus keeping its definition true.

It would be extremely difficult to achieve our goal of having unique account numbers without using a static field (or at least a static method somewhere, or adding extra parameters to the constructor), for then there would be no way to provide communication among the instances of a class. And some form of communication is needed, for how else could we ensure that different accounts have different account numbers? Using a static variable, the necessary communication become easy.

In summary, if some form of communication is needed between instances of a class, consider using static variables.

3.3.2   Static methods

Activity 3-1.3
contains anoth-
er example of
static methods,
dealing with
temperature
conversion.

In Fig. 3.8, we show class `BankAccount`'s file drawer, with one folder of the class as well as the two static components. What can be referenced from, say, the body of function `getNumber` in that folder? According to the inside-out rule (see Sec. 3.1.2), fields `person`, `number`, and `balance` as well as the static components can be referenced. Indeed, function `getNumber` references field `number`. A static method is also called a class method.

Now look at function `numberOfAccounts`. Its method body does not reference any components of instance `a1`, so there is no need to place it in the instance. Therefore, it is made static, so that there is only one copy of it, in the file drawer. Note that the inside-out rule allows the method body to reference static variable `nextAccountNumber`, which it does.

In summary, if a method body does not reference any instance components of the class in which it is defined, make the method static.

3.4   Object-oriented design

We discuss the design of a program using classes. It is an idealized design in which everything is done in a certain order, and correctly. In reality, a design may require much redoing of earlier steps when something is realized later on. Rarely can it be done in a completely idealized fashion. Nevertheless, we should strive for the ideal, for it can reduce the time and effort to complete the program.

3.4.1   The basic idea of OO design

Activity
3-8.1

Object-oriented design is the process of designing a program by focusing on the objects that the program will manipulate and designing the classes that describe the objects. We do this by focusing on the objects of the *problem domain* —the domain for which the program is being written.

Objects are things, so begin by listing objects of the program domain:

1. Write noun phrases to describe the objects to be manipulated.

For example, if a program is going to manipulate student records, here are some of the objects that we might consider:

> student name,
> student address,
> student major (e.g. English or Computer Science),
> student's advisor,
> grades in courses,
> complete student record (it contains just about all the other objects).

As another example, a program that manipulates graphical shapes and places them in a window on your monitor will deal with things like the position of a shape on the monitor, the kind of shape, the color of a shape, and the angle at which the shape is drawn.

Not all the objects listed will require new class definitions. For example, a student's name may be implemented as a `String`, which is already a class. Other objects might appear at first to be useful in the real world but may not be necessary for the program that is being written.

With the list of possible objects, we can:

2. Decide on classes and write their specifications.

The instances of these classes will be the objects.

Recall that the specification of a class describes the behavior of instances of the class, meaning that it specifies all the non-private methods of the class. It will also specify the non-private variables. This is done by picturing in your mind the behavior of the object — in terms of both the real world and how you expect it to perform in the program. In this sense, the *verbs* that come to mind end up being the method names. For example, we might have to change a student's address (method `changeAddress`), or insert a grade (`insertGrade`), or send a message to the student's advisor (`mailAdvisor`).

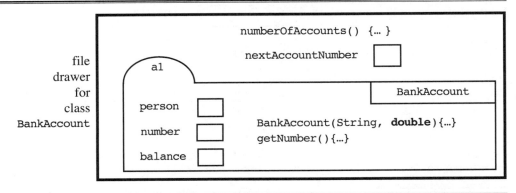

Figure 3.8: `BankAccount`'s file drawer, with one instance

Next, we can:

3. Implement the classes.

Implement one class at a time. As you implement a class, as much as possible, test its methods as soon as they are written. Do not wait until the end. Intermediate testing may give you better ideas and may cause you to change your mind about the design. Of course, intermediate testing is best done if the classes are implemented in a certain order —we will see this when we look at a design in the next several sections.

Finally,

4. Put it together.

Putting it all together in one program will be most easily done if the program parts have been incorporated one at a time into the final program as they were developed and tested.

This is a short discussion of object-oriented design. But, it should give you a bit of insight into the design process. We now give an example of object-oriented design.

3.4.2   An example of OO design

| Lesson page 3-8 provides a better intro to the game. Close this book and watch it! |

We design and implement a program that will give a child practice in reading a clock. The program starts by displaying a window that asks the player (a child) for their name (see Fig. 3.9). After the player enters their name and hits the OK button, a second window asks for the level at which they want to play —an integer in the range 1..4.

After the player types a level number and hits the OK button, a clock appears, along with text giving the player's name, level, and score thus far. Also, a

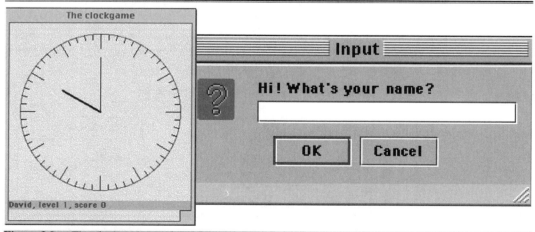

Figure 3.9:   The clock and one of the dialog windows

window appears, asking the player for the hours shown on the clock. If the player types the wrong number, a window appears that says so, and the player is asked to hit one of the buttons. If the player types the right number, a window appears that says so and the score is incremented. When the player hits the OK button, the time on the clock is changed to a new random time and the player is again asked to type in the number of hours. The game continues in this fashion.

We explain the level.

Level 1. The player is asked only for hours, and the clock always shows 0 minutes. At the other levels, the player is asked for the hours and then for the minutes.

Level 2. The clock shows 0, 15, 30, or 45 minutes.

Level 3. The clock shows minutes that are a multiple of 5.

Level 4. The clock shows any minute in the range 0..59.

The level is incremented whenever the score reaches a multiple of 5 and the level is still less than 4.

This ends the description of the game.

Identifying the objects of the game

We write down noun phrases that identify objects of the problem domain. We can think of a *clock*, which has a *time*. The clock has a *face*, a *minute hand*, and an *hour hand*.

There is a *player*. The player has a *name*, has a *score*, and is playing at a particular *level*.

The text that appears under the clock is an object; we call it the player *status*. And the whole window that contains the clock and status is an object; we call it the *clock window*.

The game itself is an object; we call it the *clock game*.

```
/** An instance is a clock with a time, painted on a canvas */
public class Clock extends Canvas {

    /** Constructor: a clock with time t */
    public Clock(Time t) { }

    /** = the time on the clock */
    public Time getTime()
        { return null; }

    /** Set the clock time to t */
    public void setTime(Time t) { }

    /** Paint the clock using g */
    public void paint(Graphics g) { }
}
```

Figure 3.10:   Specification of class `Clock`

The dialog boxes that are displayed when the player is asked for information are also objects, but of a class that already exists in the GUI package that we will be using.

We list these objects:

> clock, time, face, minute hand, hour hand
> player, name, score, level
> status, clock window, clock game, dialog box

There may be more objects to think of, but this is certainly enough to begin with. We move on to the class-design phase. We start by designing the clock.

Specifying class Clock

It is common to draw pictures like the clock on a Canvas, using methods of class Graphics, where class Canvas occurs in package java.awt. Therefore, view the clock as an extension of class Canvas.

A clock always has a time, so it makes sense to have a constructor that is given a time to display on the clock. We will design class Time in a moment.

It will be necessary to obtain and to change the clock time, so we provide getter and setter methods for the time.

We also need a method paint, as usual, that will draw on the Canvas. We collect these methods into the specification given in Fig. 3.10.

Note one thing in Fig. 3.10. We have added a return statement in method getTime, which returns **null**. Although Fig. 3.10 contains only a specification, it will soon be turned into the class itself. Before we write the method bodies, the class should compile; it should be syntactically legal. And functions must have return statements. We write such return statements in all our specifications.

```
/** An instance is a time (hours and minutes) */
public class Time {

    /** Constructor: instance with h hours, m minutes */
    public Time(int h, int m) { }

    /** = the hours of this time */
    public int getHours() { return 0; }

    /** = the minutes of this time */
    public int getMinutes() { return 0; }
    /** = a representation " hours:minutes " of this Time */

    public String toString() { return null; }

    /** = this Time equals t */
    public boolean equals(Time t) { return false; }
}
```

Figure 3.11:   Specification of class Time

Specifying class Time

We now develop the specification of class `Time` (see Fig. 3.11). An instance of `Time` contains a time on the clock. Such a time consists of an hour and a minute, so the constructor of class `Time` will have parameters for them.

The user needs getter methods for the hour and minute. Should we also provide setter methods? We decide against this; if a new time is needed, it can be obtained by creating a new instance of class `Time`. Thus, instances of class `Time` are immutable objects; they cannot be changed.

What other methods are needed? The time on the clock is probably going to be displayed somewhere, especially if the player gets it wrong. So we include method `toString`, which will provide a printable version of the time.

Looking back, we wonder whether class `Clock` should have a method `toString`. We decide that this is unnecessary. It would yield a `String` representation of the time on the clock, and this can already be obtained using `get-Time().toString()`.

When we developed this program, we found out during the implementation phase that it would be useful to have one more method in class `Time`. We discovered the need to compare the time on the clock with the player's guess at the time, so we added a method `equals` to class `Time`.

We have designed class `Clock` and class `Time`, which is used within `Clock`. Looking at the other objects that have to do with the clock (the face and hands), we decide that these objects will not have to be described by classes because they will be simply drawn on the canvas of the clock. Thus, we have finished one major portion of the design process.

Note that we did not discuss the fields we would need in classes `Clock` and `Time`. The fields will be private, so they have nothing to do with the specifications of the classes, which deal with the users' view of the classes.

Specifying class ClockWindow

The diagram in the left of Fig. 3.9 contains a clock and the game status. This window is what we have called object `clockWindow`. We now design class `ClockWindow` to describe how this window behaves (see Fig. 3.12). To have an instance appear as a window on your monitor, we make `ClockWindow` a subclass of class `JFrame`.

The constructor for `ClockWindow` will be given a clock and the `String` value that is to be placed in the status initially. The constructor's task is to add the clock and status to the window and to ensure that the window is visible.

What else do we need? The time on the clock may be changed, but the clock is given to the constructor. So the method that creates the `ClockWindow` has access to the clock, and we see no need for getter/setter methods. The status will also be changed, and we need to provide a setter method for it because otherwise it would be unchangeable. That is about all we need in class ClockWindow.

The implementation of class Time

A time consists of a number of hours and a number of minutes, and the easiest and most obvious thing to do is to introduce private instance variables to contain these two values. Based on the specification of the methods, their bodies are easy to write. See Fig. 3.13. Often, developing the class specification takes more time than the implementation.

The implementation of class Clock

Finally, we implement class Clock (see Fig. 3.14). The constructor has a Time parameter, which gives the time on the clock, so we introduce a private instance variable time to contain this Time. The constructor saves the parameter in field time. It then does something that you probably would not have known how to do: it sets the background color to a kind of pink and sets the size of the Canvas that contains the clock. For this purpose, we introduce two constants to contain the height and width.

The getter method for field time is easy to write. The setter method is also, but it has the additional task of repainting the window because the time has been changed.

The last method to implement is paint. We do not describe the stepwise refinement of this method because our focus here is on object-oriented design, not procedural design. Incidentally, this is the most difficult part of the whole implementation. Take a look at the final program if you wish.

Implementation of class ClockWindow

We do not discuss the implementation of class ClockWindow because it contains too many things with which you are not familiar. Take a look at it, if you wish; you can get it from the CD.

Testing Clock, Time, and ClockWindow

You can use the following lines in DrJava to begin testing these three classes. The first line creates a new Time and stores its name in t; the second line creates a new Clock and stores it in c; and the third line creates a new ClockWindow and stores it in g. Change the time on the first line and run again to look at a different clock.

```
/** An instance is a window with the clock and status */
public class ClockWindow extends JFrame {

    /** Constructor: window with clock c and a status with value s */
    public ClockWindow(Clock c, String s) { }

    /** Set the value of the status to s */
    public void setStatus(String s) { }
}
```

Figure 3.12: Specification of class ClockWindow

```
Time t= new Time(5, 32);
Clock c= new Clock(t);
ClockWindow g= new ClockWindow(c, " test status ");
```

Designing the player and the game

Earlier, we identified these objects:

clock, time, face, minute hand, hour hand
player, name, score, level
label, clock window, clock game, input dialog box

We have taken care of those that have to do with the clock, time, and clock window, and we now design classes for those dealing with the player and the game as a whole.

```
/** An instance is a time (hours and minutes) */
public class Time {

    /** The number of hours in the time. */
    private int hours;

    /** The number of minutes in the time. */
    private int minutes;

    /** Constructor: an instance with h hours, m minutes */
    public Time(int h, int m) {
        hours= h;
        minutes= m;
    }

    /** = the hours of this time */
    public int getHours()
        { return hours; }

    /** = the minutes of this time */
    public int getMinutes()
        { return minutes; }

    /** = a representation " hours:minutes " of this Time */
    public String toString()
        { return hours + ":" + minutes; }

    /** = this Time equals t */
    public boolean equals(Time t)
        { return this.hours == t.hours && this.minutes == t.minutes; }
}
```

Figure 3.13: Class Time

Class Player

We begin with class `Player`, whose final specification is in Fig. 3.15. According to the specification of the game, a player has a name, has a score, and is playing at some level of difficulty. Based on this, we decide that the constructor should have parameters for the player's name and the playing level, with the score initially set to 0.

It should not be necessary for a different part of the program to change these three values, but it will be necessary to access them, so we provide getter methods.

During the game, the score will be incremented —which may cause a change in the level— so we provide a method to increment the score.

Finally, we write function `toString`. Actually, we did not have `toString` initially but found out later that it would be useful. Almost always, function `toString` turns out to be useful, so put one in every class.

```java
/** An instance is the Canvas that contains the clock and status */
public class Clock extends Canvas {

    /** The time on the clock. */
    private Time time;

    /** The width and height of the canvas */
    private static final int WIDTH= 250;
    private static final int HEIGHT= 250;

    /** Constructor: a clock with time t */
    public Clock(Time t) {
        time= t;
        setBackground(new Color(255, 235, 222));
        setSize( WIDTH, HEIGHT);
    }

    /** = the time on the clock */
    public Time getTime()
        { return time;}

    /** Set the time to t and repaint the Canvas */
    public void setTime(Time t)
        { time= t;   repaint(); }

    public void paint(Graphics g) {
        Draw the face —circle and tick marks;
        Draw the hands
    }
}
```

Figure 3.14:   Class `Clock`

Designing class ClockGame

An instance of class `ClockGame` will have methods that allow a game to be played. This will involve a player, a clock, and a clock window that will contain the clock and a label that displays details of the game.

The constructor of the clock game will create the player, clock, and clock window. It will initialize the player by asking the player for their name and the level at which they want to play.

The constructor constructs the game, getting it ready to play, but it does not play it. For this, we write a method `playGame`. This completes the design of the specification of `ClockGame`. See Fig. 3.16 for the specification.

Concluding remarks

Lesson page 3-8 tells you how to get the program from the CD.

This completes the design of the specification of `Player` and `ClockGame`. The only object that we have not dealt with is the dialog box that opens when the player is asked to give some input. You can see how this object is created when you read the implementation of `ClockGame`.

We do not provide the implementations of Player and ClockGame here — our emphasis is more on designing the classes than on providing their implementation. The classes themselves can be obtained from the *ProgramLive* CD.

```java
/** An instance is a player practicing clock-reading. */
public class Player {

    /** Constructor: player with name s, score 0, and playing level lev */
    public Player(String s, int lev) { }

    /** = the name of the player */
    public String getName()
        { return null; }

    /** = the current score of the game */
    public String getScore()
        { return null; }

    /** = the level at which the player is playing */
    public String getLevel()
        { return null; }

    /** Increment the score (and level if necessary) */
    public void incrementScore() { ... }

    /** =  a representation of the player */
    public String toString()
        { return null; }
}
```

Figure 3.15: Specification of class `Player`

3.5   The model of execution

In Sec. 2.7, we discussed execution of method calls, defining the format of a *frame* for a method call, introducing the *call stack* of frames for method calls that have not yet completed, and giving the sequence of instructions for executing a method call. You will best understand method calls if you can execute them yourself, by hand. Only then will you have complete understanding of how calls work. Further, with this ability, you should have little difficulty understanding recursive calls later on (see Chap. 15).

We repeat the set of instructions for executing a method call:

> The scope box of a frame is defined in Activity 5.1. Activities 3-7.1 and 3-7.3 use synched animation to provide much better illustrations of executing method calls.

1. Evaluate the arguments of the call and push them onto the call stack.

2. Draw a frame for the call at the top of the call stack; the frame includes the argument values at the top of the stack. This frame will become the new *active frame*.

   2(a) Fill in the name of the method and set the program counter to 1.
   2(b) Fill in the scope box with the name of the entity in which the method appears: the name of a folder for a non-static method or constructor, and the name of the class for a static method.
   2(c) Draw the local variables of the method body in the frame.

   2(d) Label the argument values pushed onto the call stack in the first step with the names of the corresponding parameters.

3. Execute the method body. When referencing a name, look in the (new active) frame for it. If it is not there, look in the item given by the scope box of the frame.

4. Erase the frame —pop it from the stack. If the method is a function and the call is terminated by execution of a return statement **return** e; , push the value of e onto the call stack.

We now illustrate execution of an assignment statement that includes evaluation of a new-expression, including following the steps in executing its constructor call. We assume that the following statement occurs as the first statement

```
/** An instance has a method to play the clock game. */
public class ClockGame {
    /** Constructor: player with fields initialized and a clock window with a clock and a label.
        The player information is obtained using a dialog window. The default time is 0:00. */
    public ClockGame() { ... }

    /** Play until the player terminates the game */
    public void playGame() { ... }
}
```

Figure 3.16:   Specification of class ClockGame

of static method m in a class C and that class Coordinates is given in Fig. 3.5:

Coordinates d= **new** Coordinates(5, 6 + 2);

Part (a) of Fig. 3.17 shows the call stack with the frame for the call to method m at its top. The program counter is 1 because statement 1 is to be executed. The scope box of the frame contains the name C of the class, since m is static. The frame contains variable d.

Step 1 in evaluating the new-expression is to create a folder of class Coordinates. It is shown below. The fields have the default value 0 since their declarations do not have initializing assignments. We have arbitrarily labeled the folder a9. This folder goes in file drawer for class Coordinates.

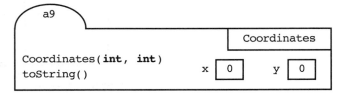

Step 2 in evaluating the new-expression is to execute the constructor call Coordinates(5, 6+2), where the method is in folder a9:

1. Step 1 is to evaluate the arguments and push their values on the call stack. This result of this step is down in part (b) of Fig. 3.17.
2. Step 2 is to create the frame for the call to Coordinates. We have done this in part (c) of Fig. 3.17. The scope box contains the name of the folder in which the called constructor appears. There are no local variables, so none are drawn. The argument values that were pushed onto the stack become the parameters. The result of this step is shown in Fig. 3.17(d).
3. Step 3 is to execute the body of the constructor. This consists of executing the assignments to x and y. Where are variables x and y? Since they are not in the frame for the call, the scope box is used to determine where they are —in folder a9. Thus, folder a9 is changed to look as shown below, and the frame for the call is changed as in Fig. 3.17(e) —the program counter has been changed to 3.

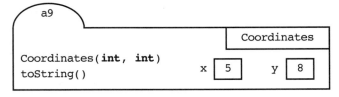

4. Step 4 of executing the constructor call is to erase the frame for the call. Execution of the call is finished. The state of affairs is as shown in Fig. 3.17(f).

Step 3 in evaluating the new-expression is to yield the name of the newly created folder, a9, as the value of the expression.

After evaluation of the new-expression, its value, a9, is stored in variable d. Since the assignment statement is finished, the program counter is incremented. The result is shown in Fig. 3.17(g); we also placed folder a9 in Fig. 3.17(g).

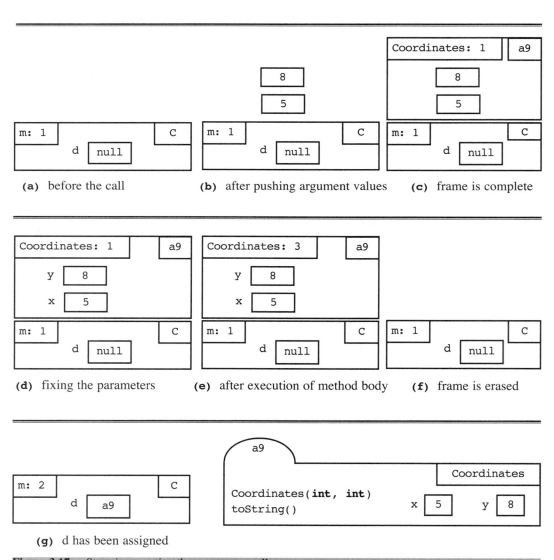

Figure 3.17:   Steps in executing the constructor call

3.6   Key concepts

- **Class**. A *class* is a file drawer that contains two kinds of items: manila folders of the class and components that were declared with modifier **static**.

- **Instances and objects.** The terms *folder*, *instance*, and *object* are used interchangeably.

- **Components: fields and methods**. The components of an *object* of a class are *instance variables* (or *fields*) and *instance methods* — variables and methods that are defined in the class without modifier **static**. Thus, the class definition is a *template* for the folders of the class.

- **Procedures, functions, constructors.** There are three kinds of method. A call to a *function* produces a value. A call to a *procedure* performs some task but does not produce a value. A call to a *constructor* initializes the fields of a newly created object. A method call can have *arguments*, which are expressions.

- **New-expression.** Evaluation of a new-expression **new** *class-name* (*arguments*) creates a new object of class *class-name*, initializes its fields by executing the call *class-name*(*arguments*), and yields the name of the new object as its value.

- **Calling a constructor.** A constructor is called either in a new-expression or as the first statement of another constructor of the class; in the latter case, keyword **this** is used instead of the class name.

- **Class as a type.** A class name may be used as a type, and a variable declared with that type can contain the name of a folder of that type.

- **Null.** The value **null** represents the absence of the name of an instance. If a variable u contains **null**, attempting to access a component using u.*component-name* is an error.

- **Information hiding.** The principle of information hiding says to hide information from those who do not need it. We usually hide fields of an object by declaring them to be **private**, although in rare cases, making them **public** is preferred.

- **Inside-out rule.** The inside-out rule, used in most programming languages, says that a program part can reference items declared or referenceable in surrounding constructs, unless a redeclaration hides them.

- **toString.** Put a function toString in (almost) every class to provide a description of the object in which the function appears.

- **Equality testing.** A relation c==b tests whether the names (of objects) that are in c and b are the same, not whether the contents of the objects are the same. Write a function equals to test whether the contents of the objects are the same.

- **Static items.** Make a variable static if it is a constant or if only one copy is needed and it provides communication between objects of the class. Make a method static if the only variables it references are its parameters and local variables and the only methods of the class that it calls are static methods.

• **Object-oriented design.** OO design lays emphasis on making a list of the nouns of the problem domain; they represent objects, and classes are designed whose instances are those objects. Verbs tend to be models for the methods of the classes.

Exercises for Chapter 3

E1. Names come in several forms, given by these examples: (1) David Gries (2) David J. Gries (3) David Joseph Gries (4) Gries, David (5) Gries, David J. and (6) Gries, David Joseph. Design a class that will allow someone to create an instance with a first name, middle name, and last name and retrieve any of these six forms from it. You might allow a person to omit the middle name if there is none. Here are two different schemes. In one scheme, there are six methods — to retrieve a name in each of the six formats. In the other scheme, there is method for indicating which of the six formats is desired and only one method for retrieving a name —using the desired form. Which of these schemes do you prefer? Why? If you use the second alternative, use constants to name the six formats.

E2. Implement and test the class of the previous exercise. How many test cases do you need to ensure that it is correct? If you need help with handling strings, see Sec. 5.2.

E3. Design a class an instance of which is a pair of dice. Each die has six faces, with the numbers in 1, 2, 3, 4, 5, 6 on them. At all times, one face is face-up. What methods will you have? You will probably want one for "rolling" the dice, so that new faces become face-up in a random manner.

E4. Implement and test the class designed in the previous exercise. In implementing a roll of the dice, you may want to look at class Random (see Sec. 5.6).

E5. Design a class whose instances are standard playing cards. Each card has a suit (one of spades, hearts, clubs, and diamonds) and a value (one of 2, 3, 4, 5, 6, 7, 8, 9, 10, Jack, Queen, King, Ace). Think carefully about what methods you incorporate in the class. Also, think about having constants to denote the suits and values. See Sec. 3.3.1.

E6. Implement and test the class of the previous exercise.

E7. Design a class that represents a list of cards (of playing cards; see exercise E5). The whole deck of 52 cards could be an instance of this class. However, a player's "hand" —say, in poker, 5 cards, could be an instance as well. In designing the methods, think of a card game that you have played and figure out what you do with the deck of cards or a hand when playing the game.

E8. Implement and test the class of the previous exercise. You may want to hold a bunch of cards in a `Vector` (see Sec. 5.3).

E9. Students in a class have received three scores on homeworks so far. Depending on the average of these three scores, they are either passing, marginal, or failing. Passing is an average in the range `70..100`, marginal is an average in the range `55..69`, and failing is an average in the range `0..54`. Design a class whose instances represent students. A student has a name and three scores. It should be possible to retrieve the name, the scores, and the average. It should also be possible to see whether a student is passing, marginal, or failing. For the latter method, introduce three constants, PASSING, MARGINAL, and FAILING, and have the function return one of them. Read Sec. 3.3.1.

E10. Implement and test the class of the previous exercise.

E11. Design a class each instance of which represents a library book, which has a title, author, and call number.

E12. Implement and test the class of the previous exercise.

E13. Design a class each instance of which represents an entry in an address book. It has a person's name, address (as a `String`), phone number, email address, and birthday (which could be of class `Date`).

E14. Implement and test the class of the previous exercise.

E15. Design a class each instance of which is an address book. Use the class of exercise E13 for the entries in the address book. Given an address book, one should be able to look for an entry by name, phone number, or address. It should be possible to delete an entry, change part of an entry, etc.

E16. Implement and test the class of the previous exercise. You may want to maintain the collection of entries in the address book using class `Vector` (see Sec. 5.3).

E17. Write a test of a class whose instances represent a time of day, i.e. it maintains the hour and minute. The user should be able to state whether the time should be seen as a 12-hour or 24-hour mechanism. In the first case, method `toString` method should produce a time that looks like `10:30AM` or `03:16PM`; in the second case, `10:30` or `15:16`. Note that the hour is always two digits. The user should be able to retrieve and set the hour, and minute.

E18. Design a class like that of exercise E17 except that it also maintains the time zone. Include just a few time zones, like GMT (Greenwich Mean Time) EST (Eastern Standard Time) and EDT (Eastern Daylight Time).

E19. Implement and test the class of the previous exercise. How many test cases do you need to ensure that it is correct? If you need help with handling Strings, see Sec. 5.2.

E20. What happens if the name of a class does not match the name of the file in which it is placed? Try it.

E21. Can you put two public classes in the same file? Try it, and explain what happens.

Chapter 4

Subclasses

OBJECTIVES

- Introduce subclasses, inheritance of components, and overriding methods.
- See how to draw an object of a subclass.
- Learn about keyword super in calling superclass methods.
- Learn how to cast from a superclass to a subclass and vice versa.
- Discuss designing object-oriented programs.
- Introduce the final model of execution.
- Discuss abstract classes.

INTRODUCTION

Activity 4-1.1 shows how class Employee would have to be changed to take different employees into account. Watch it!

In Fig. 3.1, we presented a class Employee. We now make this class more realistic by introducing several kinds of employee: the salaried and hourly employees and the executive. The yearly compensation is calculated differently for each kind of employee. Salaried employees and executives get a yearly salary, hourly employees are paid by the hour, and executives get bonuses.

With our current programming tools, changing the class of Fig. 3.1 to take three kinds of employees into account would get messy. We would have to add several fields to the class, most of which would be used in only one case. Everywhere, there would be tests to determine which kind of employee is being processed and to process the employee accordingly. Further, later changes, say, to add a new kind of employee, would be difficult to do correctly.

To help solve such problems, we introduce a new structuring mechanism: the *subclass*. It is the subclass, together with its notions of *inheritance* and *overriding* of methods, that make object-programming really useful. Java programs — including the Java API classes — make heavy use of subclasses. For example, writing GUIs would be far more difficult without subclasses.

> **Java syntax: Subclass definition**
> **public class** *subclass-name* **extends** *superclass-name* {
>   *declarations of methods and fields*
> }
>
> **Purpose**: To define a new file drawer, named *subclass-name*, and describe the contents of its manila folders (instances of the class). They have the methods and fields that are declared in superclass *superclass-name* as well as the methods and fields being declared in the subclass.

Actually, the subclass is not new to you. It was discussed in some detail in Sec.1.4, and you have already learned that the subclass is a mechanism for customizing a class to fit new needs. An instance of the subclass has all the components (instance variables and instance methods) that the superclass does, but it can define new ones. In Sec. 1.4, we also showed how to draw an instance of a subclass (see Fig. 1.9). In this chapter, we review the concepts discussed in Sec.1.4 and go into more detail on some of the issues concerning subclasses.

4.1   The subclass definition

Get class Employee and its subclasses from a footnote on lesson page 4-1 of the CD.

Figure 4.1 contains a definition of a class `Executive`. Because of the *extends clause*

        extends `Employee`

in the first line, class `Executive` is called a *subclass* of class `Employee` and class `Employee` is called a *superclass* of `Executive`. The presence of this clause means that every instance component of class `Employee` is also an instance component of class `Executive`. We say that `Executive` *inherits* the instance variables and methods of `Employee`. But subclass `Executive` can have additional instance components.

Activities 4-1.2 and 4-1.3 discuss subclasses with a slight variation of Employee and its subclasses.

Figure 4.1 contains uses of keyword **super** in the constructor and functions `toString` and `getCompensation`. Keyword **super** is explained in subsections 4.1.1 and 4.1.3.

Figure 4.2 shows how we draw an instance of subclass `Executive`. The folder has two partitions. At the top is the partition for components that are inherited from class `Employee`; the name `Employee` is in a box in the upper righthand corner of the partition. At the bottom is the partition for components that are defined in the subclass, `Executive`; the name of the subclass is in a box in the upper righthand corner of the partition.

We draw every instance of a subclass in this fashion. Having a standard way to draw such manila folders makes it easier to communicate.

Subclass `Executive` contains a private field, `bonus`. Since only `Executives`, and not other `Employees`, get bonuses, this field is placed in the subclass. Superclass `Employee` contains only fields that represent properties that all employees have.

4.1.1   Inheriting and overriding

A subclass *inherits* all the components of the superclass. This means that each instance of the subclass contains all the instance components of the superclass. The folder in Fig. 4.2 makes this clear.

Suppose a variable b contains the name a7 of the folder in Fig. 4.2 (later, we see how to create the folder and store its name in b). Then, method getName in the folder can be called using the expression

> b.getName()

This expression evaluates to the string "Gries". This expression calls an *inherited* method. In the same way, method getBonus in the folder can be called using

> b.getBonus()

There are two instance functions getCompensation in folder a7. Which one does the expression

> b.getCompensation()

call? It calls the method that is declared in subclass Executive. We say that method getCompensation in class Executive *overrides* the inherited method.

Comparing the two methods, we can see that this makes sense. Since the

```
/** An executive: an employee with a bonus. */
public class Executive extends Employee {

    /** Yearly bonus */
    private double bonus;

    /** Constructor: a person with name n, year hired d, salary 50,000, and bonus b */
    public Executive(String n, int d, double b) {
        super(n, d);
        bonus= b;
    }

    /** = this executive's bonus */
    public double getBonus()
        { return bonus; }

    /** = this executive's yearly compensation */
    public double getCompensation()
        { return super.getCompensation() + bonus; }

    /** = a representation of this executive */
    public String toString()
        { return super.toString() + ", bonus " + bonus; }
}
```

Figure 4.1: Subclass Executive

> **Do not override instance variables**. Overriding instance methods is common. Overriding instance variables —called *shadowing* rather than overriding— is allowed but rare. We do not explain the rules for referencing shadowed variables in this text, and we assume throughout that variables will not be shadowed.

employee described in the folder is an executive, the compensation should be the salary together with the bonus, not just the salary alone.

We capture this important point about object-oriented programming in the following rule. The rule is written in such a way that it will work in later cases, when we discuss subclasses of subclasses.

> **Public method overriding rule**. When determining the instance method to call (within a folder) for a call *method-name(arguments)*, start at the bottom of the folder and search upward until the appropriate method is found.

Searching from the bottom upward ensures that the overriding method is called.

Notice that all the instance variables are private; they cannot be seen outside the class in which they are defined. In fact, variables `name`, `start`, and `salary` cannot be referenced in the methods of subclass `Executive`! However, their values can be retrieved using public, inherited, getter methods.

Using super to get at an overridden method

Activity 4-2.3

Look at function `getCompensation` in Fig. 4.1. It is supposed to yield the sum of the `salary` and the `bonus`. How is the `salary` retrieved? The function body cannot reference the field because it is private. Moreover, a call `getCompensation()` within the function would call itself, since it is the overriding method!

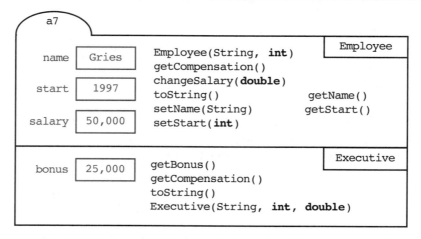

Figure 4.2: An instance of subclass `Executive`

Java provides a way out of this dilemma. To call the method getCompensation in the superclass, prefix the call with **super.**:

> **super**.getCompensation()

Notice that a reference **super**.salary is illegal because field salary is private. If it were not private, **super**.salary would be legal. But then the use of "**super**." would be unnecessary.

Here is a step by step look at how the expression

> **super**.toString() + ", bonus " + bonus

of function toString in instance a7 is evaluated.

(a) Evaluate **super**.toString(), yielding the value

```java
/** An hourly employee */
public class HourlyEmployee extends Employee {

    /* Class invariant: salary = hourlyPay * hoursWorked */

    /** Amount payed per hour and hours worked */
    private double hourlyPay;
    private int hoursWorked;

    /** Constructor: a person with name n, year hired d, hourly pay p, and hours worked h */
    public HourlyEmployee(String n, int d, double p, int h) {
        super(n, d);
        hourlyPay= p;
        hoursWorked= h;
        super.changeSalary(hourlyPay * hoursWorked);
    }

    /** = the hourly pay of this employee */
    public double getHourlyPay()
        { return hourlyPay; }

    /** = the hours worked by this employee */
    public double getHoursWorked()
        { return hoursWorked; }

    /** = This method currently has no effect.*/
    public double changeSalary(double d) {   }

    /** = a representation of this hourly employee */
    public String toString() {
        return super.toString() + ", pay " + hourlyPay + ", hours " + hoursWorked;
    }
}
```

Figure 4.3: Subclass HourlyEmployee

                `"Gries, year 1997, salary 50000"`

(b) Catenate to it the string `", bonus "`, giving thus far

          `"Gries, year 1997, salary 50000, bonus "`

(c) Catenate to it the value of field `bonus`, giving the result

          `"Gries, year 1997, salary 50000, bonus 25000"`

Functions `getCompensation` and `toString` in Fig. 4.1 make use of keyword **super** to call inherited methods.

4.1.2   The class invariant

Style Note 13.4 describing variables

Figure 4.3 shows a second subclass of `Employee`: `HourlyEmployee`. Hourly employees are paid by the hour, so the class has two private fields to contain the hourly pay and the number of hours worked. The class also has two getter methods for obtaining the values of these fields.

Handling the inherited salary field of this class is a bit tricky. The superclass has a procedure `changeSalary(d)` whose purpose is to change the salary to `d`, but we can't allow that procedure to be used for hourly employees because their salary is based on the hourly pay and the number of hours worked. Therefore, the subclass has an overriding procedure `changeSalary(d)` that does nothing.

Now look near the top of the class in Fig. 4.3. There is a comment, which we call the *class invariant*. It states the relationship that must always hold between the fields of an instance:

      `/* class invariant: salary = hourlyPay * hoursWorked */`

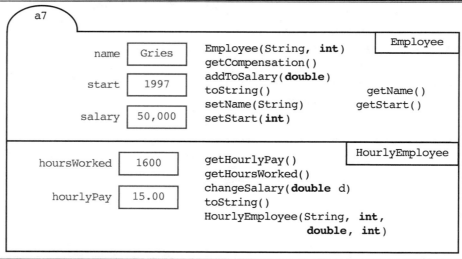

Figure 4.4:   An instance of subclass `HourlyEmployee`

Java syntax: call inherited function/procedure	Java syntax: call superclass constructor
super.m(*arguments*)	**super** (*arguments*);
Example: super.toString()	**Example: super**("Gries", 1966, 2500);
Purpose: To call method m of the superclass. Use only when an overriding method was defined and the superclass method is wanted.	**Purpose**: Call a constructor of the superclass. Can be used only as the first statement of a constructor body.

This comment is a reminder to whomever is writing or maintaining the class (or simply reading it) to keep this relation true. The relation is called an *invariant* because it is unchanging; it is "invariantly true" in each instance. Field salary *always* contains the product of the hourly pay and the hours worked.

The constructor has a call on class changeSalary of the superclass, which truthifies the class invariant initially. And, since none of the other methods of the class change the hours worked, pay per hour, or salary, it remains true.

Of course, there should be some way to change the hours worked or pay per hour. Self-help exercises ask you to write setter methods for these fields. In writing them, the class invariant reminds you to change field salary whenever you change the hours or the pay per hour. Without the class invariant, you would not know that this had to be done, and this would lead to a logical error in the class.

In any class that has several fields, there may be some relationship among their values that has to be maintained. It is important to express this relationship as a comment near the declarations of the fields and to make the comment thorough, precise, and clear. You, the programmer, will rely on it when implementing the methods of the class, and others will have an easier time reading and understanding the class.

4.1.3   Constructors in a subclass

Activity
4-2.1

The purpose of a constructor in any class is to initialize some (or all) of the fields of an instance when the instance is created. In class Executive, four fields have to be initialized: three inherited fields and field bonus.

A general rule is to initialize inherited fields using a constructor of the superclass. In class Executive, we *have* to do this because the inherited fields are private. But even if they were public, it would be better to use a superclass constructor to initialize them. Since they are declared in the superclass, let the superclass take care of them. This policy helps isolate parts of the program and makes the program easier to maintain.

Within a constructor, a call to another constructor *must* be the first statement of the body. That makes sense; initialize the inherited fields before the newly declared ones.

In the constructor of class Executive, the first thought on calling the superclass constructor would be to write:

```
Employee(n, d);
```

but that is not the syntax Java uses to call the superclass constructor. Instead, use:

```
super(n, d);
```

Thus, to call a constructor of the superclass, write a conventional call to the superclass constructor but replace the name of the class name with **super**. Note that there is no period following keyword **super**, as there is in the other use of **super** (see Sec. 4.1.1).

If you do not call a superclass constructor

The first statement of a subclass constructor *must* be a call on a superclass constructor. If you do not put one in, Java inserts this one:

```
super();
```

In this case, the superclass must have a constructor with no parameters —if not, the program is illegal and a syntactic-error message will appear when you try to compile the program. The error message may be so confusing that you have trouble determining what the mistake is —unless you remember the rules that Java inserts a superconstructor call if you do not. This error will happen more often than you expect, unless you get in the habit of explicitly writing a call to the superclass constructor as the first statement in the subclass constructor.

4.2   Casting about, or about casting

4.2.1   Apparent and real classes

An instance of class Executive of Fig. 4.1 can be created and stored using an initializing assignment like

```
Executive c= new Executive("Gries", 1966, 25000);
```

An executive is an employee; in the same way, we say that an instance of class Executive, like c, is also an Employee. And, we can assign it to an Employee variable:

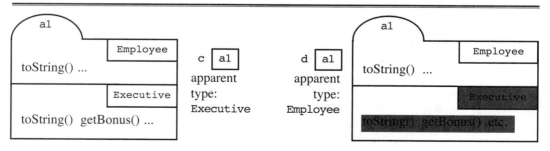

Figure 4.5:   Two different views of the same object

> **Polymorphism.** *Polymorphism*, from a Greek word meaning *multiform*, means "capable of having or occurring in several distinct forms". The ability for a call like `e1.getCompensation()` to call one of many different methods depending on the value of `e1` is a far more flexible form of polymorphism than the ad hoc polymorphism mentioned in Chap. 2.
>
> In ad hoc polymorphism, the method to be called is a syntactic property; it determined at compile-time. In *object-oriented polymorphism*, the method to be called cannot be determined until the call is to be executed at runtime, because it depends entirely on e1's value, which can change at runtime.
>
> Without OO polymorphism —the ability to have the real type determine which method to call— OO would not be half as useful as a structuring tool.
>
> If method `getCompensation` is overloaded, e.g. there is a method by that name with an **int** parameter as well as a method with no parameters, `e1.get-Compensation()` exhibits both ad hoc and OO polymorphism.

```
Employee d= c;
```

Just as Java automatically widens an **int** value to a **double**, Java widens the instance of a class to an instance of one of its superclasses.

But what does widening an object mean? Widening an **int** to a **double** takes time because a 4-byte value is changed into an 8-byte value with different characteristics. Widening an object takes no time (at runtime) but just changes the *syntactic view* of the object. Widening is best illustrated with an example.

Figure 4.5 shows on the left the syntactic view of object `a1` as seen from `c`. Apparently, c contains the name of an `Executive`, and references to all components that are available in any instance of `Executive` are legal. So, calls `c.toString()` and `c.getBonus()` are legal. We say that the *apparent type* of c is `Executive`.

On the right is the syntactic view of the same object `a1` as seen from `d`. Apparently, d contains the name of an `Employee`, and references to all components that are available in any instance of `Employee` are legal. So, the call `d.toString()` is legal, but the call `d.getBonus()` is illegal. We say that the *apparent type* of d is `Employee`.

We stress that the apparent type of an expression is a *syntactic* property. It determines what component names can be referenced. If you write the call `d.getBonus()` in your program, it will not compile.

The call `d.toString()` is legal. We now ask what it means —which method it calls. According to the public overriding rule (see Sec. 4.1.1), it calls the method `toString` that appears in the `Executive` partition of `a1`. Thus, even though the apparent class of d is `Employee`, `d.toString()` calls the overriding method of `Executive`.

Apparently, d contains an `Employee`, but in reality, it contains an `Executive`. We say that the *apparent type* of d is `Employee`, but its *real type* is `Executive`.

Java syntax: Class cast

(*class-name*) *class-expression*

Example: (Executive) d

Meaning: evaluation yields a view of the value of *class-expression* with apparent type *class-name*. It does not change the real type.

Java syntax: Operator instanceof

expression **instanceof** *class-name*

Example: d **instanceof** Executive

Meaning: evaluation yields **true** if the real class of *expression* is *class-name* (or a subclass of *class-name*) and **false** otherwise.

One may ask why one would want to put an Executive object in an Employee variable. Here is a reason. Below is a static function that yields the maximum compensation of two employees:

```
/** = the maximum compensation of e1 and e2 */
public static double max(Employee e1, Employee e2) {
  return Math.max(e1.getCompensation(),
                  e2.getCompensation());
}
```

Now consider the following assignments:

```
Executive e= ...;
HourlyEmployee h= ...;
double m= max(e, h);
```

In the call max(e, h), argument e is of class Executive and the corresponding parameter e1 is of class Employee. Therefore, during evaluation of the call, the apparent type of e1 is Employee but its real type is Executive. Hence, when the call e1.getCompensation() in the method body is evaluated, it will call the overriding function getCompensation that is defined in class Executive. This makes sense: e1 is an Executive, so its compensation should be calculated according to executive's rules. Similarly, the call e2.getCompensation() in the method body will call the overriding method that is in the HourlyEmployee partition of folder h.

Below, we summarize the important points about the apparent class and real class of an expression:

- The *apparent class* (or apparent type) of an expression is a syntactic property; it is used to determine what component references are syntactically legal. For a class variable, its apparent class is the class with which it was declared.
- The *real class* (or real type) of an expression is a semantic property. It is the class of the value of the expression, and it can change while the program is executing. The real class of an expression determines which components are actually referenced —for a call to a public method, the overriding method in the real class is called.

4.2.2   Explicit widening and narrowing

To cast an expression to some class, use the class name, within parentheses, as a prefix operator. Such a cast changes the apparent type of an expression. For example, this expression has apparent class `Executive`:

```
new Executive("Gries", 1966, 25000)
```

but this expression has apparent type `Employee`:

```
(Employee) (new Executive("Gries", 1966, 25000))
```

A cast `(C) e` is *widening* if `C` is already the apparent type of `e` or if `C` is a superclass of the apparent type of `e`. A class is *narrowing* if `C` is a subclass of the apparent type of `e`. Below, the cast of `x` is a widening cast, while the cast of `y` is a narrowing cast:

```
Executive x= new Executive("Gries", 1966, 25000);
Employee y= (Employee) x;
Executive z= (Executive) y;
```

Widening casts are unnecessary because Java does them automatically.

You have to be careful with narrowing casts. You can cast an expression only to its real type or any superclass of its real type. To see the errors you might make, consider this expression:

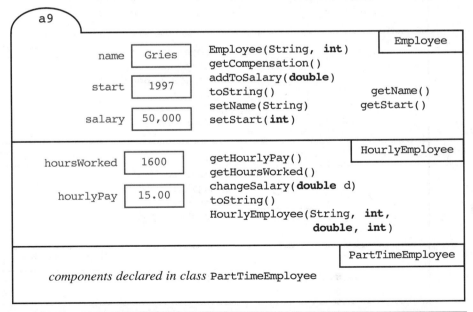

Figure 4.6:   An instance of subclass `ParttimeEmployee`

(HourlyEmployee) y

The real type of y is Executive, so to cast it to HourlyEmployee is a mistake, and this mistake is sure to lead to a runtime error and abortion of execution.

4.2.3   Operator instanceof

At times, you may want to test what the real class of a variable is, so that you do not make the mistake of casting an object to something that it is not. Use operator **instanceof** to do this. As an example, the following statement determines whether the real type of x is HourlyEmployee and, if so, executes its then-part.

```
if (x instanceof HourlyEmployee) {
   ...
}
```

Operator **instanceof** can be useful. But if you find it necessary to use it frequently, perhaps the structure of your classes is not adequate and some redesign may be in order. If you find yourself writing code like that below, where you have to test all possible subclasses, think about redesigning.

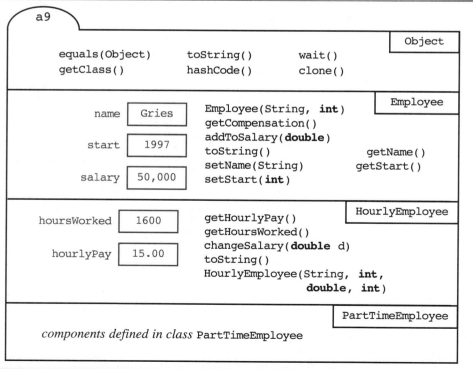

Figure 4.7:   An instance of subclass PartTimeEmployee, showing the Object partition

```
if (d instanceof Executive) {
    ...
} else if (d instanceof HourlyEmployee) {
    ...
} else if (d instanceof OvertimeEmployee) {
    ...
} else if ...
```

4.3   The class hierarchy

Subclasses of subclasses

We could extend class `HourlyEmployee` of Fig. 4.3 in at least two ways. We could have a subclass `PartTimeEmployee` —part-time employees work only part time (so they do not get health and retirement benefits), and the number of hours worked is restricted in some fashion. We could also have a subclass `Overtime-Employee`. Overtime employees are allowed to work overtime, usually at 1.5 times their normal hourly pay.

A folder of class `PartTimeEmployee` appears in Fig. 4.6. In it, there is one partition for each class: `PartTimeEmployee` at the bottom, its superclass `HourlyEmployee` above that, and its superclass `Employee` above that. The overriding rule for public methods (see Sec. 4.1.1) works for such folders; to find the method to call (within the folder), always search the folder from bottom to top.

In this case, both `Employee` and `HourlyEmployee` are called superclasses of `PartTimeEmployee`. A subclass inherits the components of *all* its superclasses.

Subclasses of subclasses appear often in object-oriented programming. In fact, the hierarchy can go quite deep. For example, class `JFrame`, which you studied in Chap. 1 and is part of the GUI classes for Java, is a subclass of `Frame`, which is a subclass of `Window`, which is a subclass of `Container`, which is a subclass of `Component`, which is a subclass of `Object`. This hierarchy was designed to create a flexible set of GUI classes.

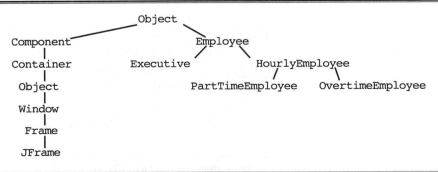

Figure 4.8:   The subclass tree

4.3.1   Class Object

Class `Object`, in package `Java.lang`, is automatically available in every Java program. It enjoys a special status: every class that does not explicitly extend another class, like `Employee`, automatically extends class `Object`. `Object` is the superclass of all classes that do not extend other classes. `Object` is the "superest" class of them all.

Figure 4.8 shows some classes in a "tree". The root of the tree is class `Object` (computer scientists draw trees with their roots at the top). Attached to it with lines underneath are two of its subclasses, `Component` and `Employee`; attached to them with lines underneath are their subclasses; and so on.

Class `Object` has a number of public instance methods, some of which are:

```
equals(Object)        toString()
getClass()            hashCode()
clone()               wait()
```

These methods are inherited by every object, so there should be an `Object` partition in every manila folder that we draw, as shown in Fig. 4.7. We usually do not draw this partition because it would clutter the folders and because we know it is in every folder.

You already know about function `toString`, whose purpose is to produce a `String` representation of the folder in which it appears. It is a good practice to override it in almost every class that you write.

Most of the methods in class `Object` are outside the scope of this text. But one needs a full discussion: function `equals`.

4.3.2   Boolean function equals

Boolean function `equals` tests for the equality of the names of objects. Here is its definition:

```
/** = "the name of this object is the same as the name of obj" */
public boolean equals(Object obj)
     {  return this == obj;  }
```

Function `equals` is often overridden to compare the contents of folders instead of their names. Care must be taken when overriding it to ensure that it has properties that are usually associated with equality. The specification of `equals` in the Java API indicates this clearly: The overriding function should be an *equivalence relation*. This means that it should have the following properties:

- It is *reflexive*: for any folder x, x.equals(x) is **true**.
- It is *symmetric*: for any folders x and y, x.equals(y) and y.equals(x) have the same value.
- It is *transitive*: for any folders x, y, and z, if x.equals(y) and y.equals(z) are **true**, then x.equals(z) is **true**.

In addition, it should have two other properties:

- It is *consistent*: x.equals(y) consistently returns **true** or consistently returns **false**, provided no information used in equals comparisons on the object is modified.
- For any folder x, x.equals(**null**) is **false**.

The spec of function equals says that it is generally necessary to override method hashCode whenever equals is overridden to maintain the general contract for method hashCode, which states that equal objects must have equal hash codes. But the topic of method hashCode is outside the scope of this text.

An example of overriding equals

In Sec. 3.2.4, we discussed aliasing and equality and wrote this boolean function in class Employee:

```
/** = "This Employee and e contain the same fields" */
public boolean equals(Employee e) {
    return name == e.name
          && start == e.start
          && salary == e.salary;
}
```

We now rewrite this function so that it overrides function equals of class Object. Thus, its parameter must be Object. Further, we must make sure that e is not **null** and that its real class is Employee. Here is the function:

```
/** = "e is an Employee, with the same fields as this Employee" */
public boolean equals(Object e) {
    return e != null
          && e instanceOf Employee
          && name == e.name
          && start == e.start
          && salary == e.salary;
}
```

4.4   Access modifiers

This section need be studied only if you are going to write your own packages (see Chap. 11).

As you know, a *private* component in a class C can be accessed only in class C, and not even in subclasses of C. A *public* component can be accessed anywhere. Classification *private* is extremely restrictive; public is extremely liberal. Java has two other access schemes, which we call *protected* and *package*, that fall between these two extremes. Below, we list all four schemes, from least to most restrictive:

- A *public component* —a component declared with modifier **public**— is accessible everywhere.
- A *protected component* —a component declared with modifier **protected**— of a class C is accessible in subclasses of C and in classes in the same package as C.
- A *package component* —a component declared without an access modifier— of a class C is accessible in classes in the same package as C.
- A *private component* —a component declared with modifier **private**— of a class C is accessible only in class C.

With most of the programs that you write, you do not use a package statement, so all the classes are automatically in the *default* package. Since all your classes are in the same package, there is no recognizable difference between access schemes protected, package, and public. Therefore, you can stick to using just private and public.

4.5   Object-oriented design

In Sec. 3.5, we discussed the design of programs that contained classes. We focused on the objects of the problem domain. We made a list of noun phrases that described the objects that we thought the program would be manipulating, and then we developed classes that would describe (some of) them. Some of the verbs of the problem domain became methods of the classes.

In this section, we extend our notion of object-oriented design to include subclasses.

4.5.1   The is-a relation

Consider designing a program to maintain a database of people associated with a university. We start by constructing noun phrases for the objects that the program will manipulate. What kind of people do we have? Well, there are grad students, undergraduates, and non-degree students who are just taking a course. There are professors, associate professors, and assistant professors. There are secretaries, lab technicians, janitors, alumni, and so on.

Such a jumbled list of people is not easy to work with, so we organize them into broad categories, such as student, faculty, staff, and alumni:

        university member
            student
                graduate
                undergraduate
                nondegree student
            faculty member
                professor

associate professor
assistant professor
staff member
  secretary
  technician
  janitor
alumni

The indentation used above is used to describe the *is-a* relation. For example, the three lines indented underneath the entry *staff member* indicate that a secretary *is a* staff member, a technician *is a* staff member, and a janitor *is a* staff member. Also, a student *is a* university member, a professor *is a* faculty member *is* a university member, and so on.

The *is-a* relation is fundamental in dealing with subclasses: if c *is a* b, then when constructing classes, we make C a subclass of class B. For example, suppose we write a class for each of the objects in this hierarchy. Then, class UniversityMember has no superclass (except Object). Class Student is a subclass of UniversityMember, Professor is a subclass of FacultyMember, and so on. So, we have a general guideline:

Make a class B a subclass of class C if each instance of B *is a* C.

Commonality of behavior

We explain why we structure classes and subclasses according to the *is-a* relation, using students as an example. The three kinds of students share common behavior, which will be reflected in the instance methods in class Student. For example, all students have a name, so there will probably be a method to get this name. And they pay tuition. Method getName may be defined in class Student, but *all* university members have names, so the method is better defined in UniversityMember and inherited in class Student. Only students pay tuition, so method payTuition will be defined in class Student.

Thus, we have the following principle:

Subclass principle: Structure classes so that behavior that is common to several classes can be defined in a superclass of those classes.

Sometimes, we insert new classes to make better use of this guideline. For example, all faculty and staff get pay, so we may decide to insert a new class, Employee, so that method getPay may be placed in it.

4.5.2   Example of object-oriented design

Get the classes
in this design
from a footnote
on lesson page
4-4.

Activity
4-4.2

We design classes that facilitate drawing various shapes in a graphics window — parallelograms, rhombuses, squares, etc. Later, you can augment these with classes to draw triangles, right triangles, and other shapes of your choosing.

Class Shape

Class Shape will be the superclass of all shape classes —see Fig. 4.9. A basic property of any shape is its placement in a graphics window, and its placement is determined by the coordinates of the upper left corner of a bounding rectangle for the shape. The constructor has these two values as parameters, and we provide getter methods for them. We also have method toString, which may be useful when debugging programs that create and use shapes.

The only other method is drawShape. This method should never be called, since instances of Shape contain not shapes but only positions of shapes! As we will see, it is included only so that it can be overridden in subclasses.

In the design of Fig. 4.9, we have written the function bodies with return statements that return the default value for the return type. This is so that this class definition is syntactically legal and will compile.

```java
import java.awt.*;

/** A shape at an (x, y) coordinate. */
public class Shape {

    /** Constructor: a shape that fits in a bounding rectangle with upper-left corner (x, y) */
    public Shape(int x, int y){}

    /** = x-coordinate of the upper-left corner of the bounding rectangle */
    public int getX()
        { return 0; }

    /** = y-coordinate of upper-left corner of the bounding rectangle */
    public int getY()
        { return 0; }

    /** = a description of this Shape, of the form (x-coordinate, y-coordinate) */
    public String toString()
        { return ""; }

    /** draw this shape using Graphics g --not to be called */
    public void drawShape(Graphics g) {}
}
```

Figure 4.9:   The design of class Shape

Subclass Parallelogram

We design the class for the first shape, class `Parallelogram`. This class is a subclass of class `Shape`, which provides the position of the parallelogram.

We determine what is needed to define a parallelogram whose bounding rectangle has upper-left corner (`x`, `y`). A parallelogram has two horizontal sides of length `l1` (say) and two vertical sides of length `l2` (say). But this does not define how much the parallelogram leans. For this purpose, we use a value `d`, which we call the *leaning factor* of the parallelogram. If `d` is at least 0, the parallelogram is as defined by the diagram on the left in Fig. 4.10, and if `d` is negative, it is as defined by the diagram on the right. Coordinates (`x`, `y`), lengths `l1` and `l2`, and leaning factor `d` completely determine the position, size, and shape of the parallelogram.

We develop specs of the methods in class `Parallelogram`. See Fig. 4.11. The constructor has as its parameters the five properties that define a parallelogram. The class has procedure `drawShape`, which draws the parallelogram using a `Graphics` object `g`. This procedure overrides `drawShape` in superclass `Shape`. This ends the design of class `Parallelogram`.

Figure 4.10:   Defining a parallelogram in terms of x, y, l1, l2, and leaning factor d

```
import java.awt.*;

/** A parallelogram that can be drawn. */
public class Parallelogram extends Shape {

    /** Constructor: a parallelogram with horizontal length l1, other length l2, bounding
        box with top-left corner (x, y), and leaning factor d
    */
    public Parallelogram(int x, int y, int l1, int l2, int d) { }

    /** Draw this parallelogram using g */
    public void drawShape(Graphics g) { }

    /** = a description of this parallelogram */
    public String toString()
        { return ""; }
}
```

Figure 4.11:   Specification of class `Parallelogram`

Subclass rhombus

A rhombus is a parallelogram whose sides are all the same length. Note the phrase "is a" in the previous sentence. A rhombus *is a* parallelogram. Therefore, we make Rhombus a subclass of class `Parallelogram`. Its design appears in Fig. 4.12

The constructor for class Rhombus has as its parameters the four properties that define a rhombus. We decide that we do not need to override inherited procedure drawShape. After all, a rhombus is a parallelogram, and the inherited procedure should work. However, we do override function toString because we want toString to tell us what kind of shape the instance describes. For example, toString could produce output like this:

```
"rhombus, pt (5, 20), side length 60, leaning factor 7 "
```

Class Rhombus is included just to make it a bit easier for clients. Instead of creating a `Parallelogram` with the two side lengths equal, they can create a Rhombus with only one side length.

Class Square

Finally, we design a class Square. A square is a rhombus in which each angle is 90 degrees, i.e. has leaning factor 0. Since a square is a rhombus, we make Square a subclass of Rhombus.

The constructor of Square is quite straightforward, as is method toString.

At this point, a bit of thinking about implementation creeps in. It is easy to draw a square using Graphics procedure drawRect. Therefore, we override inherited procedure drawShape so that we can have a simple implementation. Is this a good idea? In this small design of shape-drawing classes, it does not really matter whether we override drawShape or not. We do it just to show the kind of thinking that might go on in a design.

```java
import java.awt.*;

/** A rhombus that can be drawn. */
public class Rhombus extends Parallelogram {

    /** Constructor: a rhombus with side length l, bounding box with top-left corner
        (x, y), and leaning factor d.
    */
    public Rhombus(int x, int y, int l, int d) { }

    // = description of this parallelogram
    public String toString()
        { return ""; }
}
```

Figure 4.12:   The design of class Rhombus

Discussion

We designed four classes that create shapes in a graphics window. They form a chain, moving from the abstract, in which no shape but only a position is described, down to more and more restrictive shapes. This is the nature of the object-oriented approach. As one proceeds down a hierarchy of classes, one encounters more and more properties and restrictions.

We could design other shape classes. For example, a rectangle is a parallelogram in which the angles are equal (90 degrees), so we could have a subclass `Rectangle` of `Parallelogram`. That brings up a question: A square is a rectangle whose sides are equal, and a square is a rhombus whose angles are equal; should class `Square` be a subclass of `Rectangle` or of `Rhombus`? It cannot be both because "multiple inheritance" —inheriting from two difference superclasses— is not allowed in Java. This is a situation where the subclassing feature of Java cannot be made to model the problem domain exactly.

Java does have another feature, the *interface*, which could be used to model the situation with rectangle, rhombus, and square more exactly. See Chap. 12.

The actual implementation of these classes is straightforward, and we leave them to you. Also, the implementation can be found on the CD *ProgramLive*.

Using the shape classes

Activity 4-4.4 of the CD discusses a Java program that uses the shape classes to draw a figure like the one shown to the left. The design of the figure was done with pencil and paper, away from the computer. We drew the figure and determined what variables were needed and what they would represent. Attempting to design the figure while on the computer would be inefficient.

The presence of the shape classes makes this figure fairly easy to draw — imagine trying to draw it using only the original methods of class `Graphics`. And yet, the classes themselves are quite short and simple. A good design will lead to a simple, clear structure and a relatively simple program that is easy to use.

```java
import java.awt.*;

/** A square that can be drawn */
public class Square extends Rhombus {

    /** Constructor: a square with side length l and top-left corner (x, y) */
    public Square(int x, int y, int l) { }

    /** draw this square using Graphics g */
    public void drawShape(Graphics g) { }

    /** = a description of this square */
    public String toString()
        { return ""; }
}
```

Figure 4.13:   The design of class `Square`

Finally, lab 4 of Lesson 4 of *ProgramLive*, title "Practice with shapes", asks you to modify the picture in several ways.

4.6   The final model of execution

Activities
4-3.1, 4-3.2

In Sec. 3.5, we described the steps in executing a method call. Below, we repeat the steps, just for completeness. But there is one difference. Now that we have subclasses, during step 4 (executing the method body), we have to be more careful about what a name refers to when it is referenced in the method body. We have changed this step slightly to refer to the discussion below the list of steps.

1. Evaluate the arguments of the call and push them onto the call stack.

2. Draw a frame for the call on top of the call stack; the frame includes the argument values at the top of the stack. This frame will become the new *active frame*.

    2(a) Fill in the name of the method and set the program counter to 1.
    2(b) Fill in the scope box with the name of the entity in which the method appears: the name of a folder for a non-static method and the name of the class for a static method.
    2(c) Draw the local variables of the method body in the frame.
    2(d) Label the argument values pushed onto the call stack in the first step with the names of the corresponding parameters.

3. Execute the method body. When referencing a name, look in the (new active) frame for it. If it is not there, look in the item given by the scope box of the frame.

4. Erase the frame —pop it from the stack. If the method is a function and the call is terminated by execution of a return statement **return** e; , push the value of e onto the call stack.

Finding the item referenced by a name

Executing the method body (step 3 above) generally requires finding the variable to which a name refers or finding a method to which a method call refers. When dealing just with classes (but not subclasses), this task is rather simple: look in the active frame, and if it is not there, look in the folder or file drawer given by the scope box of the frame. Now that we have introduced subclasses, the problem of finding a variable or method is more complicated. So we give a detailed explanation.

Remember that the program being executed is syntactically correct (if not, it could not be executed) and that it is known whether a variable is a parameter, local variable, static variable, or instance variable, and similar information is known for the method m of a method call m(*args*). Also, a reference to a variable has the form x or *expression*.x, where x is a variable name and *expression* is either a class name or an expression that yields the name of a folder of some class. (A similar statement can be made about a method call.)

With this introduction, we describe how to determine the variable or method given by a variable reference or method call during execution of a method body.

1. Find a variable x (where x is a variable name) or a method for a call m(*args*).

   1a: x (or m) is static. The scope box of the active frame contains either the name of some class C (say) or the name of a folder of some class C. Look for x (or suitable method m) in C's file drawer, then in the file drawer of its superclass, etc., until it is found.

   1b: x is a parameter or local variable. Find it in the active frame.

   1c: x is an instance method. Search the folder whose name is given in the scope box of the active frame. In searching, start at the bottom and search upward.

   1d: m(arg) is an instance method. Search the folder whose name is given in the scope box of the active frame. In searching, start at the bottom and search upward.

2. Find a variable for *expression*.x or a method for a call *expression*.m(*arguments*).

   2a: x (or m) is static. Evaluate expression to yield either a classname C or a folder of some class C. Look for x (or suitable method m) in C's file drawer, then in the file drawer of its superclass, etc., until it is found.

   2b: x is an instance variable. Evaluate *expression* to yield the name of a folder. Search that folder —start at the bottom and search upward.

   2c: m is an instance method. Evaluate *expression* to yield the name of a folder. Search that folder for a suitable method —start at the bottom and search upward.

4.7   Abstract classes

Lesson
page 4-5

Class Shape of the previous section might be used incorrectly in two ways:

1. Class Shape is present only to provide a superclass of other shape classes. Instances of Shape should not be created, but creating them is not prohibited.

2. Method drawShape in class Shape should never be called; every subclass should override it. However, overriding the method cannot be enforced.

This kind of situation occurs frequently, so Java provides a construct, the *abstract class*, to handle it better. We use class Shape of Fig. 4.9 to illustrate. It is written as an abstract class in Fig. 4.14. It differs from Shape of Fig. 4.9 in two ways.

1. The class has been changed into an abstract class. This is done by inserting keyword **abstract** before keyword **class** in the first line of the class definition:

   public abstract class Shape {

   An abstract class cannot be instantiated: expression **new** Shape(...) is illegal.

2. Method drawShape has been made into an *abstract method*. This is done by inserting keyword **abstract** in the method definition and replacing the body by a semicolon:

   public abstract void drawShape (...);

   An abstract method of an abstract class must be overridden in every subclass (unless the subclass is also abstract).

That is all there is to abstract classes and abstract methods: an abstract class cannot be instantiated, and an abstract method must be overridden. With these

```
import java.awt.*;
/** A shape on a screen. */
public abstract class Shape {

    /** Constructor: a shape that fits in a bounding rectangle with upper-left corner (x, y) */
    public Shape (int x, int y){ }

    /** = x-coordinate of upper-left corner of bounding rectangle */
    public int getX()
        { return 0; }

    /** = x-coordinate of upper-left corner of bounding rectangle */
    public int getX()
        { return 0; }

    /** = a description of this shape, of the form (x-coordinate, y-coordinate) */
    public String toString()
        { return ""; }

    /** Draw this shape using g */
    public abstract void drawShape(Graphics g);
}
```

Figure 4.14: Design of class Shape as an abstract class, with abstract method drawShape

two new features, we have removed the two problems with class `Shape`.

4.8   Key concepts

• **Subclass**. A *subclass* is a class that extends another class, called its *superclass*. The subclass *inherits* all the components of the superclass, i.e. each instance of the subclass contains the instance components of the superclass. The subclass can define its own components and *override* (redefine) the inherited methods.

• **Class invariant**. The values of the fields of a subclass generally have to satisfy certain constraints. It is a good idea to write these constraints as a comment at the beginning of the class body, just before the declarations of the fields.

• **Subclass constructor**. A constructor in a subclass should begin by calling a constructor of the superclass to initialize the inherited fields. In the constructor call, use keyword **super** instead of the superclass name.

• **Overriding an overriding method**. If a method m is overridden, a call m(...) calls the overriding method. Use the notation **super**.m(...) to call the inherited method.

• **Casting**. One can cast an expression to a class C using the prefix operator (C).

• **Apparent and real class-types**. The *apparent class* of a class expression e is syntactically determined from the class-types of its operands. A component reference e.v or e.m(...) is legal only if variable v or method m(...) is available in the apparent class of e. The *real class* of e is the class of the folder whose name is currently in e; the real class can change whenever e is assigned a value. The variable or method actually referenced by e.v or e.m(...) depends on the real class of e, and not on the apparent class of e.

• **Operator instanceof**. Expression e **instanceof** C is true if and only if the class of folder e is C or a subclass of C.

• **Class Object**. Object is the superclass of all classes that do not explicitly extend a class. Object contains instance functions toString and equals, which are often overridden in subclasses. Boolean function equals should be an equivalence relation.

• **Access mechanisms**. The four access mechanisms *public*, *protected*, *package*, and *private* provide increasing restrictions on access of components. If you are using only the default package, there is no difference between the first three.

• **Object-oriented design**. The *is-a* relation provides insight into OO design with subclasses. If a problem-domain entity x is a y (e.g. an undergrad is a student), it may make sense for the class of x to be a subclass of the class of y. Common behavior of several subclasses is moved to their superclass as much as possible.

• **Abstract classes and methods**. An abstract class cannot be instantiated; an abstract method must be overridden.

4.9   Self-review exercises

SR1. If class C1 inherits from class C2, then C1 is a _____ of C2 and C2 is a _____ of C1.

SR2. Which generally has more functionality, a subclass or its superclass?

SR3. True or false? Casting an object of a subclass to its superclass type is a narrowing cast.

SR4. True or false? Casting an object of a subclass to its superclass type can be done automatically.

SR5. Defining two methods with the same name within a class is called _____. Redefining a method of a superclass within a subclass is called _____

SR6. Give an example of each of the two ways of using keyword **this**.

SR7. Give an example of each of the two ways of using keyword **super**.

SR8. What access modifier is used to hide fields of a superclass from its subclasses?

SR9. Does it make sense to make an instance method private? Explain your answer.

SR10. What class is the "superest" class of them all, in that it is a superclass of all other classes?

SR11. Name two functions that are inherited by every single class you write?

SR12. If you override method `equals(Object)`, what properties should the new method have?

SR13. How is the "is-a" relation used in object-oriented design?

SR14. True or false? You can create an instance of an abstract class.

SR15. What is a class invariant?

SR16. What is the public method overriding rule?

Answers to self-review exercises

SR1. C1 is a subclass of C2 and C2 is a superclass of C1. **SR2.** Subclass. **SR3.** false; it is a widening cast. **SR4.** True. **SR5.** Overloading and overriding. **SR6.** meth(**this**) calls method meth, giving it this instance as an argument. **this**(62) calls the constructor of this class that has an **int** parameter. **SR7. super**.toString() calls the inherited toString function. **super**(62) calls the constructor of the superclass that has one parameter, of class **int**. **SR8. private**. **SR9.** Yes, it can make sense. In implementing a class based on its specification, it may be advantageous or necessary to add new methods for simplicity or readability (or other reasons). These new methods are not mentioned in the specification and should not be available to users of the class. **SR10.** Class **Object**. **SR11.** **equals(Object)** and **toString()**. **SR12.** It should be an equivalence relation: reflexive, symmetric, and transitive. **SR13.** If a B is a C, then B should be a subclass of C. **SR14.** False. **SR15.** A class invariant is a relation concerning the fields of the class that should be true before and after each method of the class is called. Essentially, the class invariant is given by the group of definitions of the fields of the class. **SR16.** When determining the instance method to call (within a folder) for a call *method-name (arguments)*, start at the bottom of the folder and search upward until the appropriate method is found.

Exercises for Chapter 4

E1. Obtain classes **Employee**, **Executive**, and **HourlyEmployee** that are discussed in Sec. 4.1 from a footnote on Lesson page 4-1 of the CD. Design and implement a fourth class, **SalariedEmployee**. An instance of this class represents an employee that is paid on a yearly basis; the employee gets no bonus and no overtime.

E2. Add a constructor to class **Employee** (and the other classes as well) of Exercise E1 that initializes the hire date with the date at which an instance is created. Thus, in **Employee**, this constructor has only one parameter, the name of the person.

E3. Design and implement a class **Manager**, which extends class **Salaried-Employee** of Exercise E1. An instance should contain the name of the department that the manager manages. You determine what extra methods are needed and what function **toString** should produce.

E4. Design and implement a class **Address**, which contains a house number, street name, city, state, and zip code (for a house in the United States). Add a field to class **Employee** of Exercise E1 to contain the address of an employee, and add whatever methods are needed to make it accessible from outside the class.

E5. Suppose you are going to implement a set of classes that, together, describe modes of transportation (e.g. plane, auto). Each of these modes has its own submodes (e.g. an auto could be a car, SUV, truck, etc. Develop a hierarchy of such modes of transportation, which would end up being a hierarchy of classes and subclasses. This is an open-ended question, and there is no single answer.

E6. Turn to lesson page 4-1 on the *ProgramLive* CD and click on "Proj". A window opens, with some projects in it. Carry out project "Movie reviews".

E7. Consider class Counter of Fig. 4.15. Create a subclass in which the incrementation is done by 2 instead of 1. Be sure to specify any methods you write carefully.

E8. Consider class Counter of Fig. 4.15. Create a subclass that changes the value of the counter to 0 whenever it reaches 60 (this could be used to count minutes on a clock). Thus, the range of values of this Counter is 0..59. We call this "counting mod 60". Be sure to specify carefuly any methods you write.

E9. Consider class Counter of Fig. 4.15. Create a subclass in which incrementing is done "mod n", where n ≥ 2 (see the previous exercise). The user should give n as an argument in a constructor call. Be sure to specify any methods you write carefully.

E10. Consider class Counter of Fig. 4.15. Create a subclass in which the value is interpreted as minutes and seconds, e.g. 125 is two minutes and five seconds. The only change necessary is in method toString, which should return a string that gives the counter in minutes and seconds.

E11. Design and implement a class Timer, an instance of which contains hours, seconds, and minutes. It should use three private fields to contain the hours, seconds, and minutes, and each of these field should be some form of Counter (see

```java
/** A counter, which can be incremented */
public class Counter {

    private int value= 0;   // the current value of the counter

    /** Constructor: a counter that starts at 0 */
    public Counter (){ }

    /** = this counter */
    public int getCounter()
        { return value; }

    /** Set this counter to c */
    public void setCounter(int c)
        { value= c; }

    /** increment the counter */
    public void click()
        { value= value + 1; }

    /** = this counter, as a String */
    public String toString()
        { return "" + value }
}
```

Figure 4.15: Class Counter

the previous exercises). Include at least these methods: a method `set` to set the hours, minutes, and seconds; a method `click()`, which increments the seconds by 1 (and the minutes if the seconds becomes 0, and the hours in the same manner); and method `toString`. Method `toString` should give the value in the form *hours*:*minutes*:*seconds*.

E12. Write a class `Point`, which represents an (`x`, `y`) point in the plane. Include normal methods, like `toString`, as well as instance function `length(Point)`, which yields the length from the point in which the function appears to its parameter. Now write a subclass `ThreeDPoint`, which represents a three-dimensional point in (`x`, `y`, `z`) space. Override method `length` appropriately. Is this an appropriate way to write class `ThreeDPoint`, or should it stand alone and not be a subclass of `Point`?

E13. Section 4.6.2 discussed the design of a set of classes whose instances were shapes drawn using a `Graphics g`. Design, implement, and test a similar set of classes whose superclass is `Vehicle`, which is some vehicle that appears at some (`x,y`) position. Possibilities for vehicles are cars, trucks (with subtypes pickup, flatbed, moving van, etc.), cycle (motorcycle, bicycle, unicycle), etc. This is a completely open-ended problem: you choose the vehicles, what each vehicle looks like, and the subclass hierarchy.

E14. Study the subclass hierarchy in the `javax.swing` and `java.awt` packages that includes class `JFrame`. Look at the superclasses of `JFrame` and get a basic idea of what each one is for and what its methods are.

Chapter 5

Some Useful Classes

OBJECTIVES

- Describe the wrapper classes for primitive types.
- Describe classes `String` and `StringBuffer`.
- Describe classes `Date` and `Vector`.
- Describe how to format numbers.
- Describe random-number generation.
- Describe how to do input/output.
- Describe URLs and class `URL`.

INTRODUCTION

The packages of classes that come with Java enhance the basic language tremendously. Here, we study a few of the classes that come with Java.

The wrapper classes allow us to handle values of primitive types as objects of a class. For example, an `Integer` object contains, or "wraps", an **int** value.

Classes `String` and `StringBuffer` provide strings of characters. Usually, one uses `String`, but for maximum efficiency when performing some operations on strings, it is best to use `StringBuffer`.

Class `Vector` provides for the maintenance of a list of objects. An instance of class `Date` is a particular time —down to the millisecond.

Classes `DecimalFormat` and `NumberFormat` provide functions for formatting numbers. For example, we may want decimal numbers to appear always with two places following the decimal point, e.g. `4.56`. Class `Locale` provides number formats for over 140 different "locales": a locale is a country and a language.

Class Random provides functions for calculating "random" numbers. These functions are useful in some games and in simulating various processes.

Reading from the keyboard and reading/writing files are not hard-wired into Java. Instead, the ability to do IO (input/ouput) is provided by classes. We discuss several ways of doing IO, as well as how to read from URLs.

5.1   The wrapper classes

5.1.1   Wrapper class Integer

Wrapper class int is discussed on lesson page 5-1.

A variable of a primitive type, like **int**, is handled differently from a variable of a class type. A variable of type **int** contains a value; a variable of a class type contains the name of an object of the class, which in turn can contain fields with values. It would be nice to be able to handle **int** and class-type variables in the same way. To make this possible, Java provides a class `Integer`:

```
public class Integer {
    private int val;
        ...
}
```

An object of class `Integer` contains a single instance variable `val` of type **int**. `Integer` is called a *wrapper* class since an instance of it wraps an **int** variable.

Wrapped variable `val` is private, so it cannot be referenced outside the class. In fact, we do not even know what name the variable has because the specification of class `Integer` does not say. We used the name `val` just to be able to write a declaration. There is no need to know the name because the value of this field can be accessed only using getter method `intValue`:

```
/** = the value of the wrapped int */
public int intValue()
```

Moreover, there is no setter method for the field, so there is no way to change its value. The field is *immutable*. The best you can do is to create a new instance of class `Integer` with the desired value. For example, suppose variable d contains the name of an `Integer` and we want to increment its wrapped variable. We cannot, but we can assign to d the name of a new folder with the desired value:

```
d= new Integer(d.intValue() + 1);
```

To make this point clear, to the left in Fig. 5.1 we show variable d and the folder whose name d contains. To the right, we show the state after execution of this assignment to d.

Instance methods of class Integer

Above, we showed how an instance of class `Integer` wraps an **int** value. You also saw the uses of constructor `Integer(`**int**`)` and getter function

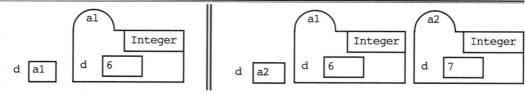

Figure 5.1:   Variable d before and after the assignment to it

intValue(). Class Integer has a few other useful instance methods.

For example, there is a second constructor, which can be used to translate a String value into a wrapped Integer. The String argument of the constructor call is converted into an **int**, and a new instance of class Integer is created that wraps it. The result of the new-expression is the name of the new instance. Here is an example of its use:

```
Integer d= new Integer("254");
```

This constructor is useful when a string is read in using, for example, GUI JLiveWindow:

```
Integer e= new Integer(JLiveWindow.getStringField(0));
```

Class Integer has methods for converting a wrapped value to a different primitive type and to a String. For example, with e containing an Integer, we can obtain its wrapped value using these function calls:

```
e.byteValue()          e.shortValue()
e.intValue()           e.longValue()
e.floatValue()         e.doubleValue()
e.toString()
```

There is a method for comparing the wrapped value with another value:

```
/** = "x is an instance of Integer and its wrapped value
        equals this wrapped value" */
public boolean equals(Integer x)
```

The argument of equals can be *any* class instance, but if it is not an instance of class Integer, the result is **false**, e.g.

```
d.equals(new Long(254))
```

is **false** no matter what value d wraps.

Static components of class Integer

Class Integer is a good place to house static components that deal with primitive type **int**. Two constants, i.e. variables with qualifier **final**, are:

Lesson page 5-1 contains info on static components of class Integer.

```
Integer.MAX_VALUE;    // Largest value of type int
Integer.MIN_VALUE;    // Smallest value of type int
```

The specification does not say what these values actually are, but you can write code to print them and use them in expressions, e.g.

```
System.out.println(Integer.MAX_VALUE);
d= Integer.MIN_VALUE + 1;
```

Class Integer contains a method for translating an **int** value x to a String; here is a call to it:

```
Integer.toString(x)
```

However, it is simpler to use the expression `"" + x` to do the job.

Class `Integer` also has static methods to get the binary, octal, and hexadecimal representations of x as `Strings`: use the function calls `Integer.toBinaryString(x)`, `Integer.toOctalString(x)`, and `Integer. toHexString (x)`.

Finally, class `Integer` has functions for converting a `String` to an **int**. We look only at method `parseInt`. Give it a `String` that represents an integer, and it converts it to an **int**:

```
/** = The integer whose decimal representation is s */
public static int parseInt(String s)
```

The `String` representation can begin with a minus sign to indicate a negative value. But it cannot have any whitespace. The presence of whitespace or of anything except the decimal representation of an integer results in an exception and, unless you have prepared for it, termination of the program.

Method `parseInt` is often used in the following way. A `String` value is obtained from the input in some manner, say, using our class `JLiveWindow`. Next, instance method `trim` of class `String` is used to strip away whitespace from either side of the `String`. The resulting `String`, with no whitespace on either side, is used as an argument to `parseInt`. Finally, the resulting **int** value is assigned to a variable:

```
d= Integer.parseInt(JLiveWindow.getStringField(0).trim());
```

5.1.2   Other wrapper classes

Lesson pages 5-1 and 5-2 contain specifications of the methods in these wrapper classes.

Wrapper classes exist in package `java.lang` for the other primitive types as well. Here are their names:

Primitive type	Wrapper class
byte	Byte
short	Short
long	Long
float	Float
double	Double
char	Character
boolean	Boolean

The wrapper classes for the numerical types and for type **boolean** are all similar, and we do not discuss them further here. Look at their API specifications, or look in Lesson 5 of *ProgramLive*.

Lesson page 5-2 discusses wrapper class Character.

Wrapper class `Character` has methods that you may find useful later on, so spend a few minutes looking at them. There are static boolean functions to tell whether a character is a lower-case character, an upper-case character, a digit, a letter, a letter or digit, a possible first character of a Java identifier, a possible other character of a Java identifier, a whitespace character (e.g. blank, tab, or new line), and a space character. These functions can come in handy when you are processing strings of characters in some fashion.

5.2 Classes String and StringBuffer

A *string* is a sequence of characters enclosed in quotes. For example, we show below a string of 16 characters, three of which are the blank character:

```
"this is a string"
```

In this section, we discuss two classes that are used for holding and manipulating strings, classes `String` and `StringBuffer`, and write a few programs that illustrate how strings can be processed. We begin by looking at how we write such strings in Java.

5.2.1 String literals

In Java, a string like `"it is"` is called a *literal* of class-type `String`. Its length is the number of characters in it, in this case, 5. The example in this paragraph shows that the single-quote character `'` and the blank character can appear in literals. In fact, almost any character can be written in a string literal. But some of them have to be written in a special way.

To place a double-quote in a string literal, precede it by the *escape character* `\`. For example, the following literal contains a blank, a double-quote character, and the digit 2: `" \"2"`.

The sequence of characters `\"` is known as an *escape sequence*. Below, we list other escape sequences and explain what they represent:

`\\`	backslash character `\`
`\"`	double-quote character `"`
`\'`	single-quote character `'`
`\n`	new-line character
`\r`	carriage-return character
`\t`	tab character
`\f`	form feed character
`\b`	backspace character

The new-line and carriage-return characters are used in operating systems to indicate the start of a new line. There are three major operating systems: Windows, Macintosh, and Unix. One of them uses the new-line character, one of them uses the carriage-return character, and one of them uses both. Such is life.

Many programs process strings of characters. For example, a text editor does, and so does the Java compiler. But often, strings are used simply to annotate output. For example, below, we write statements that print a value in the Java console:

```
System.out.print("The square of 25 is: ");
System.out.println(25 * 25);
```

5.2.2   The basics of String manipulation

A string literal has a class-type: `String`. Since `String` is a class, and not a primitive type, the literal is contained in an instance of `String`, for example,

`String` variables can be declared and assigned values. Class `String` is special in that there is no need to use a new-expression (although it can be used); just use a string literal instead. For example, execution of these statements:

```
String s= "NO!"
String t;
t=  "Yes.";
```

result in these variables and `String` folders:

We now describe various operations on strings and also introduce notation for talking about strings.

Catenation of Strings

To *catenate* two strings means to join their characters into a single string. The word *concatenation* is often used for this operation; we prefer the shorter word, *catenation*. Java uses the binary infix addition symbol + for catenation:

    "abc" + "xyz"   evaluates to   "abcxyz"

Of course, if both operands of + have numerical types, the symbol denotes addition, but if at least one operand is a `String`, the symbol denotes catenation.

If one of the operands of a catenation is a value of some primitive type, like **int** or **boolean**, it is converted to a `String`. For example, the expression

    2.5 + ", 62 "

evaluates to a `String` object whose value is " 2.5, 62 ".

Activity 5-3.4
shows execu-
tion of this
statement.

Catenation is often used in annotating output values to make them more understandable. Suppose we have two **int** variables, month and day. Here is a single statement that prints their values, but annotated with text so that the user knows what the values are:

```
System.out.println(" month  " + month + ",\nday  " + day);
```

Note that the new-line character causes the characters following it to be printed on a separate line.

When using the Java console for output when debugging programs, get in the habit of annotating the output, even in a minimal fashion, to help you decipher the output.

What is the value of the following expression?

```
2 + 5 + " apples".
```

There are two possible values, depending on which operation + is done first:

```
"7 apples"
"25 apples"
```

Since + is left associative, the operations are carried out from left to right, so the first answer is correct. To get the second one, use either of these two expressions, with the first being preferred because it requires fewer operations:

```
2 + (5 + " apples")
"" + 2 + 5 + " apples"
```

Invocation of function toString

Above, we said that if one operand of + is a String and the other is a primitive-type value, the primitive-type value is converted to a String and catenation is performed. There is one more case to consider:

```
c + s
```

where c contains the name of a folder and s is a String. In this case, the function call c.toString() is automatically invoked to produce a String representation of folder c, which is then catenated to s.

Recall that function toString has this specification:

```
/** = a description of this folder */
public String toString()
```

For reasons given in Sec. 4.3.1, function toString is present in every folder. However, it may not do what you want, and that is a good reason to redefine function toString in every class that you write.

The length of a String

Above, we made a mistake when we drew folders of class String: we omitted all the `String` instance methods. We now discuss some of these instance methods. One of them, `length`, returns the length, or number of characters, of the string that the instance contains. For example, we have:

```
"abcd".length()            is 4
("abcd" + "ef").length()   is 6
```

Non-Java notation for strings

Often, we will be talking about a particular character of a string `s` or a sequence of adjacent characters of `s`. It helps to have a notation for referring to these parts of `s`:

> `s[0]` denotes the first character of `s`.
> `s[1]` denotes the second character of `s`.
> ...
> `s[s.length()-1]` denotes the last character of `s`.

For example, if `s` is the string `"abc"`, then `s[1]` is the character `'b'`. Also, if **int** variable `i` contains 0, then `s[i+2]` is the character `'c'`. Expression `i` of `s[i]` is called the *index* of character number `i`. We stress that `s[i]` is not Java notation; we use it because it helps us discuss strings. Also, when writing `s[i]`, we assume that `i` lies in the range `0..s.length() - 1`.

A second non-Java notation describes a substring of a string:

> `s[h..k]`

is the string consisting of the characters `s[h], s[h + 1], ..., s[k]`. The length of `s[h..k]` is `k + 1 - h`. Here are examples, assuming that `s` is `"abcded"`:

```
s[2..4] is "cde";      it has length  4 + 1- 2 = 3
s[2..3] is "cd";       it has length  3 + 1- 2 = 2
s[2..2] is "c";        it has length  2 + 1- 2 = 1
s[2..1] is "";         it has length  1 + 1- 2 = 0
```

The last line above uses the convention that if the first index (2 in this case) is one more than the second index (1), then the substring is the empty string. The abbreviation `s[h..]` refers to the substring `s[h..s.length()-1]`.

Referencing the characters of a String

Function `charAt` retrieves a character from a string. The call `s.charAt(i)` evaluates to the character `s[i]`. Thus, `"At peace".charAt(1)` is `'t'`. In reference `s.charAt(i)`, `i` is the *index* of the character in `s`.

Here is a specification of instance function `charAt`:

```
/** = this[i]. Precondition: 0 <= i < this.length */
public char charAt(int i)
```

Activity 5-3.5

Function substring

For s a string, the call `s.substring(h,k)` yields the value `s[h..k - 1]`. Yes, that is right; character `s[k]` is not included in the substring `s.substring[h,k]`. Arguments h and k must satisfy:

h is the index of some character of s: $0 \le h < s.length()$.
k satisfies: $h \le k \le s.length()$.

Note: `s.substring(h,h)` denotes the empty string of s beginning at index h.

Equality of strings

When testing for equality, the important thing to remember is that a `String` value is an object. Consider `String` variables s and t as shown here:

The expression s $==$ t yields **false**, even though folders a6 and a7 contain the same value because expression s $==$ t compares the values in s and t, which are different. To compare the contents of folders, use instance function `equals`:

s.equals(t)   or   t.equals(s)

Both calls shown above yield **true**. Here is a call that would yield **false**:

"yeS.".equals(s)

Other methods of class String

Class `String` has several instance functions and one static function. We list function calls to some of them below, with brief explanations. Look at the API specs for `String` for more explanation. Below, p and q are `Strings`.

Lesson 5-3 goes into more detail in explaining these methods.

- `p.compareTo(s):`   = –1, 0, or 1 depending on whether p <, =, or > s
- `p.endsWith(s):`   = "s is a suffix of p"
- `p.indexOf(s):`   = index of first occurrence of s in p (–1 if none)
- `p.lastIndexOf(s):` = index of last occurrence of s in p (–1 if none)
- `p.startsWith(s):`   = "s is a prefix of p"
- `p.toLowerCase():`   = copy of p with all letters in upper case
- `p.toUpperCase():`   = copy of p with all letters in lower case
- `p.trim():`   = copy of p with blanks at the start and end removed
- `String.valueOf(x):` = x represented as a `String`. x can be any type

5.2.3   Changing a name format

Suppose string p contains a name in the format "last-name, first-name", with exactly one blank after the comma. The letters may be in upper or lower case.

Examples are:

```
"GRIES, david"
"gries, paul"
```

We write a program segment that stores p in string answer but in the form "first-name last-name", with the first letter of each name capitalized and the other letters small. For example, execution of the program segment with each of these inputs would produce

```
"David Gries"
"Paul Gries"
```

We start by writing code that extracts the first and last names from p. This can be done in the three steps shown below. Each step uses English or our non-Java notation because that is the simplest way to express it.

```
int i= index of the comma in p;
String lastName= p[0..i - 1];
String firstName= p[i + 2..];
```

The last two statements can be written in Java using function substring. The first is more problematic. We could write a loop to search character by character for the comma, but class String contains a function indexOf that makes the task simpler. A call p.indexOf(str) yields the first index in p of string str. Therefore, we can write this sequence as:

```
int i= p.indexOf(",");
String lastName= p.substring(0,i);
String firstName= p.substring(i + 2);
```

We can use functions toUpperCase and toLowerCase of class String to make sure that the first letters of the names are upper case and the rest lower case. Thus, the final string answer is created using this assignment:

```
answer= firstName.substring(0,1).toUpperCase() +
        firstName.substring(1).toLowerCase() +
        " " +
        lastName.substring(0,1).toUpperCase() +
        lastName.substring(1).toLowerCase();
```

The moral of this story is: become familiar with the methods of class String, for their use may save you time and energy in dealing with strings.

5.2.4 Extracting an integer from a string

Suppose a string p contains a sequence of integers, separated by blanks. There may be blanks at the beginning and end of p as well. Here is an example of p:

```
"    134 12    1   0   21  "
```

We want to write a program segment that removes the first integer from p and stores it in **int** variable d. We begin by breaking it down into a sequence of steps. This is an example of *top-down design*, or *stepwise refinement* (see Sec. 2.5).

1. Remove the blanks from the beginning of p;
2. Add a blank to the end of p (so we know p ends in a blank);
3. Find the index i of the first blank in p;
4. Store p[0..i-1], as an integer and not as a string, in d;
5. Remove p[0..i-1] from p.

These steps are written in English and our non-Java notation. This allows us to concentrate on the steps involved without worrying about how they are implemented in Java. The curious step is step 2. It was inserted so that, during step 3, we could assume that there was at least one blank after the first integer.

If you execute the sequence yourself, using p as given above, you will see that it stores 134 in d and changes p to " 12   1   0   21   ".

How do we javanize each of the steps? Looking carefully through the methods of class String, we see that we can use functions trim, indexOf, and substring, and to convert a string of digits to an integer, we use wrapper function Integer.valueOf. Here is the sequence of steps, in Java:

```
p= p.trim();
p= p + " ";
int i= p.indexOf(" ");
d= Integer.parseInt(p.substring(0,i));
p= p.substring(i);
```

5.2.5   Class StringBuffer

Lesson
page 5-4

An instance of class String is *immutable*: it cannot be changed. For example, in the program segment at the end of the previous subsection, we could not append a blank to p but had to create an entirely new string and assign it to p:

```
p= p + " ";
```

Package java.lang contains class StringBuffer, whose instances are sequences of characters that are *mutable*: they can be changed. For example, to append a blank to a StringBuffer variable q, use the procedure call:

```
q.append(" ");
```

When a string has to be changed a lot, it may be advantageous to convert it to class StringBuffer, perform the changes on the StringBuffer, and then convert the result back to a String. This can improve performance by eliminating the creation of many strings during the manipulation. We illustrate this later, but first we summarize the methods available in instances of StringBuffer.

Instance methods of StringBuffer

Below, we describe some methods of `StringBuffer` assuming that `q` is a variable of that class. There are two constructors:

- **new** `StringBuffer():` = a new `StringBuffer` that contains `""`.
- **new** `StringBuffer(p):` = a new `StringBuffer` that contains `String p`.

Functions `q.length`, `q.charAt()`, `q.substring`, and `q.toString` have their counterparts in class `String` and need no discussion.

The following procedure calls change q. We omit various restrictions on the arguments of procedure calls; see the footnotes on lesson page 5-4 of the CD for a full description, as well as examples.

- `q.setCharAt(i, c);`   Change q[i] to character c.
- `q.append(x);`   Append x to q. Arg. x can be of any primitive type or class type; if not a `String`, it is converted to a `String` and appended.
- `q.delete(h, k);`   Delete substring q[h..k - 1] from q.
- `q.deleteCharAt(k);`   Delete character q[k] from q.
- `q.insert(k, x);`   Change q to q[0..k - 1] + x + q[k..]. Convert x to a `String`, if necessary.
- `q.replace(h, k, x);`   Replace q[h..k - 1] by `String` x.
- `q.reverse();`   Reverse the characters of q, so it reads backward.
- `q.setLength(n):`   Set the length of q to n, either deleting a suffix or appending null characters `'\u0000'` as necessary.

Java's use of StringBuffers

`StringBuffers` are actually used to implement operation catenation +. For example, assuming that x is `String` variable, the statement

        x= "a " + 12;

is compiled into the equivalent of:

        x= **new** StringBuffer().append("a ").append(12).toString();

A `StringBuffer` is created, and strings are appended to it. Finally, the `StringBuffer` is converted to a `String`, which is assigned to x.

Extracting an integer from a StringBuffer

See a footnote on lesson page 5-4 to get this function.

At the end of Sec. 5.2.4, we developed a sequence of statements to remove an unsigned integer from a string. In Fig. 5.2, we define a function that removes and returns an unsigned integer from its `StringBuffer` parameter. We cannot write a similar function with a `String` parameter because `Strings` are immutable. This is indeed a situation where a `StringBuffer` should be used.

Functions `trim` and `indexOf` do not exist in `StringBuffer`, so we wrote loops to find the index of the first nonblank and the index of the first blank.

5.2.6 Exercises on strings

E1. Write (and test in your IDE —test all your work) an expression to produce a `String` that contains, in order, these things: `"variable d: "`, the value of expression d, and `"."`

E2. Write an expression to produce a `String` that contains: the value of variable `firstName`, `", "`, and the value of variable `lastName`.

E3. Write an expression to produce a `String` that, when printed, will occupy two lines. The first line should contain `"Tuesday, November "`, and the value of variable `day`. The second line should contain three blanks followed by the value of variable `weather` (e.g. `"cloudy"` or `"rainy"`. Hint: use a new-line character.

E4. Write an expression to produce a `String` that, when printed, will occupy two lines. The first line should contain `"CS100, computers and programming"`; the second line, `"instructor: "` followed by the value of variable `instructor`.

E5. Write a function that, given a `String` s, returns the number of characters before the first period `'.'` in s. If there is no period, it should return the length of s. E.g. if s is `"Gries. D."`, the answer is 5; if s is `"Gries, D"`, the answer is 8. Do not use a loop.

```
/** Remove leading and trailing spaces from q and extract and return the unsigned int that
    remains. q must begin with an unsigned integer, preceded by 0 or more blanks and ended
    by either 1 or more blanks or the end of the string. Example: if q is "   45 32", change
    q to " 32" and return 45. */
public static int extractInt(StringBuffer q) {
    // Remove beginning blanks from q
    int i= 0;
    while (q.charAt(i) == ' ') {
        i= i + 1;
    }
    q.delete(0, i);

    // Find the index i - 1 of the last character of the unsigned integer
    i= 0;
    while (i != q.length() && q.charAt(i) != ' ') {
        i= i + 1;
    }

    int v= Integer.parseInt(q.substring(0, i));
    q.delete(0, i);
    return v;
}
```

Figure 5.2: Function `extractInt`

E6. Write a function that, given a name like "Gries, Paul Christian" puts it in this form: "Paul Christian Gries".

E7. Write a function that produces the English word for a digit 0, 1, ..., or 9.

E8. Write a function that, given an integer in the range 20..99, produces the English word for it, e.g. for 30, produce "thirty" and for 42, produce "forty two". Use the function of the previous exercise.

E9. Write a function that, given a String s that contains a time like "1:15PM" or "11:00AM", produces a String that has the same time but in 24-hour format, e.g. "13:15" or "11:00". You don't need loops.

E10. Write a function that changes a date exemplified by the string "November 3, 2003" into this form: "3 November 2003".

The following exercises require loops and should be done using StringBuffers. The result of each function is a String, but the value to be returned should be first calculated as a StringBuffer and then converted to a String.

E11. Write a function that, given an integer n (≥ 0), produces a String that contains the integers in the range 0..n, separated by commas. For example, for n = 2, produce a String that contains "0, 1, 2". Do the calculation using a StringBuffer.

E12. Write a function that, given an integer n (≥ 0) and a String s, produces a String that contains n copies of s, one after the other. Do the calculation using a StringBuffer.

E13. Write a function that removes all blanks from a String.

E14. Write a function that duplicates each character of a String. For example, for the "abc", produce the "aabbcc". Build the result in a StringBuffer.

5.3   Class Vector

Lesson page 5-5

An instance of class Vector (in package java.util) contains a list of objects. It has several simple ways to refer to the objects and change them. For example, an instance could contain the email addresses of your friends, information about your compact disks, or information about students at Cornell University.

An instance of Vector is shown in Fig. 5.3. It contains three objects, numbered 0, 1, and 2, and it has room for two more (at the moment). Its *size* —the number of objects it contains— is 3, and its *capacity* —the number of objects it (currently) can contain— is 5. The instance contains many methods, which we do not show in the object. We do show functions size and capacity, which give the size and capacity of the Vector.

Two objects in this Vector are strings, and one is an Integer. Objects in a Vector can have any class, but they cannot be primitive values.

Class ArrayList. Class `Vector` has been in the API package `java.util` from the beginning. In the latest version of Java, a new class `ArrayList` was added to package `java.util`. It has roughly the same functionality as `Vector`: an object contains `size()` elements and has a capacity; elements can be added, deleted, accesssed, changed, searched for, and so on. Use either `ArrayList` or `Vector` —it is your or your instructor's choice.

We introduce non-Java notation to help us talk about the elements of a Vector `v`:

- `v[2]` refers to the element numbered 2.
- `v[h]` refers to the element given by the value of expression h.
- `v[h..k]` refers to the list of elements numbered h, h + 1, ..., k.
- `v[h..]` refers to the elements numbered h, h + 1, ..., v.size() - 1

For example, if `v` is (or contains the name of) the object in Fig. 5.3, then `v[2]` is the string `"blue"`, `v[0..1]` consists of 4, `"red"`, and `v[0..]` is the whole list of values.

In the notation `v[i]`, i is called the index of the element.

5.3.1   Creating and adding to a Vector

Activity
5-5.1

The declaration

        Vector d= **new** Vector(5);

creates an instance of class `Vector` that can hold 5 objects and stores the name of the instance in variable d. Instance d can hold 5 objects, but at the moment it does not hold any; its capacity is 5, but its size is 0. (There is also a constructor with no parameters, which creates a `Vector` with capacity 10.)

Instance function `add` is used to add elements to a `Vector`. For example, the following three statements add three objects to d, so Fig. 5.3 shows what d now looks like.

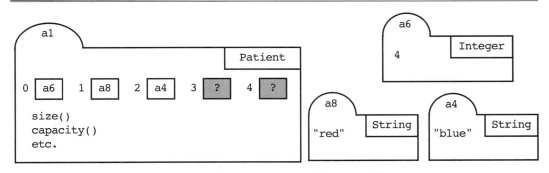

Figure 5.3:   A Vector with size 3 and capacity 5

```
d.add(new Integer(4));
d.add("red");
d.add("blue");
```

The argument of a call to add is the object to be added. It cannot be a value of a primitive type; elements of Vectors are objects. That is why we used an instance of wrapper class Integer as the argument of the first call of add. If you are not familiar with class Integer, study Sec. 5.1 on wrapper classes.

A two-parameter add procedure can be used to insert an object anywhere in the Vector. Suppose Vector d is as in Fig. 5.3. Then execution of

```
d.add(1, "yellow");
```

changes d to contain this list of objects:

```
4, "yellow", "red", "blue"
```

We use our non-Java notation for Vectors to describe this procedure: The call

```
d.add(k, obj);
```

changed Vector d to contain the list of values d[0..k-1], obj, d[k..].

The call d.add(k, obj) takes more time than the call d.add(obj) because the former has to move d[k..] to make room for the new object obj. Take this fact into account when designing and developing a program that uses a Vector.

The capacity increases automatically

If adding an element to a Vector would cause the size to exceed the capacity, the capacity is automatically increased, i.e. more memory is allocated so that the Vector can contain more elements. The capacity is not increased by 1 because that would be far too inefficient, but is always doubled. Doubling the capacity might seem like overkill, but, for purposes of efficiency, it is best.

In general, then, you do not have to worry about the capacity of a Vector because the class takes care of it automatically. However, there may be some situations where space is at a premium and you want to be sure the capacity is as close to the real size as possible. Class Vector provides methods that allow you to change the capacity and to change how many elements are added when the capacity has to be increased. We do not describe these methods because they are not necessary in a first course on programming.

5.3.2   Changing and retrieving elements

Activity
5-5.2

To replace one element of a Vector with another, use procedure SetElement. Given Vector d as in Fig. 5.3, execution of the call:

```
d.set(2, "purple");
```

changes d to contain the elements: 4 (as an Integer), "red", "purple". The first argument of a call to set can be any integer in the range 0..d.size()-1; the second can be any object. Thus, you have complete control over the list of objects in instance d.

To reference an element of Vector d, use instance function get, giving it as argument the number of the desired object. The following example writes the first two elements of d on the Java console, separated by a comma and a blank:

```
System.out.println(get(0) + ", " + get(1));
```

Suppose we want to store d[1] of Vector d in a fresh String variable s (given d as in Fig. 5.3). The following statement does *not* work:

```
String s= d.get(1); // Illegal statement
```

We state here how to fix it, without explanation. Thereafter, for those who already know about class Object and casting, we explain why it does not work.

To retrieve and use an element using function get, you generally have to know what class that element is and cast it to that class. In the above case, d[1] is class String. So, the expression to obtain object d[1] is (String) d.get(1), and this should be stored in s:

```
String s= (String) d.get(1);
```

The class of elements in a Vector

This little subsection should be read only if you know about the class hierarchy, class Object, and casting.

The elements of a Vector automatically have class Object, the superest class of them all. Therefore, when retrieving an element, you have to:

> Cast an object that is retrieved from an instance of Vector to the subclass to which it belongs so that the instance methods of the subclass can be used.

Suppose d contains the name of the object in Fig. 5.3. Then, the first and second elements of d can be retrieved and stored using these two statements:

```
Integer i= (Integer) d.elementAt(0);
String s= (String) d.elementAt(1);
```

Each element is cast from class Object down to the subclass that it really is.

Of course, if you do not know the class of a particular element, you must find out, using operation **instanceof**, before casting it. If you attempt to cast it to a class that it is not, a ClassCastException will be thrown, and your program will (probably) abort.

The safe thing to do is to make all the elements in a Vector have the same class-type, but of course this is not always appropriate.

5.3.3   Other methods in class Vector

Activity
5-5.2

Class `Vector` contains other methods that will help you create and maintain a list of objects. The ones you are most likely to use are listed below. See lesson page 5-5 of the CD for more explanation, or look at the Java API specs for `Vector`.

When removing one or more elements from v, those with higher indices than the removed ones are shifted down. Thus, the size of the v is reduced by the number of elements removed.

- `v.toString()`   = a description of v of the form [v[0], v[1], ...].

- `v.contains(obj)`   = "obj is an element of v".
- `v.indexOf(obj)`   = index of first object in v that equals obj (–1 if none).
- `v.indexOf(obj, k)`   = index of first object in v with index at least k that equals obj (–1 if none).
- `v.lastIndexOf(obj)` = index of last object in v that equals obj (–1 if none).
- `v.lastIndexOf(obj, k)`   = index of last object in v with index at most k that equals obj (–1 if none).

- `v.remove(i)`   Remove v[i] and return the removed element.
- `v.remove(obj)`   Remove from v the first object that equals obj and return the value of "an element was removed" (a boolean).
- `v.removeRange(i, j)`   Remove v[i..j] from v.
- `v.clear();`   Remove all objects from v, so that its size is 0.

5.3.4   Exercises on class Vector

E1. In the Interactions pane of DrJava, create a `Vector` vec —remember to import `java.util.*` first— and add these strings to it: "one", "two", "four". Then, type the expression vec. What is its value? Next, execute the call: `vec.add(2, "three");`. Now, what is the value of expression vec?

E2. In the Interactions pane of DrJava, create a `Vector` v1 that contains the values of these expressions: **new** `Integer(1)`, **new** Integer(3), **new** Integer(5). Then, find out the value of expression v1. Write down the values of the following expressions (let DrJava evaluate them): `v1.elementAt(1)`, `v1.elementAt(2)`, and `v1.size()`.

E3. In the Interactions pane of DrJava, create a `Vector` v1 that contains the values of these expressions: **new** `Integer(1)`, **new** Integer(3), **new** Integer(5). Then, find out the value of expression v1. What happens when you execute this assignment statement, and what do you have to do to fix it?

```
Integer middle= v1.elementAt(1);
```

E4. Write (and test) a boolean function with two arguments: a `Vector` v and an `Object` x. The function returns the value of the sentence "x occurs at least twice in v". No loop is needed. Hint: what methods in v can you call to help you determine whether x occurs at least twice in v?

E5. Suppose Vector v has at least two elements. Write a sequence of Java statements to interchange or swap v[0] and v[1]. Test the sequence.

E6. This exercise requires a loop or recursion. Suppose Vector v contains only elements of class Integer. Write a function that yields the sum of the elements.

E7. This exercise requires a loop or recursion. Write and test a function with a Vector argument v that produces a string containing the values of the elements of v in reverse order, separated by commas and delimited by "[" and "]". This is what v.toString() produces, but with the elements in the reverse order.

E8. This exercise requires a loop or recursion. Write and test a procedure that removes from its Vector argument all elements that are not of class Integer.

E9. This exercise requires a loop or recursion. Write and test a procedure with a Vector argument v that produces a new Vector whose elements are those of v but with every element duplicated. For example, if v contains ["xy", "xx"], the function produces a Vector consisting of: ["xy", "xy", "xx", "xx"].

5.4   Class Date

Lesson
page 5-6

Class Date, in package java.util, is useful when you would like to obtain the current time in your program. Execution of

```
Date d= new Date();
```

stores in variable d the name of a new Date object that represents the time, in milliseconds, that has elapsed since 1 January 1970 (Greenwich Mean Time). From d, you can get the year, month, day, hour, minute, and millisecond. And we have used it this way in the past. However, there have been changes, and many of the methods of this class are now *deprecated* —which means they have "lessened in value" because newer ones are now preferred. Below, we quote from the API spec for class Date to show you why they have been deprecated.

> Prior to JDK 1.1, class Date had two additional functions. It allowed the interpretation of dates as year, month, day, hour, minute, and second values. It also allowed the formatting and parsing of date strings. Unfortunately, the API for these functions was not amenable to internationalization. As of JDK 1.1, class Calendar should be used to convert between dates and time fields and class DateFormat should be used to format and parse date strings. The corresponding methods in Date are deprecated.

So, you see that progress in one area (internationalization) caused other changes. Java is a living, changing language.

We return to a discussion of the elapsed time. The spec of class Date tells you that this elapsed time can be obtained using this method in package java.lang.System:

public static native long currentTimeMillis();

If all you want is this time in milliseconds, use this function.

Estimating execution time

Sometimes, it is useful to get some measure of how long it takes for a method call to be executed. For example, one might want some understanding of the difference in execution time of linear search and binary search (see Chap. 8). However, the time is usually so short —less than a millisecond— that one cannot get meaningful results from executing the method call once. So one might try executing it m times, for m an integer like 10, or 100, or even 100000.

One can get the execution time in milliseconds using the following:

```
long startTime= System.currentTimeMillis();
Call the method m times;
long time= System.currentTimeMillis() - startTime;
```

The results of such a test cannot be relied on precisely because part of the elapsed time may have been allocated to other functions that had to be executed. The operating system on your computer switches between different applications (very quickly).

5.5   Formatting numbers

The way in which a number is printed using System.out.println(…) depends on its size and type. The number of characters used, as well as the format, will vary. Here are some examples:

```
System.out.println(5);                          5
System.out.println(43);                         43
System.out.println(23.56);                      23.56
System.out.println(87654321.12345678);          8.765432112345678E7
System.out.println(.0000005);                   5.0E-7
```

The conversion of a number to a string for printing in such contexts is done using a method toString in some class. In some situations, however, we would like to control the string format of a number ourselves. Perhaps we want all integers to use the same number of digits —using either leading zeros or leading spaces. Or, we might want **double** numbers to print always with two places to the right of the decimal point.

Several classes of the Java API give us this capability.

Lesson
page 5-6

5.5.1   Class DecimalFormat

Class `DecimalFormat`, in package `java.text`, allows you to describe the format into which a number should be converted. Here is an example, called a *pattern*:

> `"$###,##0.00"`

In the pattern:

- `0` represents a digit that will appear (a `0` appears if it does not exist).
- `#` represents a digit that is optional (a blank appears if it does not exist).
- `.` is the decimal separator.
- `,` is the grouping separator

Other characters that appear in a pattern, like `$` in the pattern above, appear in the converted number. Below, we show four patterns and several numbers as they appear in each. Note especially the use of `%`, which causes the number to be multiplied by `100`. Note also how the `B`'s, `C`'s, and `$` were placed when using the third pattern. Finally, note that if an integer is too big for the given pattern, more spaces are used.

number	`"$###,###,#00.00"`	`"##0.00%"`	`"B#,B#0C.$C0"`
5	`"$05.00"`	`"500.00%"`	`"B5.0BC$C"`
123.321	`"$123.32"`	`"12332.10%"`	`"B1,23.3BC$C"`
.321	`"$00.32"`	`"32.10%"`	`"B0.3BC$C"`

We have just scratched the surface of patterns in class `DecimalFormat`. The patterns and various methods are designed to make it possible to parse and format numbers in any locale (see Sec. 5.5.2), including support for Western, Arabic, and Indic digits. But this introduction is enough to get you started.

Here is how to use class `DecimalFormat`. First, create an instance of the class, using the desired pattern as the argument of the constructor call, e.g.

> `DecimalFormat decform= new DecimalFormat("##0.00");`

Then, to convert the value of an expression to a `String` using that pattern, call method `decform.format` with the expression as argument, e.g.

> `String s= decform.format(4.56);`

Is the decimal point optional?

Look at the pattern in the constructor call of the following statement:

> `DecimalFormat decform1= new DecimalFormat("###.##");`

Because there is no `0` to the right of the decimal point, the decimal point is optional and appears only if the fraction is nonzero:

> `decform1.format(25)` is `"25"`

Make the decimal point mandatory by executing the following statement:

```
decform.setDecimalSeparatorAlwaysShown(true);
```

Thereafter, `decform1.format(25)` is `"25."`

5.5.2   Formatting in locales

Lab 3 of lesson 6 contains a guided tour through the use of locales.

It is a shock to many Americans to learn that other cultures throughout the world write numbers differently. For example, here is how Americans, the English, and Russians write decimal numbers, currencies, and percentages:

US	English	Russian
1,500,012.253	1.500.012,253	1 500 012,253
$1,500.23	1.500,23	1 500,23
100,075%	100,075%	100 075%

For decimal numbers, the Americans and English give opposite roles to the comma and period! The Russians, like the English, have a "decimal comma" instead of a "decimal point" but use a space to separate groupings of digits.

It would be nice to be able to write numbers in the format of any culture. For example, a GUI could let a user indicate which format to use. This is easy to do in Java.

Class Locale

A *locale* consists of a language and country. Class `Locale`, in package `java.util`, contains information about 140 locales (but not all possible locales in the world). The English-U.S. locale is the default in most computers in the U.S, but you can probably set the default to what you want on your computer. To see what the default is on your computer, type this expression in DrJava's Interactions pane:

```
Locale.getDefault()
```

On a computer in the U.S., the value is `"en_US"`, meaning that the language is English and the country is the U.S. If the default locale for your computer is French-Canada, it will print `"fr_CA"`. The first two letters describe the language, using a code defined by the international standard ISO-639. (ISO stands for International Standards Organization). The last two letters describe the country, using a code defined by the international standard ISO-3166.

Class `Locale` has over 50 static constants that are instances of class `Locale`. For example, one of them is declared as:

```
static public final Locale KOREA= new Locale("ko","KR","");
```

Conversion using a Locale

Class `NumberFormat`, in package `java.text`, can be used to convert decimal numbers using the conventions of a particular `Locale`. Suppose you have placed an instance of `Locale` —one of the predefined ones— in variable `locale`.

Our examples use locale `"be_BY"`. Then do the following.

First, create an instance of class `NumberFormat` with `locale` as the argument of the constructor:

```
NumberFormat convertD= NumberFormat.getInstance(locale)
```

Then, use instance method `convertD.format` to convert numbers to strings using the conventions of locale `locale`, e.g.

```
convertD.format(123456543) yields the string "123 456,543"
```

To create an instance of `NumberFormat` whose `format` function converts currencies (amounts of money) of locale `locale`, use function `getCurrencyInstance`; the example shown below appears to have some unprintable characters:

```
NumberFormat convertC=
    NumberFormat.getCurrencyInstance(locale)
convertC.format(43.56) yields the string "???43,56"
```

To create an instance of `NumberFormat` whose `format` function converts percents using conventions of locale `locale`, use function `getPercentInstance`:

```
NumberFormat convertP=
    NumberFormat.getPercentInstance(locale)
convertP.format(43.56) yields the string "4 356%"
```

5.6   Random numbers

About random numbers

It is often useful in a computer program to generate and use "random" numbers. For example, if you have written a game that uses a deck of cards, to start the game you may want to shuffle the deck —place the cards in some random order. One could use 51 random numbers in the range 1..52 to indicate the order of the cards. As another example, to roll a pair of dice requires two random numbers in the range 1..6 to indicate which sides are face up. More serious applications also require random numbers. To gain insight into physical models, physicists write simulations of various physical events that require random numbers —perhaps dealing with weather, or atoms and molecules, or stars.

Random numbers are usually generated on the computer in the following way. One starts with a first value r_0 (say), called the *seed*. The first requested random number r_1 is generated from r_0 using some formula. The second requested random number r_2 is generated from r_1 using the same formula. The third one r_3 is generated from r_2 using the same formula. And so on.

So, "random numbers" are not really random. They are generated in an orderly, regulated fashion from a given seed. If you start with the same seed again, you get the same sequence of numbers (which is useful when debugging).

Nevertheless, the sequences of random numbers that are generated by Java have been shown to have properties that truly random sequences of numbers would have. They are "random enough" for people to use them with confidence in their programs.

5.6.1   Method Math.random

Static function `Math.random()` can be used to generate a sequence of random numbers. Whenever a new number is needed, call `Math.random()` again. It will give you a different random number each time.

This function produces a **double** result d (say) in the range $0 \leq d < 1$.

Suppose we want random values in the range `1..52` —for example, they might be numbers of cards in a deck of cards. Thus, we need to convert a **double** number d in the range $0 \leq d < 1$ into a value k in the range $1 \leq k \leq 52$. We show how to do this. Start with:

$$0 \leq d < 1$$

Multiply all three values by `52`:

$$0 \leq 52 * d < 52$$

Cast the middle value to an **int** —this truncates toward 0:

$$0 \leq (\textbf{int})(52 * d) < 52$$

Since the middle value is an integer, we have:

$$0 \leq (\textbf{int})(52 * d) \leq 51$$

Add 1 to each value:

$$1 \leq 1 + (\textbf{int})(52*d) \leq 52$$

So, we create and store in k a random integer in the range `1..52` using the assignment:

```
k= 1 + (int)(52*Math.random());
```

In the same way, the statements below store random numbers in the range `1..6` in two variables `die1` and `die2`, thus simulating the roll of a pair of dice:

```
die1= 1 + (int)(6*Math.random());
die2= 1 + (int)(6*Math.random());
```

5.6.2   Class Random

To gain more control over the generation of random numbers than is given by `Math.random`, use the methods of class `Random`, in package `java.util`. First, create an instance of class `Random`, using one of its two constructors:

```
Random random= new Random(long);
```

where long is any **long** integer, or

```
Random random= new Random();
```

In the first case, the seed used to start the sequence of random numbers is based on argument long. In the second case, the seed is the time in milliseconds at which the new-expression was evaluated.

Use the first case when testing a program because you may need to repeat an execution in order to help find errors. Use the second case when running so that you always use a new seed and thus get a new sequence of random numbers.

Now, whenever a new random number is generated, use one of the following function calls. There are several possibilities because one might want to generate sequences of random values in different types and ranges:

- `random.nextBoolean()`   = a **boolean** value
- `random.nextDouble()`   = a **double** d satisfying $0 \leq d < 1$
- `random.nextFloat()`   = a **float** f satisfying $0 \leq f < 1$
- `random.nextInt()`   = an **int**
- `random.nextInt(n)`   = an **int** i satisfying $0 \leq i < n$
- `random.nextLong()`   = a **long**

Class Random has other instance methods, but the ones discussed above will be used most frequently.

5.6.3   Exercises with random numbers

E1. Write a function oneOrTwo that uses function Math.random to return a random integer in the range 1..2. Test it.

E2. Function oneOrTwo produces either 1 or 2, randomly. One can think of 1 as "heads" and 2 as "tails", so we can think of a call of function oneOrTwo as simulating a flip of a coin. If we flip a coin 100 times, or 1,000 times, we would assume that half the tosses are "heads" and half are "tails". Write a program to test whether oneOrTwo is really fair, in this sense. The program will call oneOrTwo a certain number of times and report back how many of the tosses were "heads" and how many were "tails". Experiment with this program.

E3. Write a function to "throw a die (meaning one of a pair of dice)" —it should produce an integer in the range 1..6.

E4. Write a program that throws a die n times (for some given n) and counts how many times one roll is followed by exactly the same roll. E.g. the answer for the 7-roll sequence 3, 2, 2, 4, 4, 4, 3 is 3, since a 2 is followed by 2, a 4 is followed by 4, and that 4 is followed by 4. After you test it, experiment with it.

E5. Write a program that rolls a die until a 6 is rolled. Print out how many rolls were needed. Experiment with this program.

E6. Suppose an array b[0..51] (or a Vector, or a String of 52 characters) contains 52 values, e.g. it could be a deck of cards. Write a procedure that will "shuffle" b. You can do this as follows:

1. Swap b[0] and b[i], where i is a random integer in the range 0..51.
2. Swap b[1] and b[i], where i is a random integer in the range 1..51.
   . . .
51. Swap b[51] and b[i], where i is a random integer in the range 50..51.

5.7   Class JLiveRead for keyboard input

The core Java language has no facilities for reading from the keyboard or doing other input/output (I/O). Instead, all I/O is provided in the classes in package java.io. But these classes are very "low-level", forcing you to deal with reading one character at a time or a line of characters at a time, and then you have to write methods for interpreting what those characters are.

Activity 1-5.2

JLiveRead of the CD *ProgramLive* makes reading from the keyboard easier by providing static methods for reading integers, **double** values, and other items. In this section, we show how to use the methods of this class.

When running a Java program, the letters you type appear in the Java console. So, reading from the keyboard is often called "reading the Java console".

Obtain class JLiveRead from a footnote for this activity on Lesson page 1-5.

To use the methods of class JLiveRead, you have to place file JLiveRead.java in the directory for the program and make sure that it is compiled as part of the project (it will be, if the project contains call on its methods).

Suppose you want to read into a variable s an integer that the user will type on the keyboard. To do this, use the assignment statement:

```
// Read and store in s an integer typed by the user
s= JLiveRead.readLineInt();
```

When this statement is to be executed, execution waits until the user has typed an integer and pressed the enter key; the typed characters are placed in the Java console. As soon as the enter key is pressed, the integer that was typed is used as the value of the expression JLiveRead.readLineInt() and assigned to s.

If the user types anything else besides an integer (preceding and following whitespace is okay), an error message appears and the user is prompted to type in an integer.

Prompting the user

Generally, the user will not know that they must type an integer until they are told. We say that the user must be "prompted" for the input. So, when input is needed from the keyboard, a program generally prompts the user for it. (Actually, DrJava prompts automatically for keyboard input, but this is part of DrJava and not of Java itself.)

We change our program segment to prompt the user for keyboard input and, as an example, print the square of the integer that was typed:

```
// Prompt the user for an integer, store it in s, and print its square
System.out.println("Please type an integer");
s= JLiveRead.readLineInt();
System.out.println(" square is " + (s*s));
```

Reading values of other primitive types

Class JLiveRead contains methods for reading a line of input that contains values of other primitive types. In each case, the item read may be preceded and followed by blank characters. There is also a method for reading the whole line as a String. The methods are:

• readLineLong(): Read and return a **long** value.

• readLineFloat(): Read and return a **float** value.

• readLineDouble(): Read and return a **double** value.

• readLineNonwhiteChar(): Read and return the first **char** value that is not whitespace.

• readLineBoolean(): The input may contain "t", "true", "f", or "false", using lowercase or uppercase. Read it and return **true** or **false**, accordingly.

• readLineString(): Read and return a sequence of non-whitespace characters, as a String.

One more useful method can be used to read in all the typed characters:

• readString(): Read and return the typed characters, as a String. The final carriage return or line feed is not included.

Putting more than one value on a line

The methods discussed above force the user to type exactly one value before hitting the return/enter key. For example, function readLineInt will complain and ask you to type an integer again if you type the following before hitting the return/enter key:

```
25    4.0   3
```

Class JLiveRead contains methods that read a single value from a line, perhaps preceded by whitespace, leaving the rest of the line to be read later. These methods are:

```
readInt()         readLong()
readFloat()       readDouble()
readWord()
```

However, we advise against the use of the methods because using them may lead to errors. We explain.

Suppose the user types a line shown above in a situation where the program is expecting three **int**s. The user has made a mistake, since 4.0 is not an **int**. Upon trying to read 4.0, function `readInt` prints an error message and asks the reader to type the integer again, this time correctly. But then the rest of the line, containing the integer 3, will probably be discarded along with the 4.0, and most of what the user typed is thrown away and has to be typed again. It may be difficult for the user to remember what has to be typed and what does not.

Thus, allowing several items to be typed on one keyboard line makes recovery from a typing error much more difficult, and, as we all know, it is easy to make errors while typing. Thus, it is better to stick to the one-item-on-a-line mode when dealing with keyboard input.

Self-review exercises

SR1. Open class JLiveRead in DrJava and compile it. Then type the following expressions into the Interaction pane and evaluate them. During evaluation, a box will appear into which you should type an appropriate value. Experiment with making errors when typing values to see what happens.

```
JLiveRead.readLineInt()
JLiveRead.readLineBoolean()
JLiveRead.readLineNonwhiteChar()
JLiveRead.readLineString()
JLiveRead.readString()
```

SR2. Write and test a procedure to read two integers from the keyboard and print their product.

SR3. Write and test a function to read two **boolean** values from the keyboard

This instance of the GUI has four **int** fields and the ready button. Two integers were typed in the first two fields and the ready button was pressed, causing the sum of the two integers to be displayed in the third **int** field.

The GUI can have up to 7 **int** fields, 7 **double** fields, and 7 `String` fields. When the ready button is pressed, method `buttonPressed` is called. You can change this method to do whatever you want.

Figure 5.4: GUI JLiveWindow

and return their conjunction.

SR4. Write and test a function to read a **double** value and to return the floor (integer part) of the value, as an **int**. If the value is outside the range of **int**, return the maximum **int** value.

5.8   GUI JLiveWindow

GUI JLiveWindow (see Fig. 5.4) provides a window on your monitor with up to 7 **int** fields, 7 **double** fields, 7 String fields, and a "ready" button. Press the ready button, and a method buttonPressed is called. In its original version, this method places the sum of the integers in the first two **int** fields in the third **int** field, but it can be rewritten to do anything you want. Activity 1-5.3 of this CD provides a better introduction to this GUI than we can give here on paper.

Get GUI JLiveWindow from a footnote on lesson page 1-5. of the CD

For example, suppose you have written a function that changes a number of seconds to an hour-minute-seconds format (e.g. 67 could be changed to the string "0:1:7"). You can use GUI JLiveWindow to test this program. Change method buttonPressed to read the first **int** field, call your function with that integer as the argument, and place the result in the first String field. Then, test your function by repeatedly placing an integer in the first **int** field, pressing the ready button, and checking the answer that appears in the first String field.

The GUI can be used in real programs as well —wherever simple input or output is required. It can be much easier to use than keyboard input.

The GUI consists of two classes, JLiveWindow and MyJLiveWindow. MyJLiveWindow is the only one that you have to change to adapt the GUI to your needs. In fact, you will have to change only methods buttonPressed and main.

Changing the number of fields in the GUI

Open file MyJLiveWindow.java in your favorite IDE or editor and look at method main. You will see an expression that looks like this:

```
new MyJLiveWindow(4, 0, 0)
```

The first integer, 4, is the number of **int** fields; the second, 0, the number of **double** fields; the third, 0, the number of String fields —which is what the GUI in Fig. 5.4 has. Change these integers to any integer in the range 1..7. That is all there is to defining the number of fields the GUI should have.

Method buttonPressed

Method buttonPressed is called whenever the ready button is pressed. Here is the original body of the method:

```
int sum= getIntField(0) + getIntField(1);
setIntField(2,sum);
return null;
```

The assignment gets the values of the first two **int** fields and stores their sum in sum. Here, you can see that the following expression has as its value the integer that is in **int** field i (for i in the range 0..6 —the first field is numbered 0):

```
getIntField(i)
```

In the same way, it is easy to store a value in a field. The second statement,

```
setIntField(2,sum);
```

stores in **int** field 2 the value that is in variable sum. In general, the statement

```
setIntField(i,e);
```

stores the value of expression e in **int** field i, where expression i is in 0..6.

Methods also exist for accessing and changing the **double** and String fields:

```
getdoubleField(i)
getStringField(i)
setDoubleField(i,e);
setStringField(i,e);
```

Executing the GUI

Execution of the following call creates and shows the GUI window. Thereafter, you can drag the window where you want, resize it, and use the fields and ready button.

```
MyJLiveWindow.main(null);
```

An example

Consider the following method:

```
/** = the number of seconds n, but given in the form
       hours:minutes:seconds. Precondition: n >= 0 */
public static String convert(int n) {
    int hours= n / 3600;
    int remainder= n % 3600;
    return hours + ":" + (remainder / 60) +
           ":" + (remainder % 60);
}
```

To test this method, place it in class MyJLiveWindow, change it so that it has one **int** field and one String field, and write method buttonPressed as follows:

```
/** Display value convert(first int field) in the first string field */
public Object buttonPressed() {
    setStringField(0, convert(getIntField(0)));
    return null;
}
```

> **Warning**. Only one object should be linked to the keyboard or a file at a time. For example, do not have two `BufferedReaders` `br1` and `br2` linked to the keyboard and interleave expressions `br1.readLine()` and `br2.readLine()`. It will not *always* work, which is worse than something that *never* works.

We can now check many test cases by executing the program and repeatedly typing a test case into the **int** field, hitting the ready button, and checking the output in the `String` field.

Self-review exercises

SR1. Fix `MyJLiveWindow` to have four **int** fields and four String fields. Fix method `buttonPressed` so that it puts the integers 1, 2, 3, 4 in the four **int** fields and the four strings `"one"`, `"two"`, `"three"`, `"four"` in the four `String` fields.

SR2. Fix `MyJLiveWindow` to have one **int** field and one `String` field. Fix method `buttonPressed` so that it puts in the **int** field the length of the string in the `String` field.

SR3, Write a method with three parameters: a number of hours, minutes, and seconds. The method should yield the total number of seconds given by the parameters. Test the method using GUI `JLiveWindow`.

5.9   Reading the keyboard and a file

The core Java language has no facilities for doing IO (input/output). Instead, these facilities are provided in the API in package `java.io`. Here, we provide enough information to allow you to read from the keyboard and from files.

The classes that will be used in this section are:

- `InputStreamReader`: An instance can read characters from the keyboard.
- `BufferedReader`: An instance can read from any input, a line at a time.
- `File`: An instance is attached to a file in some directory on a hard drive.
- `FileReader`: An instance can read characters from a `File`.
- `JFileChooser`: An instance is a dialog window in which the user can navigate to a directory and choose a file.
- `FileOutputStream`: An instance can write bytes to a file.
- `PrintStream`: An instance has `print` and `println` methods for writing **int**s, **double**s, strings, etc.

The term *stream* is used for a sequence of data values that is processed — either read or written— from beginning to end. When the data is being read, the stream is called an *input stream*; when it is being written, the stream is called an *output stream*.

5.9.1   Reading the keyboard

Activities
5-7.1, 5-7.2

Unless your program is expecting input and contains instructions to read what you type, your program will not respond to typing. Fixing your program to read from the keyboard requires several steps, the first of which is to link to the keyboard.

Linking to the keyboard

This material is much easier to grasp from activities 5-7.1 and 5-7.2!

Variable System.in, of type InputStream, represents *standard input*. Standard input is usually the keyboard (although it can be set to some other input source). So, we can view variable System.in as containing the name of an object that *is* the keyboard.

System.in is a stream of information, and it needs a *reader* to read from it. For this purpose, we use an instance of class InputStreamReader. To create an InputStreamReader that is attached to the keyboard, use this statement:

```
InputStreamReader isr= new InputStreamReader(System.in);
```

Variable isr then contains the name of the instance that is attached to the keyboard, and its function isr.read() can be used to read from the keyboard. But this function reads only one character at a time, and this can be slow and inconvenient. Java provides a class BufferedReader that *buffers* the input: it reads lots of characters at one time, saves them, and delivers them one line at a time.

To create a BufferedReader that reads from object isr, use this statement:

```
BufferedReader br= new BufferedReader(isr);
```

Variable br is now linked to the keyboard, and its function br.readLine can be used to read the next line from the keyboard, e.g.

```
String s= br.readLine();
```

Evaluation of br.readLine() pauses until the user has typed the return/enter key on the keyboard; then, it yields the string consisting of all characters that were typed before the return/enter key was struck.

Handling IO errors

Activity
5-7.3

When reading input, problems may occur. The keyboard might get unplugged or break, something might go wrong inside your computer, etc. These events cause *exceptions*, and Java forces you to deal with them.

We illustrate this using the procedure shown in Fig. 5.5. It will not compile because the expression br.readLine() may cause an input-output exception to happen (to be thrown). The syntax error message that is printed is:

Error: unreported exception java.io.IOException; must be caught or declared to be thrown.

To make the procedure syntactically legal, remove the comment symbols that delimit the *throws clause* **Throws** IOException in the header of the method. This signals that this method may throw an IOException. Now, this method is syntactically correct, but the method that called this one may be syntactically incorrect and will also need a throws clause, and so on.

The upshot of this is that if the statement br.readLine() causes an IOException, the system will print an error message and terminate execution of the program.

For a complete discussion of handling exceptions, see Chap. 10.

Extracting numbers

Assume that a line "-77" of keyboard input has been placed in String variable line and that our task is to extract the integer from line and place it in **int** variable i. Static function parseInt of wrapper class Integer will do the job: execution of:

```
i= Integer.parseInt(line);
```

converts the string in variable line to an integer and stores the integer in variable i.

The two statements to read in a line of keyboard input and extract the integer in it can be combined to avoid declaring the unnecessary variable line:

```
i= Integer.parseInt(br.readLine());
```

But there is a problem with function parseInt: it does not allow whitespace, like blank characters, to appear before or after the integer. Thus, evaluation of this expression results in an error message and abortion of the program:

```
Integer.parseInt(" 35 ")
```

Remove the whitespace from the input using String function trim:

```
Integer.parseInt(" 35 ".trim())
```

Thus, we should read a line containing an integer, possibly with preceding

```
/** Read and print two lines from the keyboard. As written, it does not compile. Remove
    the comment delimiters around the throws clause on the first line and it will compile. */
public static void readAndProcess () /* throws IOException*/ {
    InputStreamReader isr= new InputStreamReader(System.in);
    BufferedReader br= new BufferedReader(isr);

    String line1= br.readLine();
    System.out.println(line1);

    String line2= br.readLine();
    System.out.println(line2);
}
```

Figure 5.5: A procedure to read and print two lines from the keyboard

and following blanks, with this statement:

```
i= Integer.parseInt(br.readLine().trim());
```

The other wrapper classes have their equivalents of parseInt. For example, to extract a **double** value from a string line use:

```
double d= Double.parseDouble(line.trim());
```

Iteration with input

You may want to read and process keyboard input lines until some stopping condition is met, e.g. some line contains the word "quit". This kind of task is usually done with a loop . If you know about loops, writing such a loop will be easy. See Chap. 7 for a discussion of loops.

```java
import java.io.*;
import javax.swing.*;

/** Illustrate use of class JFileChooser and reading a file */
public class FileChooserApp {

    public static void main(String[] args) throws IOException {
        BufferedReader br= getReader(); // A link to the user's file
        if (br == null) { return; }
        // Read file br and print the length of each line
        String s= br.readLine();
        // { inv: s is last line read and lengths of lines before line s have been printed }
        while (s != null) {
            System.out.println(s.length());
            s= br.readLine();
        }

        br.close();
    }

    /** Obtain a file name from the user, using a JFileChooser, and return a reader that
        that is linked to it. If the user cancels the choice, return null */
    public static BufferedReader getReader() throws IOException {
        JFileChooser jd= new JFileChooser();
        jd.setDialogTitle("Choose input file");
        jd.showOpenDialog(null);
        File f= jd.getSelectedFile();
        if (f == null) { return null; }

        return new BufferedReader(new FileReader(f));
    }
}
```

Figure 5.6:   Read lines from a file selected by user and print their lengths

5.9.2   Reading a file

Activities
5-7.5, 6-7.6

Get the program in Fig. 5.6 from a footnote on lesson page 5-7.

Reading a file is more work than reading the keyboard because the file to read must be chosen by the user. For this purpose, we suggest displaying a dialog window in which the user can navigate to a folder and choose the desired file. Such a task can be accomplished using an instance of class JFileChooser in package javax.swing.

Figure 5.6 contains a program, which obtains a file from the user and then reads the lines of the file and prints their lengths. We discuss it in two parts.

Obtaining a file from the user

Method getReader creates the BufferedReader that is attached to a file chosen by the user. Whenever you have to write a program that will read from a file selected by the user, use this method.

First, note that the header of function getReader contains a throws clause because it may throw an IO exception.

Now examine the method body. Here are the first four statements:

```
JFileChooser jd= new JFileChooser();
jd.setDialogTitle("Choose input file");
jd.showOpenDialog(null);
File f= jd.getSelectedFile();
```

The first statement creates an instance of JFileChooser and stores it in local variable jd. Attached to this instance is a dialog window on the user's monitor, which is not yet visible. The second statement set the title of the window so that the user knows what the dialog box is for. The third statement makes the dialog window visible and then waits until the user has either selected a file name or clicked the cancel button in the dialog window. The fourth statement obtains an object of class File that represents the file the user chose — f will be **null** if the user clicked the cancel button.

This is the standard way to obtain a file from the user.

Next, if f is **null**, the method returns the value **null**, as indicated in the specification of the method. If f is not **null**, this statement is executed:

return new BufferedReader(**new** FileReader(f));

It creates an instance of class FileReader that is attached to file f, creates an instance of BufferedReader that is attached to the instance of FileReader, and returns the BufferedReader.

Obtain this program from *ProgramLive* and run it so that you can see what the dialog window looks like.

Reading and processing the file

The first statement in method main calls method getReader to obtain a BufferedReader that is linked to the user's file.

The next part reads the file and prints the line lengths, using a loop that processes one line of a file at a time. There is a difference between reading a file and reading the keyboard. If there are no more lines to read in a file, function `br.readLine()` returns **null**. But there is no concept of the end of the keyboard, so the method that reads a line waits until the reader has typed another line.

Note the last statement of the method body,

```
br.close();
```

which closes the file, making it impossible to read from it anymore with variable `br`. In this program, it is not necessary to include this statement because the program will terminate right after this statement anyway. However, in general, it is a good practice to include it, just in case another part of the program attempts to open and use the same file.

```java
import java.io.*;
import javax.swing.*;
public class WriteExample {
    /** Get an output file name from the user and print two lines on it */
    public static void main(String[] args) throws IOException {
        PrintStream ps= getWriter();
        if (ps == null) {
            System.out.println(" User canceled. Nothing was written.");
            return;
        }

        // Print two lines on the file
        ps.println(" This is the first line.");
        ps.println(" This is the second line.");

        System.out.println( "File has been written." );
        ps.close();
    }

    /** Obtain a file name from the user, using a JFileChooser, and return
        a PrintStream that is linked to it. Return null if the user cancels */
    public static PrintStream getWriter() throws IOException {
        JFileChooser jd= new JFileChooser();
        jd.setDialogTitle("Choose output file");
        jd.showSaveDialog(null);
        File f= jd.getSelectedFile();

        if (f == null) { return null; }

        return new PrintStream(new FileOutputStream(f));
    }
}
```

Figure 5.7:   Print two lines on a file chosen by the user

5.10   Writing and appending to a file

Lesson
page 5-8

Figure 5.7 contains a complete program that obtains a file name from the user, using a JFileChooser, and prints two lines on it. This has the same structure as the one in Fig. 5.6, which reads a file, and it will need less discussion.

Obtaining a file name from the user

Get the program in Fig. 5.7 from a footnote on lesson page 5-8.

Method getWriter creates an instance of class PrintStream that is attached to a file chosen by the user. Whenever you have to write a program that will write a file chosen by the user, use this method.

The method stores a new JFileChooser in variable jd and gives it an appropriate title. Then it calls method jd.showSaveDialog (instead of jd.show-OpenDialog). This method opens a dialog window in which the user can navigate to a directory and type in a file name. In the dialog window, file names are grayed; the user cannot select an existing file to write. It is possible to set a switch in the instance js that allows the user to select an existing file to overwrite, but this can be dangerous.

As in the case of method getReader, a File f is created once the user has selected a file. If f is **null**, that means the user canceled the selection, and the function returns **null**. Otherwise, it creates and returns an instance of class PrintStream that is attached to the user's file.

Writing the output file

Instance ps in method main has methods print(e) and println(e). Argument e can be any expression. Its value is converted to a character representation and appended to the file, with a line separator in the case of println.

In the example of Fig. 5.7, method main simply writes two lines to the file. It then prints a message indicating that the file was written and closes the file.

```
/** Obtain a file name from the user, using a JFileChooser, and return a PrintStream that
    is linked to it and that appends to the file instead of overwriting it.
    Return null if the user cancels */
public static PrintStream getAppender() throws IOException {
    JFileChooser jd= new JFileChooser();
    jd.setDialogTitle("Choose file to append to");
    jd.showOpenDialog(null);
    File f= jd.getSelectedFile();

    if (f == null) {
        return null;
    }

    return new PrintStream(new FileOutputStream(f.getPath(), true));
}
```

Figure 5.8: Obtaining a PrintStream that appends to a file

Always call method `close` when finished with it.

I/O exceptions are suppressed by methods of class `PrintStream`. When you are finished writing, you can check whether an I/O exception occurred by calling function `ps.checkError()`; it returns **true** iff there was an I/O error.

Appending instead of overwriting

It is possible to append to a file instead of overwriting it. Figure 5.8 contains a method, `getAppender`, which obtains the name of a file to append to from the user and returns a `PrintStream`. Writing to this `PrintStream` will append to, rather than overwrite, the file.

Here are the differences between `getAppender` and `getWriter` of Fig. 5.6:

- The title of the dialog window is changed to reflect the new task.
- Instead of creating a `PrintStream` using **new** `FileOutputStream(f)`, the expression

      new FileOutputStream(f.getPath(), **true**)

  is used. The first argument is not **f** itself but a `String` that contains its name (i.e. the complete, absolute path to the file). The second argument, **true**, indicates that the file should be appended to. A second argument of **false** would cause the file to be overwritten.

In the dialog window that appears, the user cannot type a file name; they can only select one to append to.

> Get the function in Fig. 5.8 from a footnote on lesson page 5-8.

5.10.1   Exercises with files

In the following exercises, it is best to start with the appropriate class from Fig. 5.5, 5.6, or 5.7 and modify it.

E1. In the Interactions pane of DrJava, import `java.io.*`. Next, type the first three statements of method `readAndProcess` of Fig. 5.5, which will read in one line from the keyboard. Notice how DrJava gives you a place to type (in the Interactions pane). Type in something. Now see what the value of variable `line` is. You need DrJava from August 2003 or later.

E2. In DrJava, create a new class and place method `readAndProcess` of Fig. 5.5 in it. Compile the class and then test it by calling `readAndProcess` from the Interactions pane. You need DrJava from August 2003 or later.

E3. Write (and test) a procedure that (1) obtains a (text) file from the user, (2) reads its lines until a line with "END" on it is read (or until there are no more lines to read), and (3) prints the number of lines read.

E4. Assume that each line of a file contains an integer, possibly surrounded by blanks. Write (and test) a procedure that obtains the name of the file from the user, reads the file, and prints the sum of the integers.

E5. Write (and test) a procedure that compares two text files (which are obtained from the user). For each line i for which they differ, print the line number and the two lines.

E6. Write (and test) a procedure that (1) obtains the name of an output file from the user and (2) writes the first 50 squares on that output file, one on each line.

E7. Write (and test) a procedure that (1) obtains the name of an input file from the user, say the name is `"xxx"`, (2) reads the file into a `Vector`, and (3) produces an output file named `"outxxx"` that contains the lines of the input file but in reverse order.

E8. Write (and test) a procedure that (1) obtains the name of a file that is to be appended to (not simply overwritten) and appends a line containing `"THIS WAS APPENDED"` to it.

5.11 Universal resource locators

URL stands for *uniform resource locator*. URLs are used on the internet to define files and the protocols with which they should be processed. Here is an example of a URL:

`http://www.cs.cornell.edu/Courses/cs211/2001fa/index.html`

In this section, we describe URLs, look at a class in the API package whose instances maintain URLs, and show how to read the file given by a URL.

5.11.1 URLs

The URL

`http://www.cs.cornell.edu/Courses/cs211/2001fa/index.html`

consists of

1. An identification of a service or *protocol* (e.g. `http`);
2. A *domain name* or *host* (www.cs.cornell.edu), which is associated with a computer that is attached to the internet; and
3. A path on that computer (Courses/cs211/2001fa/index.html).

A URL can have other components, Here, we discuss only a restricted form of URL, which can be given as follows:

<protocol>`://`*<domain-name><path>*`?`*<query>*`#`*<fragment>*

Protocols

Here are the protocols one usually sees:

1. **http**: This stands for *HyperText Transport Protocol*, which is the most-

used protocol for accessing files over the internet. Generally, the files are html files, but they could be any files, including text files, .jpg files, and .gif files. A domain name must be given.

2. **file**: This is used for a file that is on the local computer. The domain name is generally not present.

3. **ftp**: The *File Transfer Protocol* protocol provides for files and directories of files to be transferred from one computer to another.

4. **mailto**: Used to bring up a window that can be used to send mail. The // and domain name are omitted, and instead of a path there is an email address, e.g. consider this URL: `mailto:gries@cs.cornell.edu`

Domain names, or hosts

The appearance of "//" in the URL signals the beginning of a domain name, which is a name that has been registered as being assigned to or associated with a particular computer. Here are examples of domain names:

1. www.cs.cornell.edu
2. www.cs.toronto.edu
3. www.datadesk.com

Domain names generally consist of a sequence of names separated by periods ".". It used to cost about $75 per year to register a domain name. The price has dropped to between $10 and $75. Here is the URL for the web page (http://www.icann.org/) for the company *Internet Corporation For Assigned Names and Numbers*, which maintains the rules for domain names.

The internet started with domain names that ended in: `.com` (for *commercial*), `.org` (*organization*), `.gov` (*government*), and `.mil` (*military*). Lately, new ones were added, like `.biz` (*business*), `.info` (*information*), `.net` (*internet*), and `.name` (*for individuals*) Also, any country can have a two-letter ending. Some examples are `.af` (Afghanistan), `.de` (Germany), and `.hk` (Hong Kong). The suffix `.us` exists for the United States, but it is not used much.

The domain-name part of a URL is often called the *host* —that name is used later, so remember it.

Ports

A URL can optionally specify a *port*, which is the port number to which the connection is made on the remote host machine. If the port is not specified, the default port for the protocol is used instead. For example, the default port for `http` is 80. The following example contains the port number 8080:

<code>http://www.ncsa.uiuc.edu:8080/demoweb/url-primer.html</code>

We do not deal with ports since they are usually not given in the URLs that we deal with.

Absolute paths

The *path* of a URL is a path on the computer to the file that the URL describes. For example,

```
/gries/Logic/Introduction.html
```

indicates that the hard drive of the computer whose domain name was given has a folder (directory) gries; in that folder is a folder named Logic, and in that folder is a file named Introduction.html.

The character / is used to separate entities on the path, regardless of the operating system on the computer —Unix-like, Windows, or Macintosh.

If the file name is missing at the end (so that the last entity is a folder), then a default file is chosen, usually index.html or index.htm. This default depends on the computer on which the file resides (it can be changed). On some computers, we have seen the following defaults: default.html, default.htm, home.html, and home.htm.

If the protocol is file, then the domain name is usually absent and the path is the path of a file or folder on your hard drive. The form of the beginning of such a path depends on whether a Unix-like, Windows, or Macintosh operating system is being used. You can check this out on your own computer by loading any html file that is on your hard drive into a browser like Netscape Communicator or Internet Explorer and looking at the URL that is displayed. Here are examples for the three kinds of systems:

1. Unix: /home/profs/gries/public_html/index.html
2. Windows: /C:/MyDocuments/test.html
3. Mac: /ProgramLive/Course/IC/web/ICweb.htm

Relative URLs

Within an html file, one can have a relative URL, as in:

```
href="people/faculty/faculty.htm"
```

The protocol and host are those of the current html file, and the path is assumed to be relative to the folder in which the html file appears. One can use ".." in the path to move up in the path of folders, as in all operating systems. For example, if the current folder is /gries/Logic, then relative path ../NoLogic/-test.html refers to the file /gries/NoLogic/test.html.

Fragments

The following URL has the *fragment* #chap1:

```
http://java.sun.com/index.html#chapter1
```

The fragment is often the name of a *target* within the file given by the URL, but there are other uses for it. Technically, the fragment is not part of the URL.

5.11.2   Class URL

Package `java.net` contains class URL, which is used for dealing with URLs in Java. An instance of class URL contains a description of one URL. It has methods for getting components of the url and for reading the file named by the URL.

Constructors

Usually, one uses one of two constructors when creating a new URL. First, the new-expression

new URL(s)

creates an instance for String s, which must be a URL according to the rules given above. Second, suppose URL c describes a directory and we want to create a URL for a file s that is within the directory, Use the following new-expression to create it:

new URL(c,s)

For example, we might use the following:

URL dir= **new** URL("http://www.cs.cornell.edu");
URL file= **new** URL(dir, "gries/programlive/plive.html");

Both constructors throw a `MalformedURLException` if there is a problem. Also, note that **new** URL(s) is equivalent to **new** URL(**null**, s).

The specification of the second constructor is quite detailed, indicating what happens when both c and s contain protocols and when s begins with "/". Please look at the specification in the API package for details.

Getter and toString methods

Class URL contains a number of methods for accessing the different parts of the URL that it describes. Here are some:

getFile()	the file name, as a String
getHost()	the host, or domain name, as a String
getPath()	the path, as a String
getPort()	the port number, as an **int** (-1 if port not set)
getProtocol()	the protocol, as a String

As you might expect, class URL has a `toString` method, which produces a String representation of the URL that it describes.

5.11.3   Reading the file given by a URL

A search engine like `google` seems to find appropriate files for a query almost instantaneously. The search engine is able to perform so quickly because information about web pages is already stored on its computers. Many computers in a search-engine company do nothing but browse the internet all day long, looking for new html files, extracting information from new and old files, and saving this information in a form that allows them to answer queries quickly. Google, for example, has 30,000-40,000 computers networked together, not only for answering your queries but for browsing the internet.

Thus, there is the need to read a file given by a URL. Figure 5.9 gives a method that you can use in a Java program to read such files. Here is how it works, assuming that variable url contains a URL:

1. The method call url.openStream() opens a connection to the file given by URL url. This connection is in the form of an object of class InputStream, which is stored in variable is.
2. An InputStreamReader isr is created, which can read the file one character at a time.
3. A BufferedReader is created and returned, which can read one line of the file at a time.

Suppose this statement is executed:

```
BufferedReader br= getReader(url);
```

Then, the lines of the file can be read and processed one at a time, just like the lines of any other file connected to a BufferedReader. Remember, a line of the file is read and stored in variable line using

```
line= br.readLine();
```

```
/**  = a reader for URL url (which must not be null). If url is null, if the protocol
       is not http or file, or if there is an IO error, null is returned. */
public static BufferedReader getReader(URL url) {
    if (url == null)
        return null;
    if (!url.getProtocol().equals("http") &&
        !url.getProtocol().equals("file")) {
        return null;
    }
    try {
        InputStream is= url.openStream();
        InputStreamReader isr= new InputStreamReader(is);
        return new BufferedReader(isr);
    } catch (IOException e) {
        return null;
    }
}
```

Figure 5.9:   Print two lines on a file chosen by the user

Chapter **6**

Reference on Primitive Types

OBJECTIVES

* Provide a reference on Java's primitive types.

INTRODUCTION

A *type* describes a set of values together with operations on them. For example, mathematical type *integer* describes the set of all integers together with operations like addition + and multiplication *. Each variable in a Java program has a type, which defines the values that can be associated with the variable. Each expression has a type, which depends on the type of its operands.

Java has two kinds of types: *primitive types* and *class types*. Primitive types are built into Java. A class type, or simply class, is defined in a program, by a *class definition*. In this chapter, we describe the primitive types.

Below, we list the primitive types of Java, along with the set of values in them and the amount of memory used to hold their values.

Type	Range of values	Memory used
byte	$-128..127$	1 byte (8 bits)
short	$-2^{15}..2^{15}-1$	2 bytes (16 bits)
int	$-2^{31}..2^{31}-1$	4 bytes (32 bits)
long	$-2^{63}..2^{63}-1$	8 bytes (64 bits)
float	$-3.4028235E38$ to $-1.4E-45$ $1.4E-45$ to $3.4028235E38$	4 bytes (32 bits)
double	$-1.7676931348623157E308$ to 0 0 to $1.7676931348623157E308$	8 bytes (64 bits)
char	Unicode characters	2 bytes (16 bits)
boolean	false, true	1 byte

The types are: the *integral types* (**byte**, **short**, **int**, **long**, and **char**), the *floating point types* (**float** and **double**), and type **boolean**. A beginner needs to look only at types **int**, **double**, and **boolean**.

6.1 Type int

The values of type **int** are the integers in the range:

$$-2147483648..+2147483647, \text{ or } -2^{31}..2^{31}-1.$$

A value of type **int** occupies four bytes of memory.

Use the following constants to access the minimum and maximum values of class **int**:

> Integer.MIN_VALUE   Integer.MAX_VALUE

int literals

Activity 6-2.1

The conventional representation of integers, like 108 and 0, are called *literals* in Java. Such literals are expressions of type **int**, and they denote the obvious integer values. For example, adding 108 and 9 gives the decimal value 117:

> System.out.print(108 + 9)   // Prints 117

See a footnote on lesson page 6-2 for the octal number system and for octal and hexadecimal int literals.

Conventionally, in mathematics, a decimal integer can have leading zeros, so 10, 010, and 0010 are equal. In Java, however, they are different! A leading zero means that the octal, or base 8, number system is being used, so that 10 and 010 represent different integers.

Designers of programming languages should not create notations that conflict with tradition, for they make for confusion and wasted time.

The int operations

The **int** operations are negation, unary addition, addition, subtraction, multiplication, division, and remainder. Given **int** operands, they produce an **int**. We describe these operations assuming that E, E1, and E2 are **int** expressions:

- + E is *unary addition*. Its value is the value of E.

- – E is conventional *negation*, or *unary minus*. Its value is the value of E with its sign changed (from + to – or from – to +).

Overflow! The largest **int** value is 2147483647. The value of 2147483647+1 is not 2147483648 but –2147483648! When the result of an **int** operation is outside the range of type **int**, overflow occurs, and the answer obtained is not what you expect. The answer is determined by the fact that integers are represented in *twos-complement* notation, which is outside the scope of this book. You will not be given a warning when calculated values are outside the range of **int** and your answers are not correct.

> **Remainder versus modulo.** In math, the value x **mod** y, or x *modulo* y, is the non-negative remainder r that arises from dividing x by y. The value x **mod** y satisfies:
>
> x = y * q + r and 0 ≤ r < y (for some *quotient* q, which is unique)
>
> For x ≥ 0, x % y and x **mod** y are the same. Consequently, many people call % the *mod operator*. But % and **mod** differ when x is negative. For example:
>
> –7 **mod** 5 = 3, but –7 % 5 = –2
>
> For x < 0, % and **mod** are related by the formula:
>
> x **mod** y = x % y + y

- E1 + E2 is conventional *addition*, e.g. 4 + 10 evaluates to 14.

- E1 – E2 is conventional *subtraction*, e.g. 4 – 10 evaluates to –6.

- E1 * E2 is conventional *multiplication*, e.g. 4 * 10 evaluates to 40.

- E1 / E2 is *un*conventional *division*. To compute its value, compute conventional division and throw away the fractional part of the result to yield an integer. For example,

  10 / 2 evaluates to 5
  10 / (–2) evaluates to –5
  13 / 3 evaluates to 4 (i.e. the integer part of 4.333...)
  14 / 3 evaluates to 4 (i.e. the integer part of 4.666...)
  13 / (–3) evaluates to –4 (that is, the integer part of –4.333...)
  14 / (–3) evaluates to –4 (that is, the integer part of –4.666...)

  Note that for E1 < 0 , E1 / E2 = –(E1 / E2).

- E1 % E2 is the remainder operation. For E1 ≥ 0 and E2 > 0, E1 % E2 is the remainder when E1 is (conventionally) divided by E2. For example,

  6 % 3 evaluates to 0
  7 % 3 evaluates to 1
  8 % 3 evaluates to 2

  For E1 ≥ 0 and E2 < 0, E1 % E2 = E1 % –E2.
  For E1 < 0, –E1 % E2 = –(E1 % E2).
  It is an error if E2 = 0 (an ArithmeticException occurs).

> **Watch out for = versus ==.** A worldwide mathematical convention is that = denotes equality: b = c evaluates to **true** or **false** depending on whether b and c have the same value or not. Java, following C and C++, has gone against this mathematical convention, using == for equality and = for the assignment statement. This one affront to convention has caused more misunderstanding, confusion, and economic loss than any other notational choice.

Java has the arithmetic relations <, <=, >, and >= on values of type **int**. They yield values of type **boolean**. For example, 1 < 2 evaluates to **true** and 2 <= 1 evaluates to **false**.

The operators == and != denote equality and inequality: 1 == 2 is **false** and 1 != 2 is **true**.

Precedence and associativity

One can always fully parenthesize expressions to make absolutely clear in which order the operators are to be evaluated. For example, in the fully parenthesized expression (5 + 5) * ((5 / 5) % 6), the order of evaluation is: the addition, the division, the remainder, and the multiplication.

However, writing so many parentheses can be a pain. To reduce the number of parentheses required in many expressions, mathematical conventions assign precedences to operators, which indicate the order of evaluation. For example, negation has precedence over * and * has precedence over +. Thus, in the expression −10 + 4 * 2, first the negation is performed, then the multiplication, and finally the addition. If two operators with different precedences appear next to each other, the one with the higher precedence is evaluated first.

The precedences of all **int** operators are as follows, with the highest first:

1. negation, or unary minus.
2. * and / and %, with the same precedence.
3. + and −, with the same precedence.

If two operators with the same precedence appear next to each other, the *associativity* of the operators determines which is evaluated first:

- Unary + and unary − are *right associative*, which means that they are evaluated right to left. For example, −−−5 is equivalent to −(−(−5))).
- The binary operators +, −, *, /, and % are *left associative*, which means that they are evaluated left to right. For example, the expression 5 − 6 − 3 is an abbreviation for the expression (5 − 6) − 3. This is different from 5 − (6 − 3). So you really have to know whether an operator is left associative or right associative when evaluating (or writing) an expression.

6.2 Types byte, short, and long

6.2.1 Types byte and short

The values of type **byte** and **short** are the integers in these ranges:

$$\textbf{byte:} \quad -128..127, \text{ or } -2^7..2^7-1.$$
$$\textbf{short:} \quad -32768..32757, \text{ or } -2^{15}..2^{15}-1.$$

A value of type **byte** occupies one byte; a value of type **short**, two bytes.

The following constants give the minimum and maximum values of these types:

```
Byte.MIN_VALUE          Short.MIN_VALUE
Byte.MAX_VALUE          Short.MAX_VALUE
```

Literals of type byte and short

There are no literals of types **byte** or **short**. However, if you use an **int** literal in a place where a **byte** (or **short**) value is required, and if the value is in the range of type **byte** (or **short**), it will be accepted. For example, the first statement below is legal, but the second is illegal because 128 is not in the range of type **byte**:

```
byte b1= 127;     // legal
byte b2= 128;     // illegal, because 158 is too big
```

Operations of type byte and short

There are no operations of type **byte** or **short**. Instead, the following happens. Suppose b1 and b2 are of type **byte**. Then the operation b1+b2 is evaluated as follows:

1. Widen the values of b1 and b2 to type **int**.
2. Add the two values using **int** addition.

This means that any expression with an operation that is assigned to a **byte** or **short** value has to be explicitly narrowed (see Sec. 6.3). Here is an example:

```
b1= (byte) (b1 + b2);
```

One might well ask why one would ever use types **byte** and **short** —why not always use **int**? Suppose one has a large collection, perhaps 1,000,000 values, each in a small range. Perhaps each is a day of the week, or the day of a month, or the temperature during the day in Ithaca, NY. Stored as **int**s, they require 4,000,000 bytes; stored as **byte**s, they require only 1,000,000. So, for reasons of economy of space, types **byte** and **short** can be useful.

6.2.2   Type long

The values of type **long** are the integers in the range:

$$-9223372036854775808 \; .. \; +9223372036854775807, \text{ or}$$
$$-2^{63} \; .. \; 2^{63} - 1.$$

A value of type **long** occupies eight bytes of memory.

The following constants give the minimum and maximum values of type **long**:

```
Long.MIN_VALUE
Long.MAX_VALUE
```

long literals

A sequence of digits is automatically an **int** value, and if it is too large to be in the range of **int**, the program in which it appears will not compile. For example, the following is syntactically incorrect even though the integer in it is in the range of type **long**:

```
long x= 2147483648;
```

To make an **int** literal into a **long** literal, append **L** to it (either upper case or lower case), with no whitespace before the **L**. The following initializing declaration is syntactically correct:

```
long x= 2147483648L;
```

Operations of type long

The operations of type **long** are similar to those of type **int**. They are: negation, unary addition, addition, subtraction, multiplication, division, and remainder. Given **long** operands, they produce a **long** result. See Sec. 6.1 for a description of the operations and Sec. 6.3 for a discussion of casting.

6.3 Casting among integral types

Every **byte** value is in the range of **short**, every **short** value is in the range of **int**, and every **int** value is in the range of **long**. We can depict this as follows:

byte ➡ short ➡ int ➡ long

We say that each type is *narrower* than the types to its right in this diagram and wider than the types to its left. For example, **short** is narrower than **long** and **long** is wider than **short**.

If an operand is supposed to be of a certain type but an expression of a narrower type appears there, Java will *promote* it to the required type. For example, suppose variable b is of type **byte** and the expression b + b is to be evaluated. Types **byte** and **short** have no operations. The addition is an **int** addition. Each operand is promoted from **byte** to **int**, the **int** addition is performed, and the value of the expression has type **int**.

This, then, shows how **byte** and **short** values can be used even though no operations —except conversions to other types— are defined on them.

Suppose **byte** variable b contains the value 9. The assignment

```
b= (b + 1);
```

is syntactically illegal because an **int** value cannot be assigned to a **byte** variable. But in this case, we know that the value of b+1 is in **byte**'s range, and we would like to store that value in b.

In this situation, we precede the expression (b+1) by keyword **byte** enclosed in parentheses:

```
b= (byte) (b + 1);
```

Prefix operator (**byte**) is called a *cast*. It casts or converts the type of the expression to type **byte**. Similarly, we can use the casts (**short**), (**int**), and (**long**).

Widening casts —casts that convert from a narrower type to a wider type— are unnecessary because Java promotes values to a wider type when needed.

Narrowing casts —casts that convert from a wider type to a narrower type— must always be written explicitly because Java will never automatically convert to a narrower type because it may lose information.

Identity casts, like (**int**)5, are also possible, but there is no need for them.

Casts have higher precedence than binary operators

A cast like (**byte**) has higher precedence than operators like addition and multiplication. For example, consider this assignment:

```
b= (byte) b + 1;          // illegal
```

The assignment is equivalent to:

```
b= ((byte) b) + 1;        // illegal
```

Thus, the addition is an **int** addition and produces an **int** result, which cannot be assigned to a **byte**, so the assignment is syntactically illegal. The assignment statement should be written this way:

```
b= (byte) (b + 1);        // legal
```

6.4   Floating-point types double and float

6.4.1   Type double

Lesson pages 6-3 and 6-4 discuss type double.

The values of type **double** are numbers that can have a fractional part, like –.000045 and 35.4. You can view these as the so-called "real numbers", but you cannot represent all real numbers exactly. For example, the number 1 / 3 = .333333... has an infinite number of 3's in it, so, because a **double** value occupies a finite amount of space (eight bytes), the number 1 / 3 cannot be represented exactly in type **double**. Similarly the square root of 2 and pi, the ratio of the circumference of a circle to its diameter, cannot be represented exactly in type **double**. Type **double** serves only as an approximation of the real numbers.

We give you enough information so that you can write programs that use type **double**. However, to really use the type well, you need to know more than we can explain in this book. A later course, perhaps in numerical analysis, will explain all the nuances of type **double**.

Literals of type double

There are three forms of **double** literal:

1. A decimal number with a decimal point in it.
   Examples: `1.34` and `3.` and `0.23333`.
   Due to the way literals are implemented, the value of a **double** literal may be only an approximation to the corresponding real value.

2. A number in scientific notation: a decimal number (the period `.` is optional), followed by `e` or `E`, followed by a (possibly signed) integer.
   Examples: `1.32e20` and `2.1E0` and `1E-5` and `3.14e62`.
   The value of a double literal `mEi` is the value of `m` with its decimal point moved i places to the right (if `i` is positive) or left (if `i` is negative). For example, `5.0e-5` is equivalent to `.00005`.

3. An **int** literal or a **double** literal, as in points 1 and 2 above, followed by `d` or `D`. Examples: `1D` and `1.2d` and `1.3e-30d` and `24E20D`.

Scientific notation, used in many scientific fields, helps to express numbers that would otherwise be infeasible to express. For example the *googol*, a name coined by Milton Sirotta, a nine-year old, in 1955 is the number consisting of 1 followed by 100 zeroes, `1e100`. Mathematicians would write this as 10^{100}. The width of a human hair is approximately `750,000` angstroms or `7.5e-7` meters.

Each **double** literal must be in the range of the type. If you type a literal that is outside its range, your program is syntactically incorrect and will not compile.

Two constants give the largest and smallest positive **double** values:

```
Double.MAX_VALUE:  1.7976931348623157E308
Double.MIN_VALUE:  4.9E-324
```

In addition, three other constants represent other "values" of type **double**:

1. `Double.NaN`, meaning "not a number". Division by 0 produces this value.
2. `Double.POSITIVE_INFINITY` is produced when the exponent of a positive number gets too big.
3. `Double.NEGATIVE_INFINITY` is produced when the exponent of a negative number gets too big.

The range of the exponent is `-324..308`.

Operations of type double

The basic arithmetic operators on type **double** work as expected:

- `-`: *Negation.* e.g. `-3D` evaluates to `-3.0`.

- `+`: *Addition.* e.g. `420. + 2D` evaluates to `422.0`.

- `-`: *Subtraction.* e.g. `42E1 - .2E1` evaluates to `418.0`.

- `*`: *Multiplication.* e.g. `42E1 * .2E1` evaluates to `840.0`.

- `/`: *Division.* e.g. `1D / 3D` evaluates to `0.3333333333333333`.
  Division `0D/0D` produces the value `Double.NaN`, meaning "Not a

Number", and from then on your results are garbage. Division x / 0D where x is nonzero produces either Double.POSITIVE_INFINITY or Double.NEGATIVE_INFINITY, and from then on your results are garbage. Do not divide by 0, except for fun.

- %: *Remainder*. e.g 5.2 % 5 evaluates to 0.20000000000000018. (You would expect it to evaluate to 0.2, but roundoff error is involved.)

The arithmetic relations <, <=, >, and >= can be used on values of type **double**. For example, 1.3241 < 1.3241001 evaluates to **true**.

The operators == and != can also be used with **double** operands. However, these operators are rarely used because **double** values are only approximations. Rather than checking for equality, one usually checks whether two **double** values are "close enough" —i.e. whether their absolute difference is small enough.

Precedence and associativity of double operators

The double operators have the same precedence and associativity properties as their **int** counterparts. See Sec. 6.1.

Discussion

Type **double** is not as simple and straightforward as the above introduction might indicate. This is because **double** numbers are only finite approximations to real numbers. For example, the value of Math.PI, the closest possible approximation to the ratio of the circumference of a circle to its diameter, is

3.141592653589793

but actually the fractional part of this ratio is not finite but goes on forever. It does not even repeat (e.g. the rational number 1 / 4 can be written as .25000...; the fraction consists of a non-repeating part 25 followed by a part, 0, which repeats forever).

Further, literals (like 3.141592653589793) are written in decimal, but they are stored in the computer in binary, and the conversion from decimal to binary is another source of error.

Finally, **double** operations cannot be exact. For example:

(1D / 48D) * 48D is printed as 1.0, but

(1D / 49D) * 49D is printed as 0.999999999999999.

So these two expressions are not equal in **double** arithmetic. Run this loop below and analyze its output to see some of the approximations that go on. Because **double** values are only approximations, do not write a loop whose loop counter is a **double**.

```
// An example of inexact results and rounding:
System.out.print("inexact results with float: ");
for (int i= 0; i < 1000; i= i + 1) {
    double z= 1.0D / i;
    if (z * i != 1.0D) {
        System.out.print( " " + i);
    }
}
```

A complete discussion of **double** numbers is beyond the scope of this book. For more information about **double**, look at the specification of Java and turn to more advanced books on programming and numerical analysis.

6.4.2   Type float

Type **float** is similar to type **double**, except that a **float** value occupies four bytes instead of eight. Its negative and positive values are:

$$-3.4028235E38 \text{ to } -1.4E-45$$
$$1.4E-45 \text{ to } 3.4028235E38$$

In most situations, type **double** is used and not **float** because the use of **double** gives much more accuracy. However, when space is at a premium and accuracy is not important, use **float**.

float literals

To change a double literal (that does not include d or D) into a float literal, follow it (with no separating whitespace) by a lower case or upper case F. For example, 3.0 and 5D are **double** literals, but 3.0F and 5F are **float** literals.

Operations of type float

The operations of type **float** are similar to those of type **double**. They are: negation, unary addition, addition, subtraction, multiplication, division, and remainder. Given **float** operands, they produce a **float** result. See Sec. 6.1 for a description of the operations and Sec. 6.6 for a discussion of casting.

6.5   Type char

Activity
13-7

Type **char** has as its values the set of characters that you can process in a Java program.

The constants of this type, called *literals* of type **char**, are single characters enclosed in single-quote marks, e.g. 'A' and ';'. A sequence of these characters enclosed within double quotes " form a literal of class **String**. For example, **String** literal

```
"A;a"
```

contains the characters 'A', ';', and 'a'. If you understand the **char** literals, you know what you can use to make String literals.

How do you write the character ' in a Java program? You cannot write ' ' '. Instead, write '\''. The backslash \ is called the *escape character*, and the sequence \' is the *escape sequence* that is used to denote a single quote. Figure 6.1 lists the more important escape sequences that you can use in Java.

Lesson page 6.5 discusses the ASCII and Unicode character sets.

There is a third kind of **char** literal, the unicode character, like '\u0041'. Unicode contains representations of almost all alphabets of the world. You do not have to know about Unicode now, and we do not describe it here. For information on it and the older 8-bit ASCII character-set representation, look at the CD.

There are no operations on type **char** (other than casts).

Type char is an integral type

Activity 6-5.2

Type **char** is actually an integral type, which means that one can convert a value of type **char** into an integer and back again. Recall from Sec. 6.3 the diagram concerning narrower and wider integral types:

byte ➧➤ **short** ➧➤ **int** ➧➤ **long**

Below, we show the same kind of diagram, which includes type **char**:

char ➧➤ **int** ➧➤ **long**

Thus, **char** is narrower than **int**.

If you cast a **char** value to **int**, you get the integer that represents it. If you cast an **int** value to **char**, you get the **char** that it represents. For example:

```
(int) 'A' equals 65
(char) 65 equals 'A'
```

Activities 6-5.3..4

Since **char** is an integral type, it is easy to write loops that sequence and process a range of characters, for example, all the lower-case letters 'a'..'z'. The CD contains activities that show you how to do this.

6.6   Casting among primitive types

In Sec. 6.3, we introduced casting among integral types. In Sec. 6.5, we discussed the fact that type **char** was an integral type and showed how to cast from **char** to **int** and back. In this section, we complete the discussion on casting by

character	escape seq.	character	escape seq.
backslash \	\\	carriage return	\r
double-quote "	\"	tab	\t
single-quote '	\'	form feed	\f
new line	\n	backspace	\b

Figure 6.1: Escape sequences

showing that you can cast from integral types to floating point types and back.

The following diagram shows one of the narrower-wider hierarchies beginning with **byte**. A type is narrower than the types to its right and wider than the types to its left.

byte ⟶ **short** ⟶ **int** ⟶ **long** ⟶ **float** ⟶ **double**

A second diagram shows how type **char** enters into the picture.

char ⟶ **int** ⟶ **long** ⟶ **float** ⟶ **double**

An expression of one type may be promoted to a wider type automatically if it appears in a context where the wider type is required. But all narrowing conversions must be given explicitly using a cast. A cast, as explained in Sec. 6.3, is a prefix operator of the form (*type*). Examples are (**double**) and (**char**).

Casting to a narrower type may result in garbage if the value being cast is not in the range of the type to which it is being cast.

6.7   Type boolean

Lesson page 6.6 contains a complete description of type **boolean**.

In Java, primitive type **boolean** describes the set of two values **false** and **true** (called literals), together with the following operations on them: negation !; conjunction (and) &&; and disjunction (or) ||. The word *boolean* comes from the name of George Boole, a famous mathematician in the 1800s who founded the area known as *logic*.

A boolean expression is an expression whose evaluation produces either **false** or **true**. For example, arithmetic relations like x < y and b != c are boolean expressions. If **int** variables x and y contain 6 and 4, respectively, then x < y evaluates to **false** because 6 is not less than 4.

Boolean expressions are used as the conditions of if-statements and loops. However, one can also assign boolean expressions to variables, as in:

```
boolean isLess;
isLess= x < y;
```

Boolean operators
We now discuss five boolean operators. We use variables b and c as their

b	c	!b	b && c	b || c	b == c	b != c
t	t	f	t	t	t	f
t	f	f	f	t	f	t
f	t	t	f	t	f	t
f	f	t	f	f	t	f

Figure 6.2:   Defining boolean operators in a truth table. t and f represent **true** and **false**

operands, although their operands could be any boolean expressions:

- !: *Not* or *negation*: !b yields true if b is **false** and **false** if b is **true**. The sign ! is the exclamation point; it is often read as *bang*.

- &&: *And* or *conjunction*: b && c is **true** only if both b and c are **true**; otherwise, it is **false**. Operands b and c are called the *conjuncts* of &&.

- ||: *Or* or *disjunction*: b || c is **true** if either b or c (or both) is **true**; otherwise, it is **false**. Operands b and c are called the *disjuncts* of ||.

- ==: *Equality* or *equivalence*: b == c is **true** if b and c evaluate to the same value (either **false** or **true**); otherwise, it is **false**.

- !=: *Inequality* or *inequivalence*: b != c has the same value as !(b == c).

Truth tables for the boolean operators

The values of the boolean operations can be defined using the *truth table* shown in Fig. 6.2. To save space, we use t for **true** and f for **false**). This truth table defines the values of all the operations for all possible values of their operands. Each row contains, in its first two columns, a pair of values for the possible operands b and c. There is one row for each combination. Choose a combination of values for operands b and c, choose a column that has an expression (for example, b || c) in the top line, and the value in that row-column entry is the value of the expression with those operands.

Precedences of boolean and arithmetic operators

One can mix arithmetic and boolean operations in an expression. Consider, for example, the expression

    x < y && y < z

In order to understand what the expression means, one has to know the relative precedences of its operators. Figure 6.3 gives the precedences of operators.

Short-circuit evaluation

Consider evaluating this expression in a state in which n is 0:

    n != 0 && 10 / n > 2

Highest:	Unary ops:	+ - ++ -- !
	Binary arithmetic ops.	* / %
	Binary arithmetic ops.	+ -
	Arithmetic relations:	< > <= >=
	Equality relations:	== !=
	Logical and:	&&
Lowest:	Logical or:	||

Figure 6.3: Table of operator precedences

The first operand, n != 0, evaluates to **false**. Since && with a **false** operand evaluates to **false** regardless of the value of the other operand, evaluation of the expression terminates with the value **false** —without evaluating the second operand.

Now evaluate the expression but with the operands of the conjunction exchanged (in a state in which n is 0):

   10 / n > 2 && n != 0

Since n is 0, evaluation of 10 / n causes execution of the program to abort. Division by 0 is not allowed.

Thus, changing the order of the operands in a conjunction can change the value of the conjunction.

Evaluation of a conjunction b && c is done using *short-circuit evaluation*: if the first operand b is **false**, the result **false** is obtained without evaluating the second operand.

We can give a definition of && using a non-Java "conditional expression":

   b && c is equivalent to: (**if** b **then** c **else** **false**)

which has the meaning: if b is **true**, then the result is whatever c is; otherwise, the result is **false**. Actually, Java has such a conditional expression with a different notation, and we can define b && c as:

   b && c is equivalent to: b ? c : **false**

In a similar fashion, disjunction || uses short-circuit evaluation; it is defined as:

   b || c is equivalent to: b ? **true** : c

Short-circuit evaluation is used to protect an operation that might be undefined in some states from being evaluated in those states. You have seen one example of this: protection against division by 0. Another operation that may need protection is referencing an element of an array because the subscript may not be in the range of the array. A third situation is protection against referring to a field of a nonexistent object. Here are the schemas for these boolean expressions:

   if (n != 0 && (boolean expression involving division by n)) ...
   if (n < b.length && (boolean expression involving b[n])) ...
   if (obj != **null** && (boolean expression involving obj.f)) ...

Do not use | and &. Java has two "bit" operators, | and &, which in many situations give the same result as || and &&. However, they are not evaluated in short-circuit mode. For example, evaluation of n = 0 | x / 0 = 5 causes a division-by-zero exception, while evaluation of n = 0 || x / 0 = 5 does not. The moral of this story is: stay away from | and & and use || and &&, unless you really are in a situation where | or & are required.

Properties of boolean operators

Lesson page 6-6 discusses boolean properties.

Sometimes, we want to manipulate a boolean expression to put it in another form. For example, we can replace an expression

$$!(x <= y \ || \ y <= z)$$

by the simpler expression

$$x > y \ \&\& \ y > z$$

Manipulating boolean expressions in this fashion requires knowing the properties of the operators. Many of these properties are similar to those of arithmetic operators. For example, $||$, like $+$, is associative: $x \ || \ (y \ || \ z) = (x \ || \ y) \ || \ z$.

The marks of a Boolean tyro

Activity 6-6.4

Suppose a program uses a boolean variable `atHome` and this variable is to be tested in an if-condition. It is common for tyros to use an if-statement with the condition

```
atHome == true
```

You may be wondering what a tyro is. It has nothing to do with the word *tyrant*. Also, it is not a greek fast food delicacy, a sloppy beef-lamb thing wrapped in pita bread; that is a *gyro*. A tyro is a neophyte, a person who is familiar with the rudiments of a subject but lacking in practical experience.

But back to programming in Java. The more experienced programmers realize that b == **true** is equivalent to b. That is one of the simple properties of operator equivalence. So they write the if-statement with a much simpler condition:

```
atHome
```

Similarly, the tyro will use the expression `atHome == false`, while the experienced programmer will use the simpler `!atHome`.

Another mark of the tyro is this if-statement:

```
if (atHome || atWork)
      b= true;
else b= false;
```

The pro would instead write a single assignment statement whose righthand side is the same as the condition of the if-statement:

```
b= atHome || atWork;
```

There is nothing wrong with being a tyro in the field of programming. After all, experienced programmers were once tyros, too. But tyros often do not want others to know that they are tyros. If you do not, stay away from the marks of a boolean tyro.

Part **II**

Other Java Constructs

This part covers additional Java constructs:

- Loops.
- Arrays.
- Exception-handling constructs.
- Packages.
- Interfaces.
- Nested and inner classes.

These topics are largely independent and can be studied at different times. For example, loops can be studied before the chapters on classes and subclasses. Arrays are best studied after loops since many algorithms that deal with arrays use loops.

The short chapter on packages is best studied quite early.

Interfaces and nested and inner classes should be studied after classes and subclasses.

Chapter 7

Loops

OBJECTIVES

- Study two repetitive statements: the while-loop and the for-loop.
- Learn how to develop and understand loops

INTRODUCTION

During execution, it is often necessary to repeat a statement many times. For example, consider printing the integers 0..n. You cannot program this without the ability to repeat a print statement an arbitrary number of times.

Java has three "repetitive" statements, called *loops*, that call for repeating a statement. Here, we study two of them: the while-loop and the for-loop.

Knowing how loops work is *not* the same as being able to write them efficiently and correctly. Loops are a wonderful source of bugs, and you can waste a great deal of time writing incorrect loops and trying to fix them. We present a methodology that will reduce the overall amount of time you spend writing loops.

7.1 The while-loop

7.1.1 Syntax and semantics of while-loops

Activity 7-1.1 covers the same material but with a different loop.

Consider a sequence of statements to print the numbers 2^2, 3^2, and 4^2:

```
System.out.println(2 * 2);
System.out.println(3 * 3);
System.out.println(4 * 4);
```

This task uses three statements. To print 100 squares in this manner would require 100 statements. But because of the repetitive nature of this task, it can be written in a shorter fashion using a Java statement called the *while-loop*. Here is a Java segment that contains a while-loop to perform this task:

```
// Print the squares of 2, 3, and 4
int i= 2;
while (i != 5) {
    System.out.println(i * i);
    i= i + 1;
}
```

The while-loop consists of:

Style Note
13.2, 13.2.3
indenting
loops

- The keyword **while**.
- The *loop condition* i != 5, within parentheses.
- The *repetend* of the loop: the block { ... }.

The loop condition can be any boolean expression, and the repetend can contain any sequence of statements. *Repetend* means "the thing to be repeated". Note that the statements within the block are indented. This follows the convention that subparts of a statement are indented.

Execution of a while-loop can be described using the following *flow chart*:

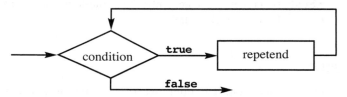

Activity 7-1.1 shows the actual execution of a loop, step by step.

According to the flow chart, execution begins by evaluating the loop condition. If it is **false**, then execution of the loop terminates; if **true**, the repetend is executed, and the process repeats, beginning with the test of the loop condition.

Each execution of the repetend is called an *iteration* of the loop. The first iteration is *iteration 0*, the second is *iteration 1*, and so on. If the loop condition is **false** initially, then zero iterations are performed during execution of the loop.

7.1.2   Tracing execution of a loop

Generally, when executing a program by hand, we draw each variable as a named box. When executing an assignment to x (say), we cross out the old value of x and put in the new one. However, when first learning about loops (and, at times, when looking for a hard-to-find error), it is helpful to draw the variables in a way that exposes the order in which the assignments were made. We call this a *timing diagram*. We illustrate by showing how to execute the following loop:

```
int x= 0;   int i= 3;
while (i != 5) {
    x= x + i * i;
    i= i + 1;
}
```

In a timing diagram, we draw the variables in a vertical column, separated by a horizontal line; next to each variable, we place its initial value:

```
x  0
i  3
```

Now, we begin executing the loop. Whenever an assignment is executed, we draw a vertical line to the right of the last value written and write in the new value of the variable to the right of the line. For example, with the above loop, because the condition i != 5 is **true** (since i is 3), the repetend is executed. First, x is assigned the value 9, yielding:

```
x  0 | 9
i  3 |
```

Then, the assignment to i is executed, yielding:

```
x  0 | 9 |
i  3 |   | 4
```

The loop condition is evaluated again; it is **true**, so the repetend is again executed. Below, to the left, we show the trace of the variables after assigning to x and, to the right, after assigning to i.

```
x  0 | 9 |   | 25 |              x  0 | 9 |   | 25 |
i  3 |   | 4 |    |              i  3 |   | 4 |    | 5
```

The loop condition is evaluated again. Because it is **false** (since i now has the value 5), the loop terminates.

Tracing the values of variables in this fashion has the advantage that we see clearly the order in which the variables were assigned and the values on which the evaluation of each expression depends. If we feel we may have made a mistake (which happens more often than most programmers like to admit), we can more easily go back and rectify it.

7.1.3 Self-review exercises

SR1. Write down the syntax of the while-loop.

SR2. Draw the flow chart of a while-loop.

SR3. Draw timing diagrams for the following loops.

(a)
```
x= 1; i= 1;
while (i != 4) {
    x= x * i;
    i= i + 1;
}
```

(b)
```
x= 1;   i= 3;
while (i != 0) {
    x= x * i;
    i= i - 1;
}
```

(c)
```
x= 1;   i= 2;
while (i <= 7) {
    x= x * i;
    i= i + 2;
}
```

(d)
```
x= 2;   y= 4;   z= 1;
while (y != 0) {
    if (y % 2 == 0) {
        x= x * x;
        y= y / 2;
    } else {
        z= z * x;
        y= y - 1;
    }
}
```

Answers to self review exercises

SR1. See beginning of Sec. 7.1.1.

SR2. See Sec 7.1.1.

SR3. (a)
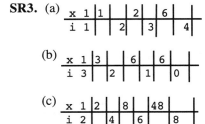

(b)

(c)

(d)

7.2   Understanding and developing loops

Style Note
13.2, 13.2.3
indenting
loops

Loops are far more complicated than assignments or if-statements, and, generally speaking, learning how to develop loops is more difficult than learning about assignments or if-statements. In this section, we go into detail about how to think about loop development and how to annotate a loop with comments that help the reader (and writer) understand it. We start with a discussion of some notation that helps simplify discussions of some loops.

A note on ranges h..k

We often want to say something about a range of integers, for example, the integers 5, 6, 7, and 8. To simplify, we use the notation 5..8 to denote this range. The notation h..k denotes the range of integers h, h + 1, h + 2, ..., k − 1, k.

For example, we might say, "the integers 5..8 have been printed", or, "x is the sum of the integers 1..n (for some integer n)".

In the table below, we give examples of ranges, giving the integers in the range and a formula (*last-value* + 1 – *first-value*) for calculating the number of integers in the range. The last line gives a general range with two variables: h..k.

range	integers in range	number of integers
5..7	5, 6, 7	7 + 1 – 5 = 3
5..6	5, 6	6 + 1 – 5 = 2
5..5	5	5 + 1 – 5 = 1
5..4	(none)	4 + 1 – 5 = 0
h..k	h, h + 1, ..., k	k + 1 – h

Take special note of the range 5..4, which denotes the range beginning at 5 but containing no integers. It may seem weird, but it follows the progression given by the preceding three, and it is quite useful, mathematically speaking.

Whenever we write a range like h..k, we assume, usually without explicitly saying so, that h ≤ k + 1, and if h = k + 1, then the range is empty. For example, we would never write a range 5..3 or 5..2 because they do not make sense. But 5..4 is ok: it denotes the set of no integers.

7.2.1 Four loopy questions

Activity 7-1.2 covers the same material but with a different loop.

This sequence of statements prints the squares of integers in the range 2..4:

```
System.out.println(2 * 2);
System.out.println(3 * 3);
System.out.println(4 * 4);
```

Below, we write a loop that does the same thing. We think of the loop shown below as *simulating* this sequence of three statements:

```
int i= 2;
while (i != 5) {
    System.out.println(i * i);
    i= i + 1;
}
```

We look for a way of commenting the loop —this particular loop is, perhaps, simple enough that it does not require comments, but most loops do. In order to figure out what kind of comments will help, we annotate the sequence of three statements, showing what is true before and after each one:

```
// { the squares of 2..1 have been printed }
System.out.println(2 * 2);
// { the squares of 2..2 have been printed }
System.out.println(3 * 3);
// { the squares of 2..3 have been printed }
System.out.println(4 * 4);
// { the squares of 2..4 have been printed }
```

Each assertion explains exactly what has been printed at that point in execution. Note the use of the range 2..1 in the first assertion to say that no squares have been printed. This notation allows us to write all four assertions in the same form, which, as you will see, is important when finding a good loop comment.

We want to place the same kind of information in the while-loop, but, since there is only one println statement in the repetend, we cannot insert all four assertions in the statement sequence! But note that the assertions are exactly the same except for the last value of the range. Thus, each assertion has the form shown below, but each has a different value in place of variable i:

loop assertion: the squares of 2..i-1 have been printed

We call this loop assertion an *invariant of the loop* because it remains invariantly true throughout execution (*invariant* means *non-changing*). We can think of this relation as a generalization of the four assertions in the sequence: the range in the assertion increases with i. Below, we have placed this invariant as a comment between the initialization and the loop:

```
// Print the squares of integers in the range 2..4
int i= 2;
// { invariant: the squares of 2..i-1 have been printed }
while (i != 5) {
    System.out.println(i * i);
    i= i + 1;
}
// { the squares of 2..4 have been printed }
```

We now look at how we understand a loop that is annotated with such an invariant. We ask ourselves four questions:

1. How does it start? This question involves the initialization. Why is variable i initialized to 2? Answer: because that initialization truthifies the invariant before any real work is done.

2. When is it done? When the loop terminates, the last assertion had better be true. In our running example, at the end, the squares of values in the range 2..4 have been printed. The invariant says this:

invariant: the squares of 2..i-1 have been printed

When the loop condition evaluates to **false**, i = 5. So, when the loop terminates, the invariant says:

> the squares of 2..5-1 have been printed

which means:

> the squares of 2..4 have been printed

which is exactly the final assertion!

3. How does it make progress? We have to be sure that the loop terminates, which means that at some point the loop condition will become **false**. In this case, i starts out at 2 and ends at 5. The statement i= i + 1; in the repetend ensures that each iteration makes progress toward the loop condition becoming **false**.

4. How does it fix the invariant? The invariant must be true each time the loop condition is evaluated. So, we have to ensure that each execution of the repetend fixes the variables to keep it **true**. In this case, before the repetend is executed, we know the following from the loop condition and the loop invariant:

> i != 5 and the squares of 2..i-1 have been printed

Therefore, the next value to print is i * i. The repetend prints this value and then increases i, after which the invariant again **true**.

The above analysis talked about a particular loop. We now discuss the same questions with regard to a general loop of this form:

> *initialization*
> // invariant: explains what is true whenever the *condition* is evaluated
> **while** (*condition*) {
>   *repetend*
> }
> // postcondition: an assertion of what is supposed to be true at the end

Again, here are the questions we ask when we are understanding a given loop or writing our own loop:

1. How does it start? In other words, what *initialization* of variables will make the invariant true initially? Here are two general strategies for this: try to make a range empty and set some variable to zero.

2. When does it stop? When it stops, the invariant is true and the loop condition is false. From these two facts, we should be able to conclude that the postcondition is true.

3. How does it make progress? What statement in the repetend ensures that after a number of iterations the loop condition will eventually become false?

4. How does it fix the loop invariant? We have to make sure that the following precondition-statement-postcondition triple holds:

```
// { condition and invariant are true }
repetend
// { invariant is true }
```

7.2.2   Developing a second loop

We develop a second loop, which stores the sum of the first n – 1 positive numbers in **int** variable x, for some n ≥ 1. Here is a subtle point: if n is 1, then we want to store the sum of the first 0 numbers in x. That is why we assign 0 to x as a separate step:

```
// Store 1 + 2 + … + (n – 1) in x (assuming n ≥ 1)
x= 0;
x= x + 1;
x= x + 2;
…;
x= x + (n – 1);
```

We develop a loop that is equivalent to this sequence of assignments.

Developing the loop invariant

The first task is to annotate this sequence so that we can derive a suitable loop invariant. We start by writing a postcondition. The postcondition is easily derived from the task of the segment, to store 1 + 2 + … + (n – 1) in x:

```
// { x = sum of 1..n–1 }
```

Working backward from the postcondition, we fill in the other assertions:

```
// { precondition: x = sum of 1..1–1 }
x= x + 1;
// { x = sum of 1..2–1 }
x= x + 2;
// { x = sum of 1..3–1 }
…
// { x = sum of 1..(n–1)–1 }
x = x + (n–1);
// { postcondition: x = sum of 1..n–1 }
```

Note that they all have the same form: the upper end of the range is an expression of the form v – 1 for some value v. Making them all have the same form is important for finding an invariant.

Like the previous example, the precondition may seem a bit odd. Again, this useful convention allows us to write assertions in a consistent manner.

A relation that generalizes all these assertions can be found by generalizing the postcondition: make a copy of the postcondition and replace identifier n by a fresh (that is, new) variable, say k:

invariant: x = sum of 1..k-1

When k is 1, this assertion looks like the precondition, when 2, it looks like the second assertion. And so on. This generalizing statement is the loop invariant. We now ask our four loopy questions to help us develop the algorithm.

1. **How does it start?** How do we initialize x and k so that the invariant is true? The sequence of statements given at the beginning of the section starts with x = 0. So, the sum of 1..k-1 has to be 0, and this happens only with k = 1. So, the initialization is this:

    ```
    x= 0;
    k= 1;
    ```

2. **When does it stop?** The loop can stop only when x = sum of 1..n-1. From the invariant, we know that x = sum of 1..k-1. So, the loop can stop when k = n. Therefore, it should continue as long as k != n.

3. **How does it make progress?** Variable k starts out at 1 and has to get up to n. Therefore, progress can be made by adding 1 to k.

4. **How does it fix the invariant?** When the repetend starts, x is the sum of 1..k-1. The repetend is going to increase k. Before this is done, the next value, k, has to be added to x. Thus, the invariant is fixed by executing x= x + k;

This ends development of the loop, which is written as:

```
// Store 1 + 2+ … + (n-1) in x
x= 0;
k= 1;
// { invariant: x = sum of 1..k-1 }
while (k != n) {
    x= x + k;
    k= k + 1;
}
```

7.2.3   A slightly different problem

In the previous section, we developed a loop that terminated with this postcondition:

x is the sum of 1..n-1

Here, we outline the development of a loop for a slightly different postcondition:

x is the sum of 1..n (where n ≥ 1)

The purpose of writing a loop for this slightly different problem is to show you how careful you have to be with the meanings of variables. You have to concentrate full attention on the given preconditions, postconditions, invariants, and other definitions. We will be brief in our explanation, for what we do here is similar to what we did in the previous section.

As before, we find the loop invariant by replacing n in the postcondition by a fresh variable k:

invariant: x is the sum of 1..k

1. **How does it start?** Since n ≥ 1, start with x equal to 1 and k equal to 1.
2. **When does it stop?** The invariant says that x is the sum of 1..k. It stops when x is the sum of 1..n. So, it stops when k = n and continues as long as k != n.
3. **How does it make progress?** By increasing k by 1.
4. **How does it fix the invariant?** By adding the next value, which is k + 1, to x.

Therefore, the loop (with initialization) is:

```
x= 1;
k= 1;
// { invariant: x is the sum of 1..k }
while (k != n) {
    x= x + (k + 1);
    k= k + 1;
}
```

7.2.4   Self-review exercises

SR1. How does it start? Each case below consists of a relation and (perhaps) values for some of the variable used in the relation. Write assignments to the other variables that make the relation true.

	Relation	Known variables	Assign to
(a)	x * y = 5 * 4	x is 5	y
(b)	x * y = a * b	x is a	y
(c)	x = sum of 1..h	x is 1	h
(d)	x = sum of 1..h	h is 2	x
(e)	x = sum of 1..h	h is 1	x
(f)	x = sum of 1..h	h is 0	x
(g)	x = sum of h..10	h is 10	x
(h)	x = sum of h..10	h is 9	x
(i)	x = sum of h..10	x is 10	h
(j)	z + x * y = a * b	z is 0	x, y
(k)	z * x^y = a^b	z is 1	x, y
(l)	sum of h..n = sum h..k		k

SR2. When does it stop? Each case below consists of an invariant and a post-condition. It is known that the invariant is true. What extra condition is needed to know that the postcondition is true?

	invariant	postcondition
(a)	x is sum of 1..k	x is sum of 1..10
(b)	x is sum of 1..k	x is sum of 1..n
(c)	x is sum of 0..k-1	x is sum of 0..10
(d)	x is sum of 1..k-1	x is sum of 1..n
(e)	x is sum of 0..k-1	x is sum of 0..n-1
(f)	x is sum of h..k	x is sum of 1..k
(g)	x is sum of h..k-1	x is sum of 1..k-1
(h)	m is the average of h..k-1	x is the average of 1..k-1
(i)	m is the average of 1..k-1	m is the average of 1..n-1
(j)	z + x * y = a * b	x * y = a * b
(k)	z + x * y = a * b	z = a * b
(l)	h..k-1 has been processed	1..k-1 has been processed

SR3. How does it make progress? Each case below consists of an initial value for a variable and a final value. Write down a simple assignment that gets the variable closer to its final value.

	initial value	final value
(a)	h is 0	h is 10
(b)	h is 10	h is 0
(c)	h is n (where n > 0)	h is 0
(d)	h is n (where n < 0)	h is 0

SR4. How does it fix the invariant? Each case below contains a relation that is assumed to be true and a statement that changes a variable. Write down a statement to execute *before* the given statement so that after both are executed, the relation is still true.

	relation	statement
(a)	s is the sum of 1..h	h= h + 1;
(b)	s is the sum of 1..h-1	h= h + 1;
(c)	s is the sum of k..n	k= k - 1;
(d)	s is the sum of k+1..n	k= k - 1;
(e)	s is the sum of 1..h	h= h - 1;
(f)	z + x * y = 100	y= y - 1;
(g)	z + x * y = 100 and y is even and y > 0	y= y / 2;

Answers to self-review exercises
SR1. (a) y = 4, (b) y = b, (c) h = 1, (d) x = 3, (e) x = 1, (f) x = 0, (g) x = 10, (h) x = 19, (i) h = 10, (j) x = a, y = b, (k) x = a, y = b, (l) k = n.

SR2. (a) k = 10, (b) k = n, (c) k - 1 = 10, (d) k - 1 = n, (e) k = n, (f) h = 1,. (g) h

= 1, (h) h = 1, (i) k = n, (j) z = 0, (k) x * y = 0 (or x = 0 || y = 0), (l) h = 1.

SR3. (a) h= h + 1; , (b) h= h - 1; , (c) h= h - 1; (d) h= h + 1;

SR4. (a) s= s + (h + 1); (b) s= s + h; (c) s= s + (k - 1); , (d) s= s + k; , (e) s= s - h; , (f) z= z + x; , (g) x= x + x; .

7.3   Examples of while-loops

7.3.1   The roach explosion

Your new apartment is infested with roaches, and they are multiplying rapidly. You would like to figure out how long it will take for them to completely fill up the apartment. You have measured the nasty things and have determined that they average .001 cubic feet each —they are big! While measuring, you found out that there were about 100 of them to start. You have been told that, if unchecked, the population more than doubles every week, increasing by 125 percent. You are going to write a program segment to figure out how many weeks it will take for them to completely fill the apartment.

The basic idea of a program is straightforward: calculate how many roaches there are after weeks 1, 2, 3, and so on, and stop as soon as the volume of the roaches is at least the volume of the apartment. This requires a loop, and we begin its development by figuring out its postcondition.

We assume that the volume of the apartment is in variable apartment-Volume. We need a variable w to contain the number of weeks and another variable population to contain the population at the end of w weeks:

> the roach population after w weeks is population

This property of w and population will hold when the program segment terminates. But there is more to say about what is true upon termination. First, the apartment volume is at most the roach volume because termination occurs when there are enough roaches to fill the apartment. Second, the roaches filled the apartment only in week w because the loop did not terminate in week w - 1. Thus, we have this postcondition:

> postcondition: the roach population after w weeks is population, and
> apartmentVolume ≤ roach volume, and
> week w - 1's roach volume < apartmentVolume

Developing the loop invariant

We now think about the loop invariant. The property of population and w should remain true and thus should be part of the invariant. The second part of the postcondition cannot be part of the invariant —that is the difficult part to calculate; that is what the loop is for. However, the third part will be true initially, when there are very few roaches. Since it is expected to be true initially and true at the end, we make sure it is always true by placing it in the loop invariant.

invariant: roach population after w weeks is `population` and
week w – 1's roach volume < `apartmentVolume`

The postcondition and the invariant differ only in that the postcondition has
one more piece: the roach volume has exceeded the apartment volume.

We now develop the loop using our methodology.

How does it start? The roach population after 0 weeks is 100. So, we use
the assignments:

```
w= 0;
population= 100;
```

When does it stop? When the roach volume is big enough: the roach volume ≥ `apartmentVolume`. So the loop condition is the complement of this relation. Remember, the roach volume is the product of a single-roach volume and the number of roaches.

How does it make progress? The postcondition requires that `apartmentVolume` ≤ roach volume. In order to make progress toward this, the number of roaches has to increase. According to the roach-population-growth rule at the beginning of this section, this means adding population * 1.25 to `population` (because the population increases by 125 percent). Here, we do the equivalent: multiply by 5 and divide by 4, so that all the operations are of type **int**.

How does it fix the invariant? Because the roach population grows weekly, the week number increases by 1.

See lesson page 7-2 to obtain this loop

```
/*   Calculate the number w of weeks it takes a roach infestation to
       completely fill an apartment */
int w= 0;
int population= 100; // roach population after w weeks
/* invariant: roach population after w weeks is population and
       week w – 1's roach volume < apartmentVolume */
while (apartmentVolume > population * .001) {
    population= population + (5 * population) / 4;
    w= w + 1;
}
```

7.3.2   Exponentiation

Activity
7-2.3

Figures. 7.1a and 7.1b contain two loops that compute the value b^c (b multiplied by itself c times) where b and c are **int**s. For example, $2^3 = 2 * 2 * 2 = 8$; and $2^0 = 1$. We use the second loop to illustrate the power of loop invariants because it is very hard to understood and develop without an invariant, and it is a *much* faster algorithm for computing an exponent.

The straightforward approach

In the first loop, y is the remaining number of times to multiply by b. Each iteration multiplies z by b and decrements y. For purposes of comparison with the second version, we discuss this algorithm using the four loopy questions.

How does it start? To see that the first conjunct of the invariant is true initially, make a copy of the conjunct and, because of the initializations, replace each occurrence of y with c and z with 1. This yields $1 * b^c = b^c$, which is true. So, the initialization truthifies the conjunct.

When can it stop? It stops when $y = 0$. Substituting 0 for y in invariant $z * b^y = b^c$ yields $z * b^0 = b^c$, which reduces to $z = b^c$.

How does it make progress? Each iteration decreases y by 1, making y closer to 0.

How does it fix the invariant? To check that the repetend maintains the invariant, we notice that we can "pull out" a factor of b:

$$z * b^y = z * b * b^{y-1}$$

Therefore, the assignments to z and y keep the value of $z * b^y$ the same, so the value of the first conjunct remains unchanged. Thus, the repetend keeps the invariant true.

Notice that y starts with value c, y decreases by one every iteration, and the loop terminates when $y = 0$. Thus, this loop takes c iterations.

Processing the binary representation of the exponent: how fast?

We first analyze how quickly the loop in Fig. 7.1b terminates. Then, we discuss its correctness.

The loop uses information about the binary representation of exponent c. For example, suppose c is 5, which is 101 in binary. The second statement assigns (binary) 101 to y. Because y is not 0, the repetend is executed. The if-condition tests whether y is even, and this test can be made by looking at the rightmost bit of the binary representation of y. Since this bit is 1, meaning y is odd, the else-part is executed, which subtracts 1 from y, yielding 100.

```
/** Set z to b^c, given c ≥ 0 */
int y= c;
z= 1;
// { invariant: z * b^y = b^c, 0 ≤ y ≤ c }
while (y != 0) {
    z= z * b;
    y= y - 1;
}
// { postcondition: z = b^c }
```

```
/** Set z to b^c, given c ≥ 0 */
int x= b; int y= c; z= 1;
// { invariant: z * x^y = b^c, 0 ≤ y ≤ c }
while (y != 0) {
    if (y % 2 == 0) {
        x= x * x;
        y= y / 2;
    } else {
        z= z * x;
        y= y - 1;
    }
}
// { postcondition: z = b^c }
```

Figure 7.1a: Slow exponentiation algorithm   **Figure 7.1b:**   Fast exponentiation algorithm

The loop condition is evaluated, and again it is true. This time, since the rightmost bit of the binary representation of y is 0, y is even, and the then-part is executed. The then-part divides y by 2. Division of an even decimal number by 2 is equivalent to deleting the last 0 of its binary representation, yielding 10.

Again, the loop condition is evaluated, and again it is true. Again, y is even, and the then-part is executed. This statement divides y by 2. This deletes the last 0 of its binary representation, yielding 1.

Again, the loop condition is evaluated, and again it is true. y is odd, and the else-part is executed. This statement subtracts 1 from y, yielding 0. This terminates the loop.

See lesson page 7-2 to obtain this loop

This analysis should convince you that this algorithm processes the binary representation of exponent y. The loop iterates once or twice for each bit of the exponent, so the total number of iterations is bounded above by twice the number of bits in the binary representation of the exponent. So, to compute 2^{15} requires at most 8 iterations (15 in binary is 1111) and to compute 2^{127} requires at most 14 iterations (127 in binary is 1111111). Compare this with the slow version in Fig. 7.1a, which requires 127 iterations to calculate 2^{127}!

Using the invariant

Focusing on y has enabled us to determine the maximum number of iterations of the loop and has given us insight into how y is used. But it hasn't helped us determine that the loop is correct. How do we know that z has the correct value upon termination?

We know of no way of explaining this without using the invariant, which gives the relation between all five variables of the algorithm.

From our earlier analysis, we can see that the second conjunct of the invariant, $0 \leq y \leq c$, is true initially and is maintained by the repetend. So, we concentrate on the first conjunct, $z * x^y = b^c$.

How does it start? To see that the first conjunct of the invariant is true initially, make a copy of the conjunct and, because of the initialization, replace each occurrence of x with b, of y with c, and of z with 1 to yield $1 * b^c = b^c$, which is true. So, the initialization truthifies the conjunct.

When can it stop? It stops when y = 0. Substituting 0 for y in invariant $z * x^y = b^c$ yields $z * x^0 = b^c$, which reduces to $z = a^b$ because $x^0 = 1$.

How does it make progress? Each iteration either decreases y by 1 or halves y, making y closer to 0.

How does it fix the invariant? Checking that the repetend maintains the invariant requires looking at two cases: y is odd or y is even.

For the case that y is even, we use this identity:

$$x^y = (x * x)^{y/2} \quad \text{(for y even)}$$

Therefore, the assignments to x and y keep the value of x^y the same, so the value of the first conjunct remains unchanged.

For the case that y is odd, we use this identity:

$$z * x^y = z * x * x^{y-1}$$

Therefore, the assignments to z and y keep the value of $z * x^y$ the same, so the value of the first conjunct remains unchanged.

In both cases —y even and y odd— the repetend keeps the invariant true.

With the aid of the invariant, we have analyzed the algorithm and seen that it is correct.

7.3.3   The spiral

Activity 7-2.4 of the CD shows you a loop that draws spirals of 2000 line segments of increasing size, with successive lines being drawn in alternating colors at the same angle. Change the angle, and you get radically different designs. Watch the activity so that you can see the colorful and beautiful designs that arise from this one loop. Amazingly different designs are drawn just by changing the angle between successive lines.

See lesson page 7-2 to obtain this loop.

On this black-and-white paper, we cannot do justice to the spirals that are drawn, to the description of what each spiral consists of, or to the loop itself. Therefore, we do not discuss the algorithm here. Look at it on the CD. Also, obtain the program from the CD and run it yourself, experimenting with different angles to see the designs that arise.

7.4   Loop patterns

A *schema* is just a "generalized presentation or a framework of reference". A loop schema is a loop (with initialization) that performs an abstract task, like:

Process the natural numbers 0..n-1

whose repetend includes an abstract statement, like:

Process k

We can use such a schema in many ways. For example, suppose we need to count the w's in a String s. We need not program this from scratch. Instead, because the characters are numbered 0 through s.length() - 1, we can start with the loop schema and refine it to fit the new task. We investigate this idea.

7.4.1   Schema to process natural numbers

We develop an abstract loop to sequence through the integers in 0..n - 1, for some natural number n, processing each one in turn. This loop is abstract because we do not say what it means to process a number.

The abstract loop should do this:

Process 0;
Process 1;

...

Process n - 1;

See lesson page
7-3 to obtain
the schema.

We can easily write down a postcondition for the loop:

> 0..n-1 have been processed

To develop a loop invariant, we make a copy of the postcondition and replace n in it by a fresh variable k:

> invariant: 0..k-1 have been processed

How does it start? The invariant has the nice property that assigning 0 to k truthifies it, because the invariant then means that no natural numbers have been processed.

When does it stop? The loop should stop when k = n because then the invariant implies that the postcondition is true. So, the loop should continue as long as k != n.

How does it make progress? Variable k starts out at 0 and is supposed to end up at n, so to make progress, increment k.

How does it fix the invariant? Since k is being incremented, the next number must be processed. The invariant tells us that the next number is k.

This leads to the loop schema of Fig. 7.2.

7.4.2   A loop to count the w's

Activity
7-3.2

We write a loop to count the number of w's in a string s, starting with the schema of Fig. 7.2. We can use this schema because the task is to process the characters of s, and these have numbers in the range 0..s.length()-1, so we are really processing the integers in this range.

The first step is to rewrite the schema in the context of our problem. We begin by replacing n in the schema by s.length().

```
// Process the n natural numbers 0..n-1 (for n ≥ 0)
int k= 0;
// { invariant: 0..k-1 have been processed }
while (k != n) {
    Process k;
    k= k + 1;
}
// { 0..n-1 have been processed }
```

Figure 7.2: A schema to process natural numbers 0..n-1

```
// Process the natural numbers 0..s.length()-1
int k= 0;
// { invariant: 0..k-1 have been processed }
while (k != s.length()) {
    Process k;
    k= k + 1;
}
// { 0..s.length()-1 have been processed }
```

Next, we replace the abstract specification, postcondition, and invariant by concrete ones:

See lesson page 7-3 to obtain the loop

```
// Set x to the number of w's in s[0..s.length()-1]
int k= 0;
// { invariant: x = number of w's in s[0..k-1] }
while (k != s.length()) {
    Process k;
    k= k + 1;
}
// { x = number of w's in s[0..s.length()-1] }
```

We must initialize so that the invariant is true initially. Since k is initially 0, to truthify the invariant, set x to 0.

The only thing left to do is to insert code to process character k. If this character is a w, then s has to be incremented. This leads to the program of Fig. 7.3.

Concluding remarks

This concludes the development of a loop from a loop schema. With this particular schema, most of the code gets copied over, without change, making the development easier (and shorter). The main creative parts are to truthify the invariant initially and to write the implementation of "Process k". To do this correctly, we first have to write the postcondition and then the invariant.

```
// Set x to the number of w's in s[0..s.length()-1]
int k= 0;
x= 0;
// { invariant: x = number of w's in s[0..k-1] }
while (k != s.length()) {
    if (s.charAt(k) == 'w') {
        x= x + 1;
    }
    k= k + 1;
}
// { x = number of w's in s[0..s.length()-1] }
```

Figure 7.3:   Counting the w's

The first time one sees the development of a loop from a schema, it seems like a lot of extra work. However, with practice, it becomes second nature to think in terms of the schema, rather than develop a loop from scratch all the time, and the whole process becomes easier and more efficient. Develop a few loops this way, and you will get to the point where you can do it without even having to look at the schema.

7.4.3   Testing primality

We use the schema of Fig. 7.2 again, but this time with slight variations on the theme. We write a loop, with initialization, to determine whether variable p is prime. Recall that a prime is an integer that is greater than 1 and whose only positive divisors are 1 and itself. The result is stored in variable b: upon termination b is true if and only if p is a prime.

We can use this schema because our task requires processing a range of natural numbers. The range starts at 2 and ends at p - 1 , so we change the schema accordingly, to start processing at 2 instead of 0. And we replace n by p.

```
// Process natural numbers 2..p-1
int k= 2;
// { invariant: 2..k-1 have been processed }
while (k != p) {
    Process k;
    k= k + 1;
}
// {2.( -1 have been processed }
```

Our concrete postcondition is the following:

postcondition: b == (p > 1 and no integer in 2..p-1 divides p)

The invariant of the schema is the same as the postcondition of the schema except that it has k in the range instead of p. Quite likely, the concrete invariant will bear the same relationship to the concrete postcondition:

invariant: b == (p > 1 and no integer in 2..k-1 divides p)

Therefore, we have this algorithm:

See lesson page 7-3 to obtain the loop

```
int k= 2;
// Assign to p to truthify the invariant;

// { inv: b == (p > 1 and no integer in 2..k-1 divides p) }
while (k != p) {
    Process k;
    k= k + 1;
}
// { b == (p > 1 and no integer in 2..p-1 divides p) }
```

We have to: (1) make sure the invariant is true initially and (2) implement the English statement "Process k".

1. The invariant is truthified using the assignment b= p > 1; —with k = 2, the range 2..k-1 is empty.
2. To process k means to add 1 to k if and only if k does not divide p.

To summarize, always increment k, and make b false if k divides p.

This gives us the algorithm of Fig. 7.4.

Optimization

We can make an optimization. Once b becomes **false**, it remains **false** because the only statement that changes b (after its initialization) is the statement b= **false**;. Therefore, it makes sense to terminate the loop if it is recognized that b is **false**. We do this by changing the loop condition to:

b && (k != p)

We can make another optimization. Suppose an integer d divides p. Then:

p = d * (p / d)

One of d and p / d is at most sqrt(p) and the other is at least sqrt(p). Therefore, only the integers in the range 2..floor(sqrt(p)) have to be checked to see whether they divide p. We leave it to you to change the algorithm to take this into account. Make sure your algorithm evaluates sqrt(p) only once. You will find the functions in class java.lang.Math helpful.

7.4.4 A schema for reading

Activity 7-3.4 develops a schema for reading a list of nonzero values from the Java console and processing them. Activity 7-3.5 uses this schema to print the sum of a sequence of nonzero values that are read from the Java console.

```
// Set b to "p is a prime"
b= p > 1;
int k= 2;
// { invariant: b == (p > 1 and no integer in 2..k-1 divides p) }
while (k != p) {
    if (p % k == 0) {
        b= false;
    }
    k= k + 1;
}
// { b = (p > 1 and no integer in 2..p-1 divides p) }
```

Figure 7.4: Testing primality

7.4.5   Self-review exercises

SR1. The range in the schema in Fig. 7.2 can be generalized. Rewrite it so that it processes the natural numbers in the range i..j-1 rather than 0..n-1.

SR2. Use the schema in Fig. 7.2 to write a loop to find the number of vowels in a String s. Hint: declare a new String that contains the five vowels, and use the fact that String method indexOf returns -1 if the char argument is not in the String of vowels.

SR3. How many numbers are there in the range i..j-1?

Answers to self review exercises

SR1.
```
// Process the  natural numbers  i..j-1 (for j ≥ i)
int k= i;
// { invariant: i..k-1 have been processed  }
while (k != j) {
    Process k;
    k= k + 1;
}
// {i..j-1  have been processed  }
```

SR2.
```
// Set x to the number of vowels in s[0..s.length()-1]
int k= 0;   x= 0;
String vowels = "aeiou";
// { invariant: x = number of vowels in s[0..k-1]  }
while (k != s.length()) {
    if (vowels.indexOf(s.charAt(k)) != -1) {
        x= x + 1;
    }
    k= k + 1;
}
// { x = number of  vowels in s[0..s.length()-1]  }
```

SR3. j - i + 1

7.5   The for-loop

7.5.1   The for-loop as an abbreviation

Activity
7-4.1

Besides the while-loop, Java has an iterative statement called the *for-loop*. The for-loop can be viewed as an abbreviation of a certain kind of while-loop. Here is an example. The following loop draws n concentric circles:

```
/** Draw n circles using Graphics g with centers (x, y)
     and radii of 4, 8, 12, ...*/
int i= 0;
// { invariant: the i smallest circles have been drawn }
while (i != n) {
    int r= 5 + 5 * i; // radius of circle i
    g.drawOval(x - i, y - i, 2 * i, 2 * i);
    i= i + 1;
}
```

This loop has a *loop counter*, i. A variable is a loop counter if (1) it is initialized just before the loop and (2) the repetend ends with a statement that increments (or decrements) it.

Below, we rewrite the while-loop as a for-loop. The first line of the for-loop (the line that begins with **for**) contains the initialization, the loop condition, and the increment of the loop counter (without the final semicolon!):

```
// Draw n circles with centers (x, y) and radii of 4, 8, 12, ...
// { invariant: the i smallest circles have been drawn }
for (int i= 0; i != n; i= i + 1) {
    int r= 5 + 5 * i; // radius of circle i
    g.drawOval(x - i, y - i, 2 * i, 2 * i);
}
```

The two program segments, one using a while-loop and one using a for-loop, execute exactly the same way. The for-loop is more compact and has a different feel to it. All the "control" part of the loop appears in the first line, and that makes it easier to understand, for some. When looking at the repetend, for example, one has to think of only one thing: *how does it fix the invariant?*

When you decide that a loop is needed in a program, if you can be positive that the loop will have a loop counter, write the loop as a for-loop. However, loops that do not have a loop counter are best written using a while-loop; and forcing these loops into the for-loop format often results in awkward code.

7.5.2 Syntax and semantics of for-loops

Activity
7-4.2

Here is the syntax of a for-loop:

> **for** (*initialization* ; *condition* ; *progress*)
> *repetend*

Style Note
13.2, 13.2.3
indenting
loops

The initialization is an assignment to the loop counter. It can also contain a declaration of the loop counter, if it has not been declared previously. But the scope of the loop counter that is declared within the loop is just the for-loop itself.

The *condition* is a boolean expression.

The *progress* is a statement that makes progress toward termination. Generally, it increments or decrements the loop counter. Note that this statement does *not* end in a semicolon.

The *repetend* is any statement. Almost always, we write it as a block: { ... }. Here is an example that prints the numbers 0..4:

```
for (i= 0; i != 5; i= i + 1) {
    System.out.println(i);
}
```

Semantics of the for-loop

To show how the for-loop is executed, we give equivalent code that uses a while-loop. First is the *initialization*, then the while-loop. The *conditions* of the while-loop and for-loop are the same. The repetend of the while-loop consists of the *repetend* of the for-loop followed by the *progress* part of the for-loop.

```
initialization
while ( condition ) {
    repetend
    progress
}
```

There is one slight difference between the general for-loop and the general while-loop when the initialization contains a declaration. The scope of a loop counter that is declared in the for-loop is only the for-loop; in the while-loop, the scope extends beyond the while-loop to include any statements that follow it.

Example

Above, we wrote a for-loop that prints the numbers 0..4. Here is the equivalent while-loop:

```
i= 0;
while (i != 5) {
    System.out.println(i);
    i= i + 1;
}
```

7.5.3   Developing a for-loop

Activity
7-4.3

Developing a for-loop is no different from developing a while-loop. The same strategy is used for both. In the next development of a for-loop, we illustrate that, in some cases, progress can be made by decrementing the loop counter.

We develop a loop to print the values 9, 8, and so on, down to 2. As the first step, we write a postcondition, which we name R.

R: 9, 8, ..., down to 2 have been printed

A possible loop invariant P can be created by making a copy of postcondition R and replacing the last integer 2 in it by a fresh variable:

invariant P: 9, 8, ..., down to k have been printed

How does it start? Initially, nothing has been printed. If k is set to 10, then the invariant implies that

9, 8, ..., down to 10 have been printed

i.e. no numbers have been printed. Therefore, setting k to 10 truthifies P.

When does it stop? Looking at the invariant and the postcondition, we see that the loop should stop when k is 2, so it should continue as long as k != 2.

How does it make progress? By decreasing k.

How does it fix the invariant? By printing the next integer, which is integer k − 1.

Putting it all together, we get this loop:

```
// Print  9, 8, ..., down to 2
// { invariant P: 9, 8, ..., down to k have been printed }
for (int k= 10; k != 2; k= k − 1)
     { System.out.println(k − 1); }
// { R: 9, 8, ..., down to 2 have been printed }
```

A different invariant, a different loop.
The loop just developed may feel a bit odd: why not start k at 9, print k, and stop when k is 1? That would work, but it would require a different invariant. A different invariant P can be created by making a copy of postcondition R and replacing the last integer 2 in it by k + 1 (instead of k); a self-review exercise in Sec. 7.5.5 asks you to develop a loop using this invariant.

invariant P: 9, 8, ..., down to k + 1 have been printed

7.5.4   A for-loop schema

Lesson
page 7-4

Earlier, we presented this schema for processing the first n natural numbers:

```
// Process natural numbers 0..n−1, for n ≥ 0
int k= 0;
// { invariant: 0..k−1 have been processed }
while (k != n) {
     Process k;
     k= k + 1;
}
// {0..n−1 have been processed }
```

This loop has a loop counter, so we can also present it as the following for-loop schema. This schema is used often for developing loops.

```
// Process natural numbers 0..n-1, for n ≥ 0
// { invariant: 0..k-1 have been processed }
for (int k= 0; k != n; k= k + 1) {
    Process k;
}
// {0..n-1 have been processed }
```

7.5.5   Self-review exercises

SR1. Write another solution to the problem in Sec. 7.5.3, but this time use this postcondition and invariant when you answer the four loopy questions:

> R: 9, 8, ..., down to 2 have been printed
> invariant P: 9, 8, ..., down to k + 1 have been printed

Answers to self review exercises

SR1. How does it start? Initially, nothing has been printed. If we set k to 9, then the invariant has the meaning:

> 9, 8, ..., down to 10 have been printed

which means that no numbers have been printed.

When does it stop? Looking at the invariant and the postcondition, we see that the loop should stop when k is 1, so it should continue as long as k != 1.

How does it make progress? By decreasing k.

How does it fix the invariant? By printing the next integer, which is integer k.

7.6   Making progress and stopping

7.6.1   Why use condition i != n?

Suppose we have a loop like this one:

```
int i= 0;
// { invariant: ... }
while (i != n) {
    Process i;
    i= i + 1;
}
```

> **The continue and break statements**. Java has a *continue statement*, whose execution causes termination of the repetend of a loop. It also has a *break statement*, whose execution causes termination of a loop or a switch statement. For information on these statements, look at the *ProgramLive* glossary as well as lesson page 7-6.

Another possibility for the loop condition of this loop is i < n. In this section, we discuss the two possible loop conditions. We have two reasons for preferring condition i != n.

> **Reason 1.** It is easier to develop i != n, rather than i < n, using our guidelines. We find a relation that indicates when the loop can stop and complement it to get the loop condition.

> **Reason 2.** Using i != n can lead to earlier detection of errors.

To understand the second reason, consider the following scenario. Suppose someone has to change this program, perhaps because of a modification in its specification to meet some new need, and they make a mistake that leads to i becoming greater than n. With the loop condition i < n, the loop terminates; with the condition i != n, the loop does not stop at all. Under these conditions, which loop condition do you prefer?

With the error in the program, the loop condition i < n would cause the loop to terminate. The error might go undetected and might never exhibit itself. When the program is used later, the error could lead to unknowingly wrong output or even to a plane crash.

But with the condition i != n, the program is in an infinite loop, and the programmer will certainly notice the problem and fix it immediately.

7.6.2   A case where i < n is needed

We develop a program to produce the reverse of a String t. Thus, if variable t initially contains the value "abcde", upon termination t contains "edcba".

Unfortunately, one cannot change the value of a String object; it is *immutable*. The standard procedure in this case is to copy the String into a variable s of class StringBuffer, which *can* be changed (is *mutable*), operate on s, and then assign s to t. See Sec. 5.2.5 for information on class StringBuffer.

Here is the outline of the program segment:

```
StringBuffer s= new StringBuffer(t);
Set s to the reverse of s;
t= s.toString();
```

Here is an idea for reversing s. The first and last characters of s have to be swapped, so we could do this first. Now, the outer two characters are in their final positions, and the next two outer characters can be swapped. And then the next two outer characters, and so on:

Swap s[0] and s[s.length() - 1];
Swap s[1] and s[s.length() - 2];
Swap s[2] and s[s.length() - 3];
...

The invariant must state what has and what has not been swapped into its final position thus far. Based on the above sequence of statements, we see that there is a prefix and a suffix of s that contain their final values, while the middle remains to be reversed. We use two variables k and n to define the boundaries of these three segments of t and write the invariant as:

inv: s[0..k-1] and s[n+1..] contain their final values, and
s[k..n] remains to be reversed

How does it start? By setting k to 0 and n to b.length() - 1, so that the prefix and suffix that contain their final values are empty.

When does it stop? The loop can stop when the middle segment contains at most one character, because then the middle segment is its own reverse. On the other hand, when the middle segment contains more than one element, that is, when k < n, more elements need to be reversed.

How does it make progress? By incrementing k or decrementing n (or both).

How does it fix the invariant? The elements s[k] and s[n] need to be swapped. Then k can be incremented and n decremented.

This completes the development of the program segment —see Fig. 7.5.

Remarks
Using k != n as the loop condition is incorrect because it is not guaranteed

---

```
// Set t to the reverse of t
StringBuffer s= new StringBuffer(t);
int k= 0;
int n= s.length() - 1;
// { invariant: s[0..k-1] and s[n+1..] contain their final values, and
//              s[k..n] remains to be reversed }
while (k < n) {
    char c= s.getChar(k);
    s.setChar(k, s.getChar(n));
    s.setChar(n, c);
    k= k + 1;
    n= n - 1;
}
t= s.toString();
```

Figure 7.5: Reversing a String

that k ≤ n. For example, if s initially contains 2 values, then initially k + 1 = n , and incrementing k and decrementing n makes k > n.

7.6.3   Off-by-one errors

Activity
7-5.4

An *off-by-one error* occurs when a loop iterates once too many or once too few times. Many people will tell you that off-by-one errors arise from carelessness, but that is all they say. They do not tell you *how* to develop the loop condition so that off-by-one errors do not occur.

If you follow the guidelines given in this text, you will rarely make off-by-one errors. As we have said earlier, to find a suitable condition for the loop, compare the invariant, for example:

> invariant: The i smallest circles have been drawn

with the postcondition, for example:

> postcondition: The n smallest circles have been drawn

and determine a relation that, together with the invariant, implies the postcondition, for example"

> relation: i = n

The complement of this relation is then the loop condition:

> loop condition: i != n

Follow this little methodology and you will rarely make off-by-one errors.

7.6.4   The bound function of a loop

Activity
7-5.1

We have been rather informal about checking that a loop makes progress toward termination. We now look in more detail at what it takes to determine this. We illustrate the technique using this loop:

```
// Draw n circles with centers (x, y) and radii of 4, 8, 12, ...
int i= 0;
// { invariant: i smallest circles were drawn and 0 ≤ i < n }
while (i != n) {
    int r= 5 + 5 * i; // radius of circle i
    g.drawOval(x - i, y - i, 2 * i, 2 * i);
    i= i + 1;
}
```

We introduce what we call a *bound function*, in this case:

> Bound function: n - i

This is an integer expression that gives an *upper bound on the number of itera-*

tions still to be performed. In this case, n – i is the exact number of iterations, but in other loops it may not be. The bound function is useful in determining worst-case execution time, since it tells us the maximum number of iterations the loop will make.

Properties of a bound function

In order to be an upper bound on the number of iterations, the bound function must satisfy two properties:

> 1. Each iteration must decrease the bound function.

In our example program, execution of the assignment to i reduces the value of expression n – i by 1.

In determining the second property, consider this. It is not enough to see that the bound function decreases at each iteration. We must also know that at some point the loop condition becomes false. We do this by requiring that as long as there is another iteration to perform, the bound function is greater than 0. We know there is another iteration to perform if (1) the invariant is true and (2) the loop condition is true.

Thus, the second property that a bound function must satisfy is this:

> 2. The invariant, together with loop condition, must imply that the bound function is greater than 0.

In our example, from the invariant and the loop condition, we conclude that i < n , and from this we conclude n – i > 0, as required.

7.7   Miscellaneous points about loops

7.7.1   There are no nested loops

Activity
7-6.1

We write a program to count the number of primes in 2..99. Recall that a prime is an integer that is greater than 1 and is divisible by only 1 and itself.

We can use the natural-number for-loop schema for this purpose and write the program, with part of it abstract, fairly quickly. The only part that is abstract and needs to be refined is the question of whether i is a prime.

```
// Set x to the number of primes in 2..99
int x= 0;
// { invariant: x = the number of primes in 2..i-1 }
for (int i= 2; i != 100; i= i + 1) {
    if (i is prime) { x= x + 1; }
}
```

Changing the task slightly to fit previously written code

In Sec. 7.4.3, we wrote code to test whether an integer is prime. To prepare for using this code, we change the program segment to set a boolean variable depending on whether i is prime and then use this task before the test and change the test accordingly:

See lesson page 7.6 to obtain the final program

```
// Set x to the number of primes in 2..99
int x= 0;
// { invariant: x = the number of primes in 2..i-1 }
for (int i= 2; i != 100; i= i + 1) {
    Set fresh variable b to "i is prime";
    if (b) { x= x + 1; }
}
```

Implementing the assignment to b

We now implement the statement b = "i is prime", using the code from Fig. 7.4, with slight adjustments. With this preparation, we can now move this code into the program. The result appears in Fig. 7.6. This completes the development of the program to compute the number of primes in 2..99.

How to read Fig. 7.6

Activity 7.6-2

When reading the program segment of Fig. 7.6 for the first time, try to understand the outer loop. In doing so, view its repetend as a sequence of two statements:

```
Set fresh variable b to "i is prime";
if (b) { x= x + 1; }
```

```
// Set x to the number of primes in 2..99
int x= 0;
// { invariant: x = the number of primes in 2..i-1 }
for (int i= 2; i != 100; i= i + 1) {
    // Set fresh variable b to "i is prime";
    boolean b= i > 1;
    int k= 2;
    // { invariant: b == i > 1 and no integer in 2..k-1 divides i }
    while (b && k != i) {
        if (i % k == 0) { b= false; }
        k= k + 1;
    }
    if (b) { x= x + 1; }
}
```

Figure 7.6:   Computing the number of primes in 2..99

> The point made in this paragraph is much better made in Activity 7-6.2!

Do *not* read the implementation of the first statement, which is given in Fig. 7.6 as a *statement-comment* (see Sec. 13.3.3). The purpose of the statement-comment is to let you focus on one thing at a time. When reading the outer loop, focus on *what* this statement does. Later, you can go back and see *how* this statement is implemented by reading the code following it up until the first blank line. And when focusing on *how* this statement is implemented, put the rest of the program out of your mind.

This ability to read at various *levels of abstraction* is important, for it lets you *separate your concerns* and focus on one thing at a time. *Focus* is the important point here.

Some people will tell you that nested loops —one loop appearing in the repetend of another— are difficult to understand. They are, if loops are not properly annotated or well structured. But in our view, the program segment of Fig. 7.6 does not have nested loops! The repetend of the outer loop is:

```
Set fresh variable b to "i is prime";
if (b) { x= x + 1; }
```

and, in this view, there is no concept of a loop.

7.7.2   How not to program

Activity 7-6.3

A student developed the code of Fig. 7.7. We have abstracted away from the task and cleaned up the code in order to make it easier to make our point. The program did not work correctly, and it took him a long time to find out that c needed to be set to 0 when r was incremented, as shown below:

```
// Process pairs (r,c), for 0 ≤ r < R, 0 ≤ r < C
int r= 0;   int c= 0;
while (r != R) {
    while (c != C)
        { Process pair (r,c); c= c + 1; }
    r= r + 1;   c= 0;
}
```

But this code is not well designed. The handling of variable c —initializing

```
// Process pairs (r,c), for 0 ≤ r < R, 0 ≤ r < C
int r= 0;   int c= 0;
while (r != R) {
    while (c != C) {
        Process pair (r,c);   c= c + 1;
    }
    r= r + 1;
}
```
Figure 7.7:   A program segment with an error

it to 0 and then setting it to 0 again at the end of the outer repetend— is just not good programming practice, as we will see in a moment.

The student's programming strategy

When asked about the absence of comments, the student replied that he had not gotten around to those yet.

> My way of programming is to write the program first, and later to fill in statement-comments and loop invariants and things.

He said this in spite of all our discussions of good programming practices and in spite of all our examples of top-down design. And his practices led to an error that took him a great deal of wasted time to find and to a bad design. In fact, providing comments after the fact is a waste of time.

When pressed for the invariant of the outer loop and for a statement-comment for the repetend of the outer loop, after some time and with help, the student said that the invariant was:

invariant: pairs (i, 0..C-1) with $0 \le i < r$ have been processed

And along with this came the statement-comment for the repetend:

Process pairs (r, 0), ..., (r, C - 1)

so that the segment could be interpreted as:

```
// Process pairs (r, c), for  0 ≤ r < R, 0 ≤ r < C
int r= 0;  int c= 0;
// inv: pairs (0..r-1, 0..C-1) have been processed
while (r != R) {
    Process pairs (r, 0), ..., (r, C - 1)
    r= r + 1;   c= 0;
}
```

```
// Process pairs (r,c), for  0 ≤ r < R, 0 ≤ r < C
int r = 0;
// invariant:  pairs (0..r-1, 0..C-1) have been processed
while (r != R) {
    // Process pairs (r, 0), ..., (r, C - 1)
    int c= 0;
    // invariant:  pairs (r, 0), ..., (r, c - 1) have been processed
    while (c != C) {
        Process pair (r, c);   c= c + 1;
    }
    r= r + 1;
}
```

Figure 7.8:   A well-designed segment to process pairs

In this version, c is not mentioned in the invariant, so why is it set to 0 in two places? What purpose does it serve? What meaning would you give c if it were to be mentioned in the invariant? Variable c has no place in the program, and it should be deleted. There is absolutely no reason for it being in there.

After removing c and then implementing the statement:

Process pairs (r, 0), …, (r, C - 1)

we wind up with the program segment of Fig. 7.8. There is a variable c, but it is local to the implementation of the above statement.

We now have a well-designed program segment.

7.8   Key concepts

• **Loop**. A *repetitive statement*, or *iterative statement*, or *loop* is a statement that calls for the repeated execution of its *repetend*.

• **While-loop**. The *while-loop* has the form: **while** (*condition*) *repetend*.

• **For-loop**. The *for-loop* has the form: **for** (*initialization ; condition ; progress*) *repetend*. It can be viewed as an abbreviation of a while-loop that has a *loop counter*.

• **Loop invariant**. A *loop invariant* is a relation that is true before and after each loop iteration. A loop is understood in terms of the loop invariant by answering four loopy questions:

1. **How does it start?** What assignments make the invariant true initially?

2. **When does it stop?** The invariant, together with the falsity of the loop condition, has to imply that the postcondition is true.

3. **How does it make progress?** Execution of the repetend has to ensure that after a finite number of iterations the loop terminates.

4. **How does it fix the loop invariant?** Each execution of the repetend begins with the invariant true, and it must end with it true as well.

• **Nested loops**. Abstraction should be used to hide nested loops: use a statement-comment that says what the repetend does, which can be used to understand the outer loop without thinking in terms of nested loops.

Exercises for Chapter 7

Many of these exercises ask you to write a loop (with initialization), given the task to be performed, a postcondition, and loop invariant. Develop the loop using the four loopy questions. This allows you to *separate your concerns*. For example, when writing the initialization, you do not worry about the loop condition or repetend, you just ask yourself what needs to be done to truthify the invariant. When you are finished writing the loop, test it in your IDE! That is the only way to be sure you did it properly.

E1. Write four loops (with initialization) to store in x the product of the integers in the range 2..10. The postcondition R is: x is the product of 2..10.

(a) Use this invariant P1. It was created by replacing constant 10 in R by k:

P1: 2 ≤ k ≤ 10 and x is the product of 2..k

(b) Use this invariant P2. It was created by replacing constant 10 in R by k − 1:

P2: 2 ≤ k ≤ 11 and x is the product of 2..k-1

(c) Use this invariant P3. It was created by replacing constant 2 in R by k:

P3: 2 ≤ k ≤ 10 and x is the product of k..10

(d) Use this invariant P4. It was created by replacing constant 2 in R by k + 1:

P4: 1 ≤ k ≤ 10 and x is the product of k+1..10

E2. Write four loops (with initialization) to determine whether an integer n is divisible by an integer in the range `first..last`, where `first ≤ last`. The answer is stored in a boolean variable b: the postcondition R is:

R: b = "n is divisible by an integer in `first..last`"

(a) Use this invariant P1, which was created by replacing `last` in R by k:

P1: b = first − 1 ≤ k ≤ last and
       "n is divisible by an integer in `first..k`"

(b) Use this invariant P2. It was created by replacing constant `last` in R by k-1:

P2: first ≤ k ≤ last + 1 and

       b = "n is divisible by an integer in `first..k-1`"

(c) Use this invariant P3. It was created by replacing constant `first` in R by k:

P3: first ≤ k ≤ last+1 and b = "n is divisible by an integer in `k..last`"

(d) Use this invariant P4. It was created by replacing constant `first` in R by k+1:

P4: first−1 ≤ k ≤ last and
       b = "n is divisible by an integer in `k+1..last`"

E3. Given is n > 0. Write a loop (with initialization) to store in k the largest power of 2 that is at most n. Note that $2^0 = 1$. The obvious way to calculate k is to successively set k to 1, 2, 4, 8, ... until the right power of 2 is reached. Use the postcondition R and invariant P shown below. Note how P is R with the last constraint $n < 2^{k+1}$ remove:

$$R:\ 1 \le 2^k \le n < 2^{k+1}$$
$$P:\ 1 \le 2k \le n$$

E4. Write a loop to calculate the quotient q and remainder r when x ≥ 0) is divided by y (> 0), using just addition and subtraction (no multiplication or division). The four variables are related by this formula:

$$x\,/\,y\ =\ q\ +\ r\,/\,y \qquad \text{where } 0 \le r < y$$
$$\text{i.e.} \qquad x\ =\ y * q\ +\ r \qquad \text{where } 0 \le r < y$$

Use the loop invariant P:

$$P:\ x\ =\ y * q\ +\ r* \quad \text{and } 0 \le r$$

which arises from the formula by deleting the constraint $r < y$.

E5. Given is x > 0 and y > 0, both integers. Find the greatest common divisor of x and y, written as x gcd y. This is the largest integer that divides both. Use these properties of gcd:

$$x \text{ gcd } y\ =\ (x-y) \text{ gcd } y$$
$$x \text{ gcd } y\ =\ x \text{ gcd } (y-x)$$
$$x \text{ gcd } x\ =\ x$$

Use two fresh variables b and c and the following postcondition and invariant:

$$R:\ b\ =\ x \text{ gcd } y$$
$$P:\ b \text{ gcd } c\ =\ x \text{ gcd } y$$

E6. Write code to delete all the vowels in `String t`. Here is the outline:

```
StringBuffer s= new StringBuffer(t);
Delete the vowels in s.
t= s.toString();
```

Answer the four loopy questions to develop the loop using the following invariant and postcondition:

> invariant: `s[0..k-1]` contains no vowels and `k != s.length()`.
> // postcondition R: `s[0..s.length()-1]` contains no vowels

Hint: Use `StringBuffer` method `deleteCharAt`. Also, be wary of your increment: you can make progress in two different ways.

E7. Deoxyribonucleic acid, or *DNA* for short, is the building block of all life. Each strand of DNA consists of two strings of *bases* twisted together to form a double helix. There are four bases, which are represented by the letters G, A, T and C. In a double helix, the letters A and T bond together, as do the letters C and G. The two sequences in a helix, then, are complements of each other. For example, these two sequences are complements of each other:

> sequence 1: `ACGTTAC`
> sequence 2: `TGCAATG`

Notice how the A's and T's line up with each other, as do the C's and G's. Write a loop to determine if two `String`s `s1` and `s2` representing DNA sequences are complements of each other. What do you need to assume about the lengths of those `String`s?

E8. Write a loop to produce the DNA complement of a `String` s.

E9. The Fibonacci numbers are the numbers 0, 1, 1, 2, 3, 5, 8, ... Each number is the sum of the previous two. This *recurrence relation* describes the sequence:

> $f_0 = 0$
> $f_2 = 1$
> $f_n = f_{n-1} + f_{n-2}$ for n > 1

Write code that finds Fibonacci number n, where n > 1. Use this invariant:

invariant: $a = f_i$ and $b = f_{i-1}$
postcondition: $i = n$ (and, therefore, $a = f_n$)

E10. Write a loop that reads a file containing integers and computes their sum.

E11. Write a loop that reads a file containing integers and computes how many even integers and how many odd integers it contains.

E12. *Compound interest* on an account is computed as follows: if an account has balance `balance`, and the annual interest rate is `rate`, the next year's balance is this:

> `balance + balance * rate`

Write a program segment that reads the initial dollar balance (a **double**), the interest rate (also a **double**, such as `.07` to represent a 7% interest rate), and the number of years to calculate (an **int**), and computes the final balance in the account.

E13. Write a loop (with initialization) that generates an approximation to e, the "base of the natural logarithm", using this formula:

> `e  =  1 + 1/1! + 1/2! + 1/3! + 1/4! +  ...  + 1/k! +  ...`

(You can see what e is by evaluating `Math.E`.) Here, `k!` is "k factorial", the quantity `1*2*...*k`. Use this invariant:

> `e  =  1 + 1/1! + 1/2! + 1/3! + 1/4! +  ...  + 1/k!` and
> `tk = 1/k!`

Use type **double** for e and tk. At each iteration, calculate the next term

`1/(k+1)`! to be calculated using `tk`. Terminate the loop when `tk` < `.1*10`^{13}. How many iterations does it take?

E14. Write a loop (with initialization) that generates an approximation to pi, the ratio of the diameter of a circle to its circumference. Do the work as in exercise E13, but use this formula to calculate approximations:

```
pi  =  4 - 4/3 + 4/5 - 4/7 + 4/9 - ...
```

Is this feasible? How many iterations does it take?

E15. Write a loop (with initialization) that generates an approximation to pi, ratio of the diameter of a circle to its circumference. Do the work as in exercise E14, but use this formula to calculate approximations, where c is `2*sqrt(3)`:

```
pi  =  c - c/(3*3¹) + c/(5*3²) - c/(7*3³) + c/(9*3⁴) - ...
```

Calculate c only once. Is this feasible —how many iterations does it take?

E16. Here is another way to calculate pi. Throw random darts at a disk of radius 1 that is inscribed in a 2x2 square. The fraction hitting the disk should be the ratio of the area of the circle, to the area of the square: `pi*r`^{2} / `(2r)`^{2}, or `pi/4`. To throw a dart, calculate two random numbers `(x, y)` in the range –2..2. The dart hits the disk if `x`^{2}`+y`^{2} `<= 1`. Write a loop (with initialization) that calculates an approximation to pi by throwing random 10,000 darts.

E17. Write a loop to count how many times the vowel "a" occurs in a string s.

E18. Write a loop to count how many vowels a string s contains.

E19. Write a loop to count how many pairs of adjacent equal characters are in a string s. The string "`bbbccd`" contains three pairs of adjacent equal values.

Chapter 8

Arrays

OBJECTIVES

- Learn how to declare an array variable.
- Understand that Java treats an array as an object.
- Learn how to create an array and store its name in a variable.
- Learn how to initialize array elements and reference them.
- Look at an array as a way to store a table of data of the same type.
- Learn fundamental algorithms for searching, sorting, and maintaining arrays.

INTRODUCTION

Suppose a program has to maintain information about students enrolled in a university. It is infeasible to declare a separate variable for each student! The Java *array* —a list of variables of the same type— can be used in such situations.

8.1   Arrays of subscripted variables

The diagram below shows an array variable b and an array object a0, which consists of four elements of type **int**:

b [a0]

```
        a0
   0     5
   1     7
   2     4
   3    −2
```

The four variables are called the *elements* of the array, and as indicated in the above diagram, they are numbered 0, 1, 2, and 3. They are referenced individually using the notation b[0], b[1], b[2], and b[3]. Mathematical notation writes the numbers below the line, as in b_2, and calls the numbers *subscripts*. Similarly,

---

Java syntax: Subscripted variable

array [**int**-*expression*]

Examples: b[5]= b[4] + 2;

Purpose: To access an array element, to either retrieve its
value (as in b[4]) or change it (above, b[5] is changed).

---

the value 2 in b[2] is called the *subscript*, or *index*, of the array element. We call
b[2] a *subscripted variable*.

The *range* of an array is the set of values that can be used as indices. The
range of b consists of 0, 1, 2, and 3; we write this range as 0..3.

The following statement stores the sum of b[0] and b[1] in variable b[3]:

    b[3]= b[0] + b[1];

Any **int** expression can be used as an index. For example, if an **int** variable
x has the value 5, b[x − 4] refers to subscripted variable b[1].

8.1.1   Declarations of arrays

Below, we show a declaration of an array:

    int[] b;

The notation **int**[] is read as "**int** array", and b's type is **int**[]. Arrays are
objects. Just as the declaration:

    String s;

does not create a String object, b's declaration does not create an array object.
It merely declares that variable b *can* contain the name of an **int** array object.

Type **int** is called the *base type* of the array. Any type can be used as the
base type. Here is a declaration for an array of strings:

    String[] s;

8.1.2   Creating an array

To create an array object and assign it to b, use a new-expression in an assignment statement. The new-expression syntax is slightly different from other new-
expressions; no constructor is called. Here is an example:

    b= new int[4];

Common error. When using a subscripted variable b[i], the value of i must be within the range
of b —one of the values in 0..b.length − 1. If i is not in range, an IndexOut-
OfBoundsException occurs and execution aborts. Get in the habit of always
asking yourself, with each variable b[i] you write, whether i is within range.

Java syntax: Array type

type [ ]

Example: `int[]`

Meaning: *type*[ ] is the type of an array whose elements are of type *type*.

Java syntax: new-array expression

new *type* [**int**-*expression*]

Example: `new double[15]`

Purpose: Evaluation creates an array object with *expression* elements, all of type *type*, and has as its value the name of the object.

Execution of this statement proceeds as follows:

1. Evaluate the new-expression: create an array of 4 **int** variables, give it a name (e.g. a0), and yield as the result of the expression the name (a0).
2. Store the name a0 in array variable b.

Once the array has been created, its size cannot be changed, so you have to figure out how many elements it should have before creating it.

You can combine declaration and initialization in an initializing declaration:

```
int[] b= new int[4];
```

8.1.3   Referencing the length of an array

Activity
8-1.2

Every array object has a fixed field `length`, which contains the number of elements in the array. Thus, if b is an array variable, the expression:

```
b.length
```

is the number of elements in, or length of, array b. Note that `length` is a variable and not a function, so no parentheses appear after it.

Activity
8-1.3 shows
execution of
such a loop

The loop below sets all the elements of array b to 72:

```
// inv: elements b[0..i-1] have been set to 72
for (int i= 0; i != b.length; i= i+1) {
    b[i]= 72;
}
```

8.1.4   Array initializers

Activities
8-1.4..5

The following sequence of statements creates an array c that contains the values 5, 6, 3, 4, and 4, but it is rather cumbersome:

```
int[] c= new int[5];
c[0]= 5; c[1]= 6; c[2]= 3; c[3]= 4; c[4]= 4;
```

Programming tip: Rather than typing 4 for the array size throughout your program, use `b.length`. That way, if you decide to change the size of the array, you need to make changes in only one place, where the array is created.

Java syntax: Array initializer

new *type* { *expr*$_1$, ..., *expr*$_n$ }

Example: **new** **int**[] {3, 5, 2}
Example: **int**[] b = {3, 5, 2};

Purpose: Create an array with the elements given in the list.
In an initializing declaration, "**new** *type*" is not needed.

Instead, you can use an *array initializer*:

```
int[] c= new int[] {5, 6, 3, 4, 4};
```

The new-expression in this assignment creates an array whose size is the number of values in the list, assigns the given values to the array elements, and yields as its value the name of the new array.

The next example illustrates two things. First, in an initializing declaration, the part "**new** *type*[]" can be omitted. Second, arbitrary expressions can be used as the expressions in an array initializer:

```
String[] s= {"Monday",
             new String("Tuesday"),
             "Wed" + "nesday"};
```

This creates a `String` array of three elements whose values are the strings "Monday", "Tuesday", and "Wednesday". (Of course, the second and third expressions can be written more simply.)

You can omit "**new** *type*[]" only in an initializing declaration and not, for example, in a simple assignment statement. Thus, the following is illegal:

```
c= {5, 6, 3, 4, 4};        // Illegal
```

8.1.5   Consequences of arrays as objects

Suppose we have two **int**[] variables b and c and a 4-element array:

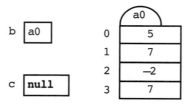

In this situation, we can create *aliasing* by executing this assignment:

```
c= b;
```

This stores in c the value that is in b:

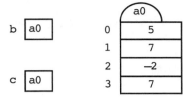

Consequently, b and c now refer to the same array. An assignment such as:

    b[1]= 6;

changes not only b[1] but also c[1], since b[1] and c[1] are one and the same.

8.1.6   Passing an array as an argument

Consider this procedure:

```
public void proc(int p1, int[] p2) {
    p1= 5;
    p2[1]= 6;
}
```

and a call to it, where b contains the name a0 of an **int**[] array object:

    proc(10, b);

The frame for the call contains parameters p1 and p2, with values 10 and a0:

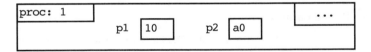

Notice that b and p2 refer to the same array object.

You already know that the assignment p1= 5; in the body of procedure proc has no effect outside the method; it changes only parameter p1, not the corresponding argument. But, since p2 contains a0, the assignment p2[1]= 6; changes array a0 and thus has an effect outside the procedure.

Because Java passes arguments "by value", it is impossible to write a procedure that is consistent with this specification:

```
/** Swap x and y */
public static void swap(int x, int y)
```

However, we can write a procedure that swaps two array elements:

```
/** Swap b[i] and b[j] */
public static void swap(int[] b, int i, int j) {
    int temp= b[i];
    b[i]= b[j];
    b[j]= temp;
}
```

This fact will be quite useful for writing code for sorting arrays.

8.1.7   Initializing class-type arrays

Be careful when creating an array whose base type is some class type, for the array element themselves are initially **null**. Consider the following statement:

```
String d= new String[4];
```

After execution, each element of d automatically contains **null**, as shown to the left in Fig. 8.1. String objects must be explicitly created; for example, after the assignment d[2]= "xyz";, the array is as shown in the right diagram of Fig. 8.1.

8.2   Talking about array segments

In every scientific field, notation is developed to concisely and clearly discuss concepts of that field. It will help us to take some time to do the same for talking about arrays.

8.2.1   Range notation: h..k

We have already introduced the notation 4..7 to stand for the range of integers 4, 5, 6, and 7. In general, we can use integer expressions instead of constants. Here are two examples:

> h..k   stands for the collection of integers h, h + 1, h + 2, ..., k − 1, k.
> The range of an array b is 0..b.length − 1.

By convention, the range h..h − 1 stands for an empty collection of integers. Thus:

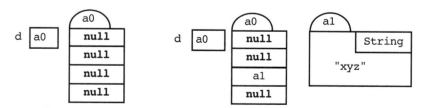

Figure 8.1:   Initializing array elements

h..h+2	stands for the set of 3 integers h, h + 1, and h + 2.
h..h+1	stands for the set of 2 integers h, h + 1.
h..h	stands for the set of 1 integer, h.
h..h−1	stands for the set of 0 integers.

The last example may seem strange to you, but this convention simplifies array discussions tremendously. We could have chosen to have h..h−1 be undefined, but that would not be as useful.

We often talk about a *segment* of an array: a sequence of adjacent elements like b[4], b[5], b[6], b[7], using the range notation in the subscript position: b[4..7]. To denote a segment b[h..b.length-1], we may omit the last index and write b[h..].

8.2.2   Horizontal descriptions of arrays.

Instead of a vertical representation of an array, we often use a horizontal version, as shown below. And we often simplify the picture: we place the name of the variable directly next to the array and omit the name of the array. (Do not change your mental picture! An array variable still contains the name of an array object.) Note that we put the indices of the array elements above the elements, not below.

	0	1	2	3
b	4	6	−5	2

It helps to think of an array as being partitioned into several segments rather than individual elements. The first segment pictured below is b[0..3]; the second is b[4..b.length−1]. We place a number after a segment boundary (e.g. 4) to indicate the subscript of the first element of a segment. We place a number before the boundary to indicate the last subscript of the segment.

As a final example, we show an array with three segments, with variables

```
        0                    3 4              b.length
  b   ┌─────────────────────────┬───────────────────┐
      │                         │                   │
      └─────────────────────────┴───────────────────┘
```

marking the boundaries. The segments are b[0..i−1], the segment consisting of the individual element b[i], and the segment b[i+1..]. If i is 3, the three segments are b[0..2], b[3..3], and b[4..].

A warning: the picture gives the impression that segment b[0..i−1] cannot

```
        0                     i               b.length
  b   ┌───────────────────────┬┬──────────────────────┐
      │                       ││                      │
      └───────────────────────┴┴──────────────────────┘
```

be empty. But if i is 0, the first segment is b[0..0−1], so it is an empty segment. In this case, the second segment consists of the first element of the array, b[0],

> **Programming tip:** When you draw horizontal arrays, do not place a variable (e.g. m) directly over a boundary, as shown below, because you cannot tell whether it marks the end of the preceding segment or the beginning of the following segment. This ambiguity leads to confusion. It will not make your instructor chuckle.
>
> ```
>           0              m
>      b  [       |            ]
> ```

and the third segment contains all but the first array element. To picture this mentally, think of dragging i all the way to 0. That squishes the first segment and stretches the right segment to take up most of the array.

8.2.3   Placing information in a segment

We can place information within a segment to describe its properties. In the example below, we place "< 3" in segment c[0..i−1] to assert that all its elements are less than 3. Similarly, we place "= 2" in the right segment to indicate that all its elements equal 2.

This picture describes a relationship between the contents of array c and

```
       0                        i              c.length
   c  [        < 3         | 5 |      = 2       ]
```

integer variable i. We call this relation P. We can write P without using a picture:

P: c[0..i−1] < 3 and c[i] = 5 and c[i+1..] = 2

Whether you prefer the picture or the formula is a matter of taste. The picture is easier to understand for most people, while the second version is usually easier to work with when developing an algorithm.

Relations may be true or false, depending on the values of the variables they reference. For example, P is a false statement if the first element of c is 4, no matter what the value of i. And P is true if i = 0 and c contains {5, 2, 2, 2} —the first segment is empty, so every element in that segment is indeed less than 3; the second segment contains a 5; and the third segment is all 2's.

Below are two more examples of relations. Relation Q1 says that the first segment b[0..i−1] is sorted, which means that its values are in non-descending order. For example, Q1 is true if i = 4 and b = {1, 3, 4, 4, −5, 2} but is false if i = 3 and b = {1, 4, 3, 3, 6, 8, 2}. Relation Q1 is used later in algorithm insertionSort, which sorts array b.

```
              0                    i            b.length
   Q1: b  [       sorted       |              ]
```

```
         0                    i              b.length
Q2: b   │ sorted, ≤ b[i..]  │ ≥ b[0..i − 1]  │
```

Relation Q2 is like Q1, but it also requires that everything in the first segment be at most everything in the second. Q2 is used in algorithm `selectionSort`, which is another sorting algorithm.

8.3   Processing array segments

8.3.1   Printing an array segment

We describe how to develop an array-printing algorithm using a relation. We can print the four values in array segment c[h..h+3] on different lines using four print statements. However, we cannot print the elements of c[h..k−1] in this manner because the number of elements is variable, and not a constant. Instead, we use a loop. To develop the loop, first write a postcondition for the task (this step is almost always easy):

   postcondition R: c[h..k−1] has been printed

To find a loop invariant P, we replace expression k by a fresh variable i:

   invariant P: c[h..i−1] has been printed

Here is a diagram for P:

```
        h                              i        k
P: b   │   these have been printed    │        │
```

How does it start? Since nothing has been printed initially, the invariant is truthified by making segment c[h..i−1] empty, i.e. by setting i to h.

When is it done? When the invariant and the postcondition are the same. That happens when i = k. Therefore, the loop should continue as long as i != k. And we now know the range of i: h ≤ i ≤ k.

How does it make progress? i starts at h and moves toward k, so to make progress toward termination, increment i.

How does it keep the invariant true? By printing c[i] before i is incremented.

Here is the final loop (with initialization):

```java
// Print c[h..k−1]
int i= h;
// inv: h ≤ i ≤ k and c[h..i−1] has been printed
while (i != k) {
    System.out.println(c[i]);
    i= i + 1;
}
```

Because this loops over a range, a **for**-loop could have been used instead:

```
// Print c[h..k-1]
// inv: h ≤ i ≤ k and c[h..i—1] has been printed
for (int i= h; i != k; i= i + 1) {
    System.out.println(c[i]);
}
```

8.3.2   A schema to process arrays

See lesson 8.3 to get these schemas from *ProgramLive*.

We step back from the loop above and make it more abstract, as shown below. First, instead of printing each array element, we say to "process it". Next, the invariant indicates what has been processed instead of what has been printed. Most of the loop remains the same! Only the repetend is changed, into an English statement to process element c[i].

```
// Process elements of c[h..k—1], in order
// inv: h ≤ i ≤ k and c[h..i—1] has been processed
for (int i= h; i != k; i= i + 1) {
    Process c[i]
}
```

Whenever you have to process an array segment, you can use this schema rather than develop the loop from scratch.

8.3.3   A schema to process in reverse

Activity
8-3.2

We develop a program schema to process the elements of array segment c[h..k—1], but in reverse order. First we write a postcondition:

postcondition: c[h..k—1] has been processed in reverse order

Now we find a loop invariant P. Since the elements are to be processed from the end to the beginning, we replace expression h by a fresh variable i:

invariant P: c[i..k—1] has been processed in reverse order

We now develop a **for**-loop.

How does it start? Because nothing has been processed initially, we truthify the invariant by setting i to k, making segment c[i..k—1] empty.

When is it done? Given the invariant, the postcondition is true when i = h. Therefore, the loop should continue as long as i differs from h. And we now know the range of i: h ≤ i ≤ k.

How does it make progress? Variable i starts at k and moves toward h, so to make progress toward termination, decrement i.

How does it keep the invariant true? From the loop invariant, we see that array element c[i − 1] should be processed.

> **Programming tip:** After you use a schema a few times, you will have digested it and will not have to look it up anymore. Be sure to always include the loop invariant because it is important for others to understand how the loop performs its task.

We end up with this algorithm:

See lesson page 8-3 to get this program.

```
//  Process the elements of c[h..k-1] in reverse order
//  inv. P: h ≤ i ≤ k and c[i..k-1] has been processed
for (int i= k; i != h; i= i − 1) {
      Process c[i - 1]
}
```

This algorithm has a somewhat awkward loop body in that it processes c[i − 1] and not c[i]. Let us change the algorithm so that the body can process c[i]. To do this, we need a new invariant for our postcondition:

postcondition: c[h..k-1] has been processed in reverse order

On the first iteration, c[k - 1] is to be processed. So i has to start at k − 1. Choosing this initialization forces us to use this invariant, replacing h with i + 1 instead of i:

inv: P: c[i + 1..k-1] has been processed

To make the range empty, i has to be initialized to k − 1. The invariant and the postcondition mean the same thing when i = h − 1. The range of i is now this: h − 1 ≤ i< k. Progress toward termination is still done by decrementing i:

```
//  Process c[h..k-1], in reverse order
//  inv: c[i + 1..k-1] has been processed and h − 1 ≤ i< k
for (int i= k − 1; i != h − 1; i= i − 1) {
      Process c[i]
}
```

Activity 8-3.3

Activity 8-3.3 develops an algorithm from this schema for reading in a list of values and printing them in reverse order.

8.3.4   Example: using a schema

Activity 8-3.4

This section illustrates the use of the loop schema from Sec. 8.3.2. We develop a function (see Fig. 8.2) that calculates the number of values in array b that are less than a given value v. For example, for array b = {8, 2, 3, 5, 7} and value v = 5, the function returns 2 because two elements of b are less than 5. Here is a specification of the function:

```
/** = number of elements of b that are less than v */
public static int numberLess(int[] b, int v)
```

How will this function be used? Given array d = {3, 5, 2, 7, 3}, the statement

```
int x= numberLess(d, d[0]);
```

stores 1 in x because one element of d is less than d[0].

The method body must process array segment b[0..b.length-1], so we use this loop schema for processing an array segment:

```
// Process elements of c[h..k-1], in order
// inv: h ≤ i ≤ k and c[h..i-1] has been processed
for (int i= h; i != k; i= i + 1) {
    Process c[i]
}
```

Instead of array c, we have b; instead of h, we have 0; and instead of k we have b.length:

```
// Process elements of b[0..b.length-1], in order
// inv: 0 ≤ i ≤ b.length and b[0..i-1] has been processed
for (int i= 0; i != b.length; i= i + 1) {
    Process b[i]
}
```

See lesson 8-3 to get this program.

Activity 8-3.5 shows you how to test it.

What does it mean to process an element b[i]? If the element is less than v, we want to count it, so we need a variable n to accumulate the result: n is the number of elements in segment b[0..i-1] that are less than v, so "Process b[i]" means to add 1 to n if b[i] is less than v.

What value should n have initially? At the beginning, no elements have been processed, so n must be initialized to 0.

The final step is to return n.

This ends the development. See Fig. 8.2 for the complete function.

```
/** = number of elements of b that are less than v */
public static int numberLess(int[] b, int v) {
    int n= 0; // number of elements less than v in b[0..j-1].

    // Process elements of b[0..b.length-1], in order
    // inv: 0 ≤ i ≤ b.length and the definition of field n
    for (int i= 0; i != b.length; i= i + 1) {
        if (b[i] < v)
            { n= n + 1; }
    }

    return n;
}
```

Figure 8.2:   Function numberLess

8.3.5   Checking equality of arrays

Suppose a1 and a2 are of type **int**[]. They contain the names of array objects (and not the arrays themselves), so a1 == a2 tests whether a1, a2 contain the same name rather than whether the array contents are equal. We write a method to compare the contents:

```
/** = "arrays a1 and a2 are equal" */
public static boolean equals(int[] a1, int[] a2)
```

The method is a function, and it returns **true** if the arrays are equal and **false** otherwise. The arrays are equal if (1) the parameters have exactly the same value or (2) the array objects have the same length and their corresponding elements are equal.

If a1 and a2 both are **null**, or if they contain the same array name, the function returns **true**. (In many situations, a method may require its array parameters to be not **null**. Here, it makes sense to allow **null** array arguments.)

If one of a1 and a2 contains **null** but the other does not, the arrays are not equal, so the function returns **false**.

If a1 and a2 have different lengths, the function returns **false**.

At this point, the arrays have the same length, so their elements have to be compared for equality. We use the loop schema from Sec. 8.3.2:

```
// Process elements of c[h..k-1], in order
// inv: h ≤ i ≤ k and c[h..i-1] has been processed
for (int i= h; i != k; i= i + 1)
    { Process c[i] }
```

Instead of array c, we have a1; instead of h, we have 0; and instead of k we have a1.length. We also update the invariant.

See lesson page 8-3 to get this program.

Activity 8-3.5 shows you how to test it.

```
/** = "arrays a1 and a2 are equal" */
public static boolean equals(int[] a1, int[] a2) {
    if (a1 == a2) { return true; }

    if (a1 == null || a2 == null) { return false; }

    if (a1.length != a2.length) { return false; }

    // Return false if a1[i] != a2[i] for some i.
    // inv: 0 ≤ i ≤ a1.length and a1[0..i-1] = a2[0..i-1]
    for (int i= 0; i != a1.length; i= i + 1) {
        if (a1[i] != a2[i])
            { return false; }
    }

    return true;
}
```

Figure 8.3:   Function equals, to check the equality of arrays

> **Programming tip:** Procedure `arraycopy` in class `System` of package `java.lang` will copy an array segment. To copy the k items in `b[i..i+k-1]` to `c[h..h+k-1]`, use
>
> ```
> System.arraycopy(b, i, c, h, k);
> ```
>
> The copy works even if b and c refer to the same array object and the two segments overlap. See the API specification for details.

```
// Process elements of a1[0..a1.length-1], in order
// inv: 0 ≤ i ≤ a1.length and a1[0..i-1] = a2[0..i-1]
for (int i= 0; i != a1.length; i= i + 1) {
    Process a[i]
}
```

What does it mean to process an element `a1[i]`? Here, it means to return **false** if `a1[i]` is not equal to `a2[i]`.

Because the loop processes every element, if the loop terminates without returning, return **true** at the end of the method.

This ends the development of the code. Fig. 8.3 contains the function.

8.3.6   Returning an array

Activity
8-3.7

Just as an array can be an argument of a method, it can be the result of a function. To indicate that the result is an array, just use the array type as the return type. We illustrate this with a function that produces a copy of an array segment:

```
/** = a copy of array segment b[x..y] */
public static int[] copy(int[] b, int x, int y)
```

See lesson
page 8-3 to get
this program.

How will the function be used? We give examples when d={3, 5, 2, 7, 3, 8}:

call	result	call range	result range
copy(d, 0, 2)	{3, 5, 2}	0..2	0..2
copy(d, 1, 4)	{5, 2, 7, 3}	1..4	0..3
copy(d, 2, 5)	{2, 7, 3, 8}	2..5	0..3
copy(d, 2, 1)	{}	2..1	0..-1
copy(d, i, j)	{...}	i..j	0..(j-i)

First, create a new array `result` in which to accumulate the result. Its size is the size of the array segment to be copied:

```
int[] result= new int[y + 1 - x];
```

We now have to write code to copy the elements of `b[x..y]` to `result[0..]`. We again use the loop schema from Sec. 8.3.2:

```
// Process elements of c[h..k-1], in order
// inv:  h ≤ i ≤ k and c[h..i−1] has been processed
for (int i= h; i != k; i= i + 1) {
     Process c[i]

}
```

We could use either b or result in place of c. We choose b, so instead of h we have x and instead of k − 1 we have y (i.e. instead of k we have y + 1):

```
// Process each element of b[x..y], in order
// inv:  x ≤ i ≤ y + 1 and b[x..i−1] has been processed
for (int i= x; i != y + 1; i= i + 1) {
     Process b[i]

}
```

Where in result do we put element b[i]? The first element b[x] goes into result[0], so b[i] goes into result[i - x]:

```
result[i - x]= b[i];
```

The invariant must say that everything before index i has been copied:

inv: b[x..i−1] has been copied to result[0..i−x−1]

After the loop terminates, the array segment has been copied to result.

This completes the development of the function to copy an array segment. See Fig. 8.4 for the function.

8.4   Storing tables of values in arrays

Consider maintaining a table of results of experiments, perhaps the number of seconds it takes a rat to run through a maze. A program may start off with no results in an array runningTimes (say) and, as the rat is run through the maze again and again, new results are added. Since the array size is given when the array is first created, the size must be large enough to contain all the experiment

```
/** = a copy of array segment b[x..y] */
public static int[] copy(int[] b, int x, int y) {
    int[] result= new int[x + 1 − y];

    // Process each element of b[x..y], in order
    // inv:  x ≤ i ≤ y + 1 and b[x..i−1] has been copied to c[0..i−x−1]
    for (int i= x; i != y+1; i= i + 1) {
        result[i - x]= b[i];
    }

    return result;
}
```

Figure 8.4:   A function to copy an array segment

results that will be added to it. We call the value `runningTimes.length` the *capacity* of the table —the total number of times the rat may be run through the maze. The program must maintain, in some fashion, the number of times the rat has been run so far, that is, the current size of the table. This is usually done using an **int** variable. The usual convention is to declare the following:

```
// Table of running times is runningTimes[0..numberOfRuns − 1]
double[] runningTimes;
int numberOfRuns;
```

Here, we have declared not only the array but variable `numberOfRuns`, which says how many running times are in the table. Further, the comment says *where* these times are stored in the array —in the first `numberOfRuns` elements. Here is an example array, which contains four running times.

0	1	2	3	numberOfRuns		runningTimes.length
29.5	99.9	99.0	47.2		?	

We place a question mark in section `runningTimes[numberOfRuns..]` to indicate that we do not know (or care) what values are in it.

Adding a new running time `t` (say) would then be done as follows —taking the approach that the insertion is done only if there is room and that a message is printed if there is no room:

```
if (numberOfRuns < runningTimes.length) {
    runningTimes[numberOfRuns]= t;
    numberOfRuns= numberOfRuns + 1;
} else {
    System.out.println("Sorry, array is full");
}
```

Sometimes we may want to delete the last value, perhaps because of a typing mistake. That is easy: simply decrement `runningTimes`:

```
runningTimes= runningTimes - 1;
```

Doing this when the table has four values, as shown above, terminates in this state:

0	1	2	numberOfRuns		runningTimes.length
29.5	99.9	99.0	47.2	?	

Element `runningTimes[3]` still contains the value 47.2. But we *do not care* about it; only elements `runningTimes[0..numberOfRuns-1]` are relevant.

In other situations, we may want to remove an arbitrary element `runningTimes[i]`, where $0 \le i < numberOfRuns$, as shown below:

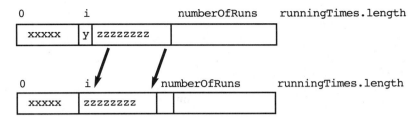

How this is done depends on whether the order of the values in the table must remain the same. If so, then code of the following form is needed:

```
numberOfRuns= numberOfRuns − 1;
Copy runningTimes[i + 1..numberOfRuns]
        to runningTimes[i..numberOfRuns−1]
```

Obviously, the time taken is proportional to the number of values to be copied.

If the order of the values does not matter, there is a much simpler and faster way to perform the task: just move the last element to `runningTimes[i]`:

```
numberOfRuns= numberOfRuns − 1;
runningTimes[i]= runningTimes[numberOfRuns];
```

(This works even if `i = numberOfRuns − 1`, in which case the last element is being removed. In this case, the second assignment has no effect, since it assigns `runningTimes[i]` to `runningTimes[i]`. It is better to leave the code like this than to use an `if`-statement to test for a special case; avoid unnecessary case analysis.)

8.4.1   Changing the size of an array

As mentioned earlier, the size of an array object is determined when the array is first created, and it cannot be changed. However, it is possible to make it look like the array size has been changed by creating a second, larger, array and copying the first array into the beginning of the second. Naturally, doing this takes time, and this copying should not be done often. To prevent frequent copying, and also limit unused space, it is common to double the size of the array. Here is code to perform this service:

```
// Double the size of array runnningTimes  (if size > 0)
double[] temp= new double[2 * runningTimes.length];
System.arraycopy(runningTimes, 0, temp,
                    0, runningTimes.length);
runningTimes= temp;
```

This code can be executed whenever array `runningTimes` runs out of space, instead of simply giving an error message and aborting program execution. See also *ProgramLive* activities 8-4.4 and 8-4.5.

8.5   Basic array algorithms

Lessons
8-5..6

There are a few fundamental array algorithms that programmers should know:

See lesson
pages 8-5..6 to
get these algorithms.

- linear search, for finding the first occurrence of a value in an array.
- finding the minimum value in an array.
- inserting a value into a sorted (in non-descending order) segment.
- partitioning an array.
- merging two sorted array segments.
- binary search for a value in an ordered array.
- insertion sort.
- selection sort.

We show some of the algorithms here; the rest can be found in *ProgramLive*.

It is difficult to memorize the code for these algorithms. Instead, *memorize the loop invariant and develop the algorithm from the invariant whenever necessary*. Here is a less threatening way to say that: remember the pictures and develop code based on them.

8.5.1   Linear search

Activities
8-5.1..2

We develop an algorithm to satisfy this specification:

```
/** = the index of the first occurrence of v in b[h..k−1]
        —or k  if v is not in b[h..k−1]  */
public static int linearSearch(int[] b, int h, int k, int v)
```

How will this function be used? Examples when d = {3, 5, 1, 7, 3, 8}:

call	result
linearSearch(d, 0, 2, 3)	0
linearSearch(d, 0, 2, 4)	2
linearSearch(d, 4, 6, 8)	5
linearSearch(d, 4, 6, 2)	6
linearSearch(d, 4, 4, 2)	4

Activity 8-5.1 of *ProgramLive* explains linear search by giving the invariant in terms of math formulas. Here, we draw diagrams. There are two possible postconditions of the method (we show only the part b[h..k−1] of the array):

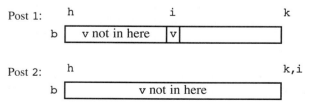

We can combine the two like this to make postcondition R:

Post R: h   i   k

b [v not in here [   ]   and (i = k or b[i] = v)

To find the loop invariant, we investigate postcondition R. It is easy to initialize i so that b[h..i-1] does not contain v: just set i to h, since then b[h..i−1] is empty and v is not in it. And, like the schema you have seen, that array segment can grow. The second part of R, "either i = k or b[i] = v", is really what we are trying to accomplish and may not be true with i = h. So, we take just the first part of R as the invariant:

inv P: h   i   k

b [v not in here [   ]

How does it start? As discussed in the previous paragraph, we set i to h.

When is the loop done? When we have the piece of the postcondition that we eliminated: when either i = k or b[i] = v. So the loop must continue as long as this condition is false. Using De Morgan's law:

not(A || B) = (**not** A && **not** B)

we see that the loop condition can be written in Java as: i != k && b[i] != v.

How does the repetend make progress? Increment i.

How does the repetend keep the invariant true? We get lucky: from the loop condition, we see that the increment happens only when b[i] != v, so no other work needs to be done.

See Fig. 8.5 for the complete method.

8.5.2   Finding the minimum value

Activity 8-5.3

We develop a function to return the index of a minimum value in an array segment:

```
/** = index of first occurrence of  v in b[h..k - 1] (= k if v is not in b[h..k − 1]) */
public static int linearSearch(int[] b, int h, int k, int v) {
    int i= h;

    // inv P: h ≤ i ≤ k and  v is not in b[h..i − 1]}
    while (i != k && v != b[i])
       { i= i + 1; }

    return i;
}
```

Figure 8.5: Function linearSearch

/** = index of minimum value of b[h..k]. Precondition: h ≤ k. */
public static int min(**int**[] b, **int** h, **int** k)

To watch this
algorithm exe-
cute, listen to
activity 8-5.3.

Calling this function makes sense only if the array segment has at least one value; hence the precondition.

How will this function be used? Examples when d = {1, 5, 1, 7, 3, 8}:

call	result
min(d, 0, 5)	0 or 2
min(d, 1, 5)	2
min(d, 3, 5)	4
min(d, 1, 1)	1

The call min(d, 0, 5) is interesting: the specification does not say which minimum value will be returned if the minimum value occurs more than once.

The heart of this function is a loop to find the index m of a minimum value. We now develop it. Because we are allowed to return the index of *any* smallest value, we choose to return the first one. Here is the postcondition:

Post R:

h		m		k
b	> v	v	≥ v	

We can get an invariant by replacing k by a fresh variable i:

inv P:

h		m	i	k
b	> v	v	≥ v	?

How does it start? At the beginning, the smallest value found so far is in b[h]. So we set both i and m to h.

When is it done? The invariant and postcondition look the same when i = k.

How does it make progress? Increment i to make unknown section smaller.

```
/** = index of minimum value of b[h..k]. Precondition: h ≤ k */
public static int min(int[] b, int h, int k) {
    int m= h;   int i= h;

    // {inv: b[m] is the minimum of b[h..i]}
    while (i != k) {
        i= i + 1;
        if (b[i] < b[m])
            { m= i; }
    }

    return m;
}
```

Figure 8.6: Function min

How does it keep the invariant true? If the new value at b[i] is smaller than
m, store m in i.

See Fig. 8.6 for the complete method. The loop could have been developed
by refining a suitable loop schema. Try this yourself!

8.5.3 Binary search

Activity
8-5.8

The linear search algorithm of Sec. 8.4.1 may have to look at all the elements of
the array segment that it is searching. If the array segment is in ascending order,
far fewer elements may have to be looked at because the search can stop as soon
as an element larger than v is detected. So, we now investigate an algorithm to
search a sorted array.

We develop an algorithm to satisfy this specification:

```
/** = index i such that R: b[h..i] ≤ v < b[i+1..k]
        Precondition: b[h..k] is in non-descending order */
public static int binarySearch(int[] b, int h, int k, int v)
```

We determine what R means, using the fact that b is in ascending order. If v
occurs in b, the postcondition indicates that the index of the rightmost occurrence
of v is to be calculated. For example, if v is 6, the index of the rightmost 6 is to
be calculated.

Second, if v is not in b, for example, v = 3, then the index of the position
after which v could be inserted should be calculated. As another example of this,
if v is less than the first element, the value h − 1 should be returned because
b[h..h−1] < v < b[h..k].

How will this function be used? Examples when d = {1, 3, 3, 5, 7, 8}:

call	result
binarySearch(d, 0, 2, 3)	2
binarySearch(d, 0, 2, 4)	2
binarySearch(d, 4, 6, 8)	5
binarySearch(d, 4, 6, 2)	4
binarySearch(d, 4, 4, 2)	4

The heart of this function is a loop to find the index i of v, which we now
develop. To find the loop invariant, note that it is easy to truthify the first part of
postcondition R by setting i to h − 1, and it is easy to truthify the second part of
assertion R by setting i to k. But, obviously, we cannot do both! We break this
dependence of both parts on i by replacing expression i + 1 by a fresh variable
j, giving us the invariant:

P: b[h..i] ≤ v < b[j..k]

If it helps, write the invariant as a diagram:

h		i		j		k
	≤ v			> v		

P is then initially truthified by assigning h − 1 to i and k + 1 to j. Then, b[h..h−1] and b[k+1..k] are empty segments.

The loop can terminate with R true only if j = i + 1. Therefore, it should continue as long as j and i + 1 are different. And, we can now place some obvious bounds on i and j in the invariant:

$$\text{P: } -1 \le i < j \le k + 1 \text{ and } b[h..i] \le v < b[j..k]$$

The repetend has to make progress by incrementing i or decrementing j. To that end, let e be the average of i and j. Because i < j + 1, e lies strictly between i and j. This means that setting either j or i to e will keep the second part of invariant P true.

There are now two cases to consider: b[e] < v and v < b[e]. In the first case, setting i to e keeps P true because b[h..e] < v. In the second case, setting j to e keeps P true because v < b[e..k]. This ends the development of the repetend and thus of the loop. The complete function is in Fig. 8.7.

Discussion

For an array segment of size 2^n for some n ≥ 0, this binary search function always makes n + 1 iterations, looking at n+1 array elements, no matter what the contents of the array. For example, if the array size is 2^{15} = 32768, it will look at only 16 elements!

It may seem that stopping as soon as the value v is found would make the algorithm faster. However, this requires a second test in the body of the loop — one has to test for v < b[i] and v = b[i] — so the loop body is less efficient.

```
/** = the value i that satisfies R: b[h..i] ≤ v < b[i+1..k]
      Precondition: b[h..k] is sorted. */
public static int binarySearch(int[] b, int h, int k, int v) {
    int i= h − 1;
    int j= k + 1;
    // inv P: h − 1 ≤ i < j ≤ k + 1 and b[h..i] ≤ v < b[j..k]
    while (j != i + 1) {
        int e= (i + j) / 2;
        // { h − 1 ≤ i < e < j ≤ k + 1 }
        if (b[e] <= v) { i= e; }
        else { j= e; }
    }
    return i;
}
```

Figure 8.7: Function binarySearch

Further, mathematical analysis has shown that stopping when v is found saves, on the average, only one iteration. Thus, it is not worth it. Further, this binary search has three other advantages over most of the other binary searches that you will see in the literature:

1. It works when the array is empty (when h = k + 1).
2. Binary searches that stop when v is found find only a random v, and not the rightmost one.
3. Binary searches that stop when v is found do not produce any indication of where v should go if v is not in the array.

Moreover, this binary search algorithm is *memorable*; just remember the post-condition and how you get the invariant from the postcondition, and you can easily develop the algorithm whenever necessary.

8.5.4   Selection sort

By an array b being "sorted" we mean that its values are in ascending order: i < j implies that b[i] ≤ b[j]. To sort an array means to place its values in ascending order. We also say that an array is sorted in descending order if i < j implies that b[i] ≥ b[j].

Sorting is a fundamental process in computing. Here, we look at one sorting algorithm, selectionSort. Another one, insertionSort, is described in *ProgramLive* activity 8-6.3. Both of these sort algorithms are "quadratic" algorithms, in both the average case and worst case. This means that for an array of size n (say), their execution times are proportional to n^2. For example, it will take 10,000 units of time to sort an array of 100 elements. Faster sorting algorithms exist. Two of them, quickSort and mergeSort, are developed in Chap. 15.

We want a procedure that satisfies this specification:

```
/** Sort b: put its elements in non-descending order */
public static void selectionSort(int[] b)
```

The body of the procedure is a loop. For its loop invariant we choose:

```
/** Sort b —put its elements in ascending order */
public static void selectionSort(int[] b) {
    // inv P: 0 ≤ i < b.length and b[0..j-1] is sorted and b[0..j-1] ≤ b[j..]
    for (int j= 0; j != b.length; j= j + 1) {
        int p= the index of the minimum value of b[j..];
        // {b[p] is min of b[j..]}
        Swap b[j] and b[p]
    }
}
```

Figure 8.8:   Abstract view of SelectionSort

```
            0                       j              b.length
P: b    ┌───────────────────┬─────────────────────┐
        │ sorted, ≤ b[j..]  │                     │
        └───────────────────┴─────────────────────┘
```

Thus, the elements of the first segment are already in ascending order. Moreover, they are no larger than those in the second segment. Remember this invariant, and you can then develop the loop from it whenever necessary, as follows.

The invariant is initially truthified by setting j to 0, since that makes the first segment b[0..j-1] empty and makes the second segment b[j..] be the whole array. Execution of the loop can terminate when j= b.length, since then the second segment is empty and the first segment is the whole array and is sorted. Therefore, the loop can continue as long as j != b.length.

Progress is made toward termination by incrementing j. However, this will maintain the invariant only if b[j] is the minimum value of b[j..]. So, the repetend consists of statements to make b[j] have this property —see Fig. 8.8.

Note that the procedure is not yet completely in Java, since the assignment to p has its expression written in English and the swap statement has to be implemented. Nevertheless, if you are explaining selection sort to someone, always present it in this fashion. We are using abstraction to hide some of the Java code and bring out the essence of selection sort.

The assignment to p can be rewritten using function min of Sec. 8.4.3. Or, the function call can be expanded inline, so that the function body would be as shown in Fig. 8.9. The function body has nested loops. But do not think of them as nested loops. When studying the outer loop, view its repetend as:

> Set p to the index of the min value of b[j..]
> Swap b[j] and b[p]

```
/** Sort b  —put its elements in ascending order */
public static void selectionSort(int[] b) {
    // inv P: 0 ≤ j ≤ b.length and b[0..j-1] is sorted and b[0..j-1] ≤ b[j..]
    for (int j= 0; j != b.length; j= j + 1) {

        // Set p to the index of the minimum value of b[j..]
        int p= j; // will contain index of minimum
        // inv: j < h ≤ b.length and b[p] is the minimum of b[j..h-1]
        for (int h= j + 1; h != b.length; h= h + 1) {
            if (b[h] < b[p])
                { p= h; }
        }

        // Swap b[j] and b[p]
        int t= b[j]; b[j]= b[p]; b[p]= t; }
}
```

Figure 8.9: Function selectionSort

When seeing how the assignment to p is implemented, look at the code underneath the statement "set p to ..."; do not look at the rest of the program. Learning to read a program on different levels of abstraction like this is important. Study activities 8-6.1, 8-6.2, and 7-6.2 of *ProgramLive* for more information on not thinking in terms of nested loops.

Analysis of execution time

We analyze the execution time of `selectionSort`. Finding the minimum of a segment of size n requires n − 1 array comparisons. Therefore, the first iteration of the loop makes `b.length` − 1 array comparisons, the next iteration makes `b.length` − 2, etc. Here is the well-known formula for the sum of these values:

$$1 + 2 + \ldots + (\texttt{b.length} - 1) = (\texttt{b.length} - 1) * \texttt{b.length} / 2$$

Thus, selection sort requires on the order of $(\texttt{b.length})^2$ array comparisons. Hence, it is *quadratic* in the size of the array to be sorted.

8.6   Parallel vs. class-type arrays

A list of item names together with their prices can be maintained in two arrays:

```
/** The item names are in items[0..size−1]
     For each items[i], its price is in prices[i] */
String[] items= new String[1000];
double[] prices= new double[1000];
int size= 0;
```

Arrays `items` and `prices` are *parallel* arrays. If one had more data for each item, say its weight, or price for buying two at a time, one would have more parallel arrays.

While parallel arrays can be used in this fashion, and in some cases may be the quickest way to get a program going, they really are not good style. One problem with them is that a method that operates on the arrays must have all the parallel arrays as parameters. Also, a method that deals with one item, say `items[t]`, must be passed `prices[t]` and the corresponding elements of other parallel arrays. Further, once the program is written, it may be difficult to change it if a new parallel array is needed to contain some new property of items.

Better is to identify the *concept* involved —in this case, an item and its associated properties— and to define a class whose instances are these items:

```
public class Item {
    /** The name and price of the item */
    private String item;
    private double price;

    // Setter and getter methods would go here
}
```

and then to declare an array whose base type is this class:

```
Item[] items= new Item[1000];
```

Using a single array of a class type instead of parallel arrays will generally simplify program structure, shorten the code that processes the data, and make later modifications (such as adding a new property of items) easier.

8.7   Key concepts

• **Arrays**. An *array* a0 is an object that is a list of elements called *subscripted variables*.

• **Array variables**. An array variable b declared as

type [] b

(*type* is any type, e.g. **int** or JFrame), initially contains **null**. An assignment

b= **new** *type* [n];

creates an array object with n elements and assigns its name to b.

• **Subscripted variables**. When b contains (the name of) an array, it has b.length elements, or subscripted variables, which are named b[0], b[1], ..., b[b.length - 1]. In a subscripted variable b[i], integer i is called the *subscript* or *index*; i must be in the range 0..b.length-1.

• **Array initializers**. The new-expression **new** *type*[] $\{x_0, x_1, ..., x_{n-1}\}$ creates an array of size n whose elements initially contain the values of expressions x_0, x_1, ..., x_{n-1}. When used in an initializing declaration (only), this new-expression can be abbreviated as $\{x_0, x_1, ..., x_{n-1}\}$.

• **Array notations**. We use non-Java notation like b[h..k] to denote the segment of array b consisting of elements b[h], b[h + 1], ..., b[k]. Pictures are also used.

• **Tables**. Sometimes, an array is used to maintain a table of values whose size is less than the size of the array. In this case, be sure to explain in a comment near the declaration of the array where in the array the table of values is stored.

• **Array schemas**. Simple schemas exist for processing all elements of an array (or a table stored in an array). Their use can reduce programming time.

• **Parallel arrays**. Instead of arrays p1[0..n] and p2[0..n], use a single array p[0..n], where p[i] is an object that contains the values p1[i] and p2[i].

• **Basic algorithms**. There are several basic array algorithms that every programmer should be able to develop. Learn such an algorithm not by memorizing code but by memorizing its spec and then practicing developing it from its spec. Among these algorithms are: linear search, finding a minimum, binary search, and selection sort.

8.8   Self review exercises

SR1. State whether each of the following is true or false. If false, explain why.
(a) One element of an array can be an **int** and another can be a **double**.
(b) An array-element subscript should normally be of type **int**.
(c) An array can be created with zero elements.
(d) The index of an array element and its subscript are the same thing.
(e) After declaring b using **int**[ ] b;, one can store a value in b[0].

SR2. Fill in the blanks:
(a) Elements of an array have the same _____.
(b) To refer to the sixth element of array b, use the notation _____.
(c) In an array element reference like b[k], b[k] is called a _____,
and k is called the _____.
(d) The number of elements in an array d is _____.

SR3. Do the following tasks regarding an array sizes.
(a) Declare a final variable sizeOfSizes that is initialized to 15.
(b) Declare variable sizes so that it can contain an array with base type **int**.
(c) Create an **int** array with n elements and store the array name in sizes.
(d) Write Java code to set all the elements of array sizes to 0.
(e) Change the fifth element of array sizes to 4.
(f) Write Java code that sets the sixth element of sizes to 6, but only if the
fifth element is even.

Exercises for Chapter 8

Many of these exercises ask for a method to be written. When writing the
method, be sure you write a suitable specification for it before writing the
method body! And test your answers on the computer.

For more exercises, turn to lesson 8 of the *ProgramLive* CD and click on
button Work.

E1. Create an array to contain the number of hours worked by someone each day
in a five-day workweek. Use the following data: Monday, 6 hours; Tuesday, 5;
Wednesday, 7; Thursday, 8; Friday, 7. Write statements to compute the total
hours worked, the average number of hours per day, and the total earnings,
assuming $7.50 per hour.

E2. A bowling alley has 100 balls with the following weight distribution:

06 pounds: 10 balls	12 pounds: 20 balls
08 pounds: 10 balls	14 pounds: 20 balls
09 pounds: 15 balls	16 pounds: 10 balls
10 pounds: 15 balls	

Create an array of 100 elements to contain the weights of the balls. Do not write

100 assignment statements; instead, use loops. Write a program segment to compute the mean, median, and total weight of the balls.

E3. A different method of storing the bowling balls of the previous exercise is to use an array of seven elements, one for each weight, and to store the number of balls with each weight. Redo the previous exercise using this method. Discuss the advantages and disadvantages of the two methods.

E4. Write (and test) statements to do the following.
   (a) Set the elements of **int** array segment b[h..k] to 0.
   (b) Print the values of b[0..3] on the Java console on one line, separated by blanks.
   (c) Print the values of array b on the Java console, three on a line, with blanks separating the three.
   (d) Print the values of array b in reverse order on the Java console, three on a line, with blanks separating the three.
   (e) Add 1 to each element of **int** array b.
   (f) Store in x the sum of the values of array segment b[h..k].
   (g) Store in x the sum of every other value of b[h..k], beginning with the first.
   (h) Store in x the sum of every other value of b[h..k], beginning with the second.
   (i) Find the largest value of **int** array segment b[h..k-1].
   (j) Find the largest value of **int** array segment b[h..k-1], considering only every other value beginning with the first.
   (k) Store the largest and smallest values of array b[h..k-1], where h < k, in variables small and large. Use a single loop.

E5. A polynomial is an expression of the form $a_0 + a_1x^1 + a_2x^2 + \ldots + a_nx^n$. Write a function that computes the value of the polynomial given, as arguments, the integer n, the value x, and an array a that contains the coefficients $a_0, \ldots, a_n$. Make sure you specify the function properly.

E6. Write a function that tells how many odd numbers an **int** array contains.

E7. Write a function that tells how many elements of an **int** array have the value x (the array and x are parameters of the method.)

E8. Write a function that computes the average of the values of a **double** array segment b[h..k].

E9. Write a procedure that does the following. Each element of array segment b[0..n−1] contains a different integer in the range 0..n-1. The array segment contains a *permutation* of the values 0..n-1. Print the elements of b[0..n−1] in the following order: Print b[0]; then, assuming that b[0]=j, print b[j]; then, assuming b[j]=k, print b[k]; etc. In other words, print b[0], b[b[0]], b[b[b[0]]], etc.

E10. Write a procedure that changes array segment b[h..k-1] to the following: each element i, h ≤ i < k, should contain the sum of the original values of b[h..i]. Thus, if b = {3, 5, 2, 7, 8} initially, upon termination b = {3, 8, 10, 17, 25}. You should do this with one loop.

E11. Rewrite selection sort of Sec. 8.5.4 to use this loop invariant:

0 ≤ j ≤ b.length and b[j..] is sorted and b[0..j-1] ≤ b[j..]

E12. Another quadratic sorting algorithm is called *bubblesort*. It works as follows. First, array b is scanned beginning at b[0], swapping each adjacent pairs of elements to put the larger of the two second. This "bubbles" the largest value to the top —to b[b.length-1]. Next, start at b[0] and bubble the next largest to b[b.length-2]. Next, start at b[0] and bubble the next largest to b[b.length-2]. Continue this process. Implement bubblesort.

E13. Modify bubblesort of the previous exercise to stop as soon as one of the bubbling-up processes does not swap any array elements.

E14. Modify bubblesort of exercise E12 to alternate bubbling a larger value upward and bubbling a smaller value downward, stopping when one upward or downward pass does not swap any elements.

Chapter 9

Multi-dimensional Arrays

OBJECTIVES

- Learn how to create and use a rectangular array.
- Learn about ragged arrays of any dimension.

INTRODUCTION

Two-dimensional tables and the mathematical *matrix* can be implemented using rectangular arrays. However, although we may abstractly think in terms of a rectangular array, Java implements it in a way that allows rows of a rectangular array to have different lengths, giving us the so-called *ragged array*. In this chapter, we use what you have already learned about arrays in the previous chapter to show how to create and manipulate ragged arrays.

9.1   Rectangular arrays

Consider the following declaration and assignment statement:

```
int[ ][ ] b;
b= new int[2][3];
```

These differ from the declaration and assignment for a one-dimensional array in that there are two pairs of brackets, not one. This means that b contains the name of a two-dimensional array, or table, and not a one-dimensional array:

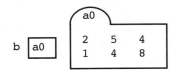

Above, we show array b as an object, assuming that some values have been assigned to its elements: Row 0 consists of the values {2, 5, 4}; row 1, the values {1, 4, 8}.

The number 2 within the first pair of brackets of the new-expression on the second line means that the array has two rows, numbered 0 and 1. The number 3 within the second pair of brackets means that the array has three columns, numbered 0, 1, and 2. Since the base type is **int**, each element is initialized to 0.

The type, or class, of b is **int**[ ][ ], so b contains either **null** or the name of an object of this type. A value of type **int**[ ][ ] is an object that is a two-dimensional array of **int** elements.

In general, any type (or class) may be used in place of **int**, and this type is the type of the array elements. It is the *base type*. Further, any **int** expression that yields a nonnegative number can be used between a pair of brackets; the expression within the first bracket pair gives the number of rows; the expression within the second bracket pair gives the number of columns.

Referencing an array element

The notation b[1][2] references the element in row 1 column 2 of two-dimensional array b. This is actually a variable, called a subscripted variable, so it could be used in the left of an assignment to change the element. For example, with b as shown above, the assignment statement:

```
b[1][2]= b[0][0] + 1;
```

changes array b to this:

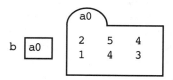

In mathematics, the notation $b_{r,c}$ would be used to reference the element, and many programming languages use the notation b[r, c]. Java has a reason for using the notation b[r][c], which will become clear in Sec. 9.3.

In an array-element reference like b[r][c], r and c must satisfy:

$0 \leq r <$ (number of rows in b)
$0 \leq c <$ (number of columns in row r of b)

Referencing the number of rows and columns of b

The number of rows of rectangular array b is given by the expression b.length. The number of columns in row i of b is given by b[i].length. Actually, since the array is rectangular, so that all rows have the same number of columns, the number of columns in any row is given by the expression b[0].length. However, in Java, we prefer to reference the number of columns in row i using b[i].length.

A non-Java notation for subarrays

Throughout this text, we have used the notation h..k to denote the range of integers h, h + 1, h + 2, ..., k. We can use this notation to describe a rectangular subarray of an array b. Here are some examples:

b[0][h..k]	Elements of row 0 with column numbers in h..k
b[0][h..]	Elements of row 0 with column numbers at least h
b[i..j][h]	Elements of column h with row numbers in i..j
b[i..j][h..k]	Elements of rows i..j with column numbers in h..k

We use this non-Java notation to provide understanding of the function in Fig. 9.1, which sums the elements of a two-dimensional array. When reading the outer loop, understand its repetend in terms of the statement-comment:

Add the elements of row r to x

which explains *what* the repetend does, not how it does it. Then, when reading the implementation of this statement-comment, put the outer loop out of your mind. It is possible to write the function without local variable p, using just local variable x. We introduced p to make the function body easier to understand.

Two-dimensional array initializers

Array initializer {2, 4, 6} can be used in creating a one-dimensional array. This notation extends to two dimensions. For example, the statement below creates and stores in c the name of a 4x3 array object —an array object that has 4 rows and 3 columns. the first row contains {2, 4, 6}, the second, {1, 1, 1}, and so on:

```
int[][] c= {{2, 4, 6}, {1, 1, 1}, {4, 5, 6}, {0, 0, 1}};
```

```
/** = the sum of the elements of array b */
public static int sum(int[][] b) {
    int x= 0;
    // invariant: x is the sum of rows 0..r-1
    for (int r= 0; r != b.length; r= r + 1) {
        // Add the elements of row r to x
        int p= 0;
        // invariant: p is the sum of elements b[r][0..c-1]
        for (int c= 0; c != b[r].length; c= c + 1)
            { p= p + b[r, c]; }
        x= x + p;
    }
}
```

Figure 9.1: A function to sum the elements of a two-dimensional array

9.2 Programs that use rectangular arrays

9.2.1 Printing a two-dimensional array

See lesson 9-23 to get the procedure to print the array.

We develop a procedure to print the elements of a two-dimensional array, one row per line. Here is its specification:

```
/** Print array d, one row per line. Precede each row by the integer
 *  1 + (the row number) */
public static void printTable(int[][] d)
```

It makes sense to use a loop schema that processes the rows of array d, one row at a time. So, here is a first refinement of its procedure body:

```
// invariant: rows 0, ..., r - 1 have been printed
for (int r= 0; r != d.length; r= r + 1) {
    Print row d[r] on one line (with its preceding integer r + 1)
}
```

We refine the repetend. We need a statement to print the integer r + 1, a loop to print the elements of the row, and a statement to write a new-line character. Again, we use a loop schema that processes an array —this time, array d[r]:

```
// Print row d[r] on one line (with its preceding integer r + 1)
System.out.print((1 + r) + "  ");
// invariant: elements d[r][0..c-1] have been printed
for (int c= 0; c != d[r].length; c= c + 1) {
    Print d[r][c]
}
System.out.println();
```

Look at the argument of the statement that prints the integer r + 1. Because the expression occurs in a place where a String value is expected, the value of r + 1 is converted to a String. Then, a String literal consisting of two blanks

```
/** Print array d, one row per line. Precede each row by the integer 1 + (row number) */
public static void printTable(int[][] d) {
    // invariant: rows 0, ..., r - 1 have been printed
    for (int r= 0; r != d.length; r= r + 1) {

        // Print row d[r] on one line, preceded by r + 1
        System.out.print((1 + r) + "  ");
        // invariant: d[r][0..c-1] has been printed
        for (int c= 0; c != d[r].length; c= c + 1)
            { System.out.print( " " + d[r][c]); }
        System.out.println();
    }
}
```

Figure 9.2: A procedure to print a two-dimensional array

is catenated to it, so that the row number is separated from the row elements.

Look also at the loop condition. The number of elements in row r is given by the expression d[r].length. The expression d[0].length could also have been used, but it is better to use d[r].length because it is correct in more situations, as we will see in Sec. 9.3.

The refinement of the statement "Print d[r][c]" is a simple print statement (see Fig. 9.2). A blank is printed before each array element so that the elements are separated. This ends the development of this procedure.

Discussion

The procedure was developed in stages, using stepwise refinement (see Sec. 2.5). We first developed the outer loop, leaving its repetend as an English statement. Then, we refined the repetend. While doing so, we obliterated the rest of the program from our minds. Concentrating on one task at a time in this fashion makes programming easier. Consciously try to *separate your concerns*.

9.2.2   A two-dimensional array schema

Get the schema from a footnote on lesson page 9-2.

We write a program schema for processing each element of a two-dimensional array d, where we assume that each element is processed in the same way.

If we think of processing the rows, one at a time, we begin with a for-loop schema and write this loop:

```
/** Process each element of d[0..][0..] */
// invariant: d[0..r-1] has been processed
for (int r= 0; r != d.length; r= r + 1)
    { Process row r }
```

We then refine the repetend. Again we use a loop schema:

```
// Process row r
// invariant: d[r][0..c-1] has been processed
for (int c= 0; c != d[r].length; c= c + 1)
    { Process d[r][c] }
}
```

This resulting schema — see Fig. 9.3 is used so often that we usually abbreviate it. Instead of the two invariants, we use a single invariant that contains the

```
// Process the elements of d[0..][0..] in row-major order.
// invariant: d[0..r-1] and d[r][0..c-1] have been processed
for (int r= 0; r != d.length; r= r + 1)
    for (int c= 0; c != d[r].length; c= c + 1)
        { Process d[r][c] }
```

Figure 9.3:   A schema for processing the elements of a two-dimensional array in row-major order

information from both. Then, we eliminate the statement-comment for the repetend of the outer loop and write the two loops together. We usually omit the braces surrounding the outer-loop repetend, since the repetend is a single statement —a for-statement. It is one of the few contexts in this text where you will find nested loops that are not separated by a statement-comment.

This schema processes the elements in *row-major order*. Processing the elements in *column-major order* means processing those in the first column, then those in the second column, etc.

9.2.3   An interesting table

Get the method from a footnote on lesson page 9-2.

Activity 9-2.3 develops a method that constructs a table of interest values. Given a number of years y and an interest number of interest rates n to calculate, the method constructs an array interest[0..y-1][0..n-1] where interest[r][c] is the balance after r years when interest accumulates at the rate of (5 + .05 * c) percent per year. Watch the development of this method on the CD.

9.2.4   Row-major search

Get the method from a footnote on lesson page 9-2.

The function of this subsection returns an instance of class Coordinates, which is given in Fig. 9.4. The function performs a row-major search of the array for a value x, as stated in this specification:

```
/** = first index (r, c) in row-major order of x in d
 * (or the pair (d.length, 0) if x not in d) */
public static Coordinates search(int[][] d, int x)
```

```
/** An instance is a pair (r, c) of integers
public class Coordinates {

    /** The row number and column number. */
    int r;   int c;

    // Constructor: an instance (r, c)
    public Coordinates(int r, int c) {
        this.r= r;
        this.c= c;
    }

    // = the string "(r, c)" (where r and c are replaced by the values in their fields)
    public String toString() {
        return "(" + r + ", " + c + ")";
    }
}
```

Figure 9.4:   Class Coordinates

For example, if d is the array {{2,8,1,7}, {5,2,7,8}, {2,3,5,6}}, then the call search(d, 5) produces the pair (1,0) because the first occurrence of 5 in d occurs in row 1, column 0.

The elements of d are to be processed in row-major order, where "processing an element" means returning from the function if the element equals x. We can use the loop schema of Fig. 9.3. The function itself is given in Fig. 9.5.

The invariant came from refining the meaning of "process an element" in this context. The loop repetend was refined as well: If x equals the array element being processed, a new instance of class Coordinates is created and returned. And, when the loop terminates normally, then, as per the specification of the method, the value returned is an instance (d.length, 0) of class Coordinates. The use of the schema made for a rapid development of this function.

9.2.5   Saddleback search

> Get the schema from a footnote on lesson page 9-2.

Suppose m by n array d satisfies this property: every row is non-descending and every column is non-descending. Under these conditions, we hope that we can search the array for a value faster than row-major order search does, which takes time proportional to m * n in the worst case. But how do we search it faster? Activity 9-2.5 of the CD develops a perfectly delightful algorithm for searching the array. The idea for the algorithm is not pulled out of a magician's hat but comes from following the principle of finding a loop invariant before writing the loop. The development is much more effective in a lecture, so we leave it to activity 9-2.5 of the *ProgramLive* CD.

9.3   Arrays of arrays

Previously, we said that a variable b declared as

```
int[][] b= {{5, 6, 2}, {1, 4, 8}};
```

contained the name of a rectangular array. While this view can be used, we gain

---

```
/** = first index (r, c) in row-major order of x in d, or (d.length, 0) if x not in d */
public static Coordinates search(int[][] d, int x) {
    // invariant: d[0..r-1] and d[r][0..c-1] do not contain x
    for (int r= 0;  r != d.length; r= r + 1)
        for (int c= 0;  c != d[r].length; c= c + 1) {
            if (d[r][c]) == x)
                { return new Coordinates(r, c); }
        }
    return new Coordinates(d.length, 0);
}
```

Figure 9.5:   A row-major search function

flexibility in our programming by understanding more clearly the Java concept of a multi-dimensional array. Actually, b contains the name of an array object of length 2, each element of which is the name of an array object of length 3:

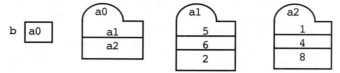

Thus, b is array object a0, b[0] is row 0, which is array object a1, and b[1] is row 1, which is array object a2. In this sense, there is no multi-dimensional array. There is simply an array, b, each element of which is an array.

Variable b, of type **int**[][], contains the name of a one-dimensional array. Array elements b[0] and b[1] have type **int**[].

Now the notation used earlier for referencing the lengths of rows and columns makes sense:

> b.length is the length of array object a0: 2
> b[0].length is the length of array object a1: 3
> b[1].length is the length of array object a2: 3

9.3.1 Ragged arrays

Consider an array b that is declared and initialized like this:

> **int**[][] c= **new int**[2][];

Array c is declared to be a two-dimensional array, but only the size of the first dimension is given (but the brackets [] for the second dimension are there). Only the elements in the first dimension are created, and they are set to **null**:

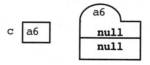

Each element of c has type **int**[], so arrays can be stored in them. Further, the arrays in the elements can have different lengths! The assignments:

> c[0]= **new int**[] {1, 3};
> c[1]= **new int**[] {2, 4, 7};

change c to look like this:

> **Java syntax: Partial-array creation**
>
> **new** *type* [*int-expression*][ ]
>
> **Example**: **new int** [n][ ]
>
> **Purpose**: Create only the first dimension of a two-dimensional array, with *int-expression* elements, all **null**.
>
> **Extension**: For an n-dimensional array, any of the first dimensions can be created, e.g. **new int**[5][3][][][].

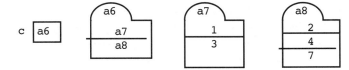

Now, row 0 of c has 2 elements and row 1 has 3 elements. We call it a *ragged array*: a two-dimensional array whose columns have different sizes.

In many cases, each row should have the same number of columns, and the old method of creating both at the same time is the method to use. However, if you want to save space by having each column have a different number of elements, use the new method, as just illustrated.

9.3.2 Pascal's triangle

In order to show one use of ragged arrays, we introduce Pascal's triangle, attributed to Blaise Pascal, a Swiss mathematician and philosopher, who first discovered this little triangle and its properties. Below, we show Pascal's triangle in the middle. On the right, we show it as we usually draw a two-dimensional array:

```
row 0                 1                    1
row 1               1   1                  1  1
row 2             1   2   1                1  2  1
row 3           1   3   3   1              1  3  3  1
row 4         1   4   6   4   1            1  4  6  4  1
row 5       1   5  10  10   5   1          1  5 10 10  5  1
  ...             ...                         ...
```

Each row r of this triangle contains r + 1 integers. The first and last elements of each row are 1. Each other element t[r][c] is the sum of the two elements above it:

$$t[r][c] = t[r-1][c-1] + t[r-1][c] \quad (\text{for } 0 < r, 0 < c < r)$$

Pascal's triangle and combinatorics

Pascal's triangle is important in the field called *combinatorics*. The integer t[r][c] is called "r **choose** c" because it is the number of ways of choosing c elements from a set of size r.

We give an example. Consider the set of integers {1, 2, 3, 4}. Its subsets of size 2 are:

$${1, 2}, {1, 3}, {1, 4}, {2, 3}, {2, 4}, {3, 4}$$

There are 6 subsets of size 2 in the set of 4, so 4 **choose** 2 is 6, and 6 appears in row 4 column 2 of Pascal's triangle.

Creating Pascal's triangle

Figure 9.6 contains a function that computes the first n rows of Pascal's triangle as a ragged array. The first statement of the function body declares two-dimensional array variable t, creates an array object of length n, whose elements are initialized to **null**, and stores the name of the array in t. Note that if n is 0, an array of size 0 is created; this is allowed in Java.

> Get the method from a footnote on lesson page 9-4.

Each iteration of the loop creates one row of array elements and stores values in them. The repetend has two steps: first, create the array object of length r + 1 and store it in t[r]; second, calculate the values of array t[r].

Calculating the values for row r is straightforward. The first value is set to 1; the inner values of the row are calculated in a loop, using the formula given earlier, and the last value is set to 1. For row 0, the single element will be calculated twice because it is both the first and the last element.

```java
/** = the first n rows of Pascal's triangle (for n >= 0) */
public static int[][] PascalTriangle(int n) {
    int[][] t= new int[n][]; // Pascal's triangle

    // invariant: rows 0..r-1 have been created
    for (int r= 0; r != t.length; r= r + 1) {
        // Create array t[r] for row r of Pascal's triangle
        t[r]= new int[r + 1];

        // Calculate the values for row r
        t[r][0]= 1;
        // invariant: elements b[r][0..c-1] have been calculated
        for (int c= 1; c < r; c= c + 1)
            { t[r][c]= t[r - 1][c - 1] + t[r - 1][c]; }
        t[r][r]= 1;
    }

    return t;
}
```

Figure 9.6:   A function to calculate n rows of Pascal's triangle

Printing Pascal's triangle

Get the method from a footnote on lesson page 9-4.

Activity 9-4.1 of the CD gives a procedure for printing the first n rows of Pascal's triangle. The major difficulty is in formatting it nicely. Each row should be centered around the vertical axis, which means that row 0, which has only one value, has to be preceded by a number of blanks that depends on how many characters the last row takes.

Further, there are two ways to print the triangle: (1) each integer value takes only the number of characters that it needs and (2) all integers are printed using the number of characters required by the largest integer.

Please see the CD for a full discussion of printing Pascal's triangle.

9.4   Key concepts

• **Array types**. *type*[ ][ ] is the type of a two-dimensional array with base type *type*, *type*[ ][ ][ ] is the type of a three-dimensional array, etc. Elements of a two-dimensional array b are referenced using b[r][c], elements of a three-dimensional array using b[r][c][d], etc.

• **Rectangular array**. A rectangular array can be created using the new-expression *type*[nrow][ncols].

• **Row-major and column-major order**. Processing an array in row-major order means processing the elements in row 0, then the elements in row 1, and so on. Processing in column-major order means processing the elements in column 0, then the elements in column 1, etc.

• **Ragged array**. In Java, multi-dimensional arrays are really arrays of arrays (of arrays, etc.). Expression **new** *type*[5][ ][ ] creates a one-dimensional array object with 5 elements, all set to **null**; each of the 5 elements has type *type*[ ][ ], so it can hold the name of an object that is a one-dimensional array of elements of type *type*[ ]. If the five elements are arrays of different lengths, the array is called a *ragged array*.

Exercises for Chapter 9

E1. A teacher is having trouble remembering the names of her 15 students, so she arranges the desks into a rectangle with 5 rows and 3 columns. The names of her students are: John, Jill, Pete, Chris, Mary, Seth, Gary, Teresa, Hanna, Amanda, Kim, Greg, George, Perry, and Mike. Write Java code to store the names of the students in a 5x3 two-dimensional array of Strings.

E2. The teacher (see exercise E1) has memorized her students' names and wants to give them new seats. Write a method to randomly shuffle the array.

E3. At the Water Hill stables, the horse stalls are arranged in a rectangle, 6 stalls by 5 stalls. Create a boolean array that will indicate which horses have been fed.

E4. The owners at the Water Hill stables (see exercise E3) would like a bit more information than just whether a horse has been fed. Create class `Horse` and make the array an array of class `Horse`. Be creative in the fields and methods you include in the class.

E5. Write a function that calculates the *transpose* of a rectangular array b. The transpose of b is b with its rows and columns interchanged. In other words, suppose b is an m-by-n array. Then the transpose c of b is an n-by-m array in which each element `c[i, j]` has the value `b[j, i]`.

E6. Write a procedure to print the first n rows of Pascal's triangle in a nice format, with each row centered. Do it two ways. First, have each element take as many characters as it needs, but no more. Second, have each element take the same number of characters: the number needed for the maximum integer to be printed.

E7. Write a function that, given an n-by-m array b, returns a one-dimensional array of size n that contains the sums of the individual rows of b.

E8. Write a function that tells whether an array is a magic square. An array is a magic square if: (1) it is an n-by-n array, for some n, (2) it contains the integers $1, 2, 3, ..., n^2$, (3) the rows, columns, and two diagonals have the same sum. Here is a magic square:

```
{{8, 1, 6}, {3, 5, 7}, {4, 9, 2}}
```

E9. Type "magic square" into a search engine on the internet and find out about magic squares. Write a function that, given an odd integer n, computes an n-by-n magic square.

E10. Think about some area where it might make sense to use a ragged array. Dream up a problem that would make use of a ragged array and write a Java program for it.

Chapter 10

Exception Handling

OBJECTIVES

- Learn about Java's Exceptional error messages.
- Learn about throwable objects and how they are thrown and caught.
- See how you can create your own throwable objects.

INTRODUCTION

When an error occurs in your program, an *exception* is *thrown*. This may lead to abortion of program execution. In the first section of this chapter, we study the error messages that are printed when abortion occurs.

We then discuss *error handling* in Java. Basically, if something untoward happens, an object of a *throwable class* is thrown, and another part of the program can *catch* it and *handle* it. The try-statement gives you the ability to catch thrown objects and handle them. Or, you can simply let another part of the program — the part that called the method in which the object was thrown— handle them.

The Java exception-handling mechanism allows you to isolate the problems of handling errors from the part of the program that does calculation in a normal fashion. Used properly, the exception-handling mechanism is a useful tool.

10.1 Output of thrown Exceptions

Method `main` of the class shown below tries to print the value of `5 / 0`:

```
public class Ex {
    public static void main(String[] args) {
        System.out.println(5 / 0);
    }
}
```

Division by 0 is not defined, so the attempt to divide by 0 is an error. Java handles this error by *throwing an exception*, which causes the program to terminate abnormally with the following messages in the Java console:

> Exception in thread "main" java.lang.ArithmeticException: / by zero
> at Ex.main(Ex.java:3)

(The first part of the first line, which says that an exception occurred in thread main, may be missing.) The important information on the first line is that an ArithmeticException occurred, a division by zero. The second line says where the exception occurred: in method main of class Ex, on line three of file Ex.java.

The information following the second line (if present) is not important for understanding the reason for program termination, and you can disregard it.

The call-stack trace

When the program aborts because of an exception, you have to study it to find out why and correct the error. The messages in the Java console tell you the kind of Exception that occurred and the method being executed at the time, and this can be helpful. But the Java console contains more. To illustrate, we change the program so that the division by 0 occurs within a different method:

```
public class Ex {
    public static void main(String[] args)
        { first(); }

    public static void first()
        { second(); }

    public static void second()
        { System.out.println(5 / 0); }
}
```

Suppose method main is called. Method main calls method first, which calls method second, which attempts to divide by 0.

This list of calls that have been started but have not completed is called the *call stack*. When the attempt to divide by zero occurs, the same exception is thrown, and the following appears in the Java console:

```
java.lang.ArithmeticException: / by zero
at Ex.second(Ex.java:7)
at Ex.first(Ex.java:5)
at Ex.main(Ex.java:3)
```

As before, the first line says that an ArithmeticException occurred, a division by zero. The second line says that the Exception occurred in method second, at line seven of file Ex.java. The third line says that method second was called from method first, and the fourth line says that first was called from main.

Thus, when an Exception occurs:

About the null pointer. Suppose you declare a variable of some class-type, say

```
JFrame jframe;
```

but forget to store anything in it. Variable `jframe` contains **null** rather than the name of a folder. If you then try to access a method, say with `jframe.get-Width()`, Java will give this message: `java.lang.NullPointerException`. By "null pointer", they mean "**null** folder name".

A Java-console message describes the call stack: the stack of methods that have been called but that have not yet completed.

You can use this stack of calls to help figure out how your program got to the point of throwing an `Exception`.

Output of an Error

A runtime error can lead to throwing either an `Exception` or an `Error`. Throwing an `Exception` may or may not cause immediate termination; as you will see later, it depends on whether your program "handles" it. Throwing an `Error` always causes immediate termination of a program. `Errors` are too severe to consider continuing execution. Here are examples of `Errors` that you may see:

```
OutOfMemoryError
InternalError
UnknownError
```

```
/** = the value r that satisfies x = q * y + r and 0 <= r < y for some q.
     Throw an IllegalArgumentException if y = 0.*/
public static int mod(int x, int y) {
    if (y == 0)
        { throw new IllegalArgumentException("x mod 0 is illegal"); }
    /* { Because q*y = (-q)*(-y), we have: mod(x,y) = mod(x,-y). } */
    y= Math.abs(y);

    int r= x % y;

    /* For x >= 0, mod(x, y) = x % y */
    if (x >= 0)
        { return r; }
    /* For x < 0, x % y is the value r' that satisfies
              x = q * y + r' and -y < r' <- 0
         =       <manipulate>
              x = (q - 1) * y + (r' + y) and -0 < r' + y <= y
       Hence, x mod y is x % y + y */
    return r + y;
}
```

Figure 10.1:   A throw-statement in function mod

Java syntax: throw-statement
throw *throwable-object* ;

Example: **throw new** NumberFormatException();

Purpose: Terminate normal execution and "throw" the *throwable-object*, which must be an instance of class Throwable. Unless the thrown object is caught, execution terminates with a message.

In the first case, you have to find out why your program used too much memory. In the other two cases, which should rarely occur, it is difficult to say what to do. Something caused things to become really messed up. Perhaps recompiling all files may help.

Message printed for thrown Errors and Exceptions are similar.

10.2   The throw-statement

Many exceptions and errors are thrown by the Java system itself. But you can write your own statements to "throw an exception". For example, consider this little program:

```java
public class Ex {
    public static void main(String[] args) {
        throw new ArithmeticException("/ by zero");
    }
}
```

```java
public class Throwable implements ... {
    private transient Object backtrace;
    private String detailMessage;

    /** Constructor: an instance with no detail message */
    public Throwable() { ... }

    /** Constructor: an instance with detail message  m  */
    public Throwable(String m) { ... }

    /** = the detail message (null if none) */
    public String getMessage() { ... }

    /** = localized message. If not overridden, same as getMessage() */
    public String getLocalizedMessage() { ... }

    /** = short description of this instance */
    public String toString() { ... }
}
```

Figure 10.2: Class Throwable (not all methods are shown)

When method `main` is called and the throw-statement in it is executed, an instance of class `ArithmeticException` is created and the program terminates with the message `"/ by zero"`. In fact, the output will be the same as if a division by zero had actually occurred.

Not all objects can be thrown. For example, you cannot throw a `JFrame`:

throw new `JFrame(); //` This statement is syntactically illegal

Only objects that are of class `Throwable` (or its subclasses) can be thrown.

Figure 10.1 contains an example of a throw-statement. Function `mod` throws an `IllegalArgumentException` if `y` is `0`, as required by its specification. Function `mod` could have been written without this test, in which case an `ArithmeticException` would be thrown (if `y` is `0`) when the expression `x % y` is calculated. But by explicitly throwing the exception, we can give a better message.

> Get method mod from page 10-2 of *ProgramLive*.

10.3   The throwable object

> Lesson page 10-2

An object can be thrown only if it is an instance of class `Throwable`, which is in package `java.lang`. Figure 10.2 contains the definition of class `Throwable`. We explain its components.

Field `backtrace` automatically contains the call stack at the point where the abnormal event occurred. Field `detailMessage` can contain a description of the error. For example, for the abnormal event division by `0`, this field contains `" / by zero"`. Every `Throwable` object has these two pieces of information.

There are two constructors; one allows the caller to give the detail message.

Getter method `getMessage` returns the detail message, and method `get-LocalizedMessage` can be overridden to return a message that is particular to a subclass. The usual method `toString` is there as well.

We do not show methods that deal with saving and printing the call stack.

```
Throwable                           The root of all throwable classes
  Error                             The root of serious errors that cause termination
    VirtualMachineError
      OutOfMemoryError
      StackOverflowError
  Exception                         The root of exceptions that may be caught and processed
    RuntimeException                The root of exceptions that need not be checked
      ArithmeticException
      IllegalArgumentException
        NumberFormatException
    IOException
    ClassNotFoundException
```

Figure 10.3:   The hierarchy of throwable classes (a partial list)

Classification of throwable classes

There are hundreds of different kinds of errors or exceptions that could happen at runtime, ranging from division by 0 to an input-output error to memory overflow. With so many different possibilities of exceptions, some structure must be put on them to keep them manageable. Java does this by providing a subclass structure for them. Figure 10.3 shows a few of the subclasses, with indenting to denote subclassing. Thus, class `Throwable` has two direct subclasses: `Error` and `Exception`. If an instance of class `Error` is thrown, something serious happened and the program terminates. If an instance of class `Exception` is thrown, then either the program *catches* it and processes it in some way or the program terminates with an error message.

Classes Exception, RuntimeException, and ArithmeticException

<table>
<tr><td>

See lesson page 10-2 to obtain a template for a subclass of class RuntimeException

</td><td>

To the left in Fig. 10.4 is an object of class `Exception`. As you can see, the only components defined in class `Exception` are two constructors: one with no parameters and one with one parameter, which, through a super-constructor call, will be assigned to inherited field `detailMessage`.

</td></tr>
</table>

On the right side of Fig. 10.4 is an object of class `RuntimeException`, which extends class `Exception`. It also contains only two components, both constructors. This illustrates the general pattern. There is no need to define anything in a throwable class besides two constructors. The different subclasses are defined only to give structure and classification to the large list of exceptions that can occur during execution of a program.

So that you can see what a throwable class looks like, Fig. 10.5 contains the definition of class `ArithmeticException`. It has two simple constructors; that is all. If you want to write your own throwable class, use this one as a model.

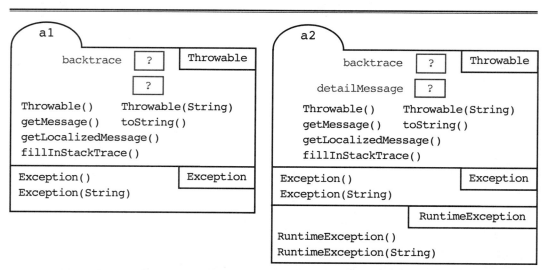

Figure 10.4:   Objects of class `Exception` and `RuntimeException`

10.4   Catching a thrown Exception

10.4.1   The try-statement

Activity
10-3.1

The program segment below contains a *try-statement*:

```
Calculate x;
try {
    y= 5 / x;
} catch (ArithmeticException ae) {
    System.out.println("x was 0; using 0 for 5 / x");
    y= 0;
}
third statement
```

The second is a *try-statement*, of the form:

```
try {
    try-block
} catch ( parameter-declaration ) {
    catch-block
}
```

The parameter-declaration must declare an object of some throwable class. In the try-block above, parameter `ae` is `ArithmeticException`, a throwable class.

Execution of the try-statement begins with execution of the try-block. We have three cases to consider, depending on whether an object is thrown and, if one is thrown, whether this try-statement catches it.

1. If no object is thrown, execution of the try-statement terminates when execution of the try-block does. This is the usual case.

2. If some object `ob` is thrown, the try-block is abnormally terminated. What happens next depends on the catch clause that follows the try-block.

   2a. If the class of the catch-clause parameter matches the class of instance

```
/** Thrown when an exceptional arithmetic condition has occurred. For example, an integer
    "divide by zero" throws an instance of this class. */
public class ArithmeticException extends RuntimeException {
    /** Constructor: an instance with no detail message */
    public ArithmeticException()
        { super(); }

    /** Constructor: an instance with detail message s */
    public ArithmeticException(String s)
        { super(s); }
}
```

Figure 10.5:   Class `ArithmeticException`

> **Java syntax: Try-statement**
> **try** *try-block*
> **catch** (*parameter-declaration*) *catch-block*
> **finally** *finally-block*
>
> **Restrictions**: The *try-block*, *catch-block*, and *finally-block* are blocks of the form { ... }. There may be zero or more *catch-phrases* of the form **catch** (*parameter-declaration*) {...}. The *finally-phrase* is optional, unless there is no *catch-phrase*.
>
> **Execution**: Discussed in this section. See the CD, lesson page 10.3, for an explanation of the finally-phrase.

ob, the catch-block catches the thrown ob: ob is assigned to the parameter and the catch-block is executed, after which execution of the try-statement terminates.

2b. If the class of the catch-clause parameter does not match the class of object ob, Exception ob is thrown to another place. In other words, ob is handled just as it would have been had there not been a try-statement. Something is guaranteed to catch the thrown object ob and handle it. Just how this works is discussed later.

In the example given above, evaluation of 5 / x throws an ArithmeticException, since x is 0. This is caught by the catch-block. So the program prints "x was 0; using 0 for 5 / x", sets y to 0, and then executes the third statement.

We emphasize that if the try-block does not throw an exception, execution proceeds normally to the statement following the try-statement. But if the try-block throws an exception, execution of the try-block is finished. Then, either the catch-block catches the exception and processes it, after which execution proceeds to the statement following the try-statement, or the catch-block does not catch the exception and the thrown object is thrown further —which we explain later.

```
/** = the integer in b[f]
     --= -1 if f is outside the range of b; = 0 if b[f] is not an integer */
public int getIntField(String[] b, int f) {
    try {
        return Integer.parseInt(b[f]);
    } catch (ArrayIndexOutOfBoundsException e) {
        return -1;
    } catch (NumberFormatException e) {
        return 0;
    }
}
```

Figure 10.6:   Realistic example of a try-statement

Example of a realistic try-statement

In Fig. 10.6, we present a function that catches two types of errors: a subscript out of range and an attempt to convert a `String` that does not contain an integer into an `int`. Class `JLiveWindow`, which provides a GUI with some `int` fields into which a user is expected to type integers, provides the motivation for this example. Take a look at the code in that class to see a real use of exception handling.

The body of the try-statement in Fig. 10.6 converts the value of b[f] —a `String`— to an `int` and returns it. This return statement is enclosed in a try-block because its execution may cause two kinds of `Exception`: a subscript out of range and a `NumberFormatException`, which may be thrown by method `parseInt`. Both of these exceptions are caught by catch clauses. This example shows that a try-statement may have any number of catch clauses, not just one.

We could have used an if-statement to test whether f was in the subscript range of array b. Here, catching it using a try-statement leads to a simpler, more consistent method body since the try-statement has to be used anyway to catch the second kind of object that could be thrown.

10.4.3   Propagation of a thrown exception

We explain the throwing of an object. The program of Fig. 10.7 contains three methods. Suppose it is executed, by calling method `main`. Method `main` calls method `first`, which then calls method `second`.

Now suppose that an object ob is thrown within method `second`, signaling some sort of error, and that the throw does not occur within a try-block. Since there is no catch clause to catch the object, it is thrown further, *to the calling method*. Thus, in this example, it appears that the call on method `second` throws ob. And if this call on method `second` does not appear within a try-block, object ob is thrown out further, to calling method `main`. So it looks like method call

```
public class C {
    public static void main(String[] args) {
        try {
            first();
        } catch ( ... )
            { ... }
    }

    public static void first()
        { second(); }

    public static void second()
        { ... }
}
```

Figure 10.7:   Propagating a thrown exception

> **Java syntax: throws-clause**
> **throws** *class-name* **,** *...,* *class-name*
>
> **Example**: **throws** ArithmeticException
>
> **Purpose**: Placed in the header of a method, the throws-clause indicates that the method may throw objects of the given *class-name*s and relieves the method of the responsibility of catching them —that responsibility is passed to methods that call this method. The throws-clause is needed for "checked Exceptions".

first() throws ob.

The call to method first is within a try-block, so if one of its catch clauses catches ob, that ends the throwing. But, if the catch clauses do not catch ob. Then ob is thrown outside the try-statement, so that it looks like the try-statement throws the object. In our example, the try-statement is not in a try-block, so ob is thrown to the caller of method main, which is within the Java system.

The call of method main within the system is within the try-block of a try-statement that catches all Throwable objects, and its catch-block is guaranteed to print the information about ob.

The general rules for throwing an object

We have shown with an example how an object is thrown. We now give a more formal description of throwing an object ob. The following cases can arise:

1. Object ob was thrown in a try-block and is caught by a catch clause. That catch clause processes ob.

2. Object ob was thrown in a try-block and is not caught by a catch clause. Then ob is thrown out to the try-statement —it is as if the try-statement itself threw ob.

3. Object ob was thrown by a statement that is not within a try-block. This statement occurs within a method body that is being executed for some method call. Then ob is thrown out to that call —it is as if the method call threw ob.

This process is repeated over and over until ob is caught. If the program does not catch ob, it will be caught by the Java system: the call that started execution of the program is within a try-statement that catches all thrown objects.

Throwing an object while another is being handled or propagated

Nothing prevents a catch-block from throwing another object a1 (say) —by mistake or otherwise— while a previously thrown object a0 is being handled. If this happens, the previously thrown object a0 is ignored and the newly thrown object a1 is propagated, as described earlier.

To test this yourself, place the method of Fig. 10.8 into a Java program, execute it, and compare the output messages with the method.

Catching and throwing an Exception further

Figure 10.1 contains method mod. Its first statement throws an exception if y = 0. We wrote the function this way so that we could give our own detail message. But there is another way to get the same result, as shown in Fig. 10.9.

We remove the if-statement and place the whole body in a try-statement that catches ArithmeticExceptions. Then, in the catch-block, we throw a new exception with the desired message. The new method body does not rethrow object ae; instead, it creates a new object and throws it. This is done because it is not possible to change the detail message of a throwable object.

But there are cases where rethrowing ae makes sense. For example, one might catch the exception only to dispose of some resources —which is beyond the scope of this text— and then rethrow the same exception.

This second way of detecting that y is 0 is more in keeping with the exception-mechanism philosophy. Rather than intersperse lots of tests for errors, which might double the size of the code, let the exception-handling facilities do that work. Of course, in this case, this second way yields a longer program, but in general, using the exception-handling facilities can help.

10.5 Checked Exceptions

A Java compiler checks to make sure that certain thrown objects are caught by your program; if they are not caught, the compiler issues an error message and refuses to compile the program. For example, consider this silly program:

```
public class C {
    public static void main(String[] args)
        { first(); }

    public static void first()
        { throw new Exception(); }
}
```

Method first may throw an Exception but does not catch it, and this makes the

---

```
public static void main(String[] args) {
    try {
        System.out.println("try-block 0 ");
        throw new ArithmeticException("fake exception 1 ");
    } catch (ArithmeticException ae) {
        System.out.println("catch-block 0 ");
        System.out.println(ae);
        throw new ArithmeticException("fake exception 2 ");
    }
}
```

Figure 10.8: A catch-block itself can throw an exception

program syntactically illegal. The compiler will issue the following error message and refuse to compile the program:

> Error: Exception java.lang. Exception must be caught or it must be declared in the throws-clause of this method C.first().

To get around this problem, place a *throws-clause* "**throws** Exception" in the method header:

```
public static void first() throws Exception {
    throw new Exception();
}
```

The occurrence of the throws-clause relieves the method of the responsibility of catching objects of the mentioned classes and places that burden on any method that calls it. In the program given above, method main is now responsible for thrown Exceptions. It can relieve itself of this responsibility by having its own throws-clause.

```
/** = the value r that satisfies x = q * y + r and 0 <= r < y for some q.
      Throw an IllegalArgumentException if y = 0. */
public static int mod2(int x, int y) {
    try {
        /* { Because q * y = (-q) * (-y), we have: mod(x, y) = mod(x, -y). } */
        y= Math.abs(y);

        int r= x % y;

        /* For x >= 0, mod(x, y) = x % y */
        if (x >= 0)
            { return r; }
        /* For x < 0: x % y is the value r' that satisfies
                x = q * y + r' and -y < r' <= 0
           =        <manipulate>
                x = (q - 1) * y + (r' + y) and -0 < r' + y <= y
           Hence, x mod y is x % y + y */
        return r + y;

    } catch (ArithmeticException ae) {
        throw new IllegalArgumentException("x mod 0 is illegal");
    }
}
```

Figure 10.9:   A second version, mod2, of function mod

```
public class C {
    public static void main(String[] args)
                            throws Exception
        { first(); }

    public static void first() throws Exception
        { throw new Exception(); }
}
```

The Java runtime system now has the responsibility of catching `Exceptions`, since it calls `main`, and it will catch them.

Checked and unchecked objects

Checking that thrown objects are caught is a good idea, for it forces the programmer to think carefully about how thrown objects should be handled. But the Java compiler does not check *all* thrown objects in this manner. All exceptions are called *checked exceptions* except these *unchecked exceptions*:

- Thrown objects of class `Error` and its subclasses.
- Thrown objects of class `RuntimeException` and its subclasses.

If Java forced us to put a throws-clause in the header for *all* possibly-thrown objects, each method would have a long throws-clause on it, and everything would become unwieldy. Therefore, the usual types of exceptions that might occur —like subscript out of range, and division by 0— are made subclasses of `RuntimeException`, so they are not checked. Those that are important to check, like input-output exceptions (instance of class `IOException`) are not subclasses of `RuntimeException` and therefore must be checked.

A mode of operation for handling checked exceptions

It is difficult to remember which exceptions are checked and which are not, and it is often a pain to have to go look it up. Therefore, we usually work as follows. We program without regard to which exceptions are checked or not. Then, when we compile and find the program is syntactically illegal because a certain exception is not caught, we investigate and figure out what to do for that particular case. Usually, this will mean simply putting a throws-clause on one or more methods.

10.6   Hints on using exceptions

Lesson
page 10-6

We make a few remarks on using exceptions.

1. Do not overuse exceptions.

Do not use exception handling to replace simple tests. Exception handling takes more time than an equivalent simple test, but that is not the real reason for not using exception handling. The ability to throw an exception in a method is there to take care of really abnormal errors that the method itself cannot be expected to handle and that should therefore be handled by the calling method (or its caller ...).

   2. Throw an exception when the method in which an abnormal event occurs is not the best place to handle it.

For example, if you are writing a method that processes a sequence of characters of a particular form and a sequence is given that does not have the form, the error is the caller's, and the calling place is the best place to handle it.

   3. Do not make try-blocks too small.

All other things being equal, it is better to have the whole body of a method enclosed in a single try-statement with several catch clauses than to have many smaller try-statements each with one catch clause.

   4. Do not hide exceptions.

When an error message says that a checked exception needs a try-block, the tendency is to write one hurriedly, like this one:

```
try {
    some code
} catch (Exception ex) {}
```

The catch-block does nothing, and the program just goes on as if nothing happened. You do this because you do not expect the exception to happen. But when it does, and it takes you several days to find the problem, you will be sorry.

10.7   Key concepts

• **Throwable object**. A throwable object is an object that is an instance of class `Throwable`. Typically, it is an object of one of two subclasses of `Throwable`: `Error` (these should not be caught and handled) and `Exception` (these may be caught and handled).

• **Throwing an exception**. Java *throws* an exception —an object of (a subclass of) class `Throwable`— if an abnormal event happens. If it is not *caught*, a message is printed and program execution aborts.

• **The throw statement**. A program can throw an exception using the statement **throw** *throwable-object*;.

• **Catching an exception**. A program can catch an exception using the try-statement:

    try *try-block* **catch** (*parameter-declaration*) *catch-block*

• **Checked exceptions**. Every possibly-thrown exception that is *not* an instance of `Error` or `RuntimeException` is called a *checked exception*. A method m (say) that possibly throws a checked exception is syntactically illegal unless m either catches it or mentions it in a throws-clause in the method header — in which case any method that calls m is viewed also as throwing the checked exception.

10.8   Self-review exercises

SR1. If execution of a try-block does not throw an exception, what happens when execution of the try-block finishes?

SR2. What happens if several catch-clauses can catch an object that is thrown in a try-block?

SR3. If a thrown exception is not handled by a method, what happens to it?

SR4. What message do you get if you reference `obj.x` and `obj` contains **null**? What does it mean?

SR5. What kinds of exceptions have to be declared with a throws-clause? What are such exceptions called?

SR6. Does throwing an `Exception` have to cause abortion of the program? What about throwing an `Error`?

SR7. When is it mandatory to have at least one catch-clause in a try-statement?

SR8. Write a catch-clause that will catch *all* thrown exceptions (but not `Errors`).

SR9. Can a throwable object be thrown in a catch-block?

SR10. Can a catch-block throw the object that it caught? If so, why would one want to do this?

Exercises for Chapter 10

E1. Write a procedure to print the real roots of the quadratic formula $ax^2 + bx + c$. These are the values `(-b + sqrt(`b^2` - 4ac))/2a` and `(-b - sqrt(`b^2` - 4ac))/2a`, and they are real if (and only if) the discriminant $b^2 - 4ac$ is non-negative. If the discriminant is negative, something drastic must be done. Be sure to specify your procedure. Now, this procedure should be written in two ways: (1) throw an exception if the discriminant is real and (2) do not use exceptions at all but print an error message. Which way is better?

E2. Write a function to return the real root`(-b + sqrt(`b^2` - 4ac))/2a` of the quadratic formula $ax^2 + bx + c$ (see the previous exercise). If the discriminant is negative, the function should throw an `IllegalArgumentException`. Be sure to write a good specification of the function, and be sure to test the function thoroughly.

E3. Write a function that changes its `String` argument of the form *"first-name last-name"* into the form *"last-name, first-name"*. Throw an `IllegalArgumentException` if the argument does not have the right form. Write the function specification first, and be sure to state what "right form" means to you. Test your function thoroughly.

E4. Write a function to compute (factorial n), for `int` value n ≥ 0, i.e. the value `1*2*...*n`. (Remember, factorial 0 is 1.) Throw an `IllegalArgumentException` if overflow occurs. Specify your function before writing it, and test it thoroughly.

E5. Write a function to compute the largest value (factorial n) that can be calculated using type `int`. Do this by calculating (factorial 1), (factorial 2), (factorial 3), ... using the function of Exercise E4, until a function call causes an exception. This is an inefficient way to calculate the value, but it gives you practice with exception handling.

E6. Write a function to read in and return an integer that the user types on their keyboard. (See Sec. 5.7.1 for reading from the keyboard.) When a line is read as a string from the keyboard, it has to be converted to an `int`, say, by using function `Integer.parseInt`. This function throws an exception if its argument cannot be converted to an `int`, and if this happens, your function should again ask the user to type an integer on their keyboard.

E7. Create an exception class and several subclasses of it. Then write a program to demonstrate that a catch-clause parameter with the class type actually catches exceptions with the subclass types. This will require using the catch-clause parameter in the catch-block.

Chapter **11**

Packages

OBJECTIVES

- Provide an understanding of packages in Java.
- Learn how to set variable CLASSPATH.

INTRODUCTION

People invent classifications and categories in order to make things manageable. In that old game of twenty questions, things of the world are divided into three categories: animal, mineral, or vegetable. Animals are further categorized into different kinds, as are minerals and vegetables. And, books in a library are classified using the Dewey Decimal system. A hierarchy of categories goes as deep as need be to provide structure and make things manageable.

Because there are hundreds of Java classes to deal with, Java provides a mechanism for classifying them: the package.

11.1   Using packages

Placing a class in a package

A *package* is a collection of classes that have been grouped together and reside in the same folder, or directory, on a computer.

Suppose we have a class OneClass in a file OneClass.java. To specify that this class belongs to a package named package1, place a package statement on the first line of file OneClass.java:

```
package package1;
public class OneClass {
    ...
}
```

It is your obligation to see to it that file OneClass.java is placed in directory `package1`, although your IDE should help you do it.

The name of a package, like `package1`, as well as the placement of directory `package1`, must satisfy certain rules, which we will look at later.

The default package

Actually, you probably will not be using the package statement for some time. The classes you write do not have a package statement, so they are automatically placed in a "default" package and appear in the project directory for the program you are writing. If you are using an IDE, various files produced by the IDE are also in this directory, as well as the `.class` files that are produced when classes are compiled.

But you need to know about packages so that you can use the *import statement*, which we explain momentarily.

Referencing classes in other packages

Suppose we have a second class, `TwoClass`, which is in a file `TwoClass.java` and belongs in the default package, since it does not contain a package statement. We put a method m in this class:

```
public class TwoClass {
    public void m() {
        OneClass d= new OneClass(); //SYNTACTIC ERROR!
        ...
    }
}
```

Generally, to refer to a class, one simply uses the class name, as in the two references to `OneClass` in the initializing declaration of d above. However, since class `OneClass` appears in a different package (package `package1`), all references to it must be preceded by the name of the package. The rule is:

> **Package-reference rule**: A reference to a class that appears in another, non-default, package, must be preceded by the name of the package followed by a dot.

Example: `package1.OneClass d= new package1.OneClass();`

The import statement

This package-reference rule makes referring to classes in other packages cumbersome. But there is a way around it. If we import the class using a suitable *import statement* just before the class definition:

```
import package1.OneClass;
```

we do not need to prefix a reference to the class with the package name.

A package may contain many classes, and to write an import statement for each one can be a chore. Hence, Java provides an abbreviation. The statement

---
Java syntax: Import statement
import *package-name* . *;

Example: **import** javax.swing.*;

Purpose: Allow classes in package *package-name* to be referenced directly.

```
import package1.*;
```

imports all the classes of package package1. This form of the import statement, used in the following definition of class TwoClass, is used frequently:

```
import package1.*;
import package1.OneClass;

public class TwoClass {
    public void m() { ... }
}
```

File TwoClass.java now imports method OneClass twice —in the first and second import statements. There is nothing wrong with this, although the second import statement is unnecessary and can be deleted.

11.2   Package names

The directory that contains package package1 may be buried a few levels down on hard drive C in a Windows environment. Here is the path to the directory on one laptop:

> Windows: C:\Gries\prog\vc\package1

In a Unix environment, the forward slash symbol is used to separate the items on the path, and a slash typically begins the path as well:

> Unix: /usr/Gries/prog/vc/package1

On the Macintosh, the first item of a path is the name of a hard drive or some other device, and the colon is used to separate items on the path:

> Macintosh: Macdisk:Gries:prog:vc:package1

All three systems use the same hierarchical concepts for storing directories and files; they just use different formats to display paths.

In Java, this path is written without the beginning drive name and with periods separating the directory names:

> Java-path: Gries.prog.vc.package1

In Java, then, we define a package name as follows:

> **Package name**: a package name is any suffix of a Java-path that

begins with a directory name.

Here are package names that can be used to reference class `OneClass`:

```
package1
vc.package1
prog.vc.package1
Gries.prog.vc.package1
```

Such complicated package names are used because packages can contain other packages. For example, package `java` contains no classes but many subpackages. One of these is package `java.lang`, which contains classes `String` and `Math` and the wrapper classes like `Integer`. Package `java.lang` also contains subpackage `java.lang.reflect`.

So you see that there is good reason to allow a package name to be a sequence of directory names separated by periods.

The class path

Java has to know where the directories corresponding to packages are placed on your computer. Each operating system has a different way of indicating this. We discuss the issue assuming that we are working on a Windows system.

Class `TwoClass`, above, imports the classes of package `package1` using :

```
import package1;
```

The path to this directory is:

```
C:\Gries\prog\vc\package1
```

The import statement tells Java what the suffix of the path is: `package1`. But how is Java supposed to know where this directory is located? In other words, how does Java know the prefix that precedes `package1` on this path? Java does not know unless it is told. This is done using an environment variable of the operating system, called `CLASSPATH`.

Your program may be using several packages that are on totally different paths, so variable `CLASSPATH` may have to contain several different prefixes. Here is an example of `CLASSPATH` with two prefixes. The prefixes are terminated with semicolons:

```
C:\Gries\prog\vc;C:\VisualCafe\Java\Src;
```

If you are using an IDE, you do not have to worry about `CLASSPATH`. The IDE either sets it for you automatically or provides a way for you to change it.

If you are using just a compiler and not a full IDE, you need to know more about setting `CLASSPATH`. We explain this briefly, but get help before you try it.

On a Windows NT computer, look in the Control panel and click on the System icon; in the window that emerges, click on the System Properties tab. You should then be able to set variable `CLASSPATH`.

On Windows 95, you can use a set statement e.g.:

```
set CLASSPATH=C:\Gries\prog\vc;C:\jdk\;
```

In Unix systems

In a Unix system, how you look at and change `CLASSPATH` depends on which "shell" you are using, so we give only a brief discussion here. Statement `set` or `setenv` may be used to store a value in `CLASSPATH`. In this example:

```
set CLASSPATH=/usr/Gries/prog/vc:/usr/jdk/lib
```

the colon is used to separate paths and a slash is used to separate directory names. But do not set `CLASSPATH` until you know what is already in it —you may want to add paths to it, not just store a new set of paths in it.

To look at the contents of `CLASSPATH`, try statement `set` without arguments. Also, look in files like `.login` and `.cshrc` for statements that set `CLASSPATH`.

11.3   The packages that come with Java

An implementation of Java comes with over forty packages, some of which contain subpackages. We mention the more important ones.

Package `java.lang` The most important package ("lang" stands for "language"). It is automatically imported, so you do not need an import statement for it. It extends the core language with several classes that you will use often. Here are the more important classes.

Class `Object` is the root of the hierarchy of classes. Every other class has `Object` as a superclass, so its methods are inherited by all classes. See Sec. 4.3.1.

Classes `String` and `StringBuffer` provide implementations of sequences of characters. See Sec. 5.2.

The eight wrapper classes, including `Integer` and `Character`, provide instances that contain the values of primitive types. Class `Void` is used to represent the primitive Java type **void**. See Sec. 5.1.

Class `Math` contains useful methods, like `abs`, `sin`, and `max`. See Sec 1.1.7.

Class `Class` has methods that provide information about an object. For example, get the name of the class of object `obj` using `obj.getClass.getName`.

Classes `Throwable`, `Error`, `Exception`, and `RuntimeException` are involved with exception handling. See Chap. 10.

Package **java.applet** Provides the basic class, `Applet`, for implementing Java programs that run on the world wide web. See Chap. 16.

Package **java.awt** Contains the classes of the "Abstract Window Toolkit", which is used to build GUIs. Some of these classes have been superceded by the Swing classes —see package `javax.swing`, below.

Package **java.io** Contains the classes that help you do input-ouput, or IO. For example, consider the statement `System.out.println(2);`. Static variable `out` of class `System` is an instance of class `PrintStream`, which belongs to package `java.io`, and `println` is a method of this class.

Package **java.text** Contains classes for formatting numbers.

Package **java.util** Contains a number of useful utilities, e.g. classes that represent dates, provide a Gregorian calendar, give methods for processing `Strings` into "tokens", provide dynamic arrays, and provide random numbers.

The Swing package, package **javax.swing** Provides replacements for some of the GUI classes in package `java.awt` and introduces some new GUI classes. For example, class `javax.swing.JFrame` is now used instead of class `java.-awt.Frame`. See Chap. 17 for a discussion of writing GUIs in Java.

11.4   Key concepts

• **Package.** A package is a collection of files for Java classes —perhaps organized as subpackages— that reside in one directory on a hard drive.

• **Package name.** A package name is a suffix of the path-name on your computer of the directory of the package. However, periods are used to separate components on the path, not / or \.

• **Class path.** You can set variable CLASSPATH in your operating system to contain some paths to directories that contain packages.

• **Using a class in a package.** To reference a class in a package, use the form *<package-name>*.*<class-name>*. Some path in variable CLASSPATH catenated with *<package-name>* must yield the actual path on your computer to the directory the package.

• **Import statement.** To remove the need to use the form *<package-name>*.*<class-name>* everywhere in your program, use an import statement **import** *<package.name>*.**;*. Thereafter, you can just use *<class-name>*.

• **Java packages.** Java comes with hundreds of prewritten classes organized into tens of packages. Package `java.lang` is automatically imported in every Java program.

• **Your packages.** Your classes are placed in a default package. If you want to place a class in another package, put a package statement on the first line of the file for the class —then store the file in the appropriate directory.

Chapter 12

Interfaces and Nested Classes

OBJECTIVES

- Learn what an interface is.
- Study interfaces that provide comparisons: `Comparable` and `Comparator`.
- Study interfaces for enumerating data: `Enumerator` and `Iteration`.
- Learn about nested static classes, inner classes, and anonymous classes.
- Learn about the flattened view of nested classes, which is used by Java.

INTRODUCTION

We study two object-oriented features of Java. The *interface* provides a way of ensuring syntactically (at compile time) that a class contains certain methods. The *nested class* allows one to define one class inside another. This means that an object of the inner class can reside in an object of the outer class, allowing the inner-class object to reference directly the components of the outer-class object.

The two features are independent, and either can be studied first.

12.1 Interfaces

Lesson page
12-1

In Chap. 4, we discussed the notion of an abstract class, like the following one:

```
public abstract class C {
    public abstract void doIt(int par);
    public abstract int giveInt(char c);
}
```

Methods `doIt` and `giveInt` are abstract —first, because they include keyword **abstract**; second, because their bodies have been replaced by semicolons. Any (non-abstract) class that extends `C` must implement these two methods.

We now introduce another mechanism, the Java *interface*, which provides

<table>
<tr><td>

Java syntax: Interface definition
```
public interface interface-name {
    abstract-method definitions and
    constant definitions
}
```
Purpose: To define an interface.

</td><td>

Java syntax: Method declaration in an interface
type method-name (*par-dec* , ..., *par-dec*) ;

Example: `int max(int x, int y);`
Note: Use **void** instead of a *type* for a procedure.

Purpose: To give (only) the header of a method, and not its body.

</td></tr>
</table>

the same capability of forcing a class to implement some methods, but in a different way.

The prefix *inter* means *between*, so the word *interface* means *between faces*. In a dictionary, you will find a definition like: a plane or other surface forming a common boundary of bodies or spaces. In programming, we generally think of an interface as something that describes how two program parts interact. For example, the interface might be a specification that describes how one of the program parts, the server, can be used by the other part, the client.

Activity 12-1.1

In Java, the word *interface* has a more restricted meaning: an *interface* is a specification of the syntax of methods that a class must implement. For example, this interface indicates that a class must implement method `actionPerformed`:

```
/** Interface for receiving action events */
public interface ActionListener {
    /** Process event e */
    void actionPerformed(ActionEvent e);
}
```

Each abstract method in an interface definition is like a conventional method except that its body has been replaced by a semicolon. It is called "abstract" because there is no implementation, i.e. no method body.

The only modifiers allowed are **public** and **abstract**, but you are discouraged from using even these since they are the defaults and the only possibility.

Definitions of constants can also appear in an interface definition, but we save their description for later.

Java will check that any class that purports to implement `ActionListener` —we see what this means later— does indeed implement method `actionPerformed`. Java will not check to make sure that the implementation satisfies the specification given by the comment on the method. Nevertheless, always place such a comment-specification on each method that is defined in the interface so that the reader knows what the method is supposed to do.

Implementing an interface

Activity 12-1.2

Below, we give a class `C1` that implements interface `ActionListener`, as indicated by the *implements clause* **implements** `ActionListener`:

Java syntax: Implements clause

implements *interface-name* , ..., *interface-name*

Example: **implements** I, Comparable

Purpose: Placing this implements clause in a class header indicates that the class implements all the methods of interfaces I and Comparable.

```
public class C1 implements ActionListener {
        void actionPerformed(ActionEvent b)
            { code in method body }
    }
```

The presence of the clause **implements** ActionListener forces class C1 to provide an implementation of the methods described in interface ActionListener; otherwise, the class definition is syntactically illegal.

12.1.1 The interface as a type

We just showed how a class could implement an interface. We now go into more detail about what this means. We show that an interface can be the type of a variable, and we discuss the ramifications of an interface being a type. The following two sections contain case studies that use interfaces, and you might want to peruse them in between studying parts of this section.

Figure 12.1 contains an interface I and two classes F and G. We use short names for the interface and its methods in order to keep diagrams and text manageable. The names are not important to our goal in this section.

To the left in Fig. 12.2 is an object a0 of class G, with the partition for class G at the bottom, then the partition for class F, and above that the partition for class Object. A variable ob contains the name a0.

We want to show how the implementation of interface I within class G affects the object. To do this most effectively, we replace the lines separating the components of subclasses by arrows and remove the box around the object —we

---

```
interface I {
    void p(C e);
}

public class F {    }

public class G extends F implements I {
    Button b;
    public G() { ... }
    void p(C e) { ... }
}
```

Figure 12.1: Interface I and classes F and G

do not need it since we are dealing with only one object. This is the middle diagram in Fig. 12.2. Thus, we see that object ob is a one-dimensional structure, moving upward to superclasses.

To the right in Fig. 12.2, we show the object modified to take into account the fact that G implements I — we added a second dimension to the object, placing at the end of the arrow the names of all components of interface I.

Casting about in the object

You already know that you can cast object ob to a superclass like F:

        F fl= (F) ob;

Activity 12-2.1 presents this material in a far more understandable fashion!

Since this is a widening cast, Java performs it automatically when necessary. Furthermore, using name f1, you can reference only components defined in F and its superclasses, even though the object contains other components. But you can always cast back to the subclass if you know what that subclass is:

        G g= (G) f1;

In the same way, interface I can be used as a type name, and you can cast object ob to I, using the expression (I) ob, as in

        I in= (I) ob;

Here, I is the type of variable in, so you see that interface names can be used as types. Also, this is a widening cast, so we can actually write this statement as:

        I in= ob;

and Java will perform the cast automatically.

In our diagrams of objects as drawn to the right in Fig. 12.2, upward casts (those that follow an arrow) will be performed automatically, while downward casts (those that follow an arrow backward) have to be given explicitly.

Consider a method that has a parameter of type I:

        void meth(I par) { ... };

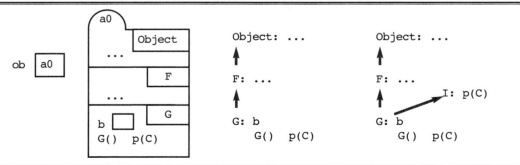

Figure 12.2:   Object a0, a 1-dimensional view, and a 2-dimensional view showing interface it implements

> **Multiple inheritance and overriding**. An interface or class inherits the methods that are defined in an interface that it implements, but it always overrides them. Because a class may implement several interfaces, a method with the same signature may be inherited from several interfaces. This is not a problem because only the signature is given in the interface, not the method body. For a complete explanation of and rules governing multiple inheritance, see the footnotes at the bottom of lesson page 12-2 of *ProgramLive*.

and a call of the method that has `ob` as its argument:

```
meth(ob);
```

Java automatically casts `ob` to type `I` when assigning `ob` to parameter `par`.

The contents of a variable of an interface type

Below, we define and initialize two variables of type `I`:

```
I x1= (I) ob;
I x2= ob;
```

Variables `x1` and `x2` contain the name of the complete object `ob`, but the only components that can be referenced are those available from apparent type `I`. Thus, component `x1.p` can be referenced. But what does `x1.p` refer to? Using the same kind of rules as for subclasses, the real type of `x1` is used to determine this: it refers to the method of the same name that is defined in class `G`. Just as with classes and subclasses, we can say that method `p` that is defined in class `G` overrides the unimplemented method in interface `I`.

Of course. You can cast `x1` from the interface-type back to `G`:

```
G h= (G) x1;
```

thus obtaining again the ability to access all components of the object.

12.1.2 Implementing several interfaces

In return for having a class `C` implement an interface, a service is provided. For example, if `C` implements `ActionListener`, the implemented method `action-Performed` in `C` will be called when a corresponding button is clicked.

As another example, in the next section, we discuss interface `Comparable`. To implement `Comparable`, a class `C` has to define method `compareTo`, which provides an ordering on the objects of class. In return, several methods can be used to search and sort arrays whose base type is class `C`.

```
/** = -1  if this object < b,
 *      0  if this object = b, and
 *      1  if this object > b */
int compareTo(Comparable b);
```

If a class needs several such services, it has to implement several interfaces. To do this, simply write the name of the interfaces (separated by commas) after keyword **implements**. For example, class G in Fig. 12.1 could implement not only I but also Comparable by changing its first line to:

public class G **extends** F **implements** I, Comparable {

Of course, class G would then have to implement method compareTo.

Figure 12.3, on the left, shows how we draw the new class G using our dimensional model. As before, there are dimensions that contain (G, F, Object) and (G, I). But there is now a third dimension, which contains (G, Comparable).

Upward casts in any dimension are performed automatically, when necessary. Downward casts must be explicitly stated. And at any point, the components that can be accessed are those at that point and upward in that dimension.

12.1.3   Extending an interface

Activity
12-2.3

Suppose we have one more interface, named S:

```
public interface S {
    void pr( int b);
}
```

Java allows one interface to extend another, so suppose that interface I extends interface S. Then our dimensional diagram is as shown to the right in Fig. 12.3. The dimension that contains I is extended to include this new interface.

The form of the extends clause within an interface definition is:

extends *interface-name* , ... , *interface-name*

In keeping with the subclass-superclass terminology, we say that S is a superinterface of I and I is a subinterface of S.

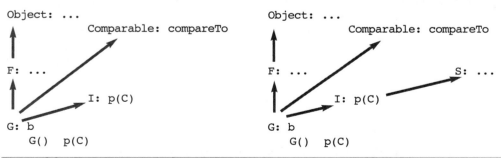

Figure 12.3:   Extending two interfaces and an interface extending an interface

12.2   Comparable and Comparator

Most of the methods we wrote to handle arrays —linear search, binary search, sorting, etc.— handle only arrays of base type **int**. We now show how to use an interface to make these methods more versatile. They will massage arrays of any base type that is a class and that has a suitable method that provides an ordering of the instances of the class.

The new versions of these methods will not sort arrays of any primitive type unless they are wrapped using one of the wrapper classes (see Sec. 5.1).

Interface Comparable

Interface java.util.Comparable has one method, compareTo, which is supposed to provide an ordering of the objects of a class. Here is the interface:

```
/** Require method compareTo, which provides an
       ordering on instances of a class */
public interface Comparable {
    /** = -1 if this object < b,
         0  if this object = b, and
         1  if this object > b */
    int compareTo(Object b);
}
```

Class Compares contains linear search and other methods that deal with arrays (see Sec. 8.5). We show how to change these methods so that they work not on an array of **int**s but on an array of any class whose elements are known to be ordered (because the class implements interface Comparable). Figure 12.4 shows class Compares with (only) one of its methods.

```
public class Compares {
    /** = position of minimum value of b */
    public static int min(int[] b) {
        int p= 0;
        // {inv: b[p] is the minimum of b[0..i-1]}
        for (int i= 1; i != b.length; i++) {
            if (b[i] < b[p]) {
                p= i;
            }
        }
        return p;
    }
}
```

Comparable b

b[i].compareTo(b[p])

change these   to these

Figure 12.4:   Class Compares, showing only method min working on an array of **int**s

Get Comparable and classes that use it from lesson page 12.3.

To modify it so that min can find the minimum of any array whose base type is known to have method compareTo defined on it, we change the base type of parameter b to the name of the interface, Comparable, and change the less-than relation within the body of the method to a call to method compareTo, as shown in Fig. 12.4. Here, you can see interface Comparable being used as a class-type, in that the interface name is used as the type of a variable.

Implementing interface Comparable

Figure 12.5 contains class Pixel, each instance of which represents a pixel in a window. It has a pair (x,y) of coordinates. Only a constructor and method compareTo are shown, but there may be other methods. We note three things about class Pixel.

1. Pixel implements Comparable, as shown in the first line of the class.

2. Parameter ob of method compareTo has type Object, as required by interface Comparable.

3. Each time parameter ob is used, it is cast back to Pixel —without this cast, fields x and y of the parameter could not be referenced. This cast will cause an exception if ob is not really a Pixel. The specification of compareTo makes clear that ob must be a Pixel.

It may seem like a lot of extra baggage to implement Comparable in class Pixel —making the parameter be an Object but then casting back to Pixel. However,

```java
public class Pixel implements Comparable {
    private int x = 0; // horizontal coordinate
    private int y = 0; // vertical coordinate
    ...
    /** Constructor: instance with horizontal coordinate xp and vertical coordinate yp */
    public Pixel(int xp, int yp)
        { x = xp; y = yp; }

    /** = 0 if this Pixel and Pixel ob are the same;
           1 if this Pixel precedes Pixel ob in row-major order;
          -1 if this Pixel follows Pixel ob in row-major order. */
    public int compareTo(Object ob) {
        if (y > ((Pixel)ob).y) return -1;
        if (y < ((Pixel)ob).y) return 1;
        if (x > ((Pixel)ob).x) return -1;
        if (x < ((Pixel)ob).x) return 1;
        return 0;
    }
}
```

Figure 12.5: Class Pixel

we have gained quite a lot. Now, method `min` of class `Compares` can be used on arrays of `Pixels`. For example, suppose we have an array `b` of base type `Pixel` and that `Pixels` have been placed in it:

Activity 12-3.3 executes a call to min, showing how casting works in a way we cannot describe on paper.

Pixel[] b= **new** Pixel[1000];

Then we find its minimum by calling method `min`:

Compares.min(b)

Automatically, method `compareTo`, which is in each element of array `b`, will be used in comparing array elements.

Implementing Comparable in other classes

Interface `Comparable` has been floating around the world for several years, but it was not officially in a Java API package until version 1.2. Some classes that do not implement `Comparable` can be subclassed to implement it. For example, Fig. 12.6 defines a subclass of class `java.util.Date`. Methods `before` and `equals` belong to `Date`. After defining `MyDate`, just use it in place of `Date`.

Classes like `String` and the wrapper classes (e.g. `Integer`) cannot be subclassed, so in Java 1.1 and earlier, to get the effect of implementing `Comparable` on them, you have to write an awkward-to-use class that wraps an **int** and implements `Comparable`. This class should have the necessary getter-setter methods, perhaps returning the value not only as an **int** but also as an `Integer`. Fortunately, interface `Comparable` was added in Java 1.2 so these sorts of shenanigans are not necessary any more.

Interface Comparator

Interface `Comparator`, in package `java.util`, provides other methods for comparing elements, one of which is an equality test:

```
import java.util.date;
public class MyDate extends Date implements Comparable {

    /** = 0  if this Date < ob;
            1  if this Date = ob;
           -1  if this Date > ob */
    public int compareTo(Object ob) {
        if (this.before((Date)ob))
            { return -1; }
        if (this.equals((Date)ob))
            { return 0; }
        return 1;
    }
}
```

Figure 12.6: Class `MyDate`, which extends `java.util.Date`

```
/** See below for specs of the two methods */
public interface Comparator {
    boolean equals(Object obj);
    int compare(Object o1, Object o2);
}
```

Function `equals` should yield **true** if (and only if)

1. `obj` is also a `Comparator`, and it imposes the same total ordering as this `Comparator` (see below).

2. `equals` is an equivalence relation, i.e. it is reflexive (`x.equals(x)`), symmetric (`x.equals(y)` == `y.equals(x)`), and transitive: (if `x.equals(y)` and `y.equals(z)`, then `x.equals(z)`).

3. It is *total*: any two objects in the domain can be tested for equality.

Function `compare` returns `-1`, `0`, or `1` depending on whether `o1` is less than, equal to, or greater than `o2`. Thus, this function imposes a total ordering on elements. Function `compare` should also satisfy the following:

```
sgn(compare(x, y)) == -sgn(compare(y, x))
```

In particular, if `compare (x, y)` throws an exception, so does `compare(y, x)`. Usually, `compare(x,y) == 0) == x.equals(y)`, but it is not necessary.

12.3 Enumeration and Iterator

An *enumeration* of a set of values is simply a listing of the values. For example, here is an enumeration of the first four natural numbers: 0, 1, 2, 3. To *enumerate a set of values* means to provide an enumeration of it. An enumeration of a `String` would be a list of its characters. One could also provide an enumeration of the links on an html page.

Package `java.util` contains interface `Enumeration`, which can be used to facilitate enumerating the objects of a collection of elements. In this section, we explore the use of this interface, as well as a newer one, interface `Iterator`.

Interface Enumeration

Here is interface `Enumeration`:

```
public interface Enumeration {
    /** = "there are more objects to enumerate" */
    boolean hasMoreElements();

    /** = the next object to enumerate. If there are
           no more, throw a NoSuchElementException */
    Object nextElement();
}
```

Its implementation requires two methods: `hasMoreElements` and `nextElement`. Note that `nextElement` yields an `Object`; this method has been made as general as possible.

A class that enumerates Strings

We use interface `Enumeration` to write a class (see Fig. 12.7) that provides an enumeration of the characters of a string. Class `StringEnumeration` needs two fields: the string whose characters are to be enumerated and an integer that indicates the next character to be listed. Integer `k` is initially `0` because `s[0]` is the first character in the enumeration. Note that we describe in comments what fields `k` and `s` are for. *Always* describe fields of using such a class invariant.

The constructor for `StringEnumeration` has one parameter, a string. This parameter is stored in field `s`.

Method `hasMoreElements` is easy to write. Since `k` is the next element to list, there are more elements if and only if `k` is less than the length of the `String`.

The specification of method `nextElement` requires us to check whether there is indeed another element and to throw an exception (see Chap. 10) if there is not. If there is another element, `k` can be incremented and the character can be returned. Note that a value of type **char** cannot be returned because `nextElement` has to return an `Object`. Therefore, the **char** to be returned is wrapped in an object of wrapper class `Character`.

```
/** An enumeration of the characters in a String, as instances of class Character. */
public class StringEnumeration implements Enumeration {
    private String s;   // The string to be enumerated
    private int k= 0;   // s[k] is next char. to be enumerated (none if k = s.length())

    /** Constructor: an instance to enumerate characters of sp */
    public StringEnumeration(String sp)
        { s= sp; }

    /** = "there are more elements to enumerate" */
    public boolean hasMoreElements()
        { return k < s.length(); }

    /** = The next element to enumerate —it is of class Character */
    public Object nextElement() {
        if (!hasMoreElements())
            { throw new NoSuchElementException("no more characters"); }

        k= k + 1;
        return new Character(s.charAt(k - 1));
    }
}
```

Figure 12.7: Class `StringEnumeration`

Using StringEnumeration in a procedure to print characters of a String

Now that we have class `StringEnumeration`, we write a procedure that uses it to print the characters of a `String`:

```
/** Print the chars of s */
public static void print(String s) {
    StringEnumeration e= new StringEnumeration(s);
    while (e.hasMoreElements())
        { System.out.println(e.nextElement()); }
}
```

First, the procedure body creates an instance of class `StringEnumeration` for s and stores it in local variable e. Next, a loop processes the characters of s, using e to enumerate the characters, one by one. The loop terminates when e indicates that there are no more elements. Each loop iteration retrieves the next element of e and prints it. This loop is so simple that we omit the invariant.

Pay attention to the way `Enumeration` e is used. Function `nextElement` should be called only if it is known that there is another element to process, and the only way to know that is to call `hasMoreElements`. Function `hasMoreElements` may actually be called several times in a row, but each call of function `nextElement` must be preceded by a call to `hasMoreElements` because that is the only way to determine whether there is another element to enumerate.

Casting the result of function nextElement

> Get a class with the method of Fig. 12.9 from lesson page 12.4.

By definition, the result of function `nextElement` has type `Object`. In method `print` above, we could use the fact that `Object` has function `toString` defined on it in order to print each character in turn. However, it may be necessary to cast the object back to `Character` in order to suitably process it. To illustrate this, in Fig. 12.8 we write a method that constructs a `String` that consists of every other character of its parameter.

```
/** = the string consisting of the first, third, fifth, ..., chars of s */
public static String getAlternateCharacters(String s) {
    String res= "";
    StringEnumeration e= new StringEnumeration(s);
    // inv: res contains the alternate chars of the part of s that has been enumerated, and
    //         an even number of characters has been enumerated
    while (e.hasMoreElements()) {
        res= res + (Character) (e.nextElement());
        if (e.hasMoreElements()) {
            Object throwAway= e.nextElement();
        }
    }
    return res;
}
```

Program 12.8:   Function `getAlternateCharacters`

Note several things about the loop in this method. First, each iteration processes *two* elements of the enumeration, appending the first to res and throwing the second away (if it exists). Second, the character to be appended to res is cast to class Character, as required. Third, nextElement is called only if it is known that a next element exists.

A *method to print any enumeration*

Earlier, we wrote a method to print the characters of a String using a StringEnumeration. Below, we rewrite this method to print *any* enumeration, using the fact that toString is defined on all objects. Instead of a String, the parameter is an Enumeration:

```
/** Print enumeration e */
public static void print(Enumeration e) {
    while (e.hasMoreElements())
        { System.out.println(e.nextElement()); }
}
```

We give a simple example of the use of method print:

```
print(new StringEnumeration(" abcde   "));
```

Also, if a class ArrayEnumeration enumerates the elements of an array, we can print the elements of an array b using:

```
print(new ArrayEnumeration(b));
```

Interface Iterator

Java 1.2 introduced interface java.util.Iterator (see Fig. 12.9) The names of the methods are different, and there is a new method that allows the removal of elements from the collection during the iteration.

```
public interface Iterator {
    /** = the enumeration (or iteration) has more elements */
    boolean hasNext();

    /** = next element in the enumeration. Throw NoSuchException if there is none. */
    Object next();

    /** Remove the last element returned by method next(). Call remove at most once per
        call to next. The behavior of an iterator is unspecified if the underlying collection is
        modified while the iteration is in progress in any way other than by calling remove. If
        remove is not supported, throw an UnsupportedOperationException.
        If remove is called illegally (e.g. twice for one call of method next), throw an
        IllegalStateException. */
    void remove();
}
```

Figure 12.9: Interface Iterator

12.4 Nested classes

Thus far, we have said that each class may contain variable declarations and method definitions, and method bodies may contain local variable declarations. We have always placed the definition of a class C (say) in a file C.java.

We now state that a class may be defined in another class, and even in a method body. Such a class is called a *nested class*. In this section, we explain why nested classes are useful, explain restrictions on them, and give examples.

12.4.1 Static nested classes

We look first at a *static nested class*: a class that is declared with attribute **static** within another class. Consider writing a class WireForm, as in Fig. 12.10, whose instances represent three-dimensional wire models. The model consists of a bunch of wires, or straight lines.

The components of class WireForm are of no interest in this discussion, and we have placed three components in it only to illustrate. However, WireForm will probably use something like class Line, shown also in Fig. 12.10, which has three fields to describe the beginning of a line and another three to describe the end of the line. Class Line would be placed in its own file, Line.java.

This organization has a big disadvantage. There is a proliferation of classes for users of WireForm to contend with. Why should users have to see class Line when it is used only by class WireForm, and not directly by users? In fact, the designers of WireForm may not *want* users to see class Line. The principle of information hiding (see Sec. 3.1.1) says to make visible only what users need to see, and this principle is violated here.

We can move toward the principle of information hiding by placing the definition of class Line within class WireForm instead of in its own file, as shown in Fig. 12.11. We make class Line a static class, as shown in Fig. 12.12, so it is a *static nested class*.

```
/** A wire form */
public class WireForm {
    public static int x;
    private int y;
    public int meth(...) {...}
    ...
}

/** An instance represents a line in 3 dimensions */
public class Line {
    double x1, y1, z1; // Coordinates of start of line
    double x2, y2, z2; // Coordinates of end of line
}
```

Program 12.10: Classes WireForm and Line (in different files)

Now, there is no need for a file `Line.java`, so that is one less file to deal with. Moreover, although we can leave class `Line` public, we prefer to make it private so that the user cannot refer to it. We have followed the principle of information hiding.

Static nested classes and the inside-out rule

Most programming languages adhere to the *inside-out rule*, which was discussed in Sec. 3.1.2. You have used this rule already. For example, statements within the body of method `meth` (in class `WireForm`) can reference variables `y` and `x`, which are declared in the enclosing class. This inside-out rule applies to static nested classes, as follows:

1. A static nested class may refer to static items of the outer class. Therefore, within `Line`, `x` can be referenced (see Fig. 12.11).

2. A static nested class may *not* refer to non-static items of the outer class, so within `Line`, variable `y` and method `meth` may not be referenced.

When to use a static nested class

Here is a general guideline for when to use a static nested class:

> If the purpose of a class `In` is simply to support another class `Out` —meaning that `In` is used only in `Out` and in no other part of the program— and if `In` makes no reference to non-static components of `Out`, then make `In` a static nested class of `Out`.

Thus, use static nested classes to improve the structure of your program and to make the program more manageable. Also, use static nested classes to hide classes that the user need not know about —follow the principle of information hiding (see Sec. 3.1.1).

```
/** An instance represents a wire form */
public class WireForm {
    public static int x;
    private int y;
    public int meth(...) {...}

    ...

    /** An instance represents a line in 3 dimensions */
    private static class Line {
        double x1, y1, z1; // Coordinates of start of line
        double x2, y2, z2; // Coordinates of end of line
        ...
    }
}
```

Figure 12.11:   Class `WireForm` with static nested class `Line`

The file drawer for a static nested class

In our model of execution, each class has a file drawer in a filing cabinet. By our rules, static components of a class are placed in the file drawer for the class. Since static class Line is defined inside class WireForm, its filing cabinet belongs inside WireForm's filing cabinet —we have to cram one file drawer inside another! Figure 12.12 shows the situation, with the filing cabinet drawers drawn as boxes. The file drawer for class Line shows one instance of the class, and there are no static components.

Above, we mentioned the general inside-out rule, which is discussed in Sec. 13.1.2. Applied to a static nested class and in terms of our file-drawer model, the inside-out rule is interpreted as follows:

> **Inside-out rule for static nested classes**. Suppose the file drawer for static nested class In is inside another file drawer Out. Then In's methods can reference each static component x of Out directly (unless In redefines x).

All instances of Line are in Line's file drawer, so they can reference x.

12.4.2 Inner classes

An *inner class* In (say) is a class that is defined within another class Out (say) without modifier **static**. Class In could be defined as a component of Out, or it could be defined within a method. Here, we discuss the case that class In is defined as a component of class Out, and not within a method.

We describe the use of an inner class using the following example. Class BankAccount, outlined in Fig. 12.13, is used to maintain bank accounts. Each instance of the class maintains the account number and the balance. There are methods for depositing an amount and withdrawing an amount. There could be other types of transactions as well —adding interest, charging a service fee, and

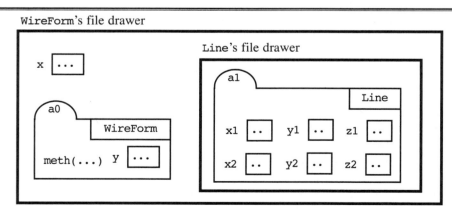

Figure 12.12: The file drawer for a static nested class

so forth. The class contains all the necessary getter/setter methods, but we do not show all methods, for lack of space.

The bank must maintain records of transactions. For this purpose, we define class `Transaction`, also in Fig. 12.13. An instance of this class maintains the account number, the kind of the transaction, and the amount of the transaction.

We must modify methods `deposit` and `withdraw` in class `BankAccount` to create instances of class `Transaction`, but first, we discuss the structure of this program. Class `Transaction` is in its own file and is public, so the user of this bank-account program sees it and can reference it. The principle of information hiding (see Sec. 3.1.1) would have us hide class `Transaction` since the user does

```
/** A bank account */
public class BankAccount {
    /** account number, amount in account, and last transaction carried out
        ("deposit" or "withdrawal") */
    private int account;
    private int balance;
    private Transaction lastTransaction;

    // Getter and setter methods omitted.

    /** Deposit amount in this account */
    public void deposit(int amount)
        { balance= balance + amount; }

    /** Withdraw amount from this account */
    public void withdraw(int amount)
        { balance= balance - amount; }
}

/** An instance is a bank-account transaction */
public class Transaction {

    /** account number, type of transaction ("deposit", "withdrawal"), and amount */
    int account;
    String transaction;
    int amount;

    /** Constructor: instance for account a, kind t, and amount n */
    public Transaction(int a, int n, String t)
        { account= a; transaction= t; amount= n; }

    /** representation of this transaction */
    public String toString()
        { return account + ": " + transaction + " " + amount; }
}
```

Figure 12.13:   Classes `BankAccount` and `Transaction` (in separate files)

not need to know about it. Further, it would be nice to structure the program so that `Transactions` for an account are connected more closely to that account instead of using a field `account` to indicate which account it is.

To do this, we make class `Transaction` an inner class of `BankAccount`, as shown in Fig. 12.14. You already know that non-static fields `account` and `balance` belong in each instance of `BankAccount`. Since class `Transaction` is also nonstatic, a file drawer for it also belongs in each instance of `BankAccount`.

Since each instance of `Transaction` is within a `Transaction` file drawer,

Get the class of Fig. 12.15 from lesson page 12.6.

```
/** A bank account */
public class BankAccount {
    /** account number, amount in account, and last transaction carried out
        ("deposit" or "withdrawal" */
    private int account;
    private int balance;
    private Transaction lastTransaction;

    // Getter and setter methods omitted.

    /** Deposit amount in this account */
    public void deposit(int amount) {
        balance= balance + amount;
        lastTransaction= new Transaction(amount, "deposit");
    }

    /** Withdraw amount from this account */
    public void withdraw(int amount) {
        balance= balance - amount;
        lastTransaction= new Transaction(amount, "withdrawal");
    }

    /** A bank-account transaction */
    private class Transaction {
        /** type of transaction ("deposit", "withdrawal") and amount */
        String transaction;
        int amount;

        /** Constructor: instance for this account, kind t, amount n */
        public Transaction(int n, String t)
            { transaction= t; amount= n; }

        /** representation of this Transaction */
        public String toString()
            { return account + ": " + transaction + " " + amount; }
    }
}
```

Program 12.14:   Class `BankAccount`, with inner class `Transaction`

and since the file drawer is within some instance of BankAccount, the general inside-out rule indicates that methods in class Transaction can access fields balance and account. This means that field account of class Transaction is no longer needed, so we removed it from the inner class. We have achieved a closer bond between classes Transaction and BankAccount.

We also made class Transaction private so that it cannot be referenced outside class BankAccount, thus following the principle of information hiding.

Finally, simply to illustrate the creation of instances of class Transaction, we added a field to BankAccount to contain the last transaction that was carried out; and we added statements to methods deposit and withdraw to create a Transaction and store it in the new field trans.

This example illustrates three reasons for using an inner class:

1. To improve the structure of the program.

2. To hide a class.

3. To make it possible for the inner class to reference non-static components of instances of the outer class.

When to use an inner class

Here is a general guideline for when to make a class an inner class.

```
/** A list of bank accounts */
public class Bank {
    // Class invariant: the accounts are in bank[0..size-1]
    private BankAccount[] bank;
    private int size;

}

/** A (reverse) iterator for bank accounts */
public class BAIterator implements Iterator {

    /** bank[0..n-1] remains to be enumerated */
    private int n= size;     // ILLEGAL REFERENCE TO size

    /** = "  there is another account to be enumerated." */
    public boolean hasNext()
        { return n > 0; }

    /** = the next item to be enumerated */
    public Object next() {
        n= n - 1;
        return bank[n]; // ILLEGAL REFERENCE TO bank
    }

}
```

Figure 12.15:   Class Bank and BAIterator (as separate files)

Guideline for using an inner class. If the purpose of a class In is simply to support another class Out —meaning that In is used only in Out and in no other part of the program— and if In needs to reference non-static components of Out, then make In an inner class of Out.

An inner class that is an iterator

We provide a second example of a useful inner class, having to do with iterators. Consider a class Bank that maintains a set of bank accounts, as outlined in Fig. 12.15. The accounts are stored in array segment bank[0..size-1]. Consider writing an Iterator that will produce the accounts, but in reverse order. We show it as a separate class, also in Fig. 12.15.

```
import java.util.*;

/** An instance is an array of bank accounts */
public class Bank {
    // Class invariant: the accounts are in bank[0..size - 1]
    private BankAccount[] bank;
    private int size;

    /** A (reverse) iterator for bank accounts */
    private class BAIterator implements Iterator {
        /** bank[0..n-1] remains to be enumerated */
        private int n= size;

        /** = "there is another account to enumerate" */
        private int hasNext()
            { return n > 0; }

        /** = the next item to be enumerated */
        public Object next() {
            n= n - 1;
            return bank[n];
        }

        /** remove is not implemented */
        public void remove() {}
    }

    /** An iterator that enumerates bank accounts in reverse order */
    public Iterator iterator()
        { return new BAIterator(); }
}
```

Figure 12.16:   Class Bank, with BAIterator as an inner class

Get the class of Fig. 12.17 from lesson page 12.6.

Class `BAIterator` has several problems. For example, it cannot access the array of accounts or field `size` of class `Bank` directly (as attempted in the initialization of field n). So, `Bank` has to have getter methods for fields `bank` and `size`, and an instance of class `Bank` has to be passed to the `Iterator`. But then `BAIterator` needs a constructor that has an object of class `Bank` as parameter. Thus, several complications arise in attempting to get the two classes to communicate.

These problems arise because `BAIterator` is separate from class `Bank`. The solution to these problems is to make `BAIterator` an inner class of `Bank`, as shown in Fig. 12.16.

Now, by the inside-out rule, the references to `size` and `bank` within class `BAIterator` refer directly to fields `bank` and `size` of class `Bank`.

Note that we made class `BAIterator` private so that it cannot be referenced from outside. But we provide method `iterator` to obtain new instances of `BAIterator`. The return type of method `iterator` is not `BAIterator` but `Iterator` —the user of class `Bank` does not even know about the name `BAIterator` and can never reference it. This is the standard way of making such an iterator available outside the class.

Study this class and its inner class carefully; use this pattern whenever an inner iterator class is desired.

The file drawer for an inner class

Activity 12-6.2

In Fig. 12.17, we show a class `Out` with an inner class `In`. In our model of execution, each class has a file drawer in a filing cabinet, and the question you may ask is where the file drawer for inner class `In` goes. Each instance of `Out` is supposed to contain the non-static components of `Out`. Since `In` is now a non-static component, a file drawer for `In` is in each instance of `Out`!

Figure 12.18 contains an example of `Out`'s file drawer, with two manilla folders and the static variable. Each folder of class `Out` contains a file drawer for `In`, with one folder showing.

With respect to Fig. 12.17, the inside-out rule, which defines what a particular part of a program can reference directly, indicates the following with respect

```
public class Out {
    public static int x;
    private int y;
    public int meth() {...}

    class In {
        int z;
        void meth2()
            { z= y; }
    }
}
```

Figure 12.17: Classes to illustrate file drawers for inner classes

to method `meth2` within object `a1`:

> The body of `meth2` in `a1` can reference `z` of `a1`, method `meth` of `a0`, variable `y` of `a0`, and static variable `x` of class `Out`.

Note that:

> `meth2` in object `a1` can reference variable `y` of object `a0`;
> `meth2` of object `a3` can reference variable `y` of object `a2`.

Thus, the conventional inside-out rule, together with the fact that each instance of class `Out` contains a file drawer for class `In`, ensures that each method `meth2` references the correct components.

12.4.3   The flattened view of inner classes

Our model of execution has us cramming a file drawer for a class inside the file drawer for another class. How do we reconcile this model of execution with the fact that computer memory consists of a sequence of bytes? We can answer this question partially by providing a flattened view of the classes in which each class has its own file drawer and no file drawer appears within another. As we discuss later, this is quite close to how Java implements inner classes.

Recall class `Out` with its inner class `In`, as shown in Fig. 12.17, and Fig. 12.18, which shows `In`'s file drawer inside each instance of `Out`. Figure 12.19 displays a "flattened" view of the classes in which class `In`'s drawer is not crammed within another file drawer.

The first thing to note is that instances of `Out` do not contain a file drawer

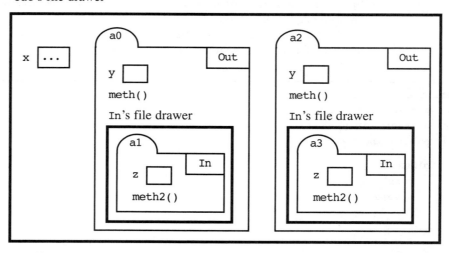

Figure 12.18:   The file drawers for an inner class

for In. Instead, they contain a variable In that contains the name Out$In of a file drawer. This name is chosen to indicate where the file drawer for class In really belongs —inside objects of class Out. As can be seen, drawer Out$In contains the contents of all of In's drawers in the inner-class view. Note that the name of the class in each instance is given as the name of the file drawer.

In the flattened view, we have lost the information that instance a1 occurs not only within In's file drawer but also within instance a0. To recover this information, each instance of In has a "scope box", which contains this information. The two objects of class In, a1 and a3, both contain a scope box.

Finally, the flattened view does not contain the information that each drawer of In is contained in Out's file drawer. To recover this information, we place a scope box in the upper right corner of In's file drawer.

The question may arise whether the flattened view is really a suitable model of memory for inner classes. To convince yourself that it is, simply convince yourself that you can unambiguously create the flattened view from the original view and the original view from the flattened view. If this is the case, they have the same information, and either view can be used.

Java uses essentially the flattened view for inner classes. You can see this for yourself. Start your IDE and set it to create a folder of the compiled classes instead of a jar file. In the folder of compiled classes you will see a file Out$1.class, which contains the information about inner class In. We have chosen the name Out$In instead of Out$1 to make it more understandable.

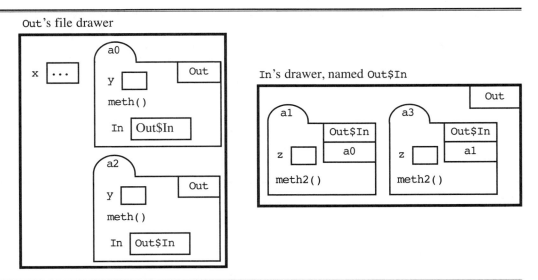

Figure 12.19:   The flattened view of an inner class

12.4.4   Local inner classes

A class that is defined within a method body is called a *local inner class*, or simply a *local class* —yes, just as a method can have local variables, it can have local classes. This means that the file drawer for the class is created within a frame for a call whenever the method in which it is defined is called.

We illustrate the use of a local class with function revIt, which yields an iterator over its parameter, array b. Thus, we show how to obtain an iterator over any array. The outline of this method is shown in Fig. 12.20. The parameter has modifier **final** for technical reasons, which we will explain later. The method is static because it does not refer to components of the class in which it was defined. The method is placed in a class Out simply to have a place to put it. It could be placed in any class.

> Get this program from lesson page 12.6.

An iterator is an instance of a class that implements interface Iterator, so we have to define that class. We place this class right in the method itself, as a local inner class. See Fig. 12.21. The return statement of the method is then changed to return (the name of) a new instance of local class ItOver.

> Activity 12-7.1 presents the memory model for local inner classes.

We do not discuss the memory model for local inner classes here. The explanation is given in a much clearer fashion than we could do here on paper, in in activity 12-7.1 of *ProgramLive*.

Parameter b of method revIt must have attribute **final** because the value of the parameter is being stored in a field of the local inner class —this is what is required to allow a simple, efficient implementation.

When to use a local class

A local class LC defined in a method m can be used to:

1. Improve the structure of the program, placing LC only where it is needed.

2. Hide LC

3. Make available to LC the final parameters and local variables of m.

4. Make available to LC the components of the class in which m appears.

```
public static class Out {

    /** = an Iterator over b's elements in reverse */
    public static Iterator revIt(final Object[] b)
        { return ?; }
}
```

Figure 12.20:   Interface Iterator

Rules for local classes

See also a foot-note on lesson page 12.7.

A local class is an inner class. Therefore, it must satisfy all the rules for an inner class. In addition, any local variable and parameter that it references must be declared **final** so they cannot be changed after its initialization. Below, we state the restrictions on a local class that is defined within another class. In the class shown in Fig. 12.22, we have made inner class In public just in order to give the rules most easily. Generally, inner classes would be made private.

Refer to Fig. 12.22 when reading the following rules for local inner classes:

1. The parameters and local variables that In accesses must have modifier **final**. In Fig. 12.22, In can access parameter p1 and local variable local1, but In cannot reference p2 and local local2, since they are not **final**. The example program shows how to access the value of a non-final parameter or local variable —assign it to a final local variable.

2. The only static components that In may have are final static fields that are initialized with expressions that contain only constants and literals.

3. Class In can access all the static components of class Out even if they are

```java
import java.util.*;

public class Out {
    /** = an Iterator over b's elements in reverse */
    public static Iterator revIt(final Object[] b) {

        /** a (reverse) Iterator over b */
        class ItOver implements Iterator {
            /** b[0..n-1] remains to be enumerated */
            int n= b.length;

            /** = "there is another element to process" */
            public boolean hasNext()
                { return n > 0; }

            /** = the next item of the iteration */
            public Object next() {
                n= n - 1;
                return b[n];
            }

            /** remove is not implemented */
            public void remove() {}
        }

        return new ItOver();
    }
}
```

Program 12.21: A local inner class

private. This is because In is defined in and is part of class Out.

4. If method meth is non-static, class In can reference all the non-static components of class Out even if they are private. This is because In is defined in and is part of class Out.

5. Inner class In may extend another class and implement interfaces. In may be extended by another class.

6. Just as local variable local1 cannot be accessed outside of method meth, class In cannot be accessed directly outside method meth.

12.4.5 Anonymous classes

We now describe the last kind of class, the *anonymous class*. An anonymous class is a class that does not have a name. That may sound kind of silly until you stop and think about it. Why does something have a name? Because it will be called by that name, usually many times. If something is never called or referred to, there is no need to give it a name. Moreover, in Java, if a class is called just once, there is a way to write it so that the name is not necessary even then.

Consider class Out, of Fig. 12.21, which contains method revIt. Local inner class ItOver is accessed in only one place, in the return statement. Therefore, it is a candidate for becoming an anonymous class. In Fig. 12.23, to describe most easily how to make ItOver into an anonymous class, we show the class with its body replaced by *<body of class>*.

To make ItOver into an anonymous class (see Fig. 12.24), do the following:

1. Replace the expression after **new** by "Iterator() *<body of class>*". Note that there is no semicolon after *<body of class>* (because it ends in a brace).

2. Remove the definition of class ItOver.

We now have an unnamed class, which implements Iterator.

When to use an anonymous class

Consider using an anonymous class when a class is accessed only once. But use anonymous classes sparingly, perhaps only when the body of the class contains one or two methods, because the syntax is difficult to follow. The body of

```
public class Out {
    void meth(final int p1, int p2) {
        final int local1= p2;
        int local2;
        public class In { ... }
    }
}
```

Figure 12.22: A local class, used to explain the rules of local classes

the anonymous class in this example is almost too long—that is why we replaced the body with *<body of class>* when explaining the creation of the anonymous class. In this fashion, you could see how simple it is to make a local inner class into an anonymous class.

12.5   Key concepts

• **Interface.** A Java interface definition can have (in its body): (1) initializing declarations of public static final variables and (2) declarations of public abstract methods.

• **Implementing an interface.** If a class *implements* an interface, the class inherits all the components that the interface declares (or inherits from superinterfaces). Since the inherited methods are abstract, the class must provide overriding declarations for all the inherited methods.

• **An interface as a type.** An interface is treated like a class-type. If a variable vc contains the name of some class c that implements an interface I, then vc can be cast to I, e.g. as in the assignment I vi= (I) vc;. This is a widening cast, and such widening casts do not have to be explicitly requested. The apparent type of variable vi is I, so that, syntactically speaking, only the components defined in I can be referenced using vi. However, such a widening cast does not lose information, and vi can be cast with a narrowing cast back to c, e.g. with (C) vc. Then, all the components declared in or inherited by c can be referenced.

• **Multiple inheritance.** A class can implement more than one interface. In doing

```
public static class Out {
    /** = an Iterator over b's elements in reverse */
    public static Iterator revIt(final Object[] b) {

        /** a (reverse) Iterator over b */
        class ItOver implements Iterator <body of class>

        return new ItOver();
    }
}
```

Figure 12.23:   Interface Iterator

```
public static class Out {
    /** = an Iterator over b's elements in reverse */
    public static Iterator revIt(final Object[] b) {
        return new Iterator() <body of class>
    }
}
```

Figure 12.24:   An anonymous class

so, it may inherit the same method signature more than once. This is no problem because the methods are abstract and must be overridden anyway.

• **Flexibility with arrays.** Interfaces provide a way of writing one method that can work with many different types. For example, using interface Comparable or interface Comparator, we can write one procedure to sort any array whose elements are of any class C that implements Comparable.

• **Writing loops.** By properly implementing interface Enumerator or interface Iterator, we can make it easy to write loops that enumerate sequences of values. For example, we can make it easy to write a loop to sequence through the characters of a string or the prime numbers in some range or the tags on an html page.

• **Listeners.** The interface is the prime mechanism for connecting an event in a GUI, like a press of a button or a keystroke, with a method, called a *listener*, to process it.

• **Nested classes.** A nested class is a class that is declared within another class. The reasons for using a nested class are: (1) to allow the nested class to refer directly to components of the outer class, (2) to reduce the proliferation of .java files, (3) to provide for better information hiding, and (4) to provide for better software engineering

• **Kinds of nested class.** A *static nested class* is a static class that is declared as a component of another class. An *inner class* is a non-static class that is declared either as a component of some class or in a method of some class — in the latter case, the class is called a *local inner class*.

• **Anonymous class.** If a local inner class is referenced in only one place, Java has a syntax for it that eliminates the need to give the class a name. When one uses this syntax, the class is called an *anonymous* class.

• **Flattened view of inner classes.** In our model, the file drawer for an inner class appears within the file drawer for the class in which it is declared. This model, along with Java's inside-out rules, helps clarify the concept of an inner class and the reasons for using them. When Java is executing a program, however, a more flattened view of the classes is implemented in which no file drawer for a class resides in the file drawer for another class.

Exercises for Chapter 12

E1. Activity 8-5.3 of the CD *ProgramLive* contains a footnote that has a link to a file, Sorting.java, that contains several methods that process arrays of **int**s. Obtain that file and modify the methods so that they process arrays of any base type that implements interface Comparable. Be sure to test your methods thoroughly.

E2. Look at the specification of class Integer in the Java API specifications. See whether it implements interface Comparable. Write a program that has an array of Integers, fill the array with values, and test some of the methods of exercise E1 using this array.

E3. Look at the specification of class Point in package java.awt. Notice that it does not implement interface Comparable. This is because there is no standard way to order points (x,y) in the plane. Write (and test) a subclass of Point that does implement class Comparable. Here is one way to compare two Points p and q. p < q if one of the following holds:

$$p.x^2 + p.y^2 < q.x^2 + q.y^2$$
$$p.x^2 + p.y^2 = q.x^2 + q.y^2 \text{ and } p.x < q.x$$
$$p.x^2 + p.y^2 = q.x^2 + q.y^2 \text{ and } p.x = q.x \text{ and } p.y < q.y$$

E4. Write a class that enumerates the indices of the letter c in a String s. The class should implement interface Enumeration. The constructor of the class should have c and s as parameters.

E5. Write a class that enumerates the factors of an integer k, where $k \geq 1$. The class should implement interface Enumeration. The constructor of the class should have k as a parameter. The factors of k are all positive integers that divide k, including 1 and k. For example, the factors of 6 are 1, 2, 3, and 6.

E6. Write a class that enumerates the primes that are at most k. The class should implement interface Enumeration. The constructor of the class should have k as a parameter. A *prime* is an integer that is at least 2 and has no factors other than 1 and itself. Can you use the Enumeration from exercise E5 to write this class?

E7. Write a class that enumerates the indices i of an array b such that either i = 0 or b[i − 1] > b[i]. The class should implement interface Enumeration. The constructor of the class should have b as a parameter. Here is an example. For the array {4,5,3,6,2,1,2,4,6,6}, the enumeration consists of the integers 0, 2, 4, 5.

E8. Write a class that enumerates the upper-case letters (i.e. characters in the range 'A'..'Z') in a String s. The class should implement interface Enumeration. The constructor of the class should have s as a parameter.

E9. Write a class that enumerates html tags in a String. The class should implement interface Enumeration. An html tag is a sequence of characters of this form:

< (any sequence of characters not containing '>', including white space) >

So, a tag begins with < and ends with >. Examples: <html>, <body>, <p>, </p>, and <br>. Do not worry about the correctness of the stuff between < and >.

E10. Write a class that enumerates the html tags in a String s that start with "<a".

There may be whitespace between the < and the a, and their *must* be whitespace after the a. The class should implement interface Enumeration. The constructor of the class should have String s as a parameter. Note that this enumeration is most easily written using the class of exercise E9 that enumerates all HTML tags.

E11. Write a class that enumerates the "words" in a String s. For this exercise, we define a word to be a sequence of non-whitespace characters. For example, the String "Love all,\nserve all." consists of the words "Love", "all,", "serve", and "all.". The class should implement interface Enumeration. The constructor of the class should have string s as a parameter.

Part III

Aspects of Programming

This part covers various aspects of programming:

Programming style.
Testing and debugging.
Exception-handling.
Recursion.
Applications and applets in Java.
GUIs and event-driven programming.

We place these topics here, rather than sprinkle them throughout the text, for organizational purposes. Programming style and testing/debugging should, of course, be taught at almost every step of a course, but it helps to have all the discussions of them in one place, for reference.

Applications and applets can be taught at almost any time, but we have found out that, if one uses an IDE like BlueJay or DrJava, later makes more sense.

Exception handling, recursion, and GUIs are usually not taught in a first programming course, but they could be.

Chapter **13**

Programming Style

OBJECTIVE

- Describe good styles for presenting programs and the reasons for them.

INTRODUCTION

Your program should be readable, because if it is not readable, the chances of its being correct are slim. Moreover, if it is unreadable, it will be difficult and time consuming to test and debug it —to find and correct the errors in it. Take the time, right from the start, to follow disciplined, careful, programming practices; it will pay off in the long run. Every time you read your program, because you are modifying it or debugging it, you will take less time if the program is readable. So,

> The major reason for using a disciplined style of programming is to save you time when dealing with your programs. The best way to reduce the burden of debugging is not to put errors in the program in the first place. Following disciplined programming practices can help immeasurably in this regard.

Your program should be readable by others as well, not just you. For example, consider a program that you have to write for a programming course. The less time a grader has to spend on your program, the more positive they will feel toward you and the better your grade will be.

In the professional world, making programs that are readable by others is even more important. Most programs live a long time and require "maintenance" —changes to adapt them to new and different requirements, upgrades in other software, new hardware, and so forth. Quite likely, the author of the program will not be around when maintenance is required, so someone else must read and understand the program enough to update it successfully.

Some of the programming habits discussed in this chapter concern syntactical measures, like indenting program parts properly and using certain conventions for names of variables. Others concern recording information in comments for the reader to understand how a program is designed and why. All are equally important; a chain is no stronger than its weakest link.

It is important to follow good programming conventions all the time. Taste and care are not things that you can turn on and off at will; either you have these qualities or you do not. So, right from the start, be disciplined and try to learn and practice good programming style.

Programming style refers not only to the presentation of a program but also to the way one goes about programming. Two people may end up with essentially the same program, but how they got there might be totally different. One person may use a disciplined, effective style, which took two hours; the other may have required fifteen hours because their ineffective programming style led to a program with many bugs, greatly increasing the testing and debugging time.

Below, we give some guidelines for programming and discuss them. Following these guidelines will reduce the time spent programming and, more importantly, the time spent testing and debugging because fewer bugs will be introduced into programs.

Guideline 1. Specify a program segment before developing it

The following guideline makes sense to most people:

> 1. Do not try to solve a problem until you know what the problem is.

In programming, this guideline is expressed in several ways. For example:

> 1a. Write a clear and precise specification for a method *before* writing the method.

This specification must include a description of all parameters of the method. Also, if a section of code is long and complicated:

> 1b. Use statement-comments to make code appear short and manageable.

Bugs creep into a program because you forget precisely what a section of code is supposed to do and you end up using it in a different way than was intended. Having a precise specification relieves you of the need to remember and thus saves you from making the error. Specifications also save time during the development process; when using a method, you have to read and understand only the specification and not the method body.

We use the program of Fig. 13.1 to see how following guideline 1 could have helped. We want to call method `numberOfPrimes`, but we forget what range of integers it investigates. A hurried glance at the method body might give us the idea that the range is `2..103`, but that is wrong. If the specification

```
/** = the number of primes in 2..102 */
```

had been written before the method body was written, the problem of figuring out what the method did and the resulting mistake in writing a call would not have arisen.

Guideline 2. Define variables

Suppose you are asked whether variable x in the method of Fig. 13.1 is initialized correctly. You will probably reply with another question, "well, how is it used, what is its meaning?" You are right to answer this way, and if you took this idea further into your own programming, you would:

2. Write down the meaning of a variable before you use it.

This meaning should appear near the declaration of the variable, be it a static variable, a nonstatic variable, or a local variable.

A student once told us that programming was easy; all you had to do was to:

Define your variables. Write the program to keep values consistent with the definition while making progress in the calculation.

Many program errors are made by inconsistent use of variables, which is caused by not writing down their definitions.

In the method of Fig. 13.1, variables x and i have to be defined together:

x is the number of primes in the range 2..i-1.

Guideline 3. Keep documentation and program consistent

Finally, do your best to keep documentation and program consistent. Here are some examples.

If you decide to change what a method does:

3a. Change the method specification, then the method body.

```
public static int numberOfPrimes() {
    int x= 1;
    for (int i= 3; i != 103; i= i + 1) {
        boolean b= i > 1;
        int k= 2;
        while (b && k != i) {
            if (i%k == 0)
                { b= false; }
            k= k + 1;
        }
        if (b)
            { x= x + 1; }
    }
    return x;
}
```

Figure 13.1:   Counting primes —with missing specifications and other comments

If you decide to change what the implementation of a statement-comment doe:,

> **3b.** Change the statement-comment, then the implementation.

Concerning variables and their meanings:

> **3c.** Change a variable definition, then statements that use it.

Obviously, documentation that is inconsistent with the program is sure to lead to bugs. Following these guidelines will help reduce the bugs in your program and thus the time spent debugging.

13.1   Naming conventions

We describe guidelines and conventions for naming variables, methods, classes, and packages.

13.1.1   Conventions for variable names

Some people will tell you to make variable names long and mnemonic in order to encapsulate what the variable means in the name itself. Others will tell you to use short names, like x and p1 because they make a program look shorter and manageable. There is a tension between using meaningful names and keeping names short. The best way to solve the dilemma is to use different rules for different situations. Java has four kinds of variable: (1) parameter, (2) local variable, (3) instance variable (or field), and (4) class variable (or static variable), and using a different, well-thought-out convention for each one makes sense.

General Guidelines

Here are some general guidelines to be followed for variable names:

1. A variable name should consist of small letters, except that all "words" within it (except the first) should be capitalized. In Java, this convention is almost universally used. Here are some variable names that follow this convention:

```
x    numberOfDogs    footSize    yCoordinate
```

2. Do not use a long mnemonic name as a substitute for a careful definition of a variable in a comment; names rarely convey the complete meaning of the entity that they name.

3. Make the length of a variable name proportional to the size of its scope. Local variables have the smallest scope, then parameters, then instance and static variables.

With these general guidelines, we now turn to more detailed ones.

Conventions for naming parameters

1. Use short, easily remembered or mnemonic names. You can do this because:

  (a) Parameters are explained in the method specification.

  (b) Method bodies are short enough to allow easy access to the parameter specs. (Many methods are short enough to fit on a computer screen.)

2. Remember that methods are usually written to be general, and parameter names should reflect that generality. For example, consider a function that finds the minimum of two variables `price` and `salePrice`. Do not name the parameters `price` and `salePrice`, name them x and y, and write a general function to find the minimum of x and y.

Conventions for naming local variables

1. Use short names for local variables, making them mnemonic if possible, but be sure to explain the use of each local variable in a comment that is placed near its declaration. You can use short names because:

  (a) Next to the declaration of each local variable is its definition.

  (b) Method bodies are short enough to allow easy access to the declaration of and comments for local variables. (A method is generally short enough to fit on a computer screen.)

2. A local variable that is used in just a few statements may not need a comment.

Conventions for naming instance variables and class variables

1. Use longer names that convey some idea of the meaning of instance variables and class variables. You should do this because their uses are often far removed from the comments describing them. Using longer names may help reduce the need to look at the definitions, thus saving the reader some time (e.g. `priceOf-Pie`). But be sure that defining comments appear near their declaration.

2. Do not use hugely long names because the longer the names, the longer and more complicated the program appears to be. Do not try to encapsulate the whole definition of an instance or class variable in its name.

Convention for naming constants (vars with modifiers `static` *and* `final`*)*

1. Use all capital letters, and use the underline character " _ " to separate words within a name (e.g. `NUMBER_OF_SIDES`).

13.1.2 Conventions for naming methods

Conventions for naming procedures

1. A procedure name should consist of small letters, except that all "words" within it (except the first) should be capitalized (e.g. printSmallest).

2. A procedure name can be a command to do something. That is, make it an action phrase or verb phrase. For example, use drawLine, not lineDrawing or drawsLine.

Here is the reason for this convention. A call on a procedure does some task; it performs an action. Make the call read like a command to perform the task, e.g.

```
printSum(5, 95, 43)
```

3. A procedure name can be the name of an algorithm (e.g. quickSort).

Conventions for naming functions

1. A function name should consist of small letters, except that all "words" within it (except the first) should be capitalized (e.g. indexOfMedian).

2. A function name can be a noun phrase that names the result (e.g. min(a,b)). Here is the reason. A function produces a value, so let the function name be a description of that value.

3. The name of a boolean function can be an abbreviation for the true-false statement that is its specification. E.g. comesBefore(date1, date2) stands for the result of "date1 comes before date2".

4. A function name may be the name of the algorithm used to compute the result (e.g. binarySearch).

13.1.3 Conventions for class names

1. Use a noun phrase for the name —a list of adjectives followed by a noun— that describes an instance of the class. Capitalize each word in the noun phrase. Examples: Date, GregorianCalendar, Checkbox, MenuItem.

2. If the class is generally not instantiated, perhaps because it consists mainly of static methods, then do not use convention 1. An example of this is class Math.

3. Capitalize all words in the class name, including the first. Class names are case sensitive. A class CheckboxMenu is stored in a file CheckboxMenu.java. Even though your operating system does not use case sensitive names, (e.g. Microsoft Windows and Macintosh OS 9), some operating systems do (e.g. Unix), so always use the same capitalization in the file name that you do in the class name. E.g. do not put a class CheckMenu in a file checkmenu.java.

13.2   Conventions for indentation

Indentation is used to help expose the structure of a program. A program that is not well indented can be hard to read because its structure may not be apparent. Watch *ProgramLive*'s activity 13-3.1 to see how hard it is to read a program that is badly indented. Also, activity 12-3.2 discusses two issues to watch out for when indenting.

Indentation conventions are based on two simple principles:

1. In a sequence of constructs —variable declarations, method definitions, statements, and the like— all the constructs are indented the same amount.

2. If a Java construct requires more than one line, its subconstructs that appear after the first line are indented.

Beyond these two principles, a few extra conventions are used to deal with the use of braces { and } to aggregate statements into a single statement. There are several ways to do this, and we comment briefly on them in the following material.

In this text, we generally indent by four blanks at a time. Your IDE probably has a preference panel where you can define how many spaces a tab indents.

13.2.1   Indenting if-statements

See lesson
page 13-3.

We put the opening brace of the then-part on the same line as the if-condition and put the closing brace on a separate line, indented the same as the **if**:

```
if (...) {
    System.out.println(x);
    System.out.println(y);
}
```

This convention is used because placing the opening brace on a line by itself takes another line, and the number of lines on the monitor is a scarce resource.

We (almost) always use a block for the then-part, even if it contains a single statement. This convention prevents us from writing an if statement:

```
if (...)
    System.out.println(x);
```

and then later adding another statement and assuming that it is part of the then-part, *which it is not*:

```
if (...)
    System.out.println(x);
    System.out.println(y);
```

If the then-part is one line, we sometimes write it like this:

```
if (...)
    { System.out.println(x); }
```

Conventions for indenting an if-else statement
Our convention is a simple extension of if-statement convention, e.g.:

```
if (...) {
    System.out.println(x);
    System.out.println(y);
} else {
    System.out.println(z);
}
```

13.2.2   Indenting assertions

An *assertion* is a relation about variables that is enclosed in braces { and } and written as a comment. It appears at the same level of indentation as the statement that precedes or follow it. Its appearance in a program asserts that it is true when execution reaches the position where it occurs. This is illustrated in the following program segment, which has a precondition and a postcondition:

```
// {  x = A and y = B (for some values A and B)  }
int t= x;
x= y;
y= t;
// { x = B and y = A }
```

13.2.3   Indenting loops

Our conventions are similar to those for an if-statement:

```
// invariant: ...
while (...) {
    System.out.println(x);
    System.out.println(y);
}
```

```
// invariant: ...
for (i= 0; i != n; i= i + 1) {
    System.out.print(i);
    System.out.println( " " + (i * i));
}
```

Convention for loop invariants
A loop invariant is a relation whose truth is maintained by execution of the repetend of the loop (under the condition that the loop invariant is initially true).

Just about every loop in this text is accompanied by a loop invariant that helps one understand the loop, and we encourage you to annotate your loops with invariants as well.

As the example above shows, a loop invariant is written as a comment just before the loop and is indented exactly the same amount as the loop. It has the identifying prefix "invariant:" or "inv:".

13.2.4 Indenting the body of a method

We place the opening brace of the body of a method after the header, we indent the statements of the body 4 spaces, and we place the closing brace on a separate line, beginning in the same column as the header of the method:

```java
/** Print x, y, and z, titled, each on a separate line. */
public static void printxyz(int x, int y, int z) {
    System.out.println("x = " + x);
    System.out.println("y = " + y);
    System.out.println("z = " + z);
}
```

Note that the specification of the method appears above the header, and the specification and method begin in the same column.

13.2.5 Indenting components of a class

It is common practice to indent all fields and methods of a class 4 spaces, as shown in Fig. 13.2. The opening brace { of the class body is on the same line as the class name and the closing brace is in the same column as the first word of the class definition.

```java
public class Example {
    public static final int PI= 3.1459;
    private int field;

    /** Constructor: an instance with field = f */
    public Example(int f) {
        field= f;
    }

    /** = a String representation of this instance */
    public String toString() {
        return " " + field;
    }
}
```

Figure 13.2: Example of indentation of components of a class

13.3   Guidelines for writing methods

This section concerns writing methods so that they are most easily read, understood, and used. Indentation within methods is covered in the previous section. Comments on declarations of local variables is covered in the next section.

Figure 13.3 contains a complete method. Users of the method, however, should look only at the specification of the method in order to see what the method does, and at its header in order to see the result type and the types of the parameters. This information is used when writing or reading calls to the method. Here is the spec and header:

```
/** = smallest of b, c, and d */
public static int smallest (int b, int c, int d)
```

13.3.1   The specification as a contract

The specification is a contract between the author of a method and its users. The author guarantees that the method does what the specification says —no more and no less— and users rely on that guarantee. It is a logical firewall. On one side is the method body, which only the author looks at; on the other are the calls to the method, which only users look at.

Thus, the specification must be consistent with the method body. It must explain precisely what the method does. If there is any discrepancy between specification and body, the author has not done their job properly, and users are forced to waste time trying to understand the method body.

Some think that a specification is not necessary, that one can tell what a method does from the name and the parameters. But this is a dangerous and error-prone practice because it is very difficult to pack a complete meaning into a name. For example, even in the example of Fig. 13.3, without the specification, some weird person might think that this method would:

Yield 1 if one of the parameters is smaller than the other two and
0 if there is no smallest.

One of the prime beneficiaries of a well-written specification is the method's

```
/** = smallest of b, c, and d */
public static int smallest (int b, int c, int d) {
    if (b <= c && b <= d)
        { return b; }

    if (c <= d)
        { return c; }

    return d;
}
```

Figure 13.3:   An example of a method

author, provided they write the specification before writing the method body. The act of writing the specification forces the author to be clear and precise; furthermore, the author can then refer to the specification when writing the body.

In conclusion, get in the habit of writing a clear and precise specification for a method before writing the method, and maintain consistency between specification and body.

The form of a specification

A specification of a method may be given in terms of a *precondition* and a *postcondition*. The precondition defines what must be true of the arguments (and any instance or class variables) when the method is called. The postcondition defines what will be true of the arguments (and any instance or class variables and, for a function, the result value) when the method call terminates.

Specification of a procedure

Since a procedure performs some task, write its specification as a command to do that task. Here are two examples:

· Swap b, c, and d so that b ≤ c ≤ d.
· Print the square of the first n natural numbers.
· Deposit d dollars in bank account ba.

Specification of a function

A function produces a value. Therefore, write its spec as an English noun phrase, mixed with math, which says what that value is. Here are examples:

· = minimum of b and c
· = square root of x, given x ≥ 0

We use = in the specification to say that the value of a call equals the value that follows = (with parameters of the function replaced by arguments of the call). Some use the word "return", as in "return the minimum of b and c". This is all right but not preferred because it is too operational. The user wants to know only what the value *is* that the function call provides, so just describe that value.

Specification of a constructor

The purpose of a constructor is to initialize (some of) the fields of a newly created object of some class. Therefore, the specification of a constructor should say simply what the initial values of all the fields are. If some of the fields are given values that depend on the parameters of the constructor, the specification must name the parameters and say how they are used to initialize the constructor. Here is an example:

```
/** Constructor: an instance with amplitude a and frequency f */
public Wave(double a, double f)
```

Javadoc specifications

A method specification or class specification that is commented using the delimiters /** and */ (yes, the opening delimiter has two asterisks) is called a *Javadoc comment*. The program Javadoc can be used to extract all Javadoc comments from a program and put them in an html format so that one then has a specification document. The Java API class specifications were extracted in this fashion. Appendix II.2 discusses Javadoc, and Sec. 2.3 of Appendix I shows how to create a Javadoc specification in DrJava.

13.3.2 Keeping body and spec consistent

Consider the method in Fig. 13.4. Part of the body is written in English. Assume the code for this statement has been written; we just do not display it here:

As an example, a call to `firstVowel` with argument `"peace"` yields the value 2 because the first vowel, `"e"` , is character number 2.

Suppose that, during development of the program for which this method was itself developed, the programmer decides that it would be better for the method to produce the *index* of the first vowel, which is 1, and not 2. So the program is changed as shown in Fig. 13.5. But the programmer does not change the specification of the function. They are in a hurry to complete the program, and they think that they will fix the specification later, after the program is working. So the specification and body are now inconsistent.

A few weeks later, while continuing to develop the program, the programmer writes a call to this function:

```
vowelNumber= firstVowel(b);
```

Having forgotten that the specification and body are inconsistent, the programmer has used the specification in writing the call. Thus, if variable b contains

---

```
/** = no. of chars. in  b up to and including the first vowel (b is known to contain a vowel) */
public static int firstVowel(String b) {
    int r;
    Store in r the no. of characters in b up to and including the first vowel of b;
    return r;
}
```
Program 13.4:   Method firstVowel

```
/** = no. of chars. in b  up to and including the first vowel (b is known to contain a vowel) */
public static int firstVowel(String b) {
    int r;
    Store in r the index of the first vowel of b;
    return r;
}
```
Program 13.5   Method firstVowel, with a modified body

"there is no longer peace", the programmer expects this statement to store 3 in vowelNumber. But it does not; it stores 2 . An error has been introduced into the program.

Such scenarios happen too often in programming. They lead to a great deal of lost time and cause immense frustration. There are at least two ways to guard against them.

1. One way is not to use method specifications at all. But this wastes a great deal of time because it forces the programmer to look at and understand the body of a method whenever a call to the method is to be written.

2. A second way to guard against these kinds of scenarios is simply to keep method specification and body consistent. This is a far better way to prevent these kinds of errors. It is best done by changing the specification first and then changing the body to fit it.

13.3.3   Using statement-comments

Lesson page 13-4

When reading or writing a program, we have many concerns, and we have to focus our attention on one at a time. The more structure that is evident in a program, the easier it is to separate our concerns and deal with one at a time.

A comment that acts as a statement —an instruction to do something—can be useful in providing structure. We call such a comment a *statement-comment*. The statement-comment says *what* to do; the code indented underneath it says *how* to do it. (Later, we discuss indentation with respect to statement-comments.)

Activities 13-4.3 – 13-4.5 are easier to understand!

Using statement comments, Fig. 13.6 is viewed as a sequence of three statements:

> *First statement*;
> // Permute x, y, z so that x <= y <= x
> *Second statement*;

First statement;

// Permute x, y, z so that x <= y <= x
   // Swap the largest of x, y, z into z
     if (x > z)
       { **int** tmp1= x; x= z; z= tmp1; }
     if (y > z)
       { **int** tmp2= y; y= z; z= tmp2; }
   // Swap the larger of x, y into y
     if (x > y)
       { **int** tmp3= x; x= y; y= tmp3; }

Second statement;

Figure 13.6:   Using statement-comments

Reading the program segment in this way, we get a first, abstract view of what it does, and if this our concern at the moment, we need read no further. If our concern is how the permutation of x, y, and z is done, we can read the indented code underneath it, for the moment putting the *first statement* and *second statement* out of our mind:

> // Permute x, y, z so that x <= y <= x
>> // Swap the largest of x, y, z into z
>> // Swap the larger of x, y into y

Thus, the permutation is done in two steps. To see how the second statement is implemented, read the indented code underneath it (see Fig. 13.6).

The use of statement-comments in this program provides us with three levels of abstraction, allowing us to read the program in three different ways. We can focus our attention on whatever concerns us at the moment.

Indentation guidelines for statement-comments and their implementations

Figure 13.6 illustrates one of our two ways of indenting statement-comments and their implementation:

1. The statement-comment itself is indented the same amount as the other statements in the sequence.
2. The implementation of a statement comment is indented four spaces underneath it.

This method of indentation is preferred because it most clearly shows the structure of the program. However, the field has not adopted this method. Instead, they generally use the following conventions, as illustrated in Fig. 13.7.

1. The statement-comment itself is indented the same amount as the other statements in the sequence.

First statement;

```
// Permute x, y, z so that x <= y <= x
// Swap the largest of x, y, z into z
if (x > z)
    { int tmp1= x; x= z; z= tmp1; }
if (y > z)
    { int tmp2= y; y= z; z= tmp2; }

// Swap the larger of x, y into y
if (x > y)
    { int tmp3= x; x= y; y= tmp3; }
```

Second statement;

Figure 13.7:   Alternative indentation for statement-comments

2. The implementation of a statement comment has the same level of indentation and has a blank line after it.

When only two levels of abstraction are used —a statement-comment and its implement, which contains no statement-comment— the second convention is satisfactory. But if the implementation of a statement-comment itself contains a statement-comment, the second convention simply does not work. In Fig. 13.7, where does the implementation of the first swap statement-comment end? At the first blank line underneath it. Then where does the implementation of the permute statement-comment end? At the first blank underneath it? The structure of the program is simply not evident from the indentation.

In this text, we tend to use the second alternative for indenting statement-comments, even though it is inferior, simply because that is what the field does. However, if the implementation of a statement-comment contains a statement-comment, we resort to the first alternative to make the structure clear.

One final point. If statement-comments get several levels deep, it is time to reorganize that piece of program, perhaps by writing a method or two, to remove some of the levels.

13.4   Describing variables

It is difficult to understand statements that use variables unless one knows what the variables mean. Typically, variables are described in comments that accompany their declarations. Here, we discuss how to write these comments.

```
/** Instance: sale of a number of items at a price, e.g.  3  for  $1.29 */
    public class ItemSale {
    private String name;      // name of item being sold
    private int groupCount;   // groupCount items cost grpPrice cents
    private int groupPrice;
    private int numSold;      // number of items sold
...
}
```

Figure 13.8   Some fields in class ItemSale

```
/** Instance: sale of a number of items at a price, e.g.  3  for  $1.29 */
public class ItemSale {
    // name  is the name of the item being sold; groupCount of them cost groupPrice cents
    private String name;
    private int groupCount;
    private int groupPrice;

    private int numSold;      // number sold
}
```

Figure 13.9   Placing field comments above their declarations

Describing instance variables and static variables

Activity
13-5.1

Figure 13.8 contains a class `ItemSale` whose instances contain information of the sale of an item. For example, one instance might represent the sale of four organic apples at a price of 3 for $1.19. We have shown only some the fields and none of the methods in the class in order to make it easier to concentrate on the issue at hand.

One might think that the names of these variables are self-explanatory and that they might be made more explanatory by making them longer. Nevertheless, the meaning of the variables will become much clearer with comments.

First, we describe `name` as the name of the item being sold. This distinguishes it, say, from the name of the salesperson.

Second, we describe `groupCount` and `groupPrice` together. This makes sense because, together, they define the price of an item.

Third, we place the obvious comment on the declaration of `numSold`.

These comments clarify two points, which are not clear from the names of the variables alone. They tell us precisely what `name` names, and they tell us that the unit for `groupPrice` is cents, and not dollars or rubles or Euros or other monetary units. This illustrates how comments can be more precise than names.

The term *class invariant* is generally used for the collection of descriptions of all the instance and class variables. Together, these descriptions describe the state of an object before and after each method of the class is called.

Cluster declarations by logical togetherness

We could have given these four declarations in some other order. However, it is not a good idea to separate the declarations of `groupCount` and `groupPrice` because, logically speaking, they belong together. Together, they describe the price of the items. This illustrates an important principle:

> Group logically related variables together and describe them with one comment.

Formatting comments

We have aligned the comments that annotate these declarations. It is not necessary to align them in this way, but it sure looks better and makes the comments easier to read! So get in the habit of aligning comments suitably. The difficulty, of course, is that if any change is made to the declarations, the alignment probably will not be proper. So some people will tell you, quite rightly, not to bother with aligning the comments.

You can use an alternative form for the comments, as illustrated in Fig. 13.9:

> Place the comments for a group of logically related variables above the declarations and follow the last declaration by a blank space.

Separate declarations of static variables from declarations of instance variables, for they generally serve a different purpose and do not have such a close logical relationship.

Take care to write good explanations of fields, for they will help not only other readers but you, as you develop the class.

Describing parameters

Lesson
page 13-5

Each parameter of a method should be described in the specification of the method, which appears just before the method as a comment. If a parameter is not mentioned in the specification, the specification is incorrect.

Describing local variables

Activity
13-5.2

Local variables are declared in the body of a method. The principles and conventions that hold for commenting instance variables hold for local variables as well. However, local variables are used in a much smaller context than instance variables. Because of this, not all local variables need defining comments. If a local variable is declared and then used only in the next line or two, it probably does not need a definition. If a local variable is used throughout the method, especially in loops, it needs a defining comment.

Use your judgment when deciding whether to place a comment next to the declaration of a local variable. Will you be able to easily understand the meaning of the variable from its use five weeks later if there is no comment? If not, annotate the declaration with an explanatory comment.

The placement of local-variable declarations

The information-hiding policy says to hide information that is not needed at a particular point so that a reader is not encumbered with unnecessary detail. This policy, in relation to local variables, says to:

```
/** Permute w.x, w.y, w.z so that w.x <= w.y < w.z */
public static permute(Triple w) {
    int tmp1;
    int tmp2;
    int tmp3;

    // Swap the largest of w.x, w.y, w.z into w.z
    if (w.x > w.z)
        { tmp1= w.x; w.x= w.z; w.z= tmp1; }

    if (w.y > w.z)
        { tmp2= w.x; w.x= w.z; w.z= tmp2; }

    // Swap the larger of w.x and w.y into w.y;
    if (w.x. > w.y)
        { tmp3= w.x; w.x= w.y; w.y= tmp3; }
}
```

Figure 13.10 Putting local variables at the beginning of a method

Place a local-variable declaration as close as possible to the first use of the variable.

To illustrate this convention, consider the method in Fig. 13.10, which uses this class `Triple`:

```java
public class Triple {
    int x; int y; int z;
}
```

Method `permute` permutes the components of its parameter `w` so that they are in a particular order. It uses three local variables, which are declared at the beginning of the method. The reader is forced to look at these variables even though they may be of no interest. For example, the reader may be satisfied with looking just at the two statement-comments. The placement of these local variables cries out for explanatory comments for them.

In Fig. 13.11, the declarations of these variables have been placed as close to their first use as possible. Now, the reader has to read them only when looking at the implement of the statement comments. Further, their use is obvious, and no comment is needed.

There may be valid reasons for placing a declaration of a local variable at the beginning of the method body. Here is one. Suppose we replace all three variables by a single local variable `tmp` and use `tmp` to make all three swaps. Variable `tmp` would be declared at the beginning of the method, perhaps like this:

```java
int tmp;     // Used in swapping variables
```

```java
/** Permute w.x, w.y, w.z so that w.x <= w.y < w.z */
public static permute(Triple w) {

    // Swap the largest of w.x, w.y, w.z into w.z
    if (w.x > w.z)
        { int tmp1= w.x; w.x= w.z; w.z= tmp1; }
    if (w.y > w.z)
        { int tmp2= w.x; w.x= w.z; w.z= tmp2; }

    // Swap the larger of w.x and w.y into w.y;
    if (w.x. > w.y)
        { int tmp3= w.x; w.x= w.y; w.y= tmp3; }
}
```

Figure 13.11 Putting local variables close to their use

Chapter **14**

Testing and Debugging

OBJECTIVES

- Learn strategies for thoroughly testing programs.
- See some tips for debugging programs.

INTRODUCTION

A *bug* is an error in a program. There are (at least) three kinds of bugs:

1. A function may not return the right value.
2. A method may incorrectly change data (for example, the values of static or instance variables, or information in a file).
3. A method may throw an exception (the bottom of the page discusses exceptions).

Testing is the process of analyzing and executing a program to determine whether it has bugs. A *test case* is a set of inputs, together with the expected output, that is used to test a section of a program, and a *test* is code that exercises a test case.

Debugging is the process of locating a bug and removing it.

The strategies and hints provided in this chapter will help reduce your overall work. At first, it will feel like you are doing more work, but after you follow these steps for several assignments, your productivity will increase, possibly dramatically.

What is an exception? When an abnormal event occurs, like division by 0 or an attempt to reference a field of a non-existent object (e.g. **null.x**) occurs, Java *throws an exception*, where an *exception* is an instance of class Throwable. Often, this results in the display of an error message and termination of the program. Section 10.1 explains the content of these errors messages, and the rest of Chap. 10 explains all the details of handling such exceptions.

> **Do better testing**! The longer bugs remain in a program, the more costly it is to remove them. This old adage has been supported by many studies, e.g. the U.S. National Institute of Standards and Technology (NIST) study in 2002. Software bugs, the study said, cost the U.S. economy about $59.5 billion a year. Further, over half the bugs in software were found late in the development process or even after the software was selling on the market. The cost could be cut by some $22 million by better testing at early stages of development.

Testing can be fun. To paraphrase a former student of the younger author, testing is a Good Thing because you approach it with a different mentality than when writing code. When writing code, you are just trying to get it done; when testing code, you are trying to "break it", you are trying your best to make it work improperly.

14.1   An introduction to testing

We begin with a discussion of testing methods since the method is generally the smallest testable unit of a program. Later, we make a few remarks about testing a class.

First, we always try to follow this guideline:

> **Guideline:** Test each method thoroughly as it is completed.

Of course, this may not always be feasible because several methods may interact in such a way that testing them together is necessary.

But there is a good reason for this guideline. Once a method is tested and its correctness is assured (as much as possible), you will be quite sure that any error that arises is not in that method. It lies elsewhere. This reduces, to a large extent, the areas of the program to be investigated when developing test cases, testing, and debugging.

The tendency, once a method is written (but not tested), is to move on to the next one. Following this tendency will assuredly end up costing you *more* time in developing and testing the program. Resist the tendency.

A second guideline is the following:

> **Guideline**: When both writing and testing a method, understand exactly what the method is supposed to do —this means that the method specification should be written before the method body.

> **Software quality teams**. Because of the high cost of leaving bugs in a program, some companies have quality assurance (QA) teams that do nothing but test software. A team is given the specification and software, and the software is not released until this team okays it. Even then, software is sold with bugs. The best way to ensure there are no bugs is not to put them there in the first place. That, of course, is hard to do.

> **Maxims and aphorisms**. A *maxim* is a general truth, fundamental principal, or rule of conduct. A synonym of *maxim* is *aphorism*, which is a concise statement of a principle or a terse formulation of a truth or sentiment.

It is impossible to test a method that is not well specified. You can read the method body, but how do you know that it does what it is supposed to do? The first job of a tester who encounters such a method is to find the person who wrote the method, find out what it is supposed to do, and then clarify the documentation. Really, they have no other choice.

We assume throughout, then, that methods and classes are well specified.

14.1.1 Five maxims for creating test cases

There are two steps in testing a program: (1) *test cases* have to be generated; (2) the program has to be *tested* with the test cases. The following maxims will guide you not only in generating test cases and testing but also in programming itself. Their application will help you write good comments for methods and variables.

Maxim 1. Test early and often.

The sooner you test a method, the sooner you will find and fix bugs. In fact, as soon as you have written a method specification, you should write an example of a call to that method. This means that you will be thinking about how the method might be used even before you write the method body. (And it will help you write better documentation.)

Maxim 2. Test only one thing at a time.

If you test several things at once and the test fails, you will have a harder time figuring out why. Also, when testing several things at once, it is easier to lose track of what you are testing and harder to make sure that you have covered all the cases.

Maxim 3. Test 0, 1, and many.

This maxim can be applied to the size of both the input and the result. *Many* usually means 2 or 3, although 5 or 10 is not unreasonable, depending on what is being tested. Why 0? Well, for example, when implementing code involving a list of items, it is easy to forget that the list might be empty (has 0 items). Why 1? It is the smallest "typical" case. If a bug is detected with size 1, it is usually easier to debug that case than on a longer list.

Maxim 4. Test null, beginning, middle, and end.

When implementing a method, it is easy to overlook what might happen if a parameter is `null`. Test at the beginning and end of the input because it is easy to forget about the two extremes while writing code. Test in the middle because it is the "regular" case.

Using a try-statement. If you have not yet studied try-statements, skip this note. Below is an advanced test that uses a try-statement to test for a **null** argument.

```
try {
    numberOfVowels(null);
    // If this point is reached there is a problem
    System.out.println("Whoops, expected an exception.");
} catch (NullPointerException e) {
    // If this point is reached, the method worked correctly,
    // so this block is empty
}
```

Maxim 5. Verify the documentation.

As you test, ask yourself questions that you would not normally think of while writing the code. Make sure the documentation answers those questions. (These are called *design decisions*.)

14.1.2   Example of creating test cases

Consider this method header and comment:

```
/** = the number of vowels in s */
public static int numberOfVowels(String s) {
    return -1;
}
```

We have written the method body with a return statement so that the method will compile. Such a method body, which does not do the right thing but is written simply to allow the program to compile, is sometimes called a *stub*. After compiling, we will begin writing the method body, but first we use the five maxims to generate test cases. Yes, we are going to generate the test cases before writing the method! At the end, we show you how to put them together into a method that you can use to easily test the method whenever you want.

Maxim 1. Test early and often. To test early, we need a test case. Below, we show a test case, which consists of a typical call to numberOfVowels and the answer we expect from it:

```
numberOfVowels("This sentence has vowels."), 7
```

Maxim 2. Test only one thing at a time. Remember the three possible kinds of bugs: incorrect value, incorrect change of data, and exception. Here, because there is no outside data to corrupt, we focus on the first: the method may return a wrong value. Later, as you test more complicated code, you might have several methods in a class. You will need to test how the methods interact, and this maxim can be used to figure out how complicated to make your testing.

Maxim 3. Test 0, 1, and many. Because we are testing vowels, we decide to use 5 for "many" —one for each vowel. In other situations it might be the number of items in a list, or the number of lines in a file, etc. Using this maxim, we generate the following tests cases:

numberOfVowels(""), 0	(the empty string)
numberOfVowels("bcd"), 0	(zero vowels, many letters)
numberOfVowels("a"), 1	(one vowel, one letter)
numberOfVowels("bad"), 1	(one vowel, many letters)
numberOfVowels("aeiou"), 5	all vowels, many letters)
numberOfVowels("facetious"), 5	(typical case)

There is another way to think of "many": many occurrences of the same vowel. When dealing with the first maxim, we wrote a test that had three e's.

Maxim 4. Test null, beginning, middle, and end. *Beginning* and *end* are covered in the penultimate test from the previous maxim. *Middle?* Yes, in several of the cases, the vowels occur in the middle of the argument. There is one item left: the parameter might be **null**. This interacts with the next maxim, and we discuss it there.

Maxim 5. Verify the documentation. In investigating the previous maxim, we found a problem with the documentation: it does not state what the result of the call numberOfVowels(**null**) should be. Should the method return 0? Or throw an Exception? Whatever decision is made, the method specification needs to be improved. Here we decide to disallow **null** and to let the code throw an exception: We add a second sentence to the method description to document this case:

```
/** = the number of vowels in s.
        Throw a NullPointerException if s is null. */
public static int numberOfVowels(String s) {
    return -1;
}
```

[It would be more appropriate to throw an IllegalArgumentException, but this requires knowledge of the try-statement or throw-statement. See Sec. 10.4.1)

The test case in this case is the following:

```
numberOfVowels(null), an exception
```

Now here is something really neat: after spending 5-10 minutes writing test cases, we have a thorough understanding of how the method behaves and have improved the method specification, *before we have written a single line of code*.

14.1.3   A test driver

Remember the second maxim: *test early and often*. When testing a method, this means that the method should be tested against all test cases when the method is first written and then tested against all test cases whenever the method is changed. Because testing is done frequently, the output from testing must be easy to read. In fact, it is typical to print information only when a test case fails, so that there is something to read only if there is a bug.

In Sec. 14.1.2, we created several test cases. Figure 14.1 contains a procedure that exercises each test case. Such a method is often called a *test driver*.

It is assumed that this procedure is placed in the same class as function `numberOfVowels`. Each test case (except the last) is wrapped in an if-statement, which compares the expected answer with the answer given by the function. Notice how we test whether the result is *not* what we expect. The last test case is exercised using a call with argument **null**. Execution of this call should cause an exception and abortion of execution.

14.1.4 Testing using JUnit

DrJava comes with a testing tool, JUnit, as do many IDEs. JUnit is the most common Java testing tool. The mechanics of using JUnit are explained in Sec. 2.4 of Appendix I. Here, we show the use of JUnit to perform the tests described in Sec. 14.1.2.

Figure 14.2 contains the same test cases as Fig. 14.1, this time to be tested using JUnit. Thus, a class extends class `TestCase`. The class contains a public

```
/** Execute some tests */
public static void testNumberOfVowels() {
   if (7 != numberOfVowels("This sentence has vowels."))
      { System.out.println("A general test failed"); }

   if (0 != numberOfVowels(""))
      { System.out.println("Empty case failed"); }

   if (0 != numberOfVowels("bcd"))
      { System.out.println("A case without vowels failed"); }

   if (1 != numberOfVowels("a"))
      { System.out.println("A case with one letter, a vowel, failed"); }

   if (1 != numberOfVowels("bad"))
      { System.out.println("A case with mixture of vowels & letters failed"); }

   if (5 != numberOfVowels("aeiou"))
      { System.out.println("A case with all vowels failed"); }

   if (5 != numberOfVowels("facetious"))
      { System.out.println("A typical case failed"); }

   numberOfVowels(null);
}
```

Figure 14.1: A method for testing function `numberOfVowels`

procedure named `test...` with no parameters for each test case, and the body of each procedure contains one call to a method of class `TestCase`. We have written independent methods for the test cases because the test cases are independent —one does not depend on another one working correctly.

This is one context where we do *not* write method specifications. Here, the context is so specific, the bodies of the methods so simple, and the names of the methods so descriptive that writing a specification for the methods would add little. In this context, we *know* implicitly what each procedure does: it exercises a test case.

14.1.5   Testing a class

Testing a class is harder than testing a method, for a class generally contains many methods. The test driver should:

1. Declare at least one and perhaps more variables with the class as their type.

2. Create instances of the class and assign them to the variables.

```
import junit.framework.TestCase;
public class TestNumberOfVowels extends TestCase {

    public void testDuplicateVowels()
        { assertEquals(7, numberOfVowels("This sentence has vowels.")); }

    public void testEmpty()
        { assertEquals(0, numberOfVowels("")); }

    public void testNoVowels()
        { assertEquals(0, numberOfVowels("bcd")); }

    public void testOneVowel()
        { assertEquals(1, numberOfVowels("a")); }

    public void testOneVowelSeveralLetters()
        { assertEquals(1, numberOfVowels("bad")); }

    public void testEveryVowelNoConsonants()
        { assertEquals(5, numberOfVowels("aeiou")); }

    public void testEveryVowelSeveralConsonants()
        { assertEquals(5, numberOfVowels("facetious")); }

    public void testNull()
        { assertEquals(0, numberOfVowels(null)); }
}
```

Figure 14.2:   An instance of `TestCase` to test `TestNumberOfVowels`

3. Check that the constructor of the class works properly. This means checking whether the fields of each new instance were properly initialized. Function toString can be useful in testing. If toString has been written, it is easy to print the contents of a class instance using it:

```
System.out.println(x.toString());
```

This test will also help test method toString.

4. Test all the other methods. This testing can follow the pattern described earlier.

When creating a subclass of TestCases to use with JUnit, a procedure setup (see Sec. 2.4 of Appendix I) can be written that creates instances of the class being tested and stores them (i.e. their names) in fields of the subclass. These fields can then be used in the test procedures of the subclass.

14.2   Approaches to creating test cases

In Sec. 14.1, we developed test cases for a method by looking only at the specification of the method —even before the method body was written. This kind of test-case development is known as *blackbox*, or *functional*, testing. There are other ways to go about developing test cases. We list three main ones here.

1. Exhaustive testing. Exhaustive testing, or testing a program on all possible inputs, sounds good but is generally infeasible for most programs

```
/** = name of 10 * n, for 2 ≤ n < 10, e.g. tensName(3) is "thirty"*/
public static String tensName(int n) {
    if (n == 2)
        { return "twenty "; }
    if (n == 3)
        { return "thirty "; }
    if (n == 4)
        { return "fourty "; }
    if (n == 5)
        { return "fifty "; }
    if (n == 6)
        { return "sixty "; }
    if (n == 7)
        { return "seventy "; }
    if (n == 8)
        { return "eighty "; }
    return "ninety ";
}
```

Figure 14.3:   Function tensName, with an error

because of the number of possible test cases. Even if a method has only one **int** parameter, exhaustive testing would require calling the method well over four billion times, and the output of each call would have to be checked for correctness.

Lesson page 14-3 has a discussion of blackbox testing and an interesting anecdote about doing it in industry.

2. **Blackbox testing, or functional testing**. In making up test cases, one looks only at the specification of the program (and not the program itself) in deciding what test cases to try. The program is a black box, and you cannot see inside it.

3. **Whitebox testing, or structural testing**. One looks at the program itself when developing test cases and uses the structure of the program to recognize possible trouble spots and develop test cases to exercise them.

The term *whitebox testing* was badly chosen. Just because a box is white does not mean you can see through it. A better term would have been *glassbox testing* or *transparent box testing*.

In the rest of this section, we discuss structural testing as a complement to functional testing. We review maxim 3:

```
/** = English equivalent of n, for 0 < n < 1000 */
public static String anglicize(int n) {
    String s= " " ; // anglicize(n) = s + anglicize(k)
    int k= n;
    if (k >= 100) {
        s= s + digitName(k / 100) + "hundred ";
        k= k % 100;
    }

    if (k >= 20) {
        s= s + tensName(k / 10);
        k= k % 10;
    }

    if (k > 10) {
        s= s + teenName(k);
        k= 0;
    }

    if (k > 0) {
        s= s + digitName(k);
        k= 0;
    }

    return s;
}
```

Figure 14.4: Method `anglicize`, to be tested (it contains an error)

Maxim 3. Test 0, 1, and many

When thinking about testing a loop, we interpret maxim 3 to mean that we should provide test cases in which a loop will execute 0 iterations, 1 iteration, and more than 1 iteration. If a program deals with an array or list of some sort, we should consider test cases for which the array (or list) has 0 elements, 1 element, and many elements.

Structural testing involves one new, extremely important, maxim:

Maxim 6. Develop test cases that provide *test coverage*.

A group of test cases provides test coverage if exercising them will cause every single part of the program to be executed at least once. When developing test cases using the functional approach, we cannot look at the method body, so there is no way to know whether complete test coverage has been achieved. So, maxim 6 is an important addition.

Here is an example that actually happened to one of us. We wrote the function of Fig. 14.3. This method is so simple that we thought we might skip testing it. But we tested it anyway, thoroughly, trying as test cases the arguments 2 through 9. All these test cases were necessary because we had to make sure that each return statement was executed at least once. It was only when looking at the output of the testing phase that we noticed the typo: we had misspelled *forty*.

As another example of test coverage, look at the function in Fig. 14.4. To provide test coverage, the then-part of each if-statement has to be executed. So, we look at calls of method *anglicize* with arguments (say) 125, 50, 15, and 5.

14.3   Approaches to testing

In Secs. 14.1.3 and 14.1.4, we introduced two approaches to exercising test cases: the use of a *test driver*, which is a method that is written to perform the tests, and the use of JUnit, an application that has been written to facilitate testing. There are other ways to exercise test cases, some of which we explore here.

Use DrJava's Interactions pane

In some cases, it is sufficient to test a method (as soon as it is written) using DrJava's Interactions pane. Suppose the method is `static`. Then you can write many calls on it in the Interactions pane and see the answer immediately.

The advantage of using the Interactions pane is that it can be done quickly and without the overhead of writing a test driver or writing a subclass of class `TestCases` (in order to use JUnit).

The disadvantage of using the Interactions pane is that it is not easily repeatable. If we make a change in the method and want to test it again, we must manually type in the calls to the method and check the answers. Using a test driver or JUnit takes more time in the beginning, but, in the end, it saves time because the same tests can be repeated whenever we want.

Use GUI JLiveWindow as a test driver

Activity 1-5.3 gives a thorough introduction to GUI JLiveWindow.

As mentioned earlier, a *test driver* is a program that has been written to test execution of another program (or program unit) on some test cases. GUI JLiveWindow can be used as a test driver in some cases. This may be easier than using DrJava's Interactions pane, but it has the same disadvantage: one must manually type in the test cases.

We provide an example of the use of GUI JLiveWindow. Suppose we have written a class that contains static methods to convert among three different temperature scales: Fahrenheit, Centigrade, and Kelvin, e.g.

```
/** Conversions to and from Fahrenheit, Centigrade, Kelvin */
public class TempConvert {

    /** = Fahrenheit equivalent of Centigrade temp c */
    public static double FahrFromCent(double c)
        { return 9 * c / 5 + 32; }

    ...

}
```

Our GUI test driver consists of two classes, JLiveWindow and MyJLive-Window. It works as follows. When you start the test driver, the GUI window will appear on your monitor. You can type a value in the first **double** field and press button Ready. The driver will use the value as the argument to method FahrFromCent and put the result in the second **double** field. It will also put text in the String fields of the GUI to label the values. You can run many test cases during one execution of the program.

Class JLiveWindow is changed in two ways to make it into our test driver. First, the call to the constructor in method main is changed to have the arguments 0, 2, and 2, so that the GUI has 0 **int** fields, 2 **double** fields, and 2 String fields.

Second, method buttonPressed, which is called when button Ready of the GUI is pressed, is changed to do the following:

1. Copy the value in the first **double** field into variable b.
2. Place the title for the first **double** field into the first String field.
3. Place the value of the call FahrFromCent(b) in the second **double** field.
4. Place the title for the second **double** field into the second String field.
5. Return the value **null**.

Figure 14.5 contains this method buttonPressed.

You can use GUI JLiveWindow as a test driver for many methods. You have control over the number of **int**, **double**, and String fields in the GUI, and you can change method buttonPressed to suit your needs.

14.4 The Java assert statement

Throughout this text, we have annotated programs with comments that contained

---

Making the assert statement work. The assert statement may not work in your system. Some IDEs have a switch that tells whether the assert statement should be allowed. For example, if your version of DrJava does not allow the assert statement, select menu **edit** item **preferences**. In the window that opens, click category **Miscellaneous** in the lefthand column and then check the box *Allow assert keyword in Java 1.4*.

If you are using a command-line window to compile a Java program, then you need the `-source 1.4` option to enable assertions, as shown below. This is needed for backward compatibility reasons.

```
javac -source 1.4 SomeClass.java
```

---

assertions. Examples are preconditions of methods, postconditions of methods, class invariants, and loop invariants. Java 1.4 has a new statement, the *assert statement*, which comes in one of two forms:

> **assert** *boolean-expression* ;
> **assert** *boolean-expression* : *expression* ;

This statement is executed as follows. The *boolean-expression* is evaluated; if it is **true**, execution of the statement is finished. If it is **false**, an `Assertion-Error` is thrown, which (for the first form above) prints the following message and terminates the program:

```
java.lang.AssertionError:
   at Funcs.testPrint(Funcs.java:28)
```

For the second form, the value of the *expression* is printed as well — it is the detail message of the thrown `AssertionError`. For example, if this value is `"hey, it is 5"`, then this is printed:

```
java.lang.AssertionError: hey, it is 5
   at Funcs.testPrint(Funcs.java:28)
```

The assert statement, inserted at judiciously chosen places, can alert you to misguided beliefs and therefore help you debug your program. For example, suppose you previously wrote the following code:

```
/** Put into double field 1 the fahrenheit value for centigrade value in double field 0 */
public Object buttonPressed() {
    double b= getDoubleField(0);
    setStringField(0, "Centigrade");
    setDoubleField(1, TempConvert.FahrFromCent(b));
    setStringField(1, "Fahrenheit");
    return null;
}
```

Figure 14.5:   Method buttonPressed used to test function `FahrFromCent`

```
if (x % 2 == 0) {
   ...
} else { // { x % 2 == 1 }
   ...
```

You can now write this code this way:

```
if (x % 2 == 0) {
   ...
} else {
   assert x % 2 == 1: "x= " + x;
   ...
```

If, for some reason, the assertion of the assert statement (the *boolean-expression*) should ever be false at that point during execution, the program will abort with a message, and you will know that there is a problem.

The assertion statement is intended to be used for internal checking of a program while a program is being developed. You are encouraged to leave assertions in a program when it is completed just in case all bugs have not been found and corrected. But assertions are not intended to be used to alert a user of a program to errors they have made. For such problems, the normal error-handling mechanisms should be used.

For example, suppose we are writing a private method, called only by our own methods, that has a precondition 0 < n < 100. We can use an assert statement to check the precondition, as shown here:

```
/** = English equivalent of n, for 0 < n < 100 */
private static String anglicize(int n) {
   assert 0 < n && n < 100: "n is " + n;
   ...
```

However, if the method is **public** and you have no control over the places from which it is called, it is better to throw the appropriate exception:

```
/** = English equivalent of n, for 0 < n < 100
      Throw an IllegalArgumentException if n out of range */
private static String anglicize(int n) {
   if (0 >= n || n >= 100)
      { throw new IllegalArgumentException("n is: " + n); }
   ...
```

Throw statements are discussed in Chap. 10 on *Exception handling*. Do not be concerned if you do not know about exceptions; if you want to test a parameter's precondition, just use the throw statement shown above, putting as the argument of the constructor of IllegalArgumentException a string that explains the problem.

Generally, you can use the assert statement to test loop invariants, postconditions of methods, and other assertions that you previously wrote as comments.

Evaluating the boolean expression of the assert statement does take time. Use it for simple tests, like the ones shown. But do not include in the boolean expression a call to a function that processes every element of a large array unless it is a temporary measure.

14.5   Debugging

Suppose a test case has detected a bug. It is now time to find the bug. This can be a time-consuming, difficult task, like finding a needle in a haystack.

There are two ways to proceed. First, one can use a debugger —your IDE probably has one. Second, one can sprinkle the program with print statements and assert statements that help you track down the error.

The use of a debugger can make the task easier because it has tools that help you analyze the program. You can step through execution of the program one statement at a time, you can look at the values of variables and expressions as execution proceeds, you can see what methods have been called, and so on.

But if a debugger is not available, or you do not know how to use it, you must resort to sprinkling the program with print and assert statements. We describe this process here.

Tracking down a bug

Suppose we are testing a program that includes the method of Fig. 14.4. In one place "nine hundred nine " is printed on the Java console, and we can tell it is wrong. We have to debug the program.

The bug might be either in a calculation or in a method that tranforms an integer to its English equivalent, like anglicize. We decide to test method anglicize. The first order of business is to:

Debugging maxim 1. Place print statements at the beginning and end of the method (to check whether its precondition is met and to check whether the value returned is correct).

In our case, the two statements to insert are:

```
System.out.println( " Start anglicize, n = " + n);
System.out.println( " End anglicize, ans = " + s);
```

```
/** = name of n, for 10 <= n <= 19 */
public static String teenName(int n)

/** = name of 10*n, for 2 <= n <= 9 */
public static String tensName(int n)

/** = name of n, for 0 < n < 10, or "" if n = 0 */
public static String digitName(int n)
```

Figure 14.6:   Specifications of some methods used in anglicizing

When we run the test case again, we see that method `anglicize` was called with n = 1210, and the result was wrong. Here is the output:

```
Start anglicize, n = 1210
End anglicize, ans = nine hundred nine
```

A look at the precondition of `anglicize` tells us that `anglicize` was called incorrectly because 1210 is not in the range for which it was written. Therefore, we will have to look for the error at the place where this call was made.

We do not pursue this particular error further. Instead, we look closer at method `anglicize` itself.

Tracking down another bug

It takes time to insert and remove print statements and to run tests in order to detect bugs. Therefore, we try to follow this maxim:

> **Debugging maxim 2.** Glean as much information as possible from each exercise of test cases.

In the case discussed above, it does not appear that calling anglicize with n = 1210 should produce the result that it did. After all, the then-part of the first if-statement will set k to 10 , so where did the "nine" come from in the answer?

If we do not see the error, we:

> **Debugging maxim 3.** Insert print statements at judiciously chosen places, in order to check values of variables.

In this case, we place the same print statement after each if-statement:

```
System.out.println("s = " + s + " , k = " + k);
```

And we execute the program again (with the same input, of course). Here is the output from that execution:

```
Start anglicize, n = 1210
s= nine hundred, k= 10
s= nine hundred, k= 10
s= nine hundred, k= 10
s= nine hundred nine, k= 0
End anglicize, ans= nine hundred nine
```

The output of the first four print statements is reasonable. But the output of the fifth print statement is not. Why did the call to `digitName` produce " nine" when its argument was 10? To find this out, we have to look at the specifications of the methods being called (see Fig. 4.6).

A look at the specification of `digitName` reveals that that method requires its argument to be less than 10, so it is our mistake to call `digitName` with 10 as the argument. But then where is the integer 10 handled?

We back up to the previous if-statement and take a look at the specification of method `teenName`. We find out that it handles arguments in the range `10..19` —even though `10` is not really a teen. Here is where reliance on the name of a method for its meaning is a mistake!

So we should be able to fix the error by changing the if-statement to the following one:

```
if (k >= 10) {
    s= s + teenName(k);
    k= 0;
}
```

Running again, with the same input, we see that the error has been fixed.

Discussion

The main goal of this section is to illustrate the debugging process. But it teaches another lesson:

> **Debugging maxim 4.** Deal carefully with *interfaces*.

The specification of a method is the interface between the method and calls to it. The bugs uncovered in this section were interface bugs: methods were called with unsuitable arguments.

Interfaces are always a problem. When building a house, baseboard molding is used where the floor meets the walls to hide the cracks, and quarter-round molding is often placed on the baseboard molding for the same reason. Plumbing interfaces are a huge source of wet trouble spots. Roofs leak mostly where the roof meets a chimney; the interface between these two quite different materials is hard to get right.

So be extremely careful with interfaces!

14.6   Key concepts

• **The cost of testing**. Testing consumes far more time than most people imagine. To reduce the time, follow good programming practices.

• **Test case**. A test case is a set of input values that are used in testing a program unit (method, class, etc.) together with the expected result. Good testing requires developing a suitable set of test cases. Some people will tell you to develop test cases before writing the program!

• **Exhaustive testing**. Such testing requires testing with every possible test case. Generally, it is infeasible.

• **Blackbox or functional testing**. Such testing requires developing test cases using only the program specification; the program and its structure is not looked at.

• **Whitebox or structural testing**. Such testing requires developing test cases while looking at the program itself. Enough test cases should be included so that *test coverage* is provided: every statement is executed at least once during testing. Also, test cases should be developed to look at boundary conditions (e.g. execution of a loop that performs 0 iterations, 1 iteration, or the maximum number of iterations).

• **Suites of test cases**. For a larger program, develop a suite of test cases and test them all whenever changes are made. If possible, write the test driver so that it does the testing automatically and prints out messages only when the answers are unexpected.

• **Debugging**. Debugging is the process of finding and removing errors once they have been detected. When looking for an error, use Java assert statements, judiciously placed print statements, and perhaps the debugging tool of your IDE to help you track down the errors.

Chapter **15**

Recursion

OBJECTIVES

- Learn what *recursion* means and see how it applies to methods.
- Learn the two perspectives on recursive calls: how to execute them and how to understand them.
- Study some interesting recursive methods.
- Learn about object recursion.
- Develop a skill in writing recursive methods.

INTRODUCTION

A recursive definition is a definition that defines something in terms of itself. For example, a *noun phrase* could be defined as either a *noun* or an *adjective* followed by a *noun phrase*. Mathematics is rampant with recursive definitions because using recursion is often the easiest way to define something.

Recursion is a powerful tool in programming. For some tasks, using recursive methods is much easier than using loops. In fact, there are *functional programming languages* that rely completely on recursion and do not have loops.

In this chapter, we study recursion and show how useful it is.

15.1   The recursive pattern

15.1.1   A simple recursive definition

A *noun phrase* is a series of adjectives (possibly empty) followed by a noun. Since *dog* is a noun, *dog* is also a noun phrase —here, the series of adjectives is empty. Since *the*, *big*, and *brown* are adjectives, *the big brown dog* is also a noun phrase.

In order to eliminate the phrase "series of" from this definition, we give a two-part *recursive definition*. A noun phrase is either:

1.   a noun

or

2.   an adjective followed by a noun phrase.

We use this definition to construct noun phrases. Since *dog* is a noun, part 1 of the definition tells us that *dog* is a noun phrase. Since *loud* is an adjective, part 2 then tells us that *loud dog* is a noun phrase. Since *big* is an adjective, part 2 tells us that *big loud dog* is a noun phrase.

The definition of noun phrase is *recursive* because it is defined in terms of itself: part 2 of the definition uses *noun phrase* to help define *noun phrase*.

Such recursive definitions occur often throughout mathematics and fields that use mathematics —for example, linguistics, which attempts (among other things) to define grammars for natural languages like English.

15.1.2   A recursive procedure

Activity
15-1.2

See lesson page 15.1 to get the procedure from the CD.

We develop a procedure that sets the elements in a segment of an array to 0:

```
/** Set elements of b[h..k] to 0.  Precondition: h <= k + 1*/
public static void setToZero(int[] b, int h, int k)
```

In writing the method body, we consider two cases: the segment is empty and it is not empty. If the segment is empty, there are no elements to be set to 0, so the method body can be terminated using a return statement. Second, if b[h..k] is nonempty, then first element, b[h], can be set to 0. Thereafter, the rest of the elements of the segment have to be set to 0. We indicate this in the method body with an English statement. The body, shown below, is correct, except that it contains an English statement.

```
if (h == k + 1)
    { return; }

// { b[h..k] is nonempty }
b[h]= 0;
```

Set elements of b[h + 1..k] to 0 // English statement

We implement the English statement. It has the same form as the procedure spec, except that it has expression h + 1 instead of parameter h. Therefore, the English statement can be implemented by a *recursive* call to this method:

```
setToZero(b, h + 1, k);
```

It is called a *recursive* call because it appears in the body of the method that it is calling. The final procedure is in Fig. 15.1.

Discussion of the recursive pattern

The body of the method consists of two cases:

- The *base case* consists of parameter values in which the task to be done can be carried out simply, with no recursive calls. Segment b[h..h-1] is empty —there are no elements to set to 0. The body simply returns.
- The *recursive case* consists of parameter values for which a recursive call is made. One step is made —set one array element to 0. Then a recursive call is made to perform the rest of the task.

The recursive call was developed using the technique for developing method calls taught in Sec. 2.2.2. The only difference is that the call is on the method in which the call occurs.

Comments on the code in Fig. 15.1

The procedure body of Fig. 15.1 is so short and simple that the comments are not needed, so we eliminate them:

```
/** Set elements of b[h..k] to 0 */
public static void setToZero(int[] b, int h, int k) {
    if (h == k + 1)
            { return; }

    b[h]= 0;
    setToZero(b, h + 1, k);
}
```

We can write this method body so that a return statement is not needed:

```
if (h <= k) {
    b[h]= 0;
    setToZero(b, h + 1, k);
}
```

However, we prefer the original body. It handles the base case first, returning as soon as it is handled. The rest of the body need not deal with it. We generally write recursive methods in the form used in Fig. 15.1.

```
/** Set elements of b[h..k] to 0. Precondition: h <= k + 1*/
public static void setToZero(int[] b, int h, int k) {
    if (h == k + 1)
        { return; }

    // { b[h..k] is nonempty }
    b[h]= 0;
    setToZero(b, h + 1, k);
}
```

Figure 15.1: Recursive procedure setToZero

> **Javanize and prepend**. We coined the word *javanize* to mean "refine into Java", or "replace by an equivalent Java statement or expression".
>
> To *append* a value to a list means to insert it at the end of the list. There exists no corresponding word to add the value at the beginning of the list, so we have coined one. To *prepend* a value to a list means to insert it at the beginning of the list.

15.1.3   A recursive function

Activity
15-1.3

We develop a function to return its `String` parameter but with blanks removed:

```
/** = p, with blank characters removed */
public static String deblank(String p)
```

For example, if the argument is the string `" a b c "`, the result of the call is the string `"abc"`:

```
deblank(" a b c ") is "abc"
```

See lesson page 15.1 to get the function from the CD.

If the argument contains only blank characters (or no characters at all), the result of the call is the empty `String`:

```
deblank(" ") is ""
```

In writing the method body, there are two cases to consider. The base case is the case that `p` is the empty `String`; there are no blanks to remove, and `p` itself can be returned.

The case that `p` contains at least one character itself breaks into two cases. (1) If the first character of `p` is a blank, the result is the rest of `p` but with blanks removed. (2) If the first character is not a blank, the result is the first character prepended to (the rest of `p` but with blanks removed). This yields this body, with some parts still in English:

```
if (p.length() == 0) {
    return p;
}

// { p has at least one character }
if (p.charAt(0) == ' ')
    { return p[1..] but with blanks removed; }

// { first character of p is not a blank }
return p.charAt(0) + (p[1..], but with blanks removed);
```

This function is correct, but it has two English expressions, which we have to Javanize. The expression (`p[1..]` but with blanks removed) is the same as the value of the function given in the specification, except that the expression has `p[1..]` instead of parameter `p`. Therefore, the expression can be implemented using the Java expression

```
deblank(p.substring(1))
```

We developed this call using our standard technique for developing function calls; the only difference is that it is a call to the function being written —it is a recursive call.

The final function is given in Fig. 15.2. And again, it consists of a base case (the empty string), in which the answer is easy to calculate, and a recursive case. The recursive case splits into two subcases; in each, the answer involves a recursive call with a smaller part of the string as argument.

Because the body of the function is so simple, the two assertions could be removed without harming readability. However, it is good to write such assertions in all your recursive methods until you have fluency with recursion.

15.1.4 A function for a math definition

See lesson page 15.1 to get the function from the CD.

The notation n! is read as "n factorial". For n ≥ 0, n! is defined as the product of the numbers in the range 1..n:

```
n! = 1 * 2 * 3 *... * n
```

By this definition, 0! is 1 because the product of 0 numbers is 1. We can write a recursive definition of n! by defining a base case and a recursive case:

```
0! = 1
n! = n * (n – 1)!  (for n > 0)
```

It is easy to javanize this recursive definition of n! as a function. For the base case, return 1. For the recursive case, return n * (n – 1), which can be done with a recursive call, as shown in Fig. 15.3.

Many recursive math definitions can be easily javanized in this manner.

```java
/** = p, with blank characters removed */
public static String deblank(String p) {
    if (p.length() == 0)
        { return p; }

    // { p has at least one character }
    if (p.charAt(0) == ' ')
        { return deblank(p.substring(1)); }

    // { p's first character is nonblank }
    return p.charAt(0) + deblank(p.substring(1));
}
```

Figure 15.2: Recursive function deblank

15.1.5   The recursive pattern

Activity
15-1.5

In the previous three subsections, three recursive methods were developed. They follow a pattern that is shared by all recursive methods.

1. There is one (possibly more) *base case*. This is a case for which no recursive calls are used; the desired result can be calculated without using recursion. The case involves the "smallest" possible arguments. In method `setToZero`, the base case was an empty array segment. In method `deblank`, it was a string of length 0. In method `factorial`, it was an integer 0.

2. There is one (possibly more) *recursive case*. This case requires a recursive call. In method `setToZero`, the recursive case was a nonempty array segment. In method `deblank`, it was a string with at least one character. In method `factorial`, it was an integer that is greater than 0.

In the recursive case, the idea is to identify a "smaller" problem of the same type and write a recursive call for it. Thus, in developing the recursive case, we look for a problem that has the same specification but on smaller values; this generally requires doing some processing before or after solving this smaller problem. This leads to recursive calls whose arguments are "smaller" than the parameters.

In method `setToZero`, the arguments of the recursive call were `b, h + 1, k`. In method `deblank`, the argument was `p[1..]`. And in method `factorial`, the argument was `n-1`.

How are the arguments of the recursive calls smaller? In method `setToZero`, the size of segment `b[h + 1..k]` is one less than the size of `b[h..k]`. In method `deblank`, the length of `p[1..]` is one less than the length of parameter `p`. And in method `factorial`, `n - 1` is smaller than `n`.

The big idea

Developing a recursive method will follow naturally as long as you hold consciously to the idea that in the recursive case, you have to:

> **Recursion strategy**. Identify a problem that is the same as the specification of the method but on a smaller scale.

```
/** = n! (assuming n ≥ 0) */
public static int factorial(int n) {
    if (n == 0)
        { return 1; }

    // { n > 0 }
    return n * factorial(n - 1);
}
```
Figure 15.3:   Recursive function `factorial`

15.1.6   Self-review exercises

SR1.   Define the term *ancestor* recursively —the way *noun phrase* was defined in Sec. 15.1.1.

SR2.   Define the syntax of decimal integers, like 5432 and 041, recursively.

The rest of these exercises ask you to write small recursive methods, which are quite similar to those developed in this Sec. 15.1. For each, we give a specification and method header. Write each one and then test it. It does no good to write a function that you think is right but is wrong. When testing, first write calls that test the base case; then slowly work your way up to calls with larger arguments.

SR3.   `/** Set each array element b[i] of b[h..n] to i */`
`public static void setToI(int[] b, int h, int n)`

SR4.   `/** Print the squares of the integers in the range h..n. */`
`public static void printSquares(int h, int n)`

SR5.   `/** Print n if it is not divisible by an integer in the range h..k */`
`public static void printIfNot(int n, int h, int k)`

SR6.   `/** Print x if it is one of the values b[h..] */`
`public static void printX(int[] b, int x, int h)`

SR7.   `/** Print n if it is divisible by an integer in the range h..k */`
`public static void printIf(int n, int h, int k)`

SR8.   `/** Print the square of the integers in the range 0..n`
`          in descending order of values in the range */`
`public static void printSquares(int n)`

SR9.   `/** Set every element of b[h..] with even index to zero */`
`public static void zeroEven(int[] b, int h)`

SR10.   `/** Print 5 if it is in b[h..k] */`
`public static void printIf5(int[] b, int h, int k)`

SR11.   `/** = s with each char duplicated, e.g. dup("bcd") is "bbccdd" */`
`public static String dup(String s)`

SR12.   `/** = sum of the characters in s (each character is a digit) */`
`public static int sumChars(String s)`

SR13.   `/** = s with each character lower-cased */`
`public static String lowerCase(String s)`

SR14.   `/** = s with every adjacent pair of characters swapped`
`             (e.g. swapPairs("abcde") is "badce" */`
`public static int swapPairs(String s)`

SR15. /** = s with the first, third, fifth, ..., chars removed */
   public static int removeE(String s)

Answers to self-review exercises

SR1. An ancestor is either a parent or an ancestor of a parent.

SR2. An integer is either a digit (one of 0, 1, 2, 3, 4, 5, 6, 7, 8, and 9) or an integer followed by a digit.

We present only the bodies of the methods.

SR3. **if** (h > n) { **return**; }
   b[h]= h;
   setToI(b, h + 1, n);

SR4. **if** (h > n) { **return**; }
   System.out.println(h * h);
   printSquares(h + 1, n);

SR5. **if** (h > k) {
      System.out.println(n);
      return;
   }
   if (h != 0 && n % h == 0)
      { **return**; }

   // { n is not divisible by h }
   printIfNot(n, h + 1, k);

SR6. **if** (h >= b.length) { **return**; }
   if (x == b[h]) {
      System.out.println(x);
      return;
   }
   printX(b, x, h + 1);

SR7. **if** (h > k) { **return**; }
   if (h != 0 && n % h == 0) {
      System.out.println(n);
      return;
   }
   printIf(n, h + 1, k);

SR8. **if** (n < 0) { **return**; }
   System.out.println(n * n);
   printSquares(n - 1);

SR9. **if** (h >= b.length) { **return**; }
   if (h % 2 == 0)

```
              { b[h]= 0; }
         zeroEven(b, h + 1);
```

SR10. `if (h > k) { return; }`
`if (b[h] == 5) {`
`    System.out.println(5);`
`    return;`
`}`
`printIf5(b, h + 1, k);`

SR11. `if (s.length() == 0) { return s; }`
`return s.charAt(0) + s.charAt(0) + dup(s.substring(1));`

SR12. `if (s.length() == 0) { return 0; }`
`return ((int) s.charAt(0) - (int) '0')`
`        + sumChars(s.substring(1));`

SR13. `if (s.length() == 0) { return s; }`
`return Character.toLowerCase(s.charAt(0))`
`        + lowerCase(s.substring(1));`

SR14. `if (s.length() <= 1) { return s; }`
`return s.charAt(1)`
`        + (s.charAt(0) + swapPairs(s.substring(2)));`

SR15. `if (s.length() <= 1) { return ""; }`
`return s.charAt(2) + removeE(s.substring(3));`

15.2   Some interesting recursive methods

15.2.1   Tiling Elaine's kitchen

Activity
15-3.1

Elaine has a 16-foot by 16-foot kitchen (see Fig. 15.4). In one of the squares of this kitchen is a one-foot by one-foot refrigerator. Elaine would like the floor of the kitchen, except for the refrigerator square, tiled with L-shaped tiles, each of which is a 2-foot by 2-foot square with one corner removed. Can Elaine's kitchen be tiled with such tiles? How should we go about it?

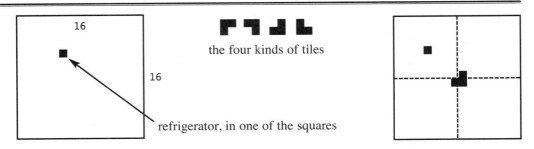

Figure 15.4:   Elaine's kitchen and the tiles

See lesson
page 15.3 to
get the method
from the CD.

We generalize to the task of tiling a 2^n by 2^n square, in which one square is already covered. This is for some $n \geq 0$:

/** Tile the 2^n by 2^n square with upper left corner (x,y). One
      square foot of it is already covered. */
public static void tile(**int** n, **int** x, **int** y)

We develop a recursive procedure to tile the kitchen. Part of our resulting program is in English, rather than Java, so that we can hide unimportant details. For example, we are not explicit about where the refrigerator is. This way, the beautiful idea behind the tiling is most easily seen.

We take $n = 0$ as the base case. Since $2^0 = 1$, a 1 by 1 square has to be tiled. But it is already covered, so no tiling needs to be done.

We want to solve the case $n > 0$ using recursion. That requires finding the same problem on a smaller scale, and the obvious thing to consider is a 2^{n-1} by 2^{n-1} kitchen. The way to get such a kitchen is to split the 2^n by 2^n kitchen into four quadrants, but then we have four 2^{n-1} by 2^{n-1} kitchens. One of them contains a covered square, but the other three do not. But we can place one tile so that it covers one square of each of these three quadrants (see the diagram on the right in Fig. 15.4). Now, all four quadrants can be tiled using recursive calls to procedure tile. The procedure is given in Fig. 15.5.

Isn't it a neat algorithm? And the key to its development was so simple. In the recursive case, consciously look for the same problem on a smaller scale.

15.2.2   Computing x^y

We develop a recursive function that computes x^y for $y \geq 0$:

/** = x^y. Precondition: $y \geq 0$ */
public static int exp(**int** x, **int** y)

If $y = 0$, then $x^y = 1$, so we use $y = 0$ as the base case.

```
/** Tile the 2ⁿ by 2ⁿ square with upper left corner (x, y).
    One sub-square is already covered. */
public static void tile(int n, int x, int y) {
    if (n == 0)
        { return; }

    Place a tile so that each quadrant has one covered square;
    tile(n - 1, x, y);
    tile(n - 1, x + 2ⁿ⁻¹, y);
    tile(n - 1, x, y + 2ⁿ⁻¹);
    tile(n - 1, x + 2ⁿ⁻¹, y + 2ⁿ⁻¹);
}
```

Figure 15.5:   Tiling Elaine's kitchen

See lesson page 15.3 to get this function from the CD.

Consider the case $y > 0$. If y is even, then x^y equals $(x * x)^{y/2}$. For example, instead of multiplying six 4s together, one can multiply three (4*4)s. Thus, if y is even, we can use a recursive call to compute $(x * x)^{y/2}$:

```
if (y % 2 == 0) { return exp(x * x, y / 2); }
```

If y is odd, we can compute x^y as $x * x^{y-1}$, using a recursive call:

```
if (y % 2 == 1) { return x * exp(x, y - 1); }
```

The function appears in Fig. 15.6. Like the previous iterative version developed in Sec. 7.3.2, it requires time proportional to $\log y$.

15.2.3 Computing Fibonacci numbers

The Fibonacci sequence 0, 1, 1, 2, 3, 5, 8, 13, ... is defined by $F_0 = 0$, $F_1 = 1$, and $F_n = F_{n-1} + F_{n-2}$ for $n > 1$. Each value in the sequence, except the first and second, is the sum of the two preceding values. It is easy to write a recursive function that calculates one of these numbers:

```
/** = Fn, for n >= 0 */
public static int Fib(int n) {
    if (n <= 1)
        { return n; }
    return Fib(n - 1) + Fib(n - 2);
}
```

The difficulty with this function is that it is extremely slow. To see this, start drawing the tree of parameters of all recursive calls:

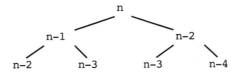

```
/** = xy. Precondition: y ≥ 0 */
public static int exp(int x, int y) {
    if (y == 0)
        { return 1 }

    if (y % 2 == 0)
        { return exp(x * x, y / 2); }

    return x * exp(x, y - 1);
}
```

Figure 15.6:   Function exp

The root of this tree indicates that the call Fib(n) calls Fib(n-1) and Fib(n-2). Then, Fib(n-1) calls Fib(n-2) and Fib(n-3), while Fib(n-2) calls Fib(n-3) and Fib(n-4). Thus, two calls Fib(n-2) are made, and one can see by drawing the next level that three calls Fib(n-3) are made. Moreover, one can prove that in calculating F_n, F_{k-1} calls of the form Fib(n-k) are made, for k = 1, 2, 3, ... That is a huge number of calls.

One can write a more efficient recursive function for calculating F_n, one that makes at most n recursive calls, by adding more parameters to the function. Here is a specification for the function:

```
/** = Fₙ, for n > 0, given k in range 1..n,  a = Fₖ,  and b = Fₖ₋₁ */
public static int Fib(int n, int k, int a, int b)
```

To calculate F_{10}, one would write the call Fib(10, 1, 1, 0). Exercise 8 asks you to write this function.

Adding parameters to help make a recursive function more efficient is akin to adding local variables to make a loop more efficient. Some of the exercises ask you to add more parameters to increase efficiency of recursive functions.

15.2.4   Merge sort

Activity 15-3.3

We develop a function that sorts array segment b[h..k]:

```
/** Sort b[h..k] */
public static void mergesort(int[] b, int h, int k)
```

This development shows a fairly simple use of recursion. However, the algorithm is less efficient than algorithm quicksort, which is shown in a later section, so it is rarely used in practice. This algorithm is called mergesort because it will make use of a method merge, which merges two sorted array segments.

We take as the base case a segment with at most one element, for such a segment is already sorted, so execution of the procedure can terminate immediately.

We consider the case of a segment with at least two elements. Suppose we view this segment as split into two separate segments, b[h..e] and b[e + 1..k]. These segments are chosen to be as close in size as possible, i.e. e = (h + k) / 2. Suppose we sort the first segment and then sort the second segment. Then it remains to merge these two sorted segments together. A procedure to do this was developed in activity 8-5.7 of the *ProgramLive* CD, and it is called using merge(b, h, e, k);. The completed method is given in Fig. 15.7.

See lesson page 15.3 to get this function from the CD.

This algorithm requires extra space of size (h - k) / 2 to hold a copied array segment during the last step of merging the two sorted segments together. However, the algorithm is much faster than insertion sort or selection sort. If the original array segment to be sorted has n elements, the algorithm always takes time proportional to n log n. In other words, if the original array segment has 2^m elements, it takes time proportional to $m*2^m$. In the worst case, insertion sort and selection sort take time proportional to 2^{2m}.

15.3 Execution of recursive calls

Understanding how a recursive method call is executed and understanding what a recursive method call does are two different activities. Separate the two completely in your mind.

Understanding what a method call does requires looking at the specification of the method. Make a copy of the specification and replace all occurrences of the method parameters by the arguments of the call; the result is a command, usually in a mixture of English and math, that is equivalent to the method call. It does not matter whether the method called is recursive or not; understanding what it does is the same.

However, you may be wondering how recursion works. Suppose in the body of a function `factorial(n)` there is a call `factorial(n - 1)`. Evaluating `factorial(n - 1)` requires executing the method body; how can the method body be executed a second time before its first execution is finished?

The answer to this is simple. If you evaluate an initial call `factorial(3)`, say, following *precisely* the steps presented in Sec. 2.7.2, you will see that those steps work for recursive as well as non-recursive calls. Nothing new has to be learned to handle recursion! Whenever a method is called, a new frame is created and pushed on the call stack, and that frame is destroyed only when the call completes. If there are 30 recursive, uncompleted calls to `factorial`, then the call stack contains 30 frames for `factorial`.

> Activity 15-2.1 shows execution of recursive calls in a way that we cannot do here. Watch that activity!

Activity 15-2.1 shows evaluation of recursive calls, showing how the call stack changes, in a way that we cannot match on paper. We urge you to watch it now to gain full understanding. You will come to understand that the steps presented in Sec. 2.7.2 work for recursive as well as non-recursive calls.

The *depth of recursion* at any point of execution in a call of a recursive method is the number of frames that are currently in use. Each of the frames takes a certain amount of space, say f bytes of memory, and it also takes time to allocate the space and to remove it. If the maximum depth of recursion during execution of a method call is m, then $m * f$ bytes of memory are required during execution. For some applications, this space requirement may be a problem, and people have been known to eschew recursion in favor of loops because of it.

```
/** Sort b[h..k] */
public static void mergesort(int[] b, int h, int k) {
    if (h >= k)
        { return; }
    int e= (h + k) / 2;
    mergesort(b, h, e);     // Sort b[h..e]
    mergesort(b, e + 1, k); // Sort b[e+1..k]
    merge(b, h, e, k);      // Merge the two sorted segments
}
```

Figure 15.7: Function `mergesort`

For certain recursive calls, called *tail-recursive* calls, no frame need be allocated, as we discuss in the next subsection. However, your Java compiler does not use this efficient implementation of tail-recursive calls. In subsection 15.3.2, we show how you can rewrite tail-recursive calls to make them more efficient.

15.3.1   Tail-recursive procedure calls

Activity 15-2.2

We use the first recursive procedure we looked at to discuss tail recursion:

```java
/** Set elements of b[h..k] to 0 */
public static void setToZero(int[] b, int k, int n) {
    if (h > k)
        { return k; }
    b[h]= 0;
    setToZero(b, h + 1, k);
}
```

Using synched animation, activity 15-2.2 explains this material better.

A recursive call of a procedure is *tail recursive* if it is the last statement in the procedure body or if it is followed directly by a return statement. In this procedure, the call:

```java
setToZero(b, h + 1, k);
```

is tail recursive, since it is the last statement in the body.

Because no statements follow this call, it can be executed without using an additional frame. We illustrate how this can be done using the call:

```java
setToZero(b, 0, 2);
```

This call creates a frame at the top of the call stack, which looks like this (we show also the array whose name is in b):

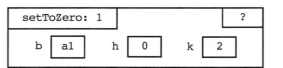

Execution of the body of setToZero begins. The value of condition h > k is **false**, so the statement following the if-statement is executed next. Since h is 0, this statement sets the first array element to 0, yielding this state:

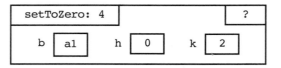

The program counter is now 4, indicating that the next statement to execute is the tail-recursive call setToZero(b, h + 1, k);. Once this call is finished, the above frame becomes active, but its contents will not be referenced because there are no more statements to execute in the method body. Since the contents of this frame are not used again, this frame can be used to hold the contents of the frame for the tail-recursive call, so a new frame for the tail-recursive call need not be created! For tail-recursive calls: a new frame need not be created because they can use the current active frame.

Execution of a tail-recursive call, then, can proceed as follows:

1. Evaluate the arguments of the call (in this case, b, h + 1, and k) and store them in the parameters of the active frame (variables b, h, and k).
2. Set the program counter to 1 so that the method body will be executed again.

Here is the frame after these two steps have been completed and just before the first statement in the method body is to be executed:

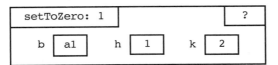

In method setToZero, the only recursive call is tail-recursive, so any call to setToZero uses only one frame! This method is almost as efficient as a loop that sets the array elements to zero.

15.3.2   Tail-recursive function calls

Consider a function f(*parameters*) {...}. Its body always terminates with a return statement:

> **return** *expression* ;

In a function f, a return statement of the form:

> **return** f(arguments);

is called *tail recursive*. A return statement of any other form is not tail recursive.

When the call f(*arguments*) in a tail-recursive return statement is evaluated, no additional frame is needed. Instead, the active frame —the one for the function body currently being executed— can be used. This is similar to the way tail-recursive procedure calls are handled, and we leave details to you.

There are many *functional languages*, like ML, Lisp, Scheme, and Haskell. When programming in these languages, the use of the assignment statement is avoided as much as possible. Instead, one writes almost all code using function definitions, function calls, and conditional expressions. Since assignments are rarely used, loops are used even more rarely. People who are fluent in recursion usually prefer it over loops because programs are easier to write and understand.

All compilers for functional languages recognize tail-recursive calls and implement them efficiently, using no extra frames for them, as shown in this and the previous sections. Thus, the additional overhead and space for recursive calls is eliminated, and the programs are just about as fast as ones that use loops.

Not all compilers recognize tail recursion and implement it efficiently. For example, Java, by design, does not. In the next section, we show you how you can rewrite a recursive procedure to make tail-recursive calls efficient.

15.3.3   Removing tail-recursion: procedures

Activity 15-2.3

We give a series of three steps for removing tail-recursive calls in a procedure. Each step preserves the correctness of the procedure. We illustrate removal of tail-recursive procedure calls using procedure `setToZero`:

```
/** Set elements of b[h..k] to 0 */
public static void setToZero(int[] b, int k, int n) {
    if (h > k)
        { return k; }

    b[h]= 0;
    setToZero(b, h + 1, k);
}
```

Using synched animation, activity 15-2.3 explains this material better.

Here are the first two steps:

Step 1. Insert a return statement at the end of the body (if it is not there).

Step 2. Place the procedure body in a while-loop with loop condition **true**. Label the while-loop and indicate its end with a comment. Use this convention whenever you implement tail-recursion efficiently yourself.

Here is the result of applying the first two steps to procedure `setToZero`:

```
/** Set elements of b[h..k] to 0 */
public static void setToZero(int[] b, int k, int n) {
    tailRecursionLoop: while (true) {
        if (h > k)
            { return k; }
        b[h]= 0;
        setToZero(b, h + 1, k);
        return;
    } // end tailRecursionLoop
}
```

Step 2 leaves the procedure correct, for the following reason. Since the last statement of the loop body is a return statement, the iteration of the loop is guaranteed to terminate by executing a return statement, so the old procedure body is executed exactly once, just as before the loop was added.

We now have the following situation. Each tail-recursive call is followed by a return statement. The final step of the transformation is as follows:

Step 3. Replace each tail-recursive call and following return statement by code that assigns the arguments to the parameters and then terminates the repetend using a continue statement.

In the case of setToZero, there is one tail-recursive call. Parameters b and k need not be assigned since they are the same as the arguments. Parameter h is assigned the value of the second argument, h + 1. The result of this transformation is shown below.

Each time you perform this transformation on a procedure, use the same label for the additional loop and the same comment at the end of the loop. Also, include the statement-comment for each recursive call, as done for setToZero above. Finally, include the continue statement even if it is the last statement in the repetend. Using these conventions will help you and others realize that this transformation was applied to the procedure.

```java
/** Set elements of b[h..k] to 0 */
public static void setToZero(int[] b, int k, int n) {
    tailRecursionLoop: while (true) {
        if (h > k)
            { return k; }
        b[h]= 0;
        // setToZero(b, h + 1, k);
        h= h + 1;
        continue tailRecursionLoop;
    } // end tailRecursionLoop
}
```

15.3.4 Removing tail-recursion: functions

Removing tail-recursive function calls is similar:

Step 1. Enclose the function body in a labeled while loop with loop condition **true**.

Step 2. Replace each tail-recursive return statement by code that assigns the arguments to the parameters and then terminates execution of the repetend using a continue statement.

We illustrate the removal of tail-recursive function calls using this function:

```
/** = k * n! (assuming n >= 0) */
public static int fact1(int k, int n) {
    if (n <= 1) {
        return k;
    }
    return fact1(k * n, n - 1);
}
```

Applying the first step of the transformation results in this function:

```
/** = k * n! (assuming n >= 0) */
public static int fact1(int k, int n) {
    tailRecursionLoop: while (true) {
        if (n <= 1)
            { return k; }
        return fact1(k * n, n - 1);
    } // end tailRecursionLoop
}
```

Applying the second step of the transformation results in the function below. Each time you perform this transformation on a function, use the same label for the additional loop and the same comment at the end of the loop. Also, include the statement-comment for each recursive call. These conventions will help you and others realize that this transformation was applied to the function.

```
/** = k * n! (assuming n >= 0) */
public static int fact1(int k, int n) {
    tailRecursionLoop: while (true) {
        if (n <= 1)
            { return k; }

        // return fact1(k * n, n - 1);
        k= k * n; n= n - 1;
        continue tailRecursionLoop;
    } // end tailRecursionLoop
}
```

15.4   Quicksort

See lesson page 15.4 to get Quicksort from the CD.

Procedure quicksort sorts array segment b[h..k]. Quicksort is the most famous and most used sorting algorithm. In the worst case, for a segment of n elements, it takes time proportional to n^2, but in the average or expected case, it takes time proportional to n log n. Moreover, it can be engineered to take space proportional only to log n.

15.4.1 Algorithm partition

Activity 8-5.5 discusses algorithm partition. A footnote tells you how to get it from the CD.

Algorithm quicksort rests heavily on algorithm partition, which is discussed in detail in activity 8-5.5 of the *ProgramLive* CD. In learning quicksort, it is important that you understand what partition does, if not how it does it. We explain it with an example. Here is its specification:

```
/** b[h..k] has at least three elements. Let x be the value initially
       in b[h]. Permute b[h..k] and return the integer j satisfying R:
    b[h..j-1] ≤ b[j] = x ≤ b[j+1..k] */
public static int partition(int[] b, int h, int k)
```

Here is an example. Suppose b[h..k] contains:

h				k	
5	4	8	7	5	2

The value in b[h] is called the *pivot* value. The call partition(b, h, k) rearranges b[h..k] to put elements smaller than the pivot value to its left and larger elements to its right. But the arrangement of the values in the two segments is not specified. Also, the placement of elements that are equal to the pivot value is not specified. We say that the specification is *nondeterministi* because different implementations can give different results and still satisfy the specification. In this case, there are several possibilities for the final arrangement of the array segment, two of which are shown here:

h		j		k				h		j	k
2	4	5	7	5	8			4	2	5	5	7	8

The value j of the index of the pivot element b[j] is returned.

The specification of this function is nondeterministic. Since we do not care about the order of values in the two final segments b[h..j-1] and b[j+1..k], function partition can be written to take time proportional to the number of elements, k + 1 – h. It makes up to k + 1 – h array comparisons.

15.4.2 Basic quicksort

Activity 15-4.1

We turn to procedure quicksort:

```
/** Sort b[h..k] */
public static void quicksort(int[] b, int h, int k)
```

We take as the base case an array segment with fewer than 10 elements. In this case, the array segment is sorted using insertionsort. Experiments have shown that this base case is efficient. Procedure quicksort is fast on large segments but relatively slow on small ones.

Consider the case of an array segment with at least 10 elements. Partitioning the segment using `partition(b, h, k)` produces an array segment that looks like this:

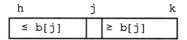

In this situation, what remains to be done? Well, segment `b[h..j-1]` has to be sorted and segment `b[j+1..k]` has to be sorted. Once they are in non-descending order, the complete segment `b[h..k]` is in non-descending order. So that is it! The complete basic `quicksort` is given in Fig. 15.8.

15.4.3   Quicksort at its best

Figure 15.9 contains procedure `quicksort` with one change. The base case occurs when the segment to be sorted has less than 2 elements, rather than 10, so that we can analyze `quicksort` on a small, 16-element array segment:

```
/** Sort b[h..k] */
public static void quicksort(int[] b, int h, int k) {
    if (k + 1 - h < 10) {
        insertionsort(b, h, k);
        return;
    }

    int j= partition(b, h, k);
    // { b[h..j-1] <= b[j] <= b[j+1..k] }
    quicksort(b, h, j - 1);
    quicksort(b, j + 1, k);
}
```

Figure 15.8:   Basic `quicksort`

```
/** Sort b[h..k] */
public static void quicksort(int[] b, int h, int k) {
    if (k + 1 - h < 2) {
        insertionsort(b, h, k);
        return;
    }

    int j= partition(b, h, k);
    // { b[h..j-1] <= b[j] <= b[j+1..k] }
    quicksort(b, h, j - 1);
    quicksort(b, j + 1, k);
}
```

Figure 15.9:   Basic `quicksort` with a base case of a segment with at most one element

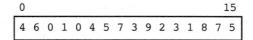

We develop an upper bound on the number of array comparisons that quicksort will make when sorting this array segment, in the best possible case, under the assumption that method partition performs one comparison for each array element that it processes.

When quicksort is given this array segment to sort, the if-condition in its body evaluates to **false**, so the assignment to j is executed. This assignment partitions as shown below —to the right of the array, we give an upper bound 16 on the number of array comparisons used to partition the array.

```
0                 j              15
┌──────────────┬─┬──────────────┐
│ 1 3 0 2 0 3 1│4│7 9 6 4 5 8 7 5│   16 comparisons
└──────────────┴─┴──────────────┘
```

The initial value in b[0], the pivot value, has been placed in b[j], everything to the left of b[j] is at most b[j], and everything to the right is at least b[j], so the comment following the assignment to j has been truthified.

Procedure quicksort sorts b[0..j-1] and then b[j+1..15]. But for this analysis, it is better to think of quicksort as partitioning both these segments and then sorting them. Below, we show the results of partitioning the two segments. Since each segment has at most 8 elements, the number of comparisons made in partitioning each of them is at most 8, for a total of at most 16.

```
      j                      j
┌──────┬─────┐      ┌──────┬─────┐
│ 0 0 1│1 3 2 3│      │ 5 5 6 4│7 8 7 9│   8 + 8 = 16 comparisons
└──────┴─────┘      └──────┴─────┘
```

Now 4 segments are to be sorted recursively: b[0..2], b[4..6], b[8..11], and b[13..15]. Each segment has at most 4 elements. The first step in sorting them is to partition them, and since each has at most 4 elements, partitioning them takes at most 4 * 4 = 16 comparisons.

On the next level, 8 segments are partitioned, each with at most 2 elements, so again it takes a maximum of 16 comparisons. This leaves 16 segments of at most 1 element each, and each is handled as a base case, so no more comparisons are done.

In summary, here is what procedure partition does on each level:

level	no. of partitions	max size of partition	max no. of comparisons
1	1	16	16
2	2	8	16
3	4	4	16
4	8	2	16

Thus, to sort a segment of 16 elements, or 2^4 elements, takes at most $4*2^4$ array comparisons. We can generalize this: to sort a segment of 2^n elements takes at most $n*2^n$ comparisons. However, this is only in the case that each call to partition partitions the segment into two segments of roughly the same size. The next section shows you a case where performance is not so good.

15.4.4   Quicksort at its worst

We do the same analysis for sorting an array that is already in ascending order:

```
0                                           15
┌─────────────────────────────────────────────┐
│ 0  1  1  2  2  3  4  5  5  6  6  7  7  8  8  9 │
└─────────────────────────────────────────────┘
```

Since the pivot value is 0, the call to partition could yield this array:

```
j                                           15
┌──┬──────────────────────────────────────────┐
│ 0│ 1  1  2  2  3  4  5  5  6  6  7  7  8  8  9 │
└──┴──────────────────────────────────────────┘
```

This call to partition took at most 16 array comparisons because each element of the array has to be looked at.

Sorting the empty segment b[0..j-1] takes no time. But sorting b[j+1..15] requires partitioning the segment, which requires up to 15 array comparisons and could produce the following:

```
j                                           15
┌──┬──────────────────────────────────────────┐
│ 1│ 1  2  2  3  4  5  5  6  6  7  7  8  8  9   │
└──┴──────────────────────────────────────────┘
```

We see that if the pivot value is the smallest value in an array segment of size n, partitioning the array takes up to n array comparisons and may produce an empty segment and a segment of size n − 1. This means that to sort the 16-element array could take up to:

16 + 15 + 14 + ... + 1 = 17 * 16 / 2

array comparisons. Generalizing, to sort an array of size n could take up to n * (n + 1) / 2 array comparisons, which is as bad as insertionsort or selectionsort. Quicksort does its worst on an array that is already sorted!

Further, the *depth of recursion in this worst case is the size of the array*, so quicksort may take space proportional to the size of the array, and that is bad.

We cannot easily reduce the worst-case time of quicksort, but we can take a few steps to reduce the probability of it happening. We can also modify quicksort to reduce the worst-case space requirements by reducing to n the maximum depth of recursion to sort an array of size 2^n. We see these changes in the next two subsections.

15.4.5 Quicksort's time/space problems

Making partition's segments closer in size

If the pivot value —the value in b[h]— is close to the smallest or largest value in the array segment, function partition will produce two segments of disparate sizes. We want the segments to be as close to the same size as possible. Making them the same size would require finding the median of b[h..k] and placing it in b[h]. However, finding the median takes so much time that the algorithm in total would be less efficient. So we don't do that.

Instead, we look at three values, b[h], b[(h + k) / 2], and b[k], and place their median in b[h]. While this doesn't guarantee that the segments are closer in size, it increases the chances that they will be. In activity 8-5.6 of *Program-Live*, we develop a procedure medianOf3(b, h, k) to swap these three array elements to place the median in b[h], and we call this procedure before calling function partition (see Fig. 15.10).

Solving the space inefficiency

Activity 15-4.4

In Sec. 15.4.4, we saw that the space required by quicksort was proportional to the maximum depth of recursion. The only way to reduce the space is to reduce the number of frames that are placed on the stack. We know how to do this in some cases, for we know how to implement tail-recursive calls without using more frames.

In the basic quicksort of Fig. 15.8, the last call is indeed tail recursive. We

```
/** Sort b[h..k] */
public static void quicksort(int[] b, int h, int k) {
    if (k + 1 - h < 10) {
        insertionsort(b, h, k);
        return;
    }

    medianOf3(b, h, k);

    // { b[h] is between b[(j + k / 2)] and b[k] }
    int j= partition(b,h,k);
    // { b[h..j-1] <= b[j] <= b[j+1..k] }

    if (j - h) <= k - j) {
        quicksort(b, h, j - 1);
        quicksort(b, j + 1, k);
    } else {
        quicksort(b, j + 1, k);
        quicksort(b, h, j - 1);
    }
}
```

Figure 15.10: Enhanced quicksort

see how to modify the algorithm to take advantage of this. We show how to minimize the maximum number of frames needed. For this explanation, assume that the number of elements, $k + 1 - h$, is a power of 2, say $k + 1 - h = 2^n$.

After partitioning, two segments are sorted. We change the body so that the *smaller* of the two subsegments is sorted first, as shown in Fig. 15.10. First, note that the new version is correct because the same two recursive calls are executed. The order in which they are executed may differ, but the order does not matter. Second, in each of the two cases, the last call is tail-recursive, so no extra frame is needed for it.

Consider the first call in each of the two cases. The segment being sorted is the smaller of the two, so it has less than 2^{n-1} elements. We use this fact to determine the maximum depth of recursion, assuming that tail-recursive calls do not need their own frames. The first frame is for a call with a segment of size 2^n. The next frame is for a call with a segment of size at most 2^{n-1}. The next frame is for a call with a segment of size at most 2^{n-2}. And so on. Thus, the frames for the calls are for segments of size 2^n, 2^{n-1}, 2^{n-2}, ... 2^3 (remember that segments of size 2^3 or less are base cases).

```
/** Sort b[h..k] */
public static void quicksort(int[] b, int h, int k) {
    tailRecursionLoop: while(true) {
        if (k + 1 - h < 10) {
            insertionSort(b, h, k);
            return;
        }

        medianOf3(b,h,k);

        // { b[h] is between b[(j + k / 2)] and b[k] }
        int j= partition(b,h,k);
        // { b[h..j-1] <= b[j] <= b[j+1..k] }

        if ((j - h) <= k - j) {
            quicksort(b, h, j - 1);
            // quicksort(b, j + 1, k);
            h= j + 1;
            continue tailRecursionLoop;
        } else {
            quicksort(b, j + 1, k);
            // quicksort(b, h, j - 1);
            k= j - 1;
            continue tailRecursionLoop;
        }
    } // tailRecursionLoop
}
```

Figure 15.11: Quicksort with tail recursion removed

Thus, we see that sorting an array of size 2^n requires at most n frames at any one time. As an example, to sort an array of size $2^{15} = 32768$, at most 15 frames are needed. We have indeed achieved a significant reduction in space requirements — if tail-recursive calls are implemented efficiently.

15.4.6   Removing quicksort's tail recursion

Activity 15-4.5

In Sec. 15.3.3, we showed how to remove tail-recursive procedure calls. We use this technique to remove the tail-recursive calls of procedure quicksort in Fig. 15.10, showing the result in Fig. 15.11. Figure 15.11, then, is our final version of quicksort. For an array segment of size n, it takes space proportional to log n. Its worst case time is proportional to n^2, but its expected time is proportional to n log n.

15.5   Object recursion

See lesson page 15.1 to get the class for generating permutations from the CD.

In a class C, we may create and store another instance of C, and, in that instance we may create and store another instance of C, and so on. This is a form of recursion, called *object recursion*. Of course, this process must stop at some point, or else an unending number of instances of C will be created. A folder of class C that contains a non-**null** field of class C is a recursive case of object recursion; a folder of class C that does not contain a non-**null** field of class C is a *base case*.

We illustrate object recursion using a class that enumerates the permutations of a String. The permutations of a String like "xyz" is the set of all its arrangements, e.g.:

> "xyz", "xzy", "yxz", "yzx", "zxy", "zyx"

The only permutation of the empty String "" is itself, "", and the only permutation of a String of one element, like "x", is itself.

We write a class PermutationGenerator with the following methods:

1. A constructor with a String parameter w.
2. A function nextElement; which returns the "next" permutation of w.
3. A function hasMoreElements, which indicates whether nextElement has been called enough times to produce all the permutations of w.

Suppose we execute:

> PermutationGenerator e = **new** PermutationGenerator("xyz");

Then, six calls of the form e.nextElement() will produce the six permutations of "xyz". Since we may not know how many permutations there are, we should always call function e.hasMoreElements() before calling e.nextElement(), to make sure another permutation exists.

Class PermutationGenerator implements interface Enumeration (see Sec. 12.3), but you do not have to understand interfaces to understand class

PermutationGenerator. Just know that by "enumerating" the permutations of w we mean returning them, one by one, as the result of calls to function next-Element. Also, the rule must be followed that nextElement is called only if it is guaranteed that another permutation of w exists to be enumerated.

Class PermutationGenerator is in Figs. 15.12. and 15.13.

Our basic idea for enumerating the permutations of a String like "xyz" is first to enumerate the permutations that begin with x, then to enumerate the permutations that begin with "y", and then to enumerate the permutations that begin with "z". We will do this using the following fields.

Variable word contains the word whose permutations are being enumerated, and hasAnother indicates whether all its permutations have been enumerated.

Variable pos contains the index of a character in word, and permutations beginning with character word[pos] are being enumerated. Variable subWord then contains the characters of word but with character word[pos] removed. Thus, we are in the process of constructing and enumerating:

word[pos] + first permutation of subWord
word[pos] + second permutation of subWord
...
word[pos] + last permutation of subWord

How do we construct these permutations of subWord? We use an instance of PermutationGenerator, whose name is stored in field subEnum. This is the recursively constructed object.

At this point, turn to the beginning of Fig. 15.12 and read carefully the class invariant, which describes the relation among the fields of the class.

Now, one can look at the constructor and see that it truthifies the representation invariant. Also, function hasMoreElements is easily seen to be correct.

Function nextElement is more complicated. First, if word is the empty string, it sets hasAnother to indicate that there are no more permutations and returns the empty string. If word is not the empty string, it first stores the next permutation in variable next —the permutation is the character word[pos] catenated with the next permutation of subWord. It then calls a private procedure getReadyForNext, which appears in Fig. 15.13. This procedure does what has to be done to make the class invariant true after permutation next is returned. Then, permutation next is returned. And that is it.

Generating permutations would be much harder if we did not use recursive objects. With them, the task turns out to be relatively simple.

15.6   Key concepts

• **Recursive definitions.** Recursive definitions play an important role in mathematics and fields that use mathematics.

• **Recursion methods and recursive objects.** In programming, recursion comes

```
import java.util.*;

/** An instance produces permutations of a string */
public class PermutationGenerator implements Enumeration {
    /* class invariant:
        (1) The definitions of word, hasAnother, and pos hold
        (2) In the case that word != "":
            (a) Definitions of subWord and subEnum hold
            (b) Permutations of word that begin with a letter in word[0..pos-1] have
                been generated.
            (c) All permutations of the form  word[pos] + e
                where e was enumerated by subEnum have been enumerated
            (d) If pos < word.length,  e has another permutation to enumerate */

    private String word;   // The word whose permutations are being enumerated
    private boolean hasAnother= true; // = "there is another permutation to enumerate"

    // if word is not "", then we use these variables:
    private int pos;        // 0 <= pos <= word.length
    private String subWord; // word but with character word[pos] removed
    private PermutationGenerator subEnum; // An enumeration for subWord

    // Constructor: an enumeration for w
    public PermutationGenerator(String w) {
        word= w; pos= 0;
        if (word.length() != 0) {
            subWord= word.substring(1);
            subEnum= new PermutationGenerator(subWord);
        }
    }

    /** = this enumeration has another element */
    public boolean hasMoreElements()
        { return hasAnother; }

    /** = the next permutation of this enumeration */
    public Object nextElement() {
        if (word.equals("")) {
            hasAnother= false;
            return "";
        }

        String next= word.charAt(pos) + (String) subEnum.nextElement();
        getReadyForNext();
        return next;
    }
}
```

Figure 15.12:   Class PermutationGenerator (see also Fig. 15.13)

in two forms: recursive methods (methods that call themselves) and recursive objects (objects of a class that contain an instance of the same class).

• **Base cases and recursive cases.** With regard to methods, a *base case* is a set of parameter values for which no recursive call is necessary; these cases are in some sense the "smallest" cases. A *recursive case* is a case in which a recursive call is made on a smaller problem of the same kind.

• **Model of execution.** The model of execution of method calls that was presented in Sec. 2.7 works even if there are recursive calls. A new frame is created whenever the method is called, so several frames for different calls to the same method may be in memory at the same time.

• **Depth of recursion.** The depth of recursion is the number of frames for calls to the same method that have not yet completed. There should be a maximum depth of recursion, or else there is infinite recursion.

• **Two perspectives on recursion.** There are two perspectives on recursive method calls. To understand a body with a recursive call in it, understand that call in terms of the spec of the method. To understand how recursion works in general, look at how recursive calls are executed, using the model of memory.

• **Tail recursion.** A recursive call is tail recursive if nothing is done in the method body once the call is completed. Tail-recursive calls can be implemented without creating another frame. However, if the system does not do that, you can remove tail-recursive calls yourself.

```
/** Variable word is not "". If subEnum has no more enumerations, then add 1 to pos,
    keeping the definition of all fields true */
private void getReadyForNext() {
    if (subEnum.hasMoreElements())
        { return; }
    pos= pos + 1;
    if (pos == word.length()) {
        hasAnother= false;
        return;
    }

    // Store in subWord the word but without character word[pos]
    // and create an enumeration subEnum for it
    subWord= word.substring(0,pos) + word.substring(pos + 1);
    subEnum= new PermutationGenerator(subWord);
    }
}
```

Figure 15.13: Class PermutationGenerator (continued)

Exercises for Chapter 15

1. (a) Define *descendent* recursively.

(b) Define the format of binary integers (sequences of 0s and 1s) recursively.

(c) Define the format of Java identifiers recursively.

(d) Define a list of integers separated by commas recursively.

2. Write a recursive definition for the product x * y of two integers x and y, where y ≥ 0.

3. Write a recursive definition for exponentiation x^y of two integers x and y, where y ≥ 0.

4. Write a recursive function to sum the values in a range. With the specification given for it, the values have to be summed from largest to smallest.

```
/** = sum of integers in the range 0..n, for n ≥ -1 */
public static int sum(int n)
```

5. The function of the previous exercise has a recursive call that is not tail-recursive. The way to change the function so that it will be tail-recursive is to add a parameter. Write the following function so that the recursive call is tail recursive.

```
/** = x + (sum of integers in the range 0..n), for n ≥ -1 */
public static int sum(int x, int n)
```

6. Rewrite the function of the previous exercise to eliminate the tail-recursive call using the technique of Sec. 15.3.4.

7. Implement the inefficient function to calculate Fibonacci numbers (see Sec. 15.2.3) and calculate some Fibonacci numbers to see how long it takes. Try calls like Fib(10), Fib(20), Fib(30), ... until you get some sense of how inefficient this function is.

8. Function fib of the previous exercise is extremely inefficient, requiring time proportional to F_n to calculate fib(n). The way to get a more efficient function is to add parameters to the function, as illustrated below. Write the function body. Make sure that any recursive calls are tail recursive.

```
/** = Fₙ, for 0 < n, given that 1 ≤ k ≤ n, a = Fₖ, and b = Fₖ₋₁ */
public static int FibLinear(int n, int k, int a, int b)
```

9. In Exercise 8, you wrote a function whose only call is tail recursive. Use the method of Sec. 15.3.4 to eliminate the tail-recursion from that function.

10. Write a recursive boolean function that tells whether a String contains a blank.

11. Write a recursive function removeDups that removes duplicate adjacent characters from a String. For example, removeDups("baaaccd") = "bacd".

12. Write a recursive function that tells how many blanks a String has.

13. Write the following function; the recursive case should involve substring s[1..]:

```
/** = the reverse of s. For example, srev("abc") is "cba" */
public static String rev(String s)
```

14. The previous exercise results in a function that has a recursive call that is not tail-recursive. The way to make it more efficient is to add an extra parameter. Write the following function, making sure that recursive calls are tail recursive:

```
/** = (the reverse of s) + t */
public static String tailrev(String s, String t)
```

15. In the previous exercise, you wrote a function to reverse a String whose only call is tail-recursive. Use the method of Sec. 15.3.4 to eliminate the tail-recursive call from that function.

16. Write the following linear search procedure, using recursion (no loops):

```
/** Return the int i that satisfies
       (0)  x is not in b[0..i-1] and
       (1)  x = b[i] or i = b.length */
public static int linearSearch(int[] b, int x, int h)
```

17. This exercise asks you to implement the binary search algorithm of Sec. 8.5.3 recursively. Write the body of the following function:

```
/** = an integer i that satisfies b[h..i] ≤ x < b[i+1..k] */
public static int binarySearch(int[] b, int x, int h, int k)
```

> Turn to lesson page 15.3 for an astonishing palindrome.

18. A palindrome is a String that reads the same backward and forward. Write the following function. The way to think about it is to understand that s is a palindrome if its first and last characters are the same and the substring between them is a palindrome. By definition, a string of length 0 or 1 is a palindrome.

```
/** = "s is a palindrome" */
public static boolean isPalindrome(String s)
```

18. Write a recursive function (no loops) to computer gcd(x, y), where x > 0 and y > 0. The gcd(x, y) is the *greatest common divisor* of x and y: the largest integer that divides both of them. Your recursive function can use (only) these properties of gcd:

- gcd(x, x) = x
- For x > y, gcd(x, y) = gcd(x - y, y)
- For y > x, gcd(y, x) = gcd(x, y - x)

19. Turn to lesson page 15-1 of the *ProgramLive* CD and click the project icon. You will see a project called Link extractor. This project is to build a Java application that produces a list of all links on a website. A recursive procedure is used to process the graph of web pages that are reachable from a given root. Do this project.

20. Recursive procedures are great for drawing geometric shapes that are repeated and drawn at increasingly smaller scales. Such shapes are called *fractals*. One example of a fractal is the Koch snowflake, due to a Swedish mathematician Helge von Koch. In the diagram on the left below is a Koch snowflake of order 0, an equilateral triangle.

The middle figure is a Koch snowflake of order 1. In each of the lines in the order-1 snowflake, the middle third of the line has been replaced by two sides of an equilateral triangle. In the order-2 snowflake on the right, again, the middle part of each line of the order-1 triangle has been replaced by two sides of an equilateral triangle. This process can go to any depth.

Write a procedure to draw a Koch snowflake of order k. You will have to put this procedure in a class that has a method `paint` —either a subclass of `JFrame` or a `JPanel`. Your instructor will give you details on this.

Here is the specification of the snowflake procedure.

```
/** Draw Koch line of order k (≥ 0) from (x1, y2) to (x5, y5) using g.
 */
public void drawFlakeLine(int k, int x1, int y1,
                          int x5, int y5, Graphics g)
```

For k = 0, the Koch line is simply a line from (x1, y2) to (x5, y5).
For k > 0, the Koch line is 4 Koch lines of order k - 1, drawn as shown here:

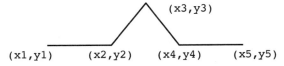

Let dx = x5 - x1, dy = y5 - y1, and p = sqrt(3.0) / 6. Then:

point (x2, y2) is (x1 + dx / 3, y1 + dy /3).

point (x4, y4) is (x1 + 2 * dx / 3, y1 + 2 * dy / 3).

point (x3, y3) is ((x1 + x5) / 2 + p * (y1 – y5),

(y1 + y5) / 2 + p * (x5 – x1)).

Points (x2, y2) and (x3, y3) are easy to figure out. The calculation of (x3, y3) is harder; it rests on trig and the fact that all four lines are the same length.

Once procedure drawFlakeLine is written, we suggest that you put it in a subclass of JFrame or JPanel along with static constants that give the coordinates (xtop,ytop), (xleft, yleft), (xright, yright) of an equilateral triangle and a variable K and then write this method paint:

```
/** Draw a Koch snowflake of order K by drawing three Koch lines of order
    K from (xtop, ytop) to (xleft, yleft), (xleft, yleft) to
    (xright, yright), and (xright, yright) to (xtop, ytop) */
public void paint(Graphics g)
```

Figure out suitable values for the points of the main equilateral triangle by experiment.

Chapter 16

Applications and Applets

OBJECTIVES

- See how to make a set of classes into a Java application.
- See how to make an application into an executable file.
- See how to write an applet and put it on an html page.

INTRODUCTION

There are two ways to make a set of Java classes into a unit that can be used elsewhere. The first is to build an *application*, which generally resides on your computer and can be executed when you want. The second is to build an *applet*, which can be called when a browser loads an html page.

16.1   Java applications

A *Java application* is a bunch of classes (in .java files) in which (at least) one class has a method main of the following form:

```
/** Called by system to start execution of the Java application */
public static void main(String[] args) { … }
```

The system calls method main to start execution of the program. The parameter, a String array, can contain information that the application uses when execution starts. The parameter is rarely used, and we will not discuss it further. So if you do not know about arrays, it does not matter.

In DrJava, there is no need for this method main because any static method in a compiled class, as well as any instance method of an accessible folder, can be called in the Interactions pane. But in other IDEs, method main is necessary, and you may have to tell the IDE which class contains method main. Each IDE has a different way to do this.

> **Manifest**. A manifest is a list of passengers or an invoice of cargo for a ship. The meaning has been generalized to a description of the contents of something, e.g. a jar file.

If you are using an IDE and you have told it which class has method `main`, any time you run the program, execution starts by calling method `main`.

Executing a Java program from the command line

In a DOS window or a command-line window, navigate to a directory that contains a file `Name.java` (say) that:

1. Has a static procedure `main` with one argument that is a `String` array.
2. Has been been compiled, so that there is a file `Name.class`.

Then, the following command executes a call to method `main` of class `java. Name`. The command should not include the suffix `.class` or `.java`.

```
java Name
```

16.2   Stand-alone applications

A Java application may consist of many classes. If you want to give someone an application, you have to give them all the `.class` files. That can be messy. Better is to put the application in a single file that can be executed easily, perhaps by double-clicking on its icon. You do this by making a *jar* file of the classes. *Jar* stands for Java ARchive —after *tar* files (TapeARchives) on Unix systems.

To make a jar file with name `app.jar`, open a DOS or command-line window and navigate to the directory where the `.java` and `.class` files are. Type in the following command (note: if command `jar` is not available, you will have to change your *path*. See the end of this Sec. 16.2):

```
jar -cf app.jar *.class
```

The "c" in –cf is for *create*. The "f" is for file, and it indicates that the name of the file to create follows, in this case, `app.jar`. The "`*.class`" is expanded to name all the `.class` files in the directory. So, this command makes up a jar file named `app.jar`, which contains all the `.class` files in the directory.

You still have to insert into the jar file something that tells it which class has method `main`. Suppose it is class `CMain`. Then do the following:

(a) Make up a file `x.mf` that contains one line of text:

```
Main-class: CMain
```

The suffix on `x.mf` stands for *manifest*. Make sure you hit the enter key after typing the text in the file because it must have a carriage-return or line-feed in it. You can create file `x.mf` in wordpad, notepad, DrJava, or any editor you want. Make sure the file is in the same directory as file `app.jar`.

(b) Type in this command in the terminal window:

```
jar -umf x.mf app.jar
```

The "u" stands for *update*, the "m" for *manifest*, and the "f" for *file*. Since the "m" precedes the "f", the manifest file name, x.mf, precedes the file name, app.jar. This command inserts into jar file app.jar the fact that method main appears in class CMain.

You can insert the classes and the main-class manifest in one step using:

```
jar -cmf x.mf app.jar *.class
```

You can now email file app.jar to anyone, and they can run it on their computer, whether it is a Unix, Macintosh, or Windows system, as long as their system runs java. To execute the program, type this (include the extension .jar):

```
java -jar app.jar
```

In some systems, you will be able to run the program by double-clicking the file.

If you want to see what is in jar file app.jar, then type this:

```
jar tvf app.jar
```

You can find out more about the jar command by typing the following and hitting the enter/return key:

```
jar app.jar
```

Variable path

If you cannot execute any of the commands java, javac, jar, and javadoc, then you probably have not set your *path* correctly. We explain this for Windows 2000; older windows systems are similar.

Your system contains a variable that lists directories that have executable files in them. Type path in a command-line window. A line will be printed that contains path names separated by semicolons. For example, one path name may be:

```
C:\WINNT\system32
```

There should be a path that looks something like this:

```
C  :\j2sdk1.4.1_02\bin
```

This is a directory called bin inside the directory where you installed the sdk. It may be different on your computer. If such a path is not there, you have to add it. Bring up the help in your Windows system, open the index, and look for *path*. There, you will find instructions on appending another directory to variable path. It may be something like the following, but read the instructions:

```
path %path%;C:\j2sdk1.4.1_02\bin
```

16.3   Java applets

Activity
16-1.2

A web page is written in a language called *html*, which stands for *HyperText Markup Language*. Web pages can contain *applets*, which are Java programs written in a special way. In this section, we show you how to write an applet. In Sec. 16.4, we discuss html and show you how to put an applet in a web page.

An applet is a Java class (together with other classes that it uses) that is a subclass of class java.applet.Applet. Class JApplet, in package `javax.swing`, is a subclass of `Applet`, and people prefer to use JApplet rather than `Applet`.

Class `Applet` (and therefore JApplet) has the five procedures listed below, which are inherited in any subclass. The procedures have empty bodies and can be overridden.

1. `paint(Graphics g)`: called to paint the applet's panel
2. `init()`: called to initialize the applet
3. `start()`: called to tell the applet to start processing
4. `stop()`: called to tell the applet to stop processing
5. `destroy()`: called to tell the applet to terminate its activities

The structure of an applet computation

Activity
16-1.3

When a browser loads a page that contains an applet, it starts the applet with these two calls:

```
init();   start();
```

Procedure `init` is supposed to initialize the applet, and procedure `start` is supposed to start any computation that the applet has to perform.

The browser also calls method `paint` to paint the applet; it will do so whenever it believes that the applet window needs painting.

If the browser window becomes hidden, perhaps because the user dragged another window in front of it or the user clicked the back button to bring up the previous page in the browser, the browser immediately calls method:

```
stop();
```

of the applet. This method is supposed to stop any computation that it is doing so that resources are not wasted. When the browser window becomes visible again, procedure `start` will be called again.

When the browser window is deleted, the browser calls:

```
destroy();
```

This procedure is supposed to relinquish any resources that the applet was using. For example, it could close a file from which it was reading or terminate any different "threads of execution" that it had started.

The use of different resources is outside the scope of this book. Hence, in this chapter, we do not discuss methods `start`, `stop`, and `destroy`. Below, we concentrate on using procedures `paint` and `init`.

A simple applet

Below, we show an an applet that paints text and a line. Figure 16.1 shows the applet as displayed in a browser window — it is the grayed rectangular area. You have seen procedure paint before in other contexts. For a discussion of this procedure, see activity 1-5.5 of the CD.

```
public class Apple extends JApplet {
    public void paint(Graphics g) {
        g.drawString(" Hello World! ", 30, 30);
        g.drawLine(30 - 2, 30 + 2, 30 + 70, 30 + 2);
    }
}
```

An applet to sum two numbers

The applet shown in Fig. 16.2 prompts the user for two floating-point numbers and then prints their sum in the applet panel. The applet does this only once because the statements that perform the request appear in init and not in paint.

Initially, the applet panel is blank. The first statement in method init calls method showInputDialog of class JOptionPane, which is in the Swing package. See Sec. 17.5.1. This method displays a dialog window on the screen, which contains the argument of the call and a text field. The user is expected to type a number and hit the return key or press button OK. When this has been done, the window disappears, and the number that was typed is returned as the value of the function call. In this case, the value is stored (as a String) in variable num0.

In the same way, the next statement displays a dialog window and stores the number that the user types into variable num1. Method showInputDialog makes it easy to obtain input from users.

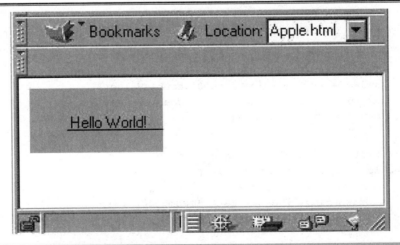

Figure 16.1: An applet to demonstrate procedure paint

Get this applet
and the next
from a footnote
on lesson page
16-3.

The values in num0 and num1 have to be converted to type **double**. This is done using static function Double.valueOf to convert a String to a value of wrapper class Double and then function doubleValue to yield the value as a **double**. The final statement stores the sum of the two values in variable sum.

Method paint is called only after init and start have finished, and inherited method start does not do anything. Method paint is straightforward. It just draws a rectangle that surrounds the text and writes the text.

An applet to paint a clock

Activity 16-3.1 discusses an applet that draws a clock on the screen. The clock is interesting because every time the clock is repainted, it obtains the time from the time on the clock on your computer. So, if you do anything to cause the system to call method paint, like resize the window, the clock is updated. The applet obtains the default Locale on your computer (see Sec. 5.5.2) and uses it

```
import java.awt.*;
import java.util.*;
import java.applet.*;
import javax.swing.*;

/** An applet that requests two double values from the user and prints their sum */
public class Summing extends JApplet {
    private double sum;     // the sum of the two values

    public void init() {
        String num0;       // First number, entered by user
        String num1;       // Second number, entered by user
        double number0; //  First number, as a double
        double number1; //  Second number, as a double

        // Read in first and second numbers
        num0= JOptionPane.showInputDialog("Enter first floating-point value");
        num1= JOptionPane.showInputDialog("Enter second floating-point value");

        // Convert the two numbers to type double and add them
        number0= Double.valueOf(num0).doubleValue();
        number1= Double.valueOf(num1).doubleValue();
        sum= number0 + number1;
    }

    /** Write the results using g */
    public void paint(Graphics g) {
        g.drawRect(10,10,120,20);
        g.drawString("The sum is " + sum, 20, 25);
    }
}
```

Figure 16.2:   An applet to sum two numbers

to obtain an instance of GregorianCalendar, which describes the time at which the instance was created in the Gregorian calendar —the calendar we use today.

We do not describe the applet in this text because it would require several pictures and a lot of text. We advise you to watch activity 16-3.1.

16.4 HTML and the web

HTML stands for *HyperText Markup Language*. Html is the language in which web pages are written. We explain the basics of html, using as an example the web page of Fig. 16.3, whose source file appears in Fig. 16.4. As you read this section, continually refer to these two figures.

The name of an html file usually has the suffix .html or .htm.

An html page consists of conventional text interspersed with html *tags*. An html tag consists of a command, possibly with arguments, within angle brackets < and >. As an example, every html page begins with the tag <html> and ends with the tag </html> Most tags come in pairs: one tag <*xxx* ...> to start something and one tag </*xxx* ...> to end it. The tags commands are case-insensitive; the tag <html> could have been written as <HTML> or <HtMl>.

The language html is also insensitive to *whitespace* (blanks, tabs, end of lines) in that several whitespace characters in a row are treated as one blank character. Thus, in an html file, you may see several blank lines, or 20 blanks at the beginning of a line, but they play the same role as a single blank in determining how the html page is formated. Therefore, you can use indentation and blank lines to help exhibit the structure of an html page, just as you do in Java.

If you want to place three blanks in a row on a web page, use the *escape sequence*   for each blank.

Between the tags <html> and </html> one generally finds two other pairs:

```
<head> ... </head>
<body> ... </body>
```

The material between the head-tags can contain various things, such as a title:

```
<title> A web page </title>
```

Within the two body-tags is the text that appears in the browser window,

---

A web page is written in HTML

Here's some red text

**Here's a different point size
and boldface** *and italics* <u>*and underline*</u>

Here's a link to <u>*Paul Gries's home page*</u> at Toronto

Figure 16.3: A web page

interspersed with various html formatting tags. For example, a new paragraph is begun with the tag <p>. The ending tag </p> is optional.

We describe a few of the formating tags-pairs that are used in html:

- <font color=red> ... </font>   The text between the tags should be red. This is the first tag that you have seen with an *argument*: In html, an argument is given by a parameter name, the = sign, and the argument value for that parameter. Java uses a *positional scheme* for giving arguments: the first argument is associated with the first parameter, etc. Html uses a *naming scheme: parameter=argument*. Therefore, the arguments can appear in any order. Arguments are sometimes called *attributes*.

- <font size=+1> ... </font>   The same font-tag pair as above, but with a different argument, which increases the point size of the material between the tags by 1.

- <b> ... </b>   Put the text between the tags in boldface.

- <i> ... </i>   Put the text between the tags in italics.

- <u> ... </u>   Underline the text between the tags.

-
   Practically the only tag without a corresponding closing tag. It gives a line break, or new line character.

The hyperlink

Surely, you have browsed web pages by clicking on a blue underlined

```
<html>
  <head><title>A web page</title>
</head>
<body>
A web page is written in HTML
<P><font color=red>Here's some red text</font></p>
<font size=+1>Here's a different point size<br>
<b>and boldface</b>
<i>and italics
<u>and underline</u><i>
</font>

<p>  Here's

a link to <a href="http://www.cs.toronto.edu/~pgries">
Paul Gries's home page </a> at Toronto
</body>
</html>
```

Figure 16.4:   The source html page for Fig. 16.1

phrase, causing the browser to load another page. We explain how this works. Consider the tag pair:

```
<a href="http://www.amazon.com">Amazon's page</a>
```

Parameter `href` of tag `<a>` has as argument the URL (*Uniform Resource Locator*) of the page that is to be loaded. Generally, the text between the commands is blue and underlined, and clicking it loads the page at the given URL. That is all there is to implementing a hyperlink in a web page!

The applet tag

Here is an example of an applet tag (and its ending partner), which can be placed in an html page:

```
<applet code = "Apple.class" width=100 height=200>
     your browser will not run this applet! </applet>
```

Parameter `code` has as its corresponding argument the name of a `.class` file that resides in the same directory as the html page in which the applet tag occurs. This `.class` file is the compiled version of a `.java` file that is a subclass of class `Applet` (in package `java.applet`). In addition, the applet tag has arguments that give the width and height (in pixels) of the rectangle that will appear in the browser page. We looked at class applet in Sec. 16.3.

When the browser opens the web page, the Java applet given in file `Apple.class` is executed. But not all browsers can run applets. A browser that cannot will instead display the text that appears between the `applet` and `/applet` tags.

If the Java `.class` files that make up the applet appear in another folder, even on a different computer, the URL of that folder should be given in a `codebase` argument. For example, suppose an IDE places the `.class` files in a folder named `Java Classes`. Then, use this applet tag, which uses a URL that is relative to the folder in which the html file appears:

```
<applet code = "Apple.class" width=100 height=200
  codebase = "Java Classes">
  Sorry, this browser does not do applets  </applet>
```

Any URL can be used to give the *codebase*, even one that refers to a folder on a different computer.

Specifying a jar file

An applet may consist of many `.class` files. If this applet is on another computer, each `.class` file must be obtained by sending a message to that computer to deliver it. Requesting and retrieving individual files in this manner is relatively time consuming —each could take several seconds or more. To overcome this problem, jar files were introduced —see Sec. 16.1.

An `archive` argument is used in an applet tag to specify that a jar file is available. For example, to indicate that the `.class` files are in file `Apple.jar`,

Activity
16-2.2

place the following archive argument in the applet tag:

```
archive = "Apple.jar"
```

Now, only one file has to be retrieved instead of many.

We have neglected to talk about passing parameters to the applet through the applet tag. See any html manual for a complete discussion of applet tags.

Concluding remarks

There are many more html tags, for example for linking to images and setting tables of data, but they should not be hard to learn.

A word of caution in using html the way we have shown. The trend is to eschew tags like <font>, <b>, <i>, and <u> and to use *styles* instead —this is not the place to explain styles. For now, there is nothing wrong with trying to write a few web pages using the commands we have described simply to get a feel for how html works.

Several software applications can help you write html pages without actually requiring you to look at the source html. *Netscape Communicator* is perhaps the simplest and is useful when one or two web pages have to be written. When a large web site is to be designed and implemented, one often use Macromedia's *DreamWeaver* or Microsoft's *FrontPage*.

Security with applets

Security is an important topic, given the current rash of attempts to break into and destroy people's web sites and computers. Lesson page 16-2 of *ProgramLive* contains a footnote that explains why applets are safe.

16.5 Key concepts

• **Java application**. An application is a set of Java classes in which some class has a static procedure main, with a single parameter of type String[ ].

• **Jar file**. A java application can be packaged in a jar file as a stand-alone application. It can then be executed with the jar command or by double clicking on it.

• **Java applet**. An applet is a Java class that is a subclass of class Applet. The subclass can override inherited procedures paint, init, start, stop, and destroy in order to have the applet do something. Use class JApplet (which is a subclass of Applet) in the Swing package, instead of Applet.

• **Html and the applet tag**. Html (HyperText Markup Language) is the language in which web pages are written. An applet can be included on a page using the applet tag. For efficiency, the classes that make up an applet can be placed in a jar file.

Chapter 17

GUIs

OBJECTIVES

- Introduce Java classes for creating Graphical User Interfaces.
- Learn to think of a program as responding to events.

INTRODUCTION

All the example programs used in this chapter can be obtained from the first footnote on lesson page 17-1.

GUI stands for *Graphical User-Interface*. GUIs consist basically of windows on your monitor that you use to communicate with an application. In this chapter, we introduce the basics for constructing GUIs in Java programs. The web page for this lesson on the CD contains links to tutorials on GUIs and to the API specs for the Java packages that deal with GUIs.

The basic classes for constructing a GUI are in package java.awt (abstract window toolkit) and in the newer package javax.swing, called the *Java Foundation Classes* (*Swing*, for short). The names of many (but not all) classes in package javax.swing are the names of their counterparts in package java.-awt but preceded with a J. For example, Button is an awt class and JButton is the corresponding Swing class.

The classes in javax.swing provide more flexibility and function than those in java.awt. The components in javax.swing are *lightweight*, while those in the awt are *heavyweight* (these terms are explained in Sec. 17.2.6). When possible, use the Swing classes.

Throughout this chapter, we explain and then summarize basic GUI methods. There are other methods that we do not have space to discuss. Get in the habit of perusing the specs so that you have some idea about how the GUI classes are structured and some familiarity with their methods.

Further, the *ProgramLive* CD contains far more material, with pictures and diagrams in color, than we can cover here. Watching the CD, rather than just reading this chapter, will be more informative as well as more enjoyable.

You can obtain source files for all programs in this chapter from the CD.

17.1 JFrames

17.1.1 The basics of JFrames

As you know from Chap. 1, an instance of class JFrame is a window that can appear on your monitor (See Fig. 17.1). The window has two visible parts: the *border* and the *content pane*. The border contains the title bar and resize control (in the lower right corner). The title bar contains the title and the usual maximize, minimize, and close buttons. The content pane contains GUI components such as buttons, scrollbars, and text areas —whatever the program has placed on it.

Creating a JFrame

The first statement below declares a variable jf and assigns to it the name of a new instance of class JFrame , with title "example". The JFrame window is initially not visible. The second statement, jf.pack(), tells the JFrame to "lay out" all the components that have been placed in it. The third statement makes the window visible. (The JFrame of Fig. 17.1 has no components.)

```
JFrame jf= new JFrame("example");
jf.pack();
jf.setVisible(true);
```

You can set the size and location of the window. Statement

```
jf.setSize(200, 70);
```

changes the window to a width of 200 pixels and a height of 70 pixels. Statement:

```
jf.setLocation(60, 30);
```

moves the window so that its top left corner is at horizontal pixel 60 and vertical pixel 30. To retrieve the current width and height of jf, use function calls:

```
jf.getWidth()    and
jf.getHeight()
```

To retrieve the position of the top-left corner, use function calls:

```
jf.getX()     and
jf.getY()
```

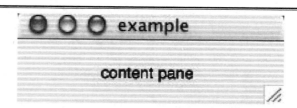

Figure 17.1: A JFrame

Preventing the user from resizing the window

Generally, the user can use the resize control to change the size of the window. To prevent such resizing, use method call:

```
jf.setResizable(false);
```

The close button

The close button can have various behaviors. The default behavior is to hide the window. Method call jf.setVisible(**true**); makes it visible again. You can change the action that is connected to the close button using the call:

```
jf.setDefaultCloseOperation( argument ) .
```

There are four possible values for the *argument*, all constants of class Window-Constants. Each provides a different effect when the close button is pressed:

Argument	Action when pressing the button
DO_NOTHING_ON_CLOSE	Nothing.
HIDE_ON_CLOSE	Hide the window.
DISPOSE_ON_CLOSE	Dispose of the window.
EXIT_ON_CLOSE	Exit program by calling System.exit(0);

Using a subclass of JFrame

We can define subclass BasicFrame of JFrame, with a suitable constructor, and place initializing statements in the constructor of the class. Other programmers using class BasicFrame will usually want to set the location themselves, delay showing the window, or alter the contents of the window. Therefore, calls to setVisible and setLocation are usually left to the user of the subclass.

```
public class BasicFrame extends JFrame {
    /** Constructor: a non-visible instance with title t */
    public BasicFrame(String t)
        { super(t); pack(); }
}
```

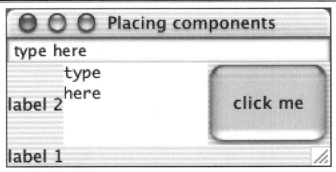

Figure 17.2: JFrame with a BorderLayout

An instance of this JFrame can then be created and made visible as follows:

```
BasicFrame bf= new BasicFrame("example");
bf.setLocation(50, 100);
bf.setVisible(true);
```

17.1.2 Placing components in a JFrame

Activity
17-1.2

A *component* is an object that can be placed in some window, like a JFrame.
Figure 17.2 shows a JFrame with five components, which we describe momentarily. That window is an instance of class ComponentExample of Fig. 17.3,
which extends JFrame. Besides a constructor, this class has a method main,
which creates an instance of the class and makes it visible.

Get the class of
Fig. 17.2 from
lesson page 17.1

There must be some means to place components in a window. In the Java
GUI system, this is done using a *layout manager*. A JFrame uses an instance of
class BorderLayout as its layout manager, and in a JFrame, the components are
placed in its *content pane*. That is why the second statement of the constructor of
ComponentExample retrieves the content pane and stores it in variable cp.

When using a BorderLayout manager, the content pane has five areas:
north, south, east, west, and center. Each area can contain one GUI component.

```
import javax.swing.*;
import java.awt.*;

/** Place components in a JFrame using default layout manager BorderLayout. Components
    in the 5 possible positions are: a JButton, two JLabels, a JTextField, a JTextArea. */
public class ComponentExample extends JFrame {

    /** Constructor: a hidden window with title t and five components */
    public ComponentExample(String t) {
        super(t);
        Container cp = getContentPane();
        cp.add(new JButton("click me"), BorderLayout.EAST);
        cp.add(new JLabel("label 1"), BorderLayout.SOUTH);
        cp.add(new JLabel("label 2"), BorderLayout.WEST);
        cp.add(new JTextField("type here", 22), BorderLayout.NORTH);
        cp.add(new JTextArea("type\nhere", 4, 10), BorderLayout.CENTER);
        pack();
    }

    public static void main(String[] args) {
        ComponentExample be = new ComponentExample("Placing components");
        be.setVisible(true);
    }
}
```

Figure 17.3: A subclass of JFrame with five components

Each of the calls `cp.add(...)` in the constructor places a component (the first argument of the call) in one of these five areas; the second argument, a constant of class `BorderLayout`, says where to put it. The diagram below shows the five areas of the content pane when using a `BorderLayout` manager.

```
.......NORTH.......

WEST   CENTER   EAST

.......SOUTH.......
```

The east contains a `JButton` (see Fig. 17.2). The argument of the call to the `JButton` constructor is the text to display on the button. Section 17.4 discusses how to make your program respond to a button click.

In the south and west of the content pane are `JLabels`, which are one-line display areas for text strings and images. Again, the argument of the constructor is the text to display. `JLabels` do not respond to mouse clicks or other events.

In the north is a `JTextField`, which is a one-line area into which the user can type. The constructor arguments are the initial text of the text field and the approximate width of the text field, in characters.

In the center is a `JTextArea`, which is a multi-line typing area. The constructor arguments are the initial text of the text area, the number of lines to display, and the approximate width of the text field, in characters.

Discussion

Basically, that is all there is to placing components in a `JFrame`. You do not have to add a component in each area. For example, if no component is placed in the east, the east part takes up no room.

Method `pack` of the constructor causes the components in the window to be resized to fit together, using the "preferred sizes" of the components. If `pack` is not called, the sizes of the components are unpredictable.

> Activity 17-1.2 shows what the JFrame looks like if it is not packed.

Even in the packed version, the center text-area is much wider than ten characters! This is because the north text field is so wide; the content pane is layed out so that each component gets at least as much room as it requested.

In the next section, we describe most of the kinds of components that can be placed in a `JFrame`.

Some older programs use the old class `Frame` of package `java.awt` instead of `JFrame`. (Actually, `JFrame` is a subclass of `Frame`.) In a `Frame`, the components are added to the `JFrame`, and not to its content pane, so local variable cp and the prefix "cp." on all calls to `add` would be removed.

17.2   Components

We give details about frequently used components, each of which is a subclass of class `JComponent`. To learn how to "listen" to a component, for example, to respond to a click of a mouse, see Sec. 17.4.

17.2.1   JButtons

A footnote on top of lesson page 17.2 gives more detail.

As shown in Fig. 17.3, an instance of class JButton is a component that can be placed in a JFrame. The creation of a new JButton is easy; the argument of the constructor in a new-expression is the string to be displayed on the button, e.g.:

```
new JButton("Yeeaaah")
```

Get a class that creates buttons from a footnote on 17.2.

JButton is a subclass of the older class Button of package java.awt, and you can create Buttons as well:

```
new Button("Nyaaaah")
```

and place them in the content pane of the JFrame.

A JButton and a Button look slightly different, as you can see in a footnote near the top of lesson page 17.2.

17.2.2   JLabels, JTextFields, JTextAreas

| Activity 17-2.2

Get a class that creates labels from a footnote. |
| --- |

Putting labels into a JFrame

An instance of class JLabel is a component that is a short text, an image, or both. In this text, we deal only with JLabels that are text. As you know from Sec. 17.1, the argument of a JLabel constructor is the text that is to be displayed. Here is an example:

```
JLabel label= new JLabel("top label");
```

If a window is resized by dragging, as activity 17.2.2 shows, a label may be partially obscured. Of course, you can drag to make the window bigger.

Retrieve and change the text in a label using getText and setText, e.g.

```
String s= label.getText();
label.setText("new text");
```

Labels are left-adjusted by default, but you can center or right-adjust them. For example, use this call to right-adjust the label:

```
label.setHorizontalAlignment(SwingConstants.RIGHT);
```

The constants of class SwingConstants that can be used as the argument are: LEFT, CENTER, RIGHT, LEADING, and TRAILING.

Change the vertical alignment using a call like the following. Possible arguments are these constants of SwingConstants: TOP, CENTER, and BOTTOM.

```
label.setVerticalAlignment(SwingConstants.TOP);
```

Putting text fields into a JFrame

An instance of class JTextField is a component that is a one-line field into which the user can type text. It is often called simply a *text field*. An example of a JTextField appears in the north part of the content pane of Fig. 17.2.

The size of a component. A JComponent has *minimum*, *preferred*, and *maximum* sizes. A layout manager tries to place a component using its preferred size, but its size will never be less than the minimum or more than the maximum.

In most situations, you do not have to deal with the size. But when a GUI does not look right, you may have to change the preferred size. Look at the API specs for JComponent, or look at activity 17-2.4 on sliders.

We found two places where it was necessary to change the preferred size of a component: (1) in using a particular slider and (2) in using a JPanel purely as a place to put graphics, without placing any components on it.

Here is an example of the creation of a text field and its placement in the center of the content pane of JFrame jf:

```
JTextField field= new JTextField("a text field", 11);
jf.getContentPane().add(field, BorderLayout.CENTER);
```

The first statement stores in field an instance of JTextField. The two arguments of the constructor call are the initial value of the text and the number of columns. The number of columns is only an approximation to the number of characters because characters have different widths. JTextField has other constructors; look them up in the API.

There are many methods for dealing with text fields. We discuss some of them below. Most of these methods are called in response to the user doing something in the GUI, like clicking a button with the mouse. You can create a JFrame with a text field on it in DrJava's Interactions pane and then experiment with these methods, with calls in the Interactions pane. So you do not have to wait until we discuss handling events before seeing the methods in action.

Making the text field uneditable

A text field is editable —the user can type in it. To make is uneditable, execute the method call:

```
field.setEditable(false);
```

To make field editable again, call the same function with argument **true**.

Playing with the text

Retrieve the text from the field using String function getText(). You can also retrieve just part of the text using a two-argument getText. For example, the following statement stores in s the substring field[start.. start+len-1] —that is, the len chars of text field field, beginning at position start:

```
String s= field.getText(start, len);
```

Change text field field to contain a string s using setText:

```
field.setText(s);
```

You can also append s to the text field or insert s at index i. The second statement below changes text field field to field[0..i-1] + s + field[i..].

```
field.append(s);
field.insert(s, i);
```

Playing with the selection

The user may select, or highlight, part the text in the text area. Your program can retrieve the selected text using the first statement shown below. Your program can also change the highlight. The second statement below selects or highlights *all* the text, while the third statement selects only field[i..j-1].

```
String selected= field.getSelectedText();
field.selectAll();
field.select(i, j);
```

Playing with the number of columns

Getter method getColumns() and a corresponding setter method exist, so it is possible to change the size of the text field while the program is running. If the size is changed, the JFrame should be packed again.

Putting text areas into a JFrame

<table>
<tr><td>Activity 17-2.2

Get a class that creates labels from a footnote.</td></tr>
</table>

An instance of class JTextArea is a two-dimensional field of editable text, called simply a *text area*. A JTextArea is shown in Fig. 17.2. That text area has a significant problem in that if too much text is placed in it —either long lines or too many lines— it will be difficult for the user to use. It would be better if the text area had scroll bars on it.

Below, we show code to create a text area with scroll bars and place it in the center of JFrame jf —the scroll bars appear only if needed.

```
JTextArea area= new JTextArea("012345678\nabc", 5, 11);
JScrollPane scrollPane= new JScrollPane(area);
jf.getContentPane().add(scrollPane, BorderLayout.CENTER);
```

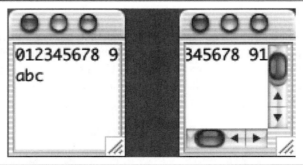

Figure 17.4:   Two snapshots of a JFrame with a JTextArea

The first statement stores in `area` an instance of `JTextArea`. The three arguments of the constructor call are the initial value of the text, the number of rows, and the number of columns. There are other `JTextArea` constructors; look them up in the API.

The second statement creates a scroll pane around text area `area`. The third statement adds the scroll pane, and with it the text area, to the center of the content pane.

Figure 17.4 contains, on the left, `JFrame jf` with a single component as created by the code above, as it appears in OS X on the Macintosh. To the right in Fig 17.4 is the same text area after three more characters have been typed by the user into the first line of the text area, causing the scroll bars to appear.

A `JTextArea` has several methods that can be used to manipulate it. Below, we describe some of them.

Playing with the text

Class `JTextArea` has the same methods as `JTextField` for retrieving and setting the text, making the text area editable or not, retrieving the selected text, and selecting a portion of the text, so we do not explain them here.

But note this: Even though the text area appears to be two-dimensional, from the internal view it is simply a `String` with new-line characters `'\n'` in it. Thus, your program will probably have to do more to process the retrieved text than it would to process the text of a text field.

Playing with the number of rows and columns

Getter methods `getColumns()` and `getRows()` and corresponding setter methods exist. So it is possible to change the size of the text area while the program is running. If the size is changed, the `JFrame` should be packed again.

Text wrapping

The default in a text area is not to wrap text. So, when the user types in a text area, the scroll bar adjusts to show the portion that contains the cursor where characters are being typed. However, you can set the text area to wrap the text using the method call:

```
area.setLineWrap(true);
```

Now, when the cursor goes past the right end of the text area, automatically the next characters are placed on the next line. When wrapping, the default is to wrap at character boundaries. Execute the following method call to wrap at word boundaries instead:

```
area.setWrapStyleWord(true);
```

17.2.3   Other components

Lesson page 17-2 describes better all the components mentioned in this section. Also, get sample classes from there.

Sections 17.2.1 and 17.2.2 describe the basic components that are used in GUIs: buttons, labels, text fields, and text areas. A number of other components can be placed in a JFrame. We list their classes here and summarize what each is.

- JSlider: A bar with a tab, which the user can move.
- JCheckBox: A titled box, which the user can check or uncheck.
- JRadioButton: a titled circle, which the user can check or uncheck.
- JComboBox: A menu of items; the user selects one, which is then shown.
- JList: A list of items, all showing (if possible); the user selects items.
- JColorChooser. An instance allows the user to choose a color. It is fun!

In addition, a class ButtonGroup can be used to group a bunch of JRadio-Buttons so that only one can be selected at any time. Select one, and the others in the group become unselected.

Activity 17-2.4 shows how sliders are created and used, and each of the other components listed above is described extensively in a footnote on lesson page 17-2 of the CD. The illustrations are in color and far better than we could do here, on paper. Further, from lesson page 17.2, you can obtain subclasses of JFrame that have the components on them. The *ProgramLive* CD is the best place to see examples of these components.

```java
import javax.swing.*;
import java.awt.*;

public class GraphicsPanelExample extends JPanel {
    /** width and height of the panel and a color for painting the panel */
    private int width;
    private int height;
    private Color color;

    /** Constructor: a JPanel that is colored c and has width w and height h */
    public GraphicsPanelExample(int w, int h, Color c) {
        super();
        color= c;
        width= w;
        height= h;
        setPreferredSize(new Dimension(width, height));
    }

    public void paint(Graphics g) {
        g.setColor(color);
        g.fillRect(0, 0, width, height);
    }
}
```

Figure 17.5:   A JPanel that is painted a certain color

17.2.4   JPanels as graphics panels

A footnote on lesson page 17-2 discusses this topic. Also, obtain a copy of the classes from page 17-2.

Component class JPanel has an inherited procedure paint, which is used to draw lines, rectangles, ovals, text, and the like using methods of class Graphics. A JPanel can be added to a JFrame, just like any other component. The class shown in Fig. 17.5 extends class JPanel, so its instances are components that can be placed in a JFrame.

In the context in which this class GraphicPanelExample is expected to be used, it will be used only for painting. Therefore, an instance of GraphicPanel has to set its own size in the constructor, using method setPreferredSize. Other than the call to this method, there is little new in this class.

Procedure paint in class GraphicPanelExample simply paints the whole rectangle that makes up the component with color c. However, you can change this procedure to draw whatever you wanted.

The subclass of JFrame that is defined in Fig. 17.6 illustrates the use of JPanel components. The constructor creates three instances of GraphicsPanel-Example and places them into the content pane of the JFrame. All three instances

```java
import java.awt.*;
import javax.swing.*;

public class GraphicsPanelExampleLay extends JFrame {
    /** Constructor: a frame with title t and three GraphicsPanelExamples */
    public GraphicsPanelExampleLay(String t) {
        super(t);
        JPanel cPane= new GraphicsPanelExample(50, 50, Color.pink);
        JPanel ePane= new GraphicsPanelExample(80, 50, Color.green);
        JPanel wPane= new GraphicsPanelExample(30, 50, Color.yellow);

        Container cp= getContentPane();
        cp.add(cPane, BorderLayout.CENTER);
        cp.add(ePane, BorderLayout.EAST);
        cp.add(wPane, BorderLayout.WEST);

        pack();
    }
}
```

Figure 17.6:   A class with three JPanels

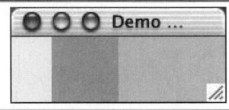

Figure 17.7:   An instance of the class in Fig. 17.6

of GraphicsPanelExample have the same height, 50, but they have different widths. An instance of this class is shown in Fig. 17.7, without colors.

17.2.5   Components versus containers

A *container* is an object that can contain displayable *components*. JFrame is an example of a container, and JButton is an example of a component.

Some components are themselves containers, so one can create components within other components. This provides a great deal of (needed) flexibility in creating GUIs.

Figure 17.8 contains a partial hierarchy of components in the GUI system. In the case of Button and JButton, Button is in the old package java.awt and JButton is in the new package javax.swing. There are many other such cases.

We have omitted many classes from the hierarchy, including layout managers (like BorderLayout) and classes that deal with menus.

```
Component
    Box, Filler, Button, Canvas
    Checkbox, Choice
    Label, List, Scrollbar
    TextComponent
      TextField, TextArea
    Container
      JComponent
         AbstractButton
            JButton
            JToggleButton
               JCheckBox
               RadioButton
         JLabel, JList
         JOptionPane, JPanel
         JPopupMenu, JScrollBar
         JSlider
         JTextComponent
            JTextField, JTextArea
      Panel
         Applet
            JApplet
      ScrollPane
      Window
         Frame
            JFrame
      JWindow
```

Figure 17.8:   Partial hierarchy of components and containers

17.2.6   Lightweight versus heavyweight

Skip this advanced topic on first reading.

You may wonder how a component is actually drawn on a window. Each component in the old `java.awt` is associated with a "native" program —one written in the machine language— that does the actual drawing. This native program is called the component's *peer*. Any component that has such an associated peer component is called *heavyweight*.

In the newer Swing package, the only heavyweight components are top-level ones: `JWindow`, `JFrame`, `JDialog`, and `JApplet`. All the others, like `JButton` and `JTextArea`, are called *lightweight* because they do not have an associated peer. They rely on the objects in which they are placed —ultimately one of the top-level components— to do the drawing for them. Since they do not have associated peer programs, they are "lighter".

In theory, you can mix lightweight and heavyweight components. In a lightweight `JPanel`, for example, you should be able to place a heavyweight `Button` and a lightweight `JButton`. But this mixing of components does not always work well because the two kinds of components have different properties. Therefore, if you have a choice, do not mix. Use components of the Swing package, wherever possible, or stick completely to the old `java.awt` package.

Here are two differences between lightweight and heavyweight components:

1. A lightweight component can have transparent pixels, so you may see whatever is underneath. A heavyweight component is always opaque.

2. Mouse events on a lightweight component fall through to its parent —the container to which it was added. Mouse events on a heavyweight component do not fall through.

There are other differences, but these should be enough for you to see why mixing lightweight and heavyweight components might create inconsistency that could lead to problems.

Sun's web page for Java discusses lightweight versus heavyweight components. The last time we looked, this issue was discussed at URL:

http://java.sun.com/products/jfc/tsc/articles/mixing/

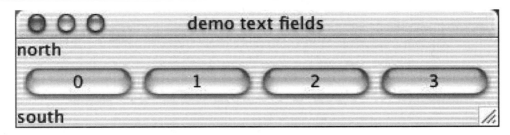

Figure 17.9:   A `JFrame` with a four-button `JPanel` in the center

> **Putting borders around JComponents**. This is an advanced topic. There is a way to put a border around any JComponent, like a JButton or a JPanel. You cannot put a border around a Box this way, but you get that effect by adding the Box as the only component of a JPanel and then putting a border around the JPanel.
>
> A footnote at the bottom of lesson page 17-3 of the CD shows you how to put borders around JComponents and gives several examples.

17.3   Containers and layout managers

Class JFrame is a subclass of class Container, which means that it can contain components like buttons and labels. JFrame, with a BorderLayout manager, may seem rather limited because it can contain only five components —in the east, north, west, south, and center.

We introduce two other containers, the Jpanel and the Box, which have layout managers FlowLayout and BoxLayout, respectively. Instances of JPanel and Box can be added as components to a JFrame —or even to another JPanel or Box. This nesting of containers allows us to construct a JFrame whose layout is quite complex and that can contain any number of components.

There are other layout managers, e.g. CardLayout, GridBagLayout, GridLayout, and OverlayLayout. We do not discuss them.

```
import java.awt.*;
import javax.swing.*;

/** An instance has labels in the north and south and a JPanel with four buttons in the center */
public class PanelDemo extends JFrame {
    JPanel p= new JPanel();

    /** Constructor: an invisible frame with title t, 2 labels, and a 4-button JPanel */
    public PanelDemo(String t) {
        super(t);
        p.add(new JButton("0"));
        p.add(new JButton("1"));
        p.add(new JButton("2"));
        p.add(new JButton("3"));

        Container cp= getContentPane();
        cp.add(new JLabel("north"),BorderLayout.NORTH);
        cp.add(new JLabel("south"),BorderLayout.SOUTH);
        cp.add(p,BorderLayout.CENTER);

        pack();
    }
}
```

Figure 17.10:   Class PanelDemo

17.3.1   JPanels and FlowLayout managers

Activity 17-3.1 does a better job than we can do on paper.

Get the class of Fig. 17.9 from a footnote on lesson page 17-3.

A JPanel is a transparent Swing container used to group related components. As an example, consider the JFrame in Fig. 17.9. It has a JPanel in the center and JLabels in the north and south. The JPanel contains four buttons.

Figure 17.9 is an instance of class PanelDemo of Fig. 17.10. The class has a field p, which is initialized to contain a JPanel. In the constructor, four buttons are added to p, one by one, using procedure p.add. Unlike previous calls of procedure add, these calls have only one argument; we explain why later.

Next, the content pane of the JFrame is stored in variable cp, and the JPanel and labels are added to the content pane. Finally, the JFrame is packed.

FlowLayout managers

Much like a JFrame's content pane, a JPanel is a subclass of Container, so a JPanel can contain other components —four buttons in this case.

By default, a JPanel uses as layout manager an instance of class FlowLayout, not BorderLayout. When using a FlowLayout manager, components are added using a one-argument method add. Any number of components can be added, and they appear from left to right, in the order added.

Activity 17-3.1 demos adding new rows.

If there is not enough room to hold components in a JPanel horizontally, new rows are added to contain them. Thus, you can see why the layout manager is called a *flow layout* manager; the components in it go with the flow.

That is all there is to FlowLayout managers.

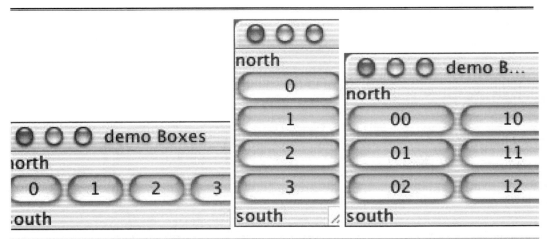

Figure 17.11:   Three JFrames with Boxes in them

17.3.2 Boxes and BoxLayout managers

The leftmost JFrame of Fig. 17.11 looks like it contains a JPanel in its center. However, the center is really an instance of class Box. Like JPanel, Box has Container as a superclass. But it uses a BoxLayout manager instead of a FlowLayout manager.

The leftmost JFrame is an instance of class BoxDemo of Fig. 17.12. We investigate its constructor.

The second statement creates and stores in variable b a Box object. The argument of the constructor call is a constant of layout manager BoxLayout, which tells the layout manager to lay out the Box horizontally. Then, the four buttons are added to Box b using a single-argument add procedure, just as with a FlowLayout manager.

Following that, the JFrame's content pane is stored in variable cp and the components are added to content pane cp, with the Box object in the center. Finally, the JFrame is packed.

When using a BoxLayout manager, components are added one at a time, using the one-argument method add. But with a BoxLayout manager, the components always stay in a row. They may get squished together, but they remain in one row.

```java
import java.awt.*;
import javax.swing.*;

public class BoxDemo extends JFrame {
    /** Constructor: an invisible frame with title t, labels in the north and south,
        and a four-button horizontal Box in the center. */
    public BoxDemo(String t) {
        super(t);

        Box b= new Box(BoxLayout.X_AXIS);
        b.add(new JButton("0"));
        b.add(new JButton("1"));
        b.add(new JButton("2"));
        b.add(new JButton("3"));

        Container cp= getContentPane();
        cp.add(new JLabel("north"), BorderLayout.NORTH);
        cp.add(new JLabel("south"), BorderLayout.SOUTH);
        cp.add(b, BorderLayout.CENTER);
        pack();
    }
}
```

Figure 17.12: Class BoxDemo

Vertical versus horizontal layout

Because the argument to the Box constructor is BoxLayout.X-AXIS, the line of components is horizontal. If we change the argument to BoxLayout.Y_AXIS, the line of components is vertical, as shown in the center of Fig. 17.11.

A rectangular layout of buttons

Class Box and layout manager BoxLayout, together with the fact that we can nest components, can be used to construct quite complex layouts. As an example of this, we show code that, when placed in the constructor, produces the rightmost JFrame of Fig. 17.11, which looks like a rectangle of buttons.

First, create variable leftBox, store in it a vertical Box, and add three buttons to it:

```
Box leftBox= new Box(BoxLayout.Y_AXIS);
leftBox.add(new JButton(" 00 "));
leftBox.add(new JButton(" 01 "));
leftBox.add(new JButton(" 02 "));
```

Second, create a rightBox, store in it a vertical Box, and add three buttons to it:

```
Box rightBox= new Box(BoxLayout.Y_AXIS);
rightBox.add(new JButton(" 10 "));
rightBox.add(new JButton(" 11 "));
rightBox.add(new JButton(" 12 "));
```

Third, create variable b, store in it a horizontal Box, and add boxes leftBox and rightBox to it:

```
Box b= new Box(BoxLayout.X_AXIS);
b.add(leftBox);
b.add(rightBox);
```

Finally, add the labels and box b to the content pane and pack it:

```
Container cp= getContentPane();
cp.add(new JLabel(" north "), BorderLayout.NORTH);
cp.add(new JLabel(" south "), BorderLayout.SOUTH);
cp.add(b, BorderLayout.CENTER);
pack();
```

The ability to nest containers in other containers, together with the ability to create horizontally or vertically placed components, makes it quite easy to construct complex GUI designs.

Leaving spaces in a Box

Look at the JFrame on the right in Fig. 17.11. Suppose we do not want the right middle button, but we do want the lower right button to remain at the bottom. To do this, instead of adding the button to `rightBox`, create an invisible component and add it:

```
rightBox.add(Box.createGlue());
```

Class `Box` has a number of static methods for generating components that create space in one fashion or another. Study the class specification to find out more about them. Here are some of them:

```
Box.createGlue();              Box.createRigidArea(…);
Box.VerticalGlue();            Box.createHorizontalGlue();
Box.createVerticalStrut(…);    Box.createHorizontalStrut(…);
```

Be careful with these procedures, for their action when the `JFrame` is resized is not always clear. When using these features, you might fix the `JFrame` so it cannot be resized by the user:

```
setResizable(false);
```

17.3.3   Using different layout managers

Obtain a class ChangeLayout Demo from a footnote on lesson page 17-3.

It is possible to change the layout manager of a `JFrame` (but not to a `BoxLayout` manager). For example, to change it to a flow layout, use:

```
getContentPane.setLayout(new FlowLayout());
```

`BoxLayout` managers are reserved only for `Box` objects. If you want to use a `BoxLayout` manager for a `JFrame`, then create a `Box` and place it as the sole component of the `JFrame`, as outlined here:

```
JFrame jf= new JFrame("title");
Box b= new Box(BoxLayout.X_AXIS);
Add components to b;
jf.add(b,BorderLayout.CENTER);
```

17.4   Listening to a GUI

Lesson page 17-4

A GUI is useful only when it reacts to events —clicking a button, typing in a text field, etc. In order to react, the program must have access to the events. In this section, we show how to listen to events. We concentrate on listening to buttons and to mouse events, for those are the most widely used events.

Figure 17.13:   A `JFrame` with two buttons, in two different states

17.4.1   Button events

To the left in Fig. 17.13 is a JFrame with two buttons. The east button is enabled, so pressing it will cause an action to be performed; the west button is disabled and appears grayed out. Clicking the east button disables it and enables the west button, changing the JFrame into the state shown to the right in Fig. 17.13. Then, clicking the west button disables it and enables the east button again.

Obtain the class of Fig. 17.13 from lesson page 17-4.

The JFrame in Fig. 17.13 is an instance of class ButtonDemo1 of Fig. 17.14. We show you how this class accomplishes its task in two steps. First, we show the part that lays out the JFrame; second, we show how to make the buttons *listen* to mouse clicks. Note that the class contains a statement to import classes of package java.awt.event; some of these classes are used in listening to events.

```java
import javax.swing.*;
import java.awt.*;
import java.awt.event.*;

public class ButtonDemo1 extends JFrame implements ActionListener {
    // Class invariant: exactly one of eastButton and westButton is enabled
    private JButton westButton= new JButton("west");
    private JButton eastButton= new JButton("east");

    /** Constructor: invisible frame with title t and 2 buttons */
    public ButtonDemo1(String t) {
        super(t);

        Container cp= getContentPane();
        cp.add(westButton, BorderLayout.WEST);
        cp.add(eastButton, BorderLayout.EAST);

        westButton.setEnabled(false);
        eastButton.setEnabled(true);

        westButton.addActionListener(this);
        eastButton.addActionListener(this);

        pack();
    }

    /** Process a click of a button */
    public void actionPerformed(ActionEvent e) {
        boolean b= eastButton.isEnabled();
        eastButton.setEnabled(!b);
        westButton.setEnabled(b);
    }
}
```

Figure 17.14:   Listening to buttons

Laying out the JFrame

In the class, two buttons are created, `eastButton` and `westButton`. The assertion for the two declarations, the *class invariant*, lets the reader know that exactly one of the buttons is enabled at any point. As might be expected, the constructor adds the two buttons to the content pane. And, two statements disable the west button and enable the east button, thus truthifying the class invariant. At the end of the constructor, the frame is packed, as usual.

Making the buttons listen

Making a button listen is a three-step process:

1. Write a procedure `actionPerformed` to process a button click. It must have one argument of type `ActionEvent`. Our procedure is given at the bottom of the class in Fig. 17.14. It stores in local variable b a boolean that indicates whether button `eastButton` is enabled and sets the enabledness of the two buttons accordingly. Here, you see calls to two methods of class `JButton`: `isEnabled` and `setEnabled`. This particular procedure does not access its parameter e. We talk about that later.

2. Have the class implement interface `ActionListener`. This ensures that `actionPerformed` appears in the class. Do this by putting an *implements clause* in the method header, as shown in Fig. 17.14. Do not worry if you do not know about interfaces and implements clauses. Just do this.

3. Add an instance of this class as an *action listener* for the button. For example, the following call adds this instance as a listener of button `westButton`. Remember that keyword **this**, used in a method, refers to the instance in which the method appears.

    `westButton.addActionListener(`**this**`);`

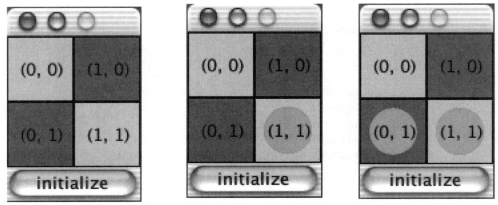

Figure 17.15: Listening to mouse events

/** A JPanel of size (WIDTH, HEIGHT) with no components. Green or red depending on whether
the sum of the parameters of the constructor is even. Click square to produce a pink disk on it;
click again to remove the disk. */

```
public class Square extends JPanel {
    /** Height and width of square */
    public static final int HEIGHT= 50;
    public static final int WIDTH= 50;

    private int x; /* x-coordinate of square on board */
    private int y; /* y-coordinate of square on board */
    private boolean hasDisk= false; /* = "the square has a pink disk" */

    /** Constructor: a square at (x, y) */
    public Square(int x, int y) {
        this.x= x;   this.y= y;
        setPreferredSize(new Dimension(WIDTH, HEIGHT));
        this.addMouseListener(new MouseEvents());
    }

    /** paint this square using g */
    public void paint(Graphics g) {
        if ((x+y)%2 == 0) { g.setColor(Color.green); }
        else { g.setColor(Color.red); }

        g.fillRect(0, 0, WIDTH - 1 , HEIGHT - 1);

        if (hasDisk) {
            g.setColor(Color.pink);
            g.fillOval(7, 7, WIDTH - 14, HEIGHT - 14);
        }
        g.setColor(Color.black);
        g.drawRect(0, 0, WIDTH - 1 , HEIGHT - 1);
        g.drawString("(" + x + ", " + y + ")", 10, 5 + HEIGHT / 2);
    }

    /** Complement the "has pink disk" property */
    public void complementDisk() { hasDisk= !hasDisk; repaint(); }

    /** Remove pink disk (if present) */
    public void clearDisk() { hasDisk= false; repaint(); }

    /** Contains methods that process mouse events */
    public class MouseEvents extends MouseInputAdapter {
        /** Complement the "has pink disk" property */
        public void mouseClicked(MouseEvent e) { complementDisk(); }
    }
}
```

Figure 17.16: Class Square

Now, whenever button westButton (say) is clicked by the user, method actionPerformed is called to process the click.

This may seem like a lot of work, but there are only three pieces that you have not seen before: (1) a procedure that processes mouse clicks, (2) the implements clause, and (3) a call to register this instance as a listener of the button.

Differentiating among buttons

Procedure actionPerformed of Fig. 17.14 does the same thing no matter which of the two buttons is clicked. In some situations, we want different actions for different buttons. We describe two ways to identify the source of an event:

1. Within actionPerformed, determine the component that caused the event. Do this using parameter e of procedure actionPerformed, which is a description of the event that caused the method to be called. Method e.getSource() yields the component on which the event occurred. So, we can test whether the component is the east button.

   if (e.getSource == eastButton) ...

2. Provide different actionPerformed procedures. This requires providing different classes to contain the different procedures and takes more work. It can sometimes best be done using an inner class. We do not discuss this here but leave it to activity 17-4.2 and a footnote on lesson page 17-4.

17.4.2   Mouse events: class Square

The leftmost JFrame in Fig. 17.15 contains a GUI, which contains the basics for constructing a checkerboard. Click on a square, and a pink disk appears in it, as shown in the middle JFrame. Well, it should be pink, and the squares themselves are in living red and green, if you look at them in activity 17-4.3. Click again on the same square and pink disk disappears. Do this any number of times, and for any square. To remove all the pink disks, click button initialize.

Each of the four squares is an instance of class Square, which extends class JPanel as shown in Fig. 17.16. We do not add components to the JPanel. We only draw on it using methods of class Graphics. Each square is 50 by 50 pixels. Two fields contain the coordinates of the square —used to print on the square— and field hasDisk indicates whether a disk is present on the square.

The constructor saves its two parameters in the fields and sets the preferred size of the JPanel to WIDTH and HEIGHT. Its last statement is explained later.

Method paint is called by the system whenever the square has to be repainted. First, it sets the pen color to the background color —green or red— and fills in the square with that color. Second, if a pink disk is to be drawn, it sets the pen color to pink and draws the disk. Last, it sets the pen color to black, draws the border, and draws the coordinates on the square. The order in which these actions are done is important since each item is drawn on top of the previous one.

```java
import javax.swing.*;
import java.awt.*;
import java.awt.event.*;

public class MouseDemo extends JFrame {
    Box leftColumn= new Box(BoxLayout.Y_AXIS);
    Square b00= new Square(0,0);
    Square b01= new Square(0,1);

    Box rightColumn= new Box(BoxLayout.Y_AXIS);
    Square b10= new Square(1,0);
    Square b11= new Square(1,1);

    JButton jb= new JButton("initialize");
    Box b= new Box(BoxLayout.X_AXIS);

    /** Constructor: an invisible JFrame with title t */
    public MouseDemo(String t) {
        super(t);
        leftColumn.add(b00);
        leftColumn.add(b01);
        b.add(leftColumn);

        rightColumn.add(b10);
        rightColumn.add(b11);
        b.add(rightColumn);

        Container cp= getContentPane();
        cp.add(b, BorderLayout.CENTER);
        cp.add(jb, BorderLayout.SOUTH);

        jb.addActionListener(new ButtonListener());

        pack();
        setResizable(false);
    }

    /** Respond to mouse click on button jb */
    public class ButtonListener implements ActionListener {
        public void actionPerformed(ActionEvent e) {
            b00.clearDisk();
            b01.clearDisk();
            b10.clearDisk();
            b11.clearDisk();
        }
    }
}
```

Figure 17.17:   Class MouseDemo

Method `complementDisk` complements the disk-present property —if there is a disk, it removes the disk, and vice versa. Method `clearDisk` makes sure there is no disk. Both methods call `repaint`, telling the system that the square must be repainted.

Registering for mouse clicks

Now look in Fig. 17.16 at class `MouseEvents`, which is defined at the bottom of class `Square`. You may not have known that one class can be declared within another. Class `MouseEvents` is an *inner class* of class `Square`. We need it to be an inner class so that, by the inside-out rule (see Sec. 2.4), its method `mouseClicked` can reference method `complementDisk`.

A complete understanding of inner classes is given in Sec. 12.4. But you do not need that complete understanding to continue here.

Class `MouseEvents` extends class `MouseInputAdapter` and overrides its method `mouseClicked`. This method is to be called when there is a mouse click on the component. Here, the method simply calls `complementDisk`, so if there was a disk, there will not be, and vice versa.

An instance of class `MouseEvents` has to be registered as a listener for the `Square`. This is done in the constructor of class `Square` using this statement:

```
this.addMouseListener(new MouseEvents());
```

That is all there is to listening to a mouse click: Write a (inner) class that has the method that responds to a mouse click and register an instance of the class as a listener.

About class MouseInputAdaptor

Class `MouseInputAdaptor` has six methods for dealing with mouse events:

1. when the mouse enters the component.
2. when the mouse leaves the component.
3. when the mouse is pressed on the component.
4. when the mouse is released on the component.
5. when the mouse is clicked on the component.
6. when the mouse is dragged beginning in the component.

These methods do not do anything unless you override them. For most simple GUI applications, `mouseClicked` is the only method you need to define.

17.4.3   Mouse events: class MouseDemo

The GUI window (in all three states) of Fig. 17.15 is an instance of class `MouseDemo` of Fig. 17.17. It makes use of class `Square`. We discuss `MouseDemo`.

Three fields, `leftColumn`, `b00`, and `b01`, are initialized with values that make up the two lefthand boxes of the GUI. Similarly, fields `rightColumn`, `b10`, and `b11` make up the two righthand boxes. There are two other fields: `Button jb` and and the horizontal box b that contain vertical boxes `leftColumn` and `rightColumn`.

Now look at the constructor of class `MouseDemo`. After the superconstructor is called, the following happens:

Obtain the class in Fig. 17.16 from lesson page 17-4.

1. The left column of boxes is created and added to `Box b`.
2. The right column of boxes is created and added to `Box b`.
3. Horizontal box b and button jb are added to the content pane.
4. A button listener is registered with button `jb` (we look at this later).
5. The `JFrame` is packed.
6. The `JFrame` is fixed so that it cannot be resized.

Registering a button listener

Button `jb`, the initialize button, needs a listener. Recall that to handle a click of a mouse button, a method `actionPerformed` has to be written and an object that contains this method has to be registered with the button, using the button's method `addActionListener`.

Class `MouseDemo` has an inner class, which provides method `actionPerformed`. This class is written as an inner class so that the method can call methods `clearDisk` of the four squares to remove any pink disks on them —notice the four calls in the body of method `actionPerformed`.

Step 4 in the list above registers an instance of this class with button `jb`, using the statement:

```
jb.addActionListener(new ButtonListener());
```

This concludes our discussion of class `MouseDemo`. Looked at as a whole, it can seem quite daunting. But broken down into its constituent pieces, it is quite logical and reasonable. We urge you to get a copy of these classes from the CD and experiment with them to see that the clicking of buttons really works.

Listening to the Squares in class MouseDemo

We placed the listener for mouse events on a square in class `Square`. This was easier because, in the `Square` constructor, we had to register only one mouse listener (although that registration happens whenever an instance is created).

Registering the mouse listeners in class `MouseDemo` is also possible. It has the disadvantage that a listener for each `Square` must be registered separately. It has the advantage that only class `MouseDemo` knows the precise location of each `Square`, and this information may be necessary when processing some mouse events, like mouse drags and releases. We do not explore this issue further.

17.4.4   Listening to other components

Listening to other components besides buttons and mouse clicks is similar to listening to buttons. One registers a listener with that component. Therefore, we do not discuss listening to other components in this paper text.

However, page 17-4 of the *ProgramLive* CD has footnotes that discuss:

1. Listening to a return/enter key-press in a text field
2. Listening to a `JList`
3. Listening to a `JSlider`
4. Listening to a `JColorChooser`
5. Listening to a `JComboBox`
6. Listening to a `JCheckBox`
7. Listening to a `RadioButton`

Further, the *ProgramLive* CD contains programs that demo most of these tasks. They can be obtained from the CD from footnotes on lesson page 17-4.

If you are designing a GUI that requires listening to one of the above components, obtain the corresponding demo program from the *ProgramLive* CD and use it as an example.

17.4.4   Using several listeners

A prime goal in designing a program is to place distinct tasks in different modules, thus *separating your concerns*. Appropriately isolating different tasks can simplify development, debugging, and later maintenance. For example, when changing the program later because of a change in specification, it will be easier to identify the modules that need changing and change them.

The system for listening to events in Java helps us isolate different tasks in different modules (in this case, different listeners). It is possible to register several listeners for the same event, and all of them will be called when that event happens —*in the reverse order in which they were registered*.

Activity 17-4.5 of the *ProgramLive* CD describes a program that has three listeners for a button press or a return/enter key-press in a text field. When the button is pressed or the return/enter key is pressed, three things happen:

> Obtain the class discussed in Activity 17.4.5 from lesson page 17-4.

1. An upper-case version of the text field is appended to a text area.
2. The text field is appended to an output file.
3. The text field is cleared.

Each of these tasks is handled by a different listener —but each listener responds to the same event.

17.5   Dialog windows

> Lesson page 17-5

In some situations, it is useful to pop up a window that asks the user for some information, wait for the information, and then proceed depending upon what the information is. Section 5.7.2 shows how to use a `JFileChooser` to request a file to read/write from the user. Here, we look at class `JOptionPane`, which provides some standard dialog windows, and class `JDialog`, which you can use to build your own dialog window from scratch.

17.5.1 Class JOptionPane

Class `JOptionPane`, in package `javax.swing`, provides several static methods for creating and showing different kinds of dialog windows. We look at four of the methods here: `showMessageDialog`, `showInputDialog`, `showConfirmDialog`, and `showOptionDialog`.

Method showMessageDialog

Activity
17-5.1

Execution of the method call shown below causes the dialog window on the left of Fig. 17.18 to appear on your monitor:

```
JOptionPane.showMessageDialog(
    null,
    "Division by 0",
    "arithmetic error",
    JOptionPane.ERROR_MESSAGE);
```

The call has four arguments. The first argument, the *parent window*, is explained later. The second is the *message* of the dialog window. The third is the *title* of the dialog window. The fourth determines the way the dialog window looks.

There are four other possibilities for the fourth argument:

- `JOptionPane.`INFORMATION_MESSAGE
- `JOptionPane.`WARNING_MESSAGE
- `JOptionPane.`QUESTION_MESSAGE
- `JOptionPane.`PLAIN_MESSAGE

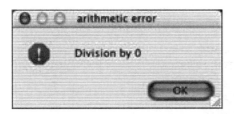
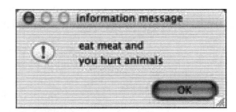

Figure 17.18: JOptionPanes

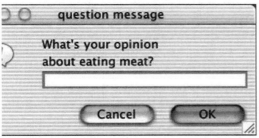
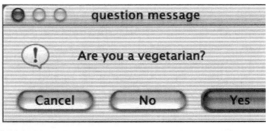

Figure 17.19: A `showInputDialog` window and a `showConfirmDialog` window

As another example, the right dialog window in Fig. 17.8 was created with fourth argument JOptionPane.INFORMATION_MESSAGE.

Modal windows

These dialog windows are *modal* dialog windows. This means that, when they are shown, they capture the focus, and clicking on other windows belonging to this execution will have no effect. You must close this window before anything else can happen in the program.

The first argument, the parent

The first argument in calls to showMessageDialog is called the *parent window* of the dialog window. If the first argument is **null**, the dialog window appears in the center of the monitor. However, suppose the first argument is the name window (say) of some window that is already showing on the monitor. Then, when the dialog window is created and shown, it is shown in front of window window.

Function showInputDialog

String function JOptionPane.showInputDialog displays a modal dialog window with a message and returns text typed by the user. An example window appears to the left in Fig. 17.19. A call has four parameters:

1. The *parent* (as with method showMessageDialog).
2. The message (a String). In the example, it is "What's your opinion about eating meat?".
3. The title (a String). In the example, it is: "question message".
4. The style of the window, which tells what picture to put in the window. It is one of the following constants of JOptionPane:

   JOptionPane.ERROR_MESSAGE
   JOptionPane.INFORMATION_MESSAGE
   JOptionPane.WARNING_MESSAGE
   JOptionPane.QUESTION_MESSAGE
   JOptionPane.PLAIN_MESSAGE

Figure 17.20:   A showOptionDialog window

The result of a call is as follows: If the user hits the cancel button, **null** is the result. If the user clicks the OK button, the result is the contents of the text field.

Function showConfirmDialog

Function JOptionPane.showConfirmDialog displays a modal dialog window with a message and returns an **int**, depending on what button was clicked. An example window appears to the right in Fig. 17.19.

We explain only the version that has five parameters. Here they are:

1. The *parent* (as with method showMessageDialog).
2. The message. In the example, it is "Are you a vegetarian?".
3. The title. In the example, it is: "question message".
4. Description of the buttons that appear in window. In the example, constant JOptionPane.YES_NO_CANCEL_OPTION was used. Here are the possible constants:

   JOptionPane.YES_NO_OPTION
   JOptionPane.YES_NO_CANCEL_OPTION
   JOptionPane.OK_CANCEL_OPTION
   JOptionPane.DEFAULT_OPTION (gives a single button, OK)

5. The style of the window, which tells what picture to put in the window. This is one of the following JOptionPane constants:

   JOptionPane.ERROR_MESSAGE
   JOptionPane.INFORMATION_MESSAGE
   JOptionPane.WARNING_MESSAGE
   JOptionPane.QUESTION_MESSAGE
   JOptionPane.PLAIN_MESSAGE

The result of a call is one of the following JOptionPane constants:

   JOptionPane.YES_OPTION
   JOptionPane.NO_OPTION
   JOptionPane.CANCEL_OPTION
   JOptionPane.OK_OPTION
   JOptionPane.CLOSED_OPTION

Function showOptionDialog

Function JOptionPane.showOptionDialog displays a modal dialog window with a message and returns an **int**, depending on what button was clicked. The caller gives the buttons that appear in the window. An example dialog window appears in Fig. 17.20.

We explain the version of the function that has these seven parameters:

1. The *parent* (as with method showMessageDialog).

Activity 17-5.2

Activity 17-5.2

2. The message (a `String`). In the example, it is `"Are you a vegetari-an?"`.

3. The title (a `String`). In the example, it is: `"question message"`.

4. Defines what buttons appear in the window if the sixth parameter is **null**. We always use 0 for the corresponding argument.

5. The style of the window, which tells what picture to put in the window. This is one of the following `JOptionPane` constants:

```
JOptionPane.ERROR_MESSAGE
JOptionPane.INFORMATION_MESSAGE
JOptionPane.WARNING_MESSAGE
JOptionPane.QUESTION_MESSAGE
JOptionPane.PLAIN_MESSAGE
```

6. An array of button titles. In Fig. 17.20, the array is `{"yes"`, `"nein"`, `"maybe"}`. Actually, this parameter is any array of objects. Array elements that are strings are turned into buttons; array elements that are not strings are simply placed in the window in some fashion.

7. The component in the array (see parameter 6) that should be highlighted when the window appears. In this example, `"nein"`. Striking the enter key is equivalent to clicking this button.

The result of a call is the index in the button array of the button that was clicked or, if the close button was clicked, value `JOptionPane.CLOSED_OPTION`.

17.5.2 Class JDialog

An instance of class `JDialog` is a bare window that can be used to create a dialog with the user. As with a `JFrame`, you can add whatever components you want to its content pane and listen to them. And, as with all the methods discussed in Sec. 17.5.1 on `JOptionPanes`, you can define the parent frame and title.

You also have the ability to make the window non-modal, which means that other processing can go on while the dialog window is visible on the monitor, which you cannot do using the `JOptionPane` methods.

To find out more about `JDialog`, look at the Java API specs for it. Look also at the tutorial for it that is referenced in the web page for lesson 17 on the *ProgramLive* CD.

17.6 Key concepts

• **GUI**. A *GUI* is a graphical user-interface. In Java, GUIs are developed using classes in the older package `java.awt` and the newer package `javax.swing`.

• **Top-level windows**. The classes whose instances can be independent windows are: `Window`, `JWindow`, `Frame`, `JFrame`, and `JDialog` (or their subclasses).

• **Containers and components**. A *container* is an instance of a class that can contain components (like buttons and text fields). A *component* is an instance of a class that can be placed in a container. Panel, JPanel, and Box are examples of components that are themselves containers. Using these three, one can nest components to any level.

• **Basic components**. The basic components are labels, buttons, text fields, text areas, checkboxes, radio buttons, combo boxes, lists, and sliders.

• **Layout managers**. A *layout manager* for a container is an instance of a class that takes care of "laying out" the components that have been added to the container. Each container has a layout manager associated with it. Each different kind of layout manager uses different rules for laying out the components. The primary layout-manager classes are BorderLayout, FlowLayout, and BoxLayout, but there are others.

• **Graphics**. An instance of container class JPanel has a method paint, which can be used to draw on the panel using methods of class Graphics.

• **Listening to a GUI**. In order to listen to an event like a mouse click, a click of a button, or the press of the enter/return key in a text field, an instance of a class that implements ActionListener has to be registered with the component on which the event takes place. The instance of the class needs a method action-Performed, which processes the event.

• **Dialog windows**. Class JOptionPane has several methods that make it easy to display a modal window on the monitor, wait for the user to close it, and then retrieve the user's response.

• **Lightweight versus heavyweight**. Top-level windows are *heavyweight* —they have associated "peers", written in machine language, that do all the window drawing. Components can be heavyweight or *lightweight*, which means that they do not have such peers. All the awt components are heavyweight, but the swing components are lightweight. Mixing lightweight and heavyweight components may lead to inconsistencies and unwanted behavior in a window. So that this does not happen, try to use all swing components, or all awt components.

Exercises for Chapter 17

E1. Write (and test) a subclass of JFrame that has two components:
  • in the west, a JLabel that contains "waist size:";
  • in the east, a JTextField with initial value "34 inches".

E2. Same as exercise E1, but right-adjust the label —see Sec. 17.2.2. Drag the window to make it wider to see what happens to the label.

E3. Like exercise E1, but make the text field uneditable.

E4. Write (and test) a subclass of `JFrame` that has five components:
- in the east, a `JLabel` that contains "EAST";
- in the west, a `JLabel` that contains "WEST";
- in the north, a `JButton` that says "north";
- in the south, a `JButton` that says "south";
- in the center, a `JTextField` that initially contains "this is a text field".

Sections 17.1.2 and17.1.3 give you the necessary information.

E5. Write (and test) a subclass of `JFrame` that contains:
- a `JLabel` in the west that contains "color";
- a `JTextField` in the east that initially contains: "red";

Include a method `getTheField()` that returns the value in the `JTextField`, a method `setTheField(s)` that changes the field to `String s`, and methods `makeFieldEditable()` and `makeFieldUneditable()` with obvious meaning. Test all this in the Interactions pane of DrJava by creating and showing an instance of the subclass, calling the methods, and changing the value in the `JTextField` (by typing into the field) several times. See Sec. 17.2.2.

E6. Write (and test) a subclass of JFrame that contains:
- a JTextArea in the west that initially contains: `"The west\nwindow"` and has no scroll bars.
- a JTextArea in the east that initially contains: `"The east\nwindow"` and has scrollbars, if necessary.

Make both of the text areas 6 rows by 10 columns. Using DrJava's Interactions pane, create and show an instance of this subclass and experiment with typing text into the two text areas.

Add methods `dontWrap()` and `wrap()` to the subclass, which cause the text not to wrap and to wrap. Create and show an instance of this subclass and experiment with typing text and the wrap-nowrap methods.

See Sec. 17.2.2.

E7. Write (and test) a subclass of JFrame that contains:
- a JTextArea in the west that initially contains: `"The west\nwindow"` and has no scroll bars.
- a JTextArea in the east that initially contains: `"The east\nwindow"` and has scrollbars, if necessary.

Make both of the text areas 6 rows by 10 columns. Include methods `getWestArea()` and `getEastArea()` that return the values in the text areas and methods `setEastArea(s)` and `setWestArea(s)` that change the fields to `String s`. Test all this in the Interactions pane of DrJava by creating and showing an instance of the subclass, calling the methods, and changing the values in the text areas (by typing into them) several times. See Sec. 17.2.2.

E8. Write (and test) a subclass of `JFrame` that contains:
- a `JCheckBox` in the east, with title "rain";
- a `JRadioButton` in the west, with title "hot".

E9. Write (and test) a subclass of JFrame that contains:
- a radio button in the east, with title "rain".
- a radio button in the center, with title "cloudy".
- a radio button in the west, with title "sunny".

Group them together in a `ButtonGroup`, and make "sunny" be checked when the window is first shown. See Sec. 17.2.3.

E10. Write (and test) a subclass of `JFrame` that contains a `JComboBox` in the center. It should have these entries: "rain", "snow", "cloudy", "sunny", with "sunny" initially checked. Write a procedure `addItem(s)` that adds an item with title s to the `JCombobox`. Experiment in DrJava's Interactions pane. See Sec. 17.2.3.

E11. Write (and test) a subclass of `JFrame` that contains a `JList` with a scroll bar (if necessary) in the center. It should have these entries: "rain", "snow", "cloudy", "sunny", "fog", "hurricane", with "sunny" initially checked. Experiment with this in DrJava's Interactions pane. See Sec. 17.2.3.

E12. Write (and test) a subclass of `JFrame` that contains a `JColorChooser` in the center. Experiment with it in DrJava's Interactions pane. See Sec. 17.2.3.

E13. Write (and test) a subclass of `JFrame` that contains:
- a `JTextField` in the north, with initial value `"red"`;
- a red `JPanel` in the center, with preferred size 100 by 100 pixels.

The class should have a `String` field that initially contains `"red"`. It should have a method `newColor(s)`, which changes the text field to s and then changes the color of the `JPanel` accordingly —but only if s is one of `"red"`, `"green"`, `"pink"`, `"white"`, `"black"`, and `"magenta"`. See Sec. 17.2.4.

E14. Write (and test) a subclass of `JFrame` that contains:
- A `JPanel` in the north, which itself contains four buttons titled "one", "two", "three", "four".
- A `Box` in the south, which itself contains four buttons titled "one", "two", "three", "four".

Create and show an instance of this class. Then, experiment with it, by dragging it to make it narrower and wider. What happens to the buttons in the `JPanel`? In the `Box`? See Sec. 17.3.

E15. Write (and test) a subclass of `JFrame` that contains a `Box` in its center. This `Box` should itself contain two rows and three columns. Each entry should be a JLabel, with these titles:

```
"(a1, b2)"      "(a1, b3)"      "(a1, b4)"
"(a2, b2)"      "(a2, b3)"      "(a2, b4)
```
See Sec. 173.2.

E16. Write (and test) a `JFrame` that contains a `Box` in its center. This `Box` should itself contain three rows:
- the first row contains two `JLabel`s with titles `"left"` and `"right"`.

- the second row contains one JTextField with 5 rows and 30 columns. Put whatever you want in it.
- the third row contains three JButtons labeled "yes", "no", and "cancel". See Sec. 17.3.2.

E17. Write (and test) a subclass of JFrame that contains the two buttons as shown in Fig. 17.13. Exactly one should be enabled at any time, and clicking one of the enabled one enables the other. See Sec. 17.4.1.

E18. Write (and test) a subclass of JFrame that contains a rectangle of four buttons labeled "top-left", "top-right", "bot-left", and "bot-right". Only one should be enabled at any time, and clicking the enabled one enables the next one in clockwise order. See Sec. 17.41.

E19. Add a JLabel to the subclass of exercise E18. The label should always have the same title that the enabled button has.

E20. Add a method change(s) to the subclass of exercise E19. Parameter s has to be one of the strings "top-left", "top-right", "bot-left", and "bot-right" (if it is anything else, a call should terminate without doing anything). Change the enabled button (and the label) to the one given by s.

E21. Write (and test) a subclass of JFrame that contains a button title "rotate" in the north and a Box of three colored JPanels in the center —make them a reasonable size, through trial and error. One JPanel should be red, one white, and one blue. Whenever button rotate is clicked, the colors should rotate one position to the right —the blue becomes white, the white becomes red, and the red becomes blue.

E22. Class Square of Fig 17.16 is either green or red and may have a pink disk on it. Change the background color to be either green or pink. Then, modify the class so that it can have either a red or a black disk (or nothing) on it, as in the game of checkers. This means having suitable methods to place a disk and to remove any disk on the square.

E23. Write (and test) a subclass of JFrame that has a row of four Squares on it, as given in exercise E22. Initially, each Square should have nothing on it. Also, the subclass should have two text fields and a button. The user should be able to type a number (1, 2, 3, or 4) into the first text field, either "" or "black" or "red" into the second text field, and click the button. This should result in the designated square having either nothing, a black disk, or a red disk on it. If the user typed something else in either of these fields, no change should be made.

Appendices

These appendices cover:
   I. Issues in dealing with Java.
   II. The Java API specifications.
   III. Outline of some Java API classes.
   IV. Correctness of programs.

Appendix I

Dealing with Java

OBJECTIVES

- Learn how to install and use DrJava.
- Learn how to edit, compile, and execute programs in a terminal window.
- Learn about the use of JUnit for testing programs.
- Learn how to make a stand-alone application.
- Learn about Java error/exception messages.

INTRODUCTION

There are two methods for developing and testing Java programs. The first is to use a *command-line window*, like an MSDOS window or a Unix terminal window. Here, you use an editor, like Notepad or BBEdit or emacs or VI, to edit the .java source files. When you think the program is ready, you compile the program and execute it, using command-line (typed from the keyboard) instructions.

The second method is to use an *integrated development environment*, or *IDE*. The IDE provides a GUI (graphical user interface) that has an editor, a button to compile the program, and another button to execute the program. It may have other bells and whistles that help you test programs, debug them, and more.

There are a dozen or more popular Java IDEs: BlueJ, CodeWarrior, DrJava, Eclipse, Forte, JBuilder, JGrasp, ProjectBuilder, Visual Cafe, and many more. Search the internet for "Java IDE" and you will find a lot of them.

In this appendix, we introduce you to the use of a command-line system and to DrJava. DrJava is quite simple to use, and yet it has a powerful feature currently unmatched in other IDEs. Since it is free and small (just over 2MB), we encourage you to download it even if you already have an IDE. You can do the early exercises in this text most easily using DrJava, and you can then switch to your other IDE when you are comfortable with Java.

I.1   Java SDK

No matter which IDE you use, you will need a Java Virtual Machine (JVM) in order to run Java programs. To compile programs, you will also need a Software Development Kit (SDK) for Java. Some IDEs come with an SDK, especially the commercial ones. If you have an IDE already, check the documentation to see if it includes an SDK. Also, Mac OS X includes an SDK.

If you do not have an SDK, download it from the Sun web page. At the time of this writing, the current version of Java, 1.4.1, is available at this URL:

```
http://java.sun.com/j2se/1.4.1/download.html
```

Download the SDK (not the JRE!) for your operating system, and *carefully* follow the instructions for installing it.

I.2   DrJava

Lesson 20 of the CD contains four activities that demonstrate DrJava. These activities, using recordings, synched animation, and snapshots of the DrJava GUI, do a better job than we can do here.

DrJava is a free IDE for editing, compiling, and executing Java programs. It was developed in Java itself by the JavaPLT group at Rice University. They are still working to improve and extend it. It was designed primarily with students in mind and is easy to use, but it does have some features that advanced programmers will appreciate. It is also *open source*, which means that you can download and read the Java source code for DrJava. DrJava was written in Java!

DrJava is the simplest IDE that we have found. It provides the fastest, most intuitive way to get started with programming of any IDE that we have used. (Other IDEs have strengths that DrJava does not.) DrJava is available here:

```
http://drjava.sourceforge.net
```

Once installed, DrJava is easy to run. Suppose you downloaded drjava-stable-200300822.jar. To run it, just double-click its icon.

Alternatively, in a command line in a terminal window, type:

```
java -jar drjava-stable-20030822.jar
```

You will see a window with three areas, as shown in Fig. I.1. This is a snapshot from a Macintosh running OS X; yours may look different. We made the window as small as possible so that it fits in this book. The left pane contains a list of files that you have opened. The right pane, called the "Definitions Pane", contains the Java code for the currently-selected file. The bottom pane, called the "Interactions Pane", allows you to try out Java statements and expressions.

Does it need tools.jar? In Windows, if you had to install the SDK, DrJava may ask you where file `tools.jar` is. If you do not navigate to find it, you will not be able to compile Java programs. Look for it where you installed the SDK, probably in folder `Program Files`. Look for a folder named `j2sdk1.4.0_01` (or something similar). Inside it will be a folder `lib`, and inside `lib` should be `tools.jar`.

I.2.1   Using the Interactions Pane

The Interactions Pane has a prompt, ">". You can type Java expressions and statements at the prompt. Try it: click in the Interactions pane, type 3 + 4 * 5 and hit the return/enter key. Underneath the expression you should see the result: 23. Notice that the 23 does not have the prompt before it.

This interactive feature, missing from most IDEs, has revolutionized how we teach because we can use it to demonstrate during our lectures.

You can type as many expressions as you like, one per line, and after each one, DrJava will show you the result. You can also declare and initialize variables in the Interactions Pane:

```
int i= 4;
```

Once a variable is declared and initialized, you can use it in expressions:

```
i * (i + 7)
```

That is all you need to know to do all the exercises in Chap. 1: just type the various expression and statements at the prompt.

I.2.2   Using the Definitions Pane

To write a Java class, type this in the Definitions Pane in the upper right:

```
public class MyPoint {
    public int x;
    public int y;
}
```

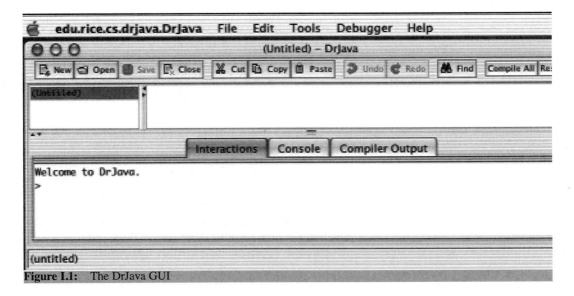

Figure I.1:   The DrJava GUI

Now save it in a file: click button "Save", and make sure the name of the file is `MyPoint.java`. The name of the file has to be the same as the name of the class plus ".java". *Capitalization is vital!* In Java, all names are case sensitive.

You also need to compile your code. Click button "Compile All"; in a few moments, you should see this:

Last compile completed successfully.

If you do not see that, you have your first syntax error. Congratulations! You will see many more syntax errors in your programming career. Get used to them; they are a fact of life for every programmer. Just go back and make sure that you typed class `MyPoint` *exactly* as we show it and that the file name is spelled correctly and has the right capitalization. Keep doing this until it compiles. Now you can use `MyPoint` in the Interactions Pane.

The lower pane has three, and sometimes four, tabs. The leftmost tab is "Interactions". Click on it to bring back the Interactions Pane.

Type the following statements and expressions. Note that when you use a semicolon, you do not see a result. Statements are terminated with semicolons; expressions are not. Expressions have values; statements do not.

```
MyPoint p= new MyPoint();
p.x= 5;
p.y= -12;
p.x
p.y
5 * (p.x + p.y)
p.x= 9;
p.x
```

You now know enough to write classes in DrJava, compile them, and test them.

The Java console

When a Java program is running, error messages are printed in a special window, the *Java console*. Also, when one of the following statements is executed, the value of the *expression* is placed in the Java console (and a new line is started, for `println`):

```
System.out.println( expression );
System.out.print( expression );
```

When using DrJava, error messages and the values of *expression*s in such `print` and `println` statements are also printed in the Interactions pane, interspersed with lines that the user types and responses from DrJava.

One of the tabs in the lower pane is titled "Console". Clicking this tab changes the lower pane into the Java console; there, you will see error messages and the values of expressions from `print` and `println` statements.

Using the Interactions history, resetting the Interactions Pane

DrJava keeps a history of lines that you have typed in the Interactions Pane. Use the up- and down-arrow keys to scroll through them.

You can remove all variables that have been declared and start afresh by pressing button Reset, in the upper right of the window. Hitting Reset does not destroy the Interactions history; it just removes all traces of execution.

Using classes from the Java APIs

If you want to use a class from one of the API packages, you have to *import* it. Import statements can be typed in the Interactions Pane. For example, type the following lines into Java (hitting return after each one), and you will see a window for the JFrame appear in the upper left corner of your monitor. You may have to resize the window to make it big enough to see the title in its title bar:

```
import javax.swing.*;
JFrame jf= new JFrame("First JFrame");
jf.show();
```

Method calls in the Interactions Pane

Click "New". This creates a new document, initially called (Untitled). In the Definitions Pane, type this class, which has one instance function and one static function:

```
public class Test {
  /** = the value 5 */
  public static int testInstance() {
    return 5;
  }

  /** = the value 6 */
  public static int testStatic() {
    return 6;
  }
}
```

Save the file with name Test.java. After the file is saved, click button Compile All. DrJava will compile the program. When it says "Last compilation completed successfully", click the Interactions tab and, in the Interactions Pane, type this expression and then hit return:

```
Test.testStatic()
```

This expression is a call to function testStatic in class Test, and you can see that it prints the value 6, as required by its specification.

Function testInstance is an instance function, so it belongs in each folder of class Test. Before we can call it, we have to have a folder. Type the following lines into the Interactions pane:

```
Test t= new Test();
t.testInstance()
```

The first line creates an instance of class `Test` and stores its name in a new variable `t`. The second line calls `t`'s function `testInstance`, which yields 5.

I.2.3   Javadoc

DrJava has a facility for creating and displaying Javadoc comments. Click the item `Javadoc` on the right of the tool bar at the top of the DrJava window. A navigation window appears, which asks you to select a folder into which the Javadoc files will be placed. We suggest that you create a new folder titled "doc" within the folder for the project you are working with and select it. After you select the folder, DrJava creates the Javadoc files — be patient; it can take a few moments. Finally, a new window will appear with the Javadoc spec in it, in the same format as the Java API specifications.

I.2.4   Using JUnit in DrJava

The application JUnit is designed to facilitate the testing of Java programs. JUnit can be used in many contexts; here, we show how to use it in DrJava.

We use as an example the testing of function `max` of class `SimpleMath` in Fig. I.2, which is assumed to be in file `SimpleMath.java`. We have deliberately

```java
public class SimpleMath {

    /** = maximum of x and y */
    public static int max(int x, int y) {
        if (x <= y)
            { return y - 1; }
        return x;
    }
}

import junit.framework.TestCase;
public class TestMax extends TestCase {
    public void testXBigger()
        { assertEquals(7, SimpleMath.max(7, 5)); }

    public void testYBigger()
        { assertEquals(5, SimpleMath.max(-5, 5)); }

    public void testXYSame()
        { assertEquals(8, SimpleMath.max(8, 8)); }
}
```

Figure I.2:   Using JUnit to test method `max`

put a mistake in the function body.

Also in Fig. I.2 is a class `TestMax`, assumed to be in file `TestMax.java`. This class contains three test cases to be used in testing method `max`. This class has the following properties:

1. It imports `junit.framework.TestCase`.

2. It extends class `TestCase`.

3. It contains three public procedures without parameters, all of whose names begin with `test`. We call these *test procedures*.

4. Each test procedure tests one test case by calling `assertEquals`. The first argument of the call is the result that is expected from the test case; the second argument, a call to method `max` that is the test case.

Suppose the two classes of Fig. I.2 are in the same directory and have been opened in DrJava and compiled. Finally, suppose that file `TestMax` is selected in DrJava and thus appears in the file window. Then, clicking button `Test` in the righthand part of the tool bar at the top of DrJava causes calls to the three test procedures to be executed. Each procedure contains a call to procedure `assert-Equals`. If the first argument of that call equals the second, nothing is printed. But if the first argument of that call does not equal the second, an error message is printed in the `Test output` pane of the lower window.

In the case of the classes of Fig. I.2, these error messages will appear in the `Test output` pane:

```
2 tests failed:
File: .../testjunit/TestMax.java  [line: 8]
Error: expected:<5> but was:<4>
File: .../testjunit/TestMax.java  [line: 12]
Error: expected:<8> but was:<7>
```

Click the mouse button on one of these error messages to highlight the line in file `TestMax` that produced the error message, so you can easily see which test case failed.

Conventions for test procedures

When button `test` in the tools bar is clicked, each test procedure is called once to exercise a test case. In class `TestMax` of Fig. I.2, each test procedure simply contains a call of `assertEquals` to perform such a test. However, the test procedure can do anything. It can have assignments, if-statements, loops — whatever is necessary to exercise the test case.

Figure I.3 describes other inherited procedures (besides `assertEquals`) that could be used to exercise test cases.

Class `TestMax` of Fig. I.2 tests a rather simple static method. When testing more complicated ones that interact in some fashion with other methods, or when testing a non-static method, it may be necessary to create objects that are to be used in several tests. So these objects may have to be created before any of the test procedures are called. To accomplish this, define this procedure in class `TestMax`:

> **protected void** setUp() { ... }

Procedure `setUp` is called before any of the procedures whose name begins with `test` are called.

Write one test procedure or many?

It is possible to include all the test cases in a single test procedure, as follows:

```
public void testAllTestCases() {
    assertEquals(7, SimpleMath.max(7, 5));
    assertEquals(5, SimpleMath.max(-5, 5));
    assertEquals(8, SimpleMath.max(8, 8));
}
```

The problem with doing this is that only one failure will be reported because a test procedure terminates as soon as *one* failure is detected and reported. In general, one wants to exercise as many test cases as possible. The guideline to follow, then, is the following:

> **Guideline:** Exercise independent test cases in different test procedures.

```
/** Display an error message if expected value ob1 does not equal ob2
    (use ob1.equals(ob2) for the test) */
assertEquals(Object ob1, Object ob2)
```

```
/** Display an error message that includes s if expected value ob1 does not equal ob2
    (use ob1.equals(ob2) for the test) */
assertEquals(String s, Object ob1, Object ob2)
```

```
/** Display a message if p1 != p2. (Methods exist for the other primitive types.) */
assertEquals(int p1, int p2)
```

```
/** Display a message that includes s if p1 != p. (also for the other primitive types)  */
assertEquals(String s, int p1, int p2)
```

```
/** Display a message that includes s if b is not true. */
assertTrue(String s, boolean b)
```

```
/** Display a message that includes s if b is not false. */
assertFalse(String s, boolean b)
```

Figure I.3: Methods of class `TestCase`

Setting variable path. If you cannot execute any of the commands `java`, `javac`, `javadoc`, or `jar`, you probably have not set your *path* correctly. We explain this for Windows 2000; older windows systems are similar.

Your system contains a variable that lists directories with executable files in them. Type "`path`" in a command-line window. The line that is printed contains path names separated by semicolons. For example, one path name may be:

```
C:\WINNT\system32
```

There should be a path that looks like this: `C:\j2sdk1.4.1_02\bin`. This is a directory called `bin` inside the directory where you installed the `sdk`. It may be different on your computer. If such a path is not there, you have to add it. Bring up the help in your Windows system, open the index, and look for "path". There, you will find instructions on appending another directory to variable path. It may be something like this (but read the instructions):

```
path  %path%;C:\j2sdk1.4.1_02\bin
```

Summary

We have shown how to use JUnit to develop test cases that can be exercised easily whenever a method is changed. What we have shown works very well for testing individual methods. JUnit also provides the ability to create *test suites —* collections of tests that can be used to test the many classes that appear in a program. A discussion of these other features is beyond the scope of this book.

I.3   Using a command-line window

We describe how to deal with Java from an MDOS window on a PC. Dealing with Java in a UNIX terminal window is similar.

In the window, navigate to the folder that contains the Java program that you want to compile and execute. Suppose the Java program is a *Java application* (see Sec. 16.1), and suppose that method `main` is in class `ClassName`.

Compiling the Java source files

To compile all the `.java` source files, type the following (`*.java` expands into a list of file names that end in `.java`). This compiles your program — it is equivalent to clicking button `Compile all` in DrJava.

```
javac *.java
```

Executing the program

To execute the program by calling static method `main` in class `ClassName`, type the command:

```
java ClassName
```

Note that the command should not include the suffix `.class` or `.java`.

Extracting Javadoc comments

Assume that you have placed Javadoc comments on classes, methods, and fields (see Appendix II.2). To extract the Javadoc comments, type the following commands:

```
mkdir doc
javadoc -d doc *java
```

(Note, in some systems, you may not have to create directory doc first; javadoc will do it for you.) Program javadoc creates in directory doc a description of your .java files in the same format as the API file specifications that you have been looking at, where the description contains all the javadoc comments.

Bring up directory doc in a window (not a command-line window). Double click on file index.html. Your browser will open with that file, and you will be able to look at the specifications of your program. It's neat!

I.4   Making a stand-alone application

A program may consist of many classes, generally in the same directory. If you want to give someone your program, you have to give them all the .class files —zip them up into a .zip file— and the someone must then unzip them. That is messy. To make things easier, you can make a *jar* file of the classes. Jar stands for *Java ARchive*; after *tar* files (*TapeARchives*) on Unix systems.

To make a jar file, get into a DOS or command-line window and navigate to the directory where the .java and .class files are. Then, type in this command:

```
jar -cf file-name.jar *.class
```

The *c* is for *create*. The *f* is for *file* and indicates that the name of the file to create follows: file-name.jar. The *.class* is expanded to name all the .class files in the directory. So, this command makes up a jar file named file-name.jar that contains all the .class files in the directory.

You still have to insert into the jar file something that tells it which class has method main. Suppose it is class MainClass. Then do the following:

(a) Make up a file x.mf that contains one line of text in it:

```
Main-class: MainClass
```

The suffix on x.mf stands for *manifest*. You do not have to use the suffix. Be sure to hit the enter key after typing the text; there must be a carriage-return or line-feed in it. You can create this file in wordpad or notepad or DrJava or any editor you want. Make sure the file is in the same directory as file file-name.jar

(b) Type this command in the window:

```
jar -umf x.mf file-name.jar
```

The *u* stands for *update*, the *m* for *manifest*, and the *f* for *file*. Since the *m* comes before the *f*, the manifest file name, x.mf, comes before the file name. This command inserts into jar file file-name.jar the fact that method main appears in class MainClass.

You can do both steps together —insert the classes and the main-class indication— by using the command:

```
jar -cmf x.mf file-name.jar *.class
```

You can email file file-name.jar to anyone, and they can run it on their computer, whether it has a Unix, Macintosh, or Windows system, as long as their system has Java in it. In some systems, you can run the program just by double-clicking on the jar file. Otherwise, type this line (include the extension .jar):

```
java -jar file-name.jar
```

If you want to see what is in jar file file-name.jar, then type this:

```
jar tvf file-name.jar
```

You can find out more about the jar command by typing simply jar.

I.5   Java error messages

Method main of the class shown below tries to print the value of 5 / 0:

```
public class Ex {
    public static void main(String[] args)
        { System.out.println(5 / 0); }
}
```

Division by 0 is not defined, so the attempt to divide by 0 is an error. Java handles this error by *throwing an exception*, which causes the program to terminate abnormally, with the following messages in the Java console:

Exception in thread "main" java.lang.ArithmeticException: / by zero
at Ex.main(Ex.java:3)

(The first part of the first line, which says that an exception occurred in thread main, may be missing, depending on which IDE you use.) The important information on the first line is that an ArithmeticException occurred, a division by zero. The second line says where the exception occurred: in method main of class Ex, on line 3 of file Ex.java.

There may be more information following the second line, depending on the IDE you use, but it is not important and you can disregard it.

The call-stack trace

When the program aborts because of an exception, you have to study the program to find out why and correct the error. The Java console messages tell you the kind of exception that occurred and the method that was being executed at the time, and this can be helpful. But it contains a bit more. To illustrate, we change the program so that the division by 0 occurs within a different method:

```java
public class Ex {
    public static void main(String[] args)
        { first(); }

    public static void first()
        { second(); }

    public static void second()
        { System.out.println( 5 / 0 ); }
}
```

Suppose method main is called. Method main calls first, which calls second, which divides by 0. The list of calls that have been started but have not completed is called the *call stack*. When the division by zero occurs, the same exception is thrown, and the following appears in the Java console:

```
java.lang.ArithmeticException: / by zero
at Ex.second(Ex.java:7)
at Ex.first(Ex.java:5)
at Ex.main(Ex.java:3)
```

As before, the first line says that an ArithmeticException occurred, which was a division by zero. The second line says that the exception occurred in second, at line 7 of file Ex.java. The third line says that second was called from first, and the fourth line says that first was called from main.

Thus, when an exception occurs:

> A message on the Java console describes the call stack: the stack of methods that have been called but have not yet completed.

You can use this stack of calls to help figure out how your program got to the point of throwing the exception.

If your program aborts with one of these errors, there is a severe problem:

```
OutOfMemoryError
InternalError
UnknownError
```

In the first case, you have to find out why your program used too much memory. In the other two cases, it is difficult to say what to do. Something caused things to become really messed up. Perhaps recompiling all files may help.

Appendix II

Java API and Javadoc

OBJECTIVES

- Describe how to locate and use the specifications of classes in the Java API.
- Investigate extracting specifications from annotated programs.

INTRODUCTION

The Java API specifications describe what each class is for and how it is to be used. It describes the methods and fields within a class that can be accessed and what they do. These specifications are on the world wide web, so you have to be connected to the internet to use them. You can download the specifications, but they take a lot of space. If you can usually work with a connection to the internet, you are better off doing that rather than downloading.

The Java API specifications were extracted from the Java API .java files automatically, using a program called Javadoc. You, too, can use Javadoc to extract specifications of your programs, provided you write your comments in a special manner. We show you how to do this in Sec. 2 of this Appendix.

II.1 The Java API Specifications

Where to find the Java API specifications

At the time of this writing, the Java API specifications were at this URL:

```
http://java.sun.com/j2se/1.4.1/docs/api/index.html
```

This is the specifications for Java 1.4.1. If there is a later version when you read this, browse until you find it or ask your instructor where a newer version might be. Actually, for what you are doing based on this book, you could use this version as well as a newer one; most of the changes will not affect you.

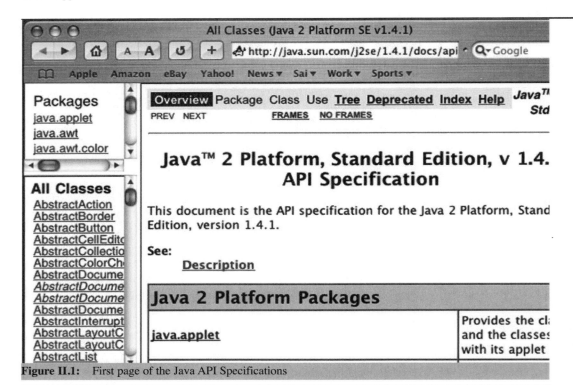

Figure II.1: First page of the Java API Specifications

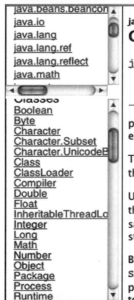

Figure II.2: The main pane shows information about class Math

Looking at the Java API specifications

Bring up the specifications in some browser. You will see something similar to the page that is displayed in Fig. II.1. The small pane on the upper left contains a list of the Java packages, and the pane on the lower left contains a list of all the classes in those packages (as well as items called *interfaces*; we do not deal with them now). Both of these panes are scrollable, so you can easily find what you are looking for (if you know what that is).

The main pane on the right contains a horizontal button bar, whose items are fairly self-explanatory. (*Deprecated* means *lessened in value*, and Java uses the term for classes and methods that have been superceded by better ones. You can still use the deprecated ones, and we do from time to time.) The lower part of the main pane contains a list of packages in the Java API.

Here is how we usually work to access the spec of a particular class, say `Math`, in package `java.lang`. First, use the scroll bar in the upper left pane to make `java.lang` visible. Click on `java.lang`. The lower left pane will change to show only the interfaces and classes in that package. Now, use the scroll bar in the lower left pane to make `Math` visible and click on it. When the main pane changes, scroll down a bit until it looks like Fig. II.2.

In the main pane, you now see a description of class `Math`. Scroll down slowly, and you will see a "summary" of the fields and of methods. These summaries tell you a little about the fields and methods of the class. For example, the

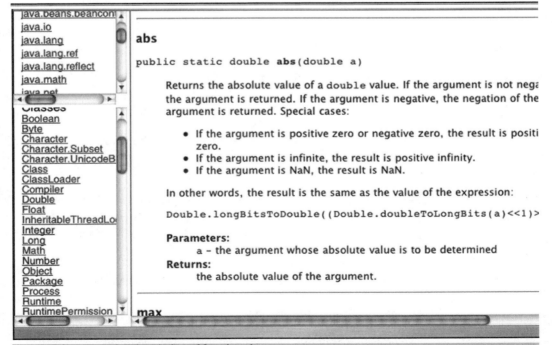

Figure II.3: Extensive description of function abs

first entry in the Method summary is for function `abs`, and we see that it has attribute **static**, that it produces a **double** value, and that it has a **double** parameter (named `a`). We also see that it returns the absolute value of a double value:

Method Summary	
static double	**abs**(double a) Returns the absolute value of a `double` value.
static float	**abs**(float a) Returns the absolute value of a `float` value.

There is a second function with the same name, which returns a **float** value.

Click on the underlined word `abs`, which is a link to another part of the same web page. The main pane changes to display a more extensive description of the method, as shown in Fig. II.3. This description even tells you what "absolute value" means.

What else can you do?

We have shown you the basic ideas of looking at specifications of classes and methods. There are a few other things you can do using the icons at the top of the web page. For example, clicking `Index` will bring up a page that contains an alphabetical listing of all the packages, classes, interfaces, methods, and fields in the API packages.

Also, if you do not like frames, click the NO FRAMES link.

Experiment with all the different features, in order to get a good idea what is available in the Java API specifications. Get used to using this tool regularly, whenever you need help with some predefined Java class.

II.2   Javadoc

You can extract specifications from your program if you annotate the program appropriately. This requires placing *Javadoc comments* —comments of the form:

```
/** ... */
```

in appropriate places. The first sentence of the comment (everything up to and including the first period ".") is used in the summary portions of the Javadoc documentation. The whole comment (without the comment delimiters) appears in the detailed portions of the Javadoc documentation.

Since Javadoc documentation is meant mainly for users of classes, Javadoc generally extracts specifications only for public classes, methods, and fields, — those that the user can use. Therefore, such public entities are the prime targets for Javadoc comments. However, it is possible to set a switch that forces Javadoc to extract comments from private entities as well.

We now discuss briefly the placement of Javadoc comments.

1. Before each class. Place a Javadoc comment that explains what an instance of the class is. For example:

/** An instance of the class is a shape, like a polygon. */

You can, of course, place a lot more details in this Javadoc comment. These details can give more information on each instance and, more importantly, explain how to use the class, give the author and date finished, and so on. Look at the Java API specifications to get some idea on this comment.

2. Before each method. Place a Javadoc comment that specifies the method. Method specifications are discussed in Sec. 13.3.

3. Before each declaration of a variable in the class. Place a Javadoc comment that describes the meaning of the variable, as discussed in Sec. 13.4.

Extracting Javadoc comments

The end of Appendix I.2 contains instructions for extracting Javadoc comments when using DrJava. Appendix I.3 contains instructions for extracting Javadoc comments in a command-line window or MDOS window.

Appendix **III**

Number Systems and Logarithms

OBJECTIVES

- Learn the binary, octal, decimal, and hexadecimal number systems.
- Be able to abbreviate binary numbers as octal or hexadecimal numbers.
- Be able to convert an **int** to its binary representation and back.
- Understand the basics of base-2 logarithms.

INTRODUCTION

In Sec 1.1, we introduced briefly binary, octal, decimal, and hexadecimal systems. The binary number system was said to be important because computers store integers using binary. But binary numbers —and base-2 logarithms, which we explain in this Appendix— arise in more ways than simply the storage of integers. For example, they arise in the explanation of the running time of many algorithms, such as exponentiation x^y, binary search, and quick sort.

We explain these number systems in more detail, showing how one can convert an integer from one number system to another. With regard to logarithms, we explain them only enough so that the running times of various algorithms can be understood, and we keep the explanation simple.

III.1   Number systems

Below, we show the "digits" that are used in counting in four number systems:

```
binary:        0 1
octal:         0 1 2 3 4 5 6 7
decimal:       0 1 2 3 4 5 6 7 8 9
hexadecimal:   0 1 2 3 4 5 6 7 8 9 A B C D E F
```

The number of digits used is called the *base* of the number system. The binary system has base 2; the octal system, base 8; the decimal system, base 10; and the hexadecimal system, base 16. In the hexadecimal system, we run out of the usual one-character digits so we use the first six capital letters of the alphabet for the last six digits.

Each of these systems uses a *positional notation* to represent the integers. For example, consider the decimal number 536, which, to make clear that a base-10 number is meant, we write as:

$$(536)_{10}$$

The 6 is in the *units* position, the 3 is in the *tens* position, and the 5 is in the *hundreds* position. This number is a representation for the quantity

$$5*10^2 + 3*10^1 + 6*10^0$$

Each of the digits 5, 3, and 6 is a base-10 digit, i.e. is in the range $0..9$. A k-digit decimal integer in the form $d_{k-1}...d_2d_1d_0$, where each d_i is in the range $0..9$ and d_{k-1} is not 0, represents the integer:

$$d_{k-1}*10^{k-1} + ... + d_1*10^1 + d_0*10^0$$

Here is an integer in the binary, or the base-2, number system:

decimal	octal	hexadecimal	binary	power of 2
0	0	0	0	
1	1	1	1	2^0
2	2	2	10	2^1
3	3	3	11	
4	4	4	100	2^2
5	5	5	101	
6	6	6	110	
7	7	7	111	
8	10	8	1000	2^3
9	11	9	1001	
10	12	A	1010	
11	13	B	1011	
12	14	C	1100	
13	15	D	1101	
14	16	E	1110	
15	17	F	1111	
16	20	10	10000	2^4
20	24	14	10100	
64	80	40	1000000	2^6

Figure III.1: Integers in four number systems

$$(10110)_2$$

The base is 2. The rightmost digit (or bit), 0, is in the *units* position, the 1 to its left is in the *twos* position, the 1 to its left is in the *fours* position, the 0 to its left is in the *eights* position, and the leading 1 is in the *sixteens* position. Because the base is 2, this number is a representation for the integer that is the value of this expression:

$$1*2^4 + 0*2^3 + 1*2^2 + 1*2^1 + 0*2^0$$

In general, a positive integer in the base 2 system has the form

$$(d_{k-1}\ldots d_1 d_0)_2,$$

where each d_i is either 0 or 1 and $d_{k-1} = 1$. Thus, k is the number of bits needed to represent the integer without leading zeros. The value $(d_{k-1}\ldots d_1 d_0)_2$ is:

$$d_{k-1}*2^{k-1} + \ldots + d_1*2^1 + d_0*2^0,$$

i.e.

$$\sum_{i \text{ in } 0..k-1} d_i*2^i$$

In keeping with this representation, we represent zero by k = 0, i.e. with 0 bits.

The connection between binary, octal, and hexadecimal

Below, we show the first `eight` integers in binary and, underneath them, their representation in octal:

000	001	010	011	100	101	110	111	(binary)
0	1	2	3	4	5	6	7	(octal)

Based on this description, you can see that to produce the octal representation from the binary representation, just replace each sequence of three bits (starting with the least significant) by its octal representation. For example:

$(101011)_2$	is	$(53)_8$
$(1110101111)_2$	is	$(1657)_8$

In the same way, we can translate from binary to hexadecimal by replacing each four-bit segment (starting with the least-significant bit, i.e. starting at the right) by its one-character hexadecimal equivalent. Here are examples:

$(1011)_2$	is	$(B)_{16}$
$(101011)_2$	is	$(2B)_{16}$
$(1011001110101111)_2$	is	$(B3AF)_{16}$

We often write numbers in hexadecimal rather than binary notation, even though they are maintained in binary in a computer, because the hexadecimal notation is more compact and easy to read and because we can easily translate from one notation to the other.

For example, in a Java program, we can use the Unicode literal `'\u0041'` to represent the character 'A' because $(0041)_{16}$ is the hexadecimal representation of the integer $(65)_{10}$ that represents the character A, but in the computer, this is maintained as the binary integer $(1000001)_2$.

Maintaining the binary representation in an array

When we keep the binary representation of a nonnegative integer n in an array d with the minimum number of elements, we place bit d_0 in element d[0], d_1 in d[1], and so on. Thus, we can write:

$$n = \sum_{i \text{ in } 0..d.length-1} d[i]*2^i$$

This means that if n = 0, the array has 0 elements —yes, in Java, you can create an array with 0 elements. If n = 8, array d is {0, 0, 0, 1} —our conventional way of writing the array puts the least significant bit first, so we have to look at the array in reverse to see it as a binary integer: 1000.

Converting an integer to base 2

Suppose **int** variable n contains a non-negative integer. We write a function that produces the binary representation of n in an array d of exactly the right length. Thus, each bit d_i shown above will be in array element d[i]. We investigate how to calculate the bits of the binary representation of n > 0, where:

$$n = d_{k-1}*2^{k-1} + \ldots + d_1*2^1 + d_0*2^0$$

From this formula, we see that:

$$n \% 2 = d_0$$

```
/** = an array d[0..] that contains exactly the binary representation of n (n ≥ 0) */
public static int[] IntToBinary(int n) {
    int[] d= new int[32];
    int x= 0;
    int k= 0;

    // inv: the binary representation of n is:
    //      the binary representation of x followed by the reverse of b[0..k-1]
    while (x != 0) {
        d[k]= x % 2;
        x= x / 2;
        k= k + 1;
    }

    int[] dc= new int[k];
    System.arraycopy(d, 0, dc, 0, k);
    return dc;
}
```

Figure 1II.2: Function `IntToBinary`

and

$$n/2 = d_{k-1}*2^{k-2} + \ldots + d_1*2^0$$

Therefore, the binary representation of n is:

the binary representation of n / 2 followed by the bit n % 2.

We can then find the next bit d_1 in the same way from n / 2. This gives us the idea for a loop invariant. We introduce a variable x and use the invariant:

invariant: the binary representation of n is:
the binary rep. of x followed by the reverse of d[0..k-1]

The function is in Fig. III.2. Initially, we don't know how many bits there are in the representation of n. Therefore, an array of the largest size possible is created and used. We know the maximum size, 31, because the parameter is an **int**. Then, at the end of the function body, we create an array of the right size and copy the digits into this new array. Note that if n = 0, then k = 0 at the end, and we are creating an array of 0 elements and copying 0 elements into it.

Converting from base 2 to an int

In Fig. III.3, we present a function to compute n from its binary representation in an array. The value of n is given by:

$$n = \sum_{i \text{ in } 0..d.length-1} d[i]*2^i$$

The formula for n is a polynomial whose coefficients are in array d, and n is most efficiently calculated using a method called *Horner's scheme*. To see this scheme, write the polynomial as:

$$d[0] * 2^0 + d[1] * 2^1 + d[2] * 2^2 + \ldots + d[3] * 2^3 + \ldots$$

and factor out multiples of 2:

$$d[0] + 2 * (d[1] + 2 * (d[2] + 2 * (d[3] + \ldots)))$$

```
/** = the integer whose binary representation is in array d */
public static int BinaryToInt(int[] d) {
    int x= 0;
    int k= d.length;
    // inv: 0 <= k <= b.length and
    //      x = d[k] + 2*(d[k + 1] + 2 * (d[k + 2] + 2 * (d[k + 3] + …)))
    while (k != 0) {
        k= k - 1;
        x= x * 2 + d[k];
    }
    return x;
}
```

Figure III.3: Function BinaryToInt

Now, we can compute this formula from the inside out, maintaining always the following value x, for some k:

```
x = d[k] + 2* (d[k+1] + 2 * (d[k+2] + 2* (d[k+3] + …)))
```

The elements of d that appear in this formula are d[k..d.length-1]. If k = d.length, no elements of d are involved in the sum, and x is 0.

III.2 Base-2 logarithms

Figure III.4 contains the first five powers of two. The first column gives the integers in base 10; the second column, the integers written as a power of two; and the third column, the integers written in binary. You can see a general rule for writing powers of two in binary: the integer 2^n is 1 followed by n zeros.

For a positive integer 2^n, n is called the *base-2 logarithm of* n, written $\log_2$ n, or, when it is clear from the context, simply as log n. The last column of Fig. III.4 gives the logarithms of the first five powers of 2.

We can define *logarithm* in another way:

For an integer $k = 2^n$, log k is the number of times you have to multiply 2 by itself to get k.

We have described logarithms using examples that were powers of 2, but log k is defined for any positive number k. For example: log 12 is 3.5849625007211565... because:

$$12 = 2^{3.5849625007211565...}$$

However, in this book, we never require calculation of logarithms of arbitrary numbers, and if you understand logarithms only for powers of 2, that is fine.

integer	as a power of 2	in binary	logarithm
1	2^0	1	0
2	2^1	10	1
4	2^2	100	2
8	2^3	1000	3
16	2^4	10000	4

Figure III.4: Powers of 2 and their logarithms

Appendix **IV**

Correctness of Programs

OBJECTIVES

- Outline the basic ideas of proving a sequence of statements correct.
- Outline how to develop a program and its proof hand in hand, with the proof ideas leading the way.

INTRODUCTION

In this appendix, we show how to specify a program segment in terms of a precondition and postcondition. We then look at how the assignment statement, if-statement, and loop can be defined —not in terms of how they are executed but in terms of when a precondition-statement-postcondition triple {Q} S {R} is true. We discuss how these ideas can be used to develop sequences of statements, with the proof ideas leading the way.

We use the boolean implication operator => (which will be defined at the appropriate time). We also introduce the notion of an *axiom*. An axiom is a basic true-false statement that we assume to be true —it is a postulate, a theorem accepted without proof. Also, we will introduce *inference rules*, which are used to generate new theorems from old ones.

We confine our attention to the empty statement, the assignment statement, the conditional statement, and the while-loop.

A major principle is that the task is not to prove an existing program correct but to develop a program and its proof hand-in-hand —with the proof ideas leading the way. A second principle is that parts of a program can be *calculated*, rather than guessed. Most of our examples are necessarily very simple, in order to explain the ideas. But see Sec. IV.6 for a real illustration of the power of the methodology.

While the ideas concerning program correctness may be formal, they can (and perhaps should) be utilized in an informal manner in most cases. In fact, we do use them all the time when we develop an invariant for a loop from its specification and then develop the loop from the invariant, as shown in Chap. 7.

This material necessarily is terse and compact. It is not a tutorial but a brief summary of the material. For more information, turn to a text like *The Science of Programming*, by David Gries (Springer-Verlag, 1981).

IV.1   Hoare triples

Recall from Sec. 2.6.2 that an *assertion* is simply a true-false statement placed before or after a statement in a program, with the intent that it should be true at that place. An assertion placed before a statement is a precondition of the statement; an assertion placed after the statement is a postcondition of the statement. For example, consider the following:

```
{x = 0}
x= x + 1;
{x > 0}
```

In this appendix, we write assertions within bold braces. The field of formal development of programs uses plain braces { and }, but they cannot be used here because they already have a meaning in Java. We could place the assertion within comment symbols, but this gets too cumbersome.

Such an assertion-statement-assertion triple is called a *Hoare triple*, after Tony Hoare, who invented the notation in about 1969. It has this meaning:

> Suppose the precondition (in the above case, x = 0) is true and the statement (x= x + 1;) is executed. Then, execution is guaranteed to terminate, and when it does, the postcondition (x > 0) will be true.

Note that the Hoare triple is itself a true-false statement. We can write false (or erroneous) ones. Below, we give some Hoare-triples and indicate whether they are true or not.

{x = 0}   x= x − 1;   {x < 0}
This triple is **true**.

{x = 0}   x= x − 1;   {x = 0}
This triple is **false**.

{true}   if (x > y)   Swap x and y **{** x ≤ y**}**
This triple is **true**.

{false}   x= 1;   {x = 0}
This triple is **true**. In no state is **false** true. Hence, in every state in which the precondition is true (there are none), execution terminates with the postcondition true. If the precondition is **false**, the postcondition can be anything.

`{x > 0}` **while** `(x > 0)` `x= x+1;` `{x = 0}`
This triple is **false**. The statement does not terminate in all states in which the precondition is true.

`{true}` `x= 1;` `{false}`
This triple is **false**. The statement is guaranteed to terminate, but when it does, the postcondition will not be true.

`{true}` **while** `(Math.random() != .5)` `{false}`
This triple is **false**. Termination of the loop is not guaranteed.

Specification of a program segment

We can use the Hoare triple to specify what a program segment —say, a sequence of statements— is supposed to do. Generally, we also have to say what variables the program segment may or should change. Here are examples. Each example specifies the statement by giving a command that says what it should do and then writes the specification as a Hoare triple.

1. Specification of a statement s: Given $y > 0$, store x^y in z. In other words, write a program segment S that satisfies the following Hoare triple, where S changes only z (S may, of course, change local variables declared in it):

$$\{y \geq 0\} \quad S \quad \{z = x^y\}$$

2. Specification of a statement s: Set z to the maximum of x and y. In other words, write S to store in z so that:

$$\{\text{true}\} \quad S \quad \{z = \max(x, y)\}$$

3. Specification of a program s: Sort array b. The specification:

$$\{\text{true}\} \quad S \quad \{b \text{ is in ascending order}\}$$

is not completely satisfactory because S could simply set all elements of array b to 0. We could say in English that S may only swap elements of b. But to place the requirement that S only permute the elements of b in the Hoare triple itself, do the following. First, introduce boolean function `perm(b, B)` with definition:

`perm(b, c)` = "array b is a permutation of array c"

Then, write the Hoare triple as:

$$\{\text{perm(b, B)}\} \quad S \quad \{\text{perm(b, B) and } b \text{ is in ascending order}\}$$

Here, B is taken to be a virtual constant —meaning that it cannot be used in statement S, so it cannot be changed. The specification says that if b is a permutation of some array B, then after execution of S, b is still a permutation of B and, furthermore, b is in ascending order.

4. Specification of a program s: Swap x and y, if necessary, to truthify $x \leq y$. We use two virtual constants X and Y:

$\{\text{perm}(\{x, y\}, \{X, Y\})\}$ S $\{\text{perm}(\{x, y\}, \{X, Y\})$ and $x \le y\}$

5. Specification of a program s. Print x on the Java console, followed by a line feed. We can write this as a Hoare triple if we use a String variable javaConsole (say) to denote the Java console. Again using a virtual constant, we have:

$\{\text{javaConsole} = \text{JV}\}$ S $\{\text{javaConsole} = \text{JV} + x + \text{"\textbackslash n"}\}$

This example shows how we can deal with statements that print on the Java console or some file.

IV.2   Two inference rules

Suppose we know that the following Hoare triple is true:

$\{x \ge 0\}$ S $\{y = x$ and $z = x{+}1\}$

Then, we can also conclude that statement S does its job in an initial state in which x = 0 and in a final state in which z = x+1:

$\{x = 0\}$ S $\{y = x$ and $z = x{+}1\}$
$\{x \ge 0\}$ S $\{z = x{+}1\}$

That is, we can replace the precondition by something that implies it, and we can replace the postcondition by something that it implies. We might write this as:

$\{x = 0\}$
$\{x \ge 0\}$
S
$\{y = x$ and $z = x{+}1\}$
$\{z = x{+}1\}$

Thus, if we have two adjacent assertions, the rule is that the first must imply the second, i.e. whenever the first is true, the second must be true too. We might do something like this if we are interested only in the "stronger" precondition, in this case x = 0, or the "weaker" postcondition, in this case, z = x+1.

To formalize these notions, we use the logical operator *implication operation* b => c, which is defined as follows:

Definition of implication =>

false	=> false	is	**true**
false	=> true	is	**true**
true	=> false	is	**false**
true	=> true	is	**true**

Note: Boolean expression P is stronger than boolean expression Q if P is true in fewer states than Q. We also then say that Q is weaker than P. Here is a more precise definition:

Definition of stronger/weaker: P is stronger than Q and Q is weaker than P if P => Q is always true.

An *inference rule* allows us to infer that some *conclusion* is true based on some initial *premises*. We write an inference rule in this form:

inference rule: Provided *premise 1*, *premise 2*,
we conclude: *conclusion*

For example, the first inference rule below allows us to strengthen the precondition, while the second allows us to weaken the postcondition:

Strengthen precondition rule: Provided P => Q,   {Q} S {R}
we conclude: {P} S {R}

Weaken postcondition rule: Provided R => T,   {Q} S {R}
we conclude: {Q} S {T}

IV.3   Axiomatic definition of statements

We now define the skip statement, assignment statement, sequence of statements, conditional statements, and while-loop using Hoare triples. We call the definitions *axioms* because they are "truths" that we take to hold without formal proof. This is necessarily a brief introduction, and some explanations as well as some of the nuances are left untold. We first introduce notation. The notation:

    [v\e]R

denotes a copy of assertion R in which each occurrence of variable v has been replaced by expression e. For example:

[v\v+1](v ≥ w)	is	v+1 ≥ w
[v\x+y](x*v = v)	is	x*(x+y) = (x+y)

We extend this notation to the following, to denote a copy of R in which v and w have been simultaneously replaced by expressions —extension to more than two variables is assumed as well:

    [v,w\e,f]R

denotes a copy of expression R in which occurrences of v and w have been simultaneously replaced by expressions e and f. Here are examples:

[v,w\w,v](v ≥ w)	is	w ≥ v

[x,n= x+b[n],n+1](x is the sum of b[0..n−1])
is   x+b[n] is the sum of b[0..n+1−1])
which can be rewritten as   x is the sum of b[0..n−1])

IV.3.1   Empty statement

The empty block {} does absolutely nothing, but very fast. In some languages, it can be written as **skip**. In others, a semicolon by itself denotes a skip statement. Thus:

```
x= x+1; ;
```

consists of two statements: the first increments x; the second does nothing.

We can define the **skip** as follows:

skip axiom. For all assertions R,
{R} **skip** {R}

This makes sense. If R is true, and nothing is done, then R is still true.

IV.3.2   Assignment statement

The assignment statement is defined as follows:

Assignment statement axiom. For all assertions R,
{e is well-defined and [v\e]R} v= e; {R}

At first glance, this definition looks backward; one feels that the postcondition, not the precondition, should include [v\e]R, since the assignment stores e in v. However, the definition is correct. It shows how one can compute the necessary and sufficient precondition such that execution of the assignment terminates with R true. We will give examples in a moment.

The first part of the precondition, "e is well-defined", is present in order to ensure that evaluating e does not cause an exception. Here are possible expressions e and the accompanying expression "e is well defined":

b[i]	$0 \leq i < b.length$
x / y	$y \;!= 0$
s.charAt(k)	$0 \leq k < s.length()$

One can use different versions of "e is well-defined", depending on one's needs. For example, suppose x and y have type **int**. Here are two possibilities for "x+y is well-defined". Use the first to get a general handle on correctness of a program, assuming that "God's integers" are being used; use the second when complete correctness, down to not having arithmetic overflow, is required:

(1) First alternative: **true**
(2) Second alternative: abs(x+y) $\leq$ INTEGER.MAX_VALUE

Below, we give examples of uses of the assignment statement axiom. We omit the term "e is well-defined" when it is **true**.

1. $\{0 = 0\}$ x= 0; $\{x = 0\}$

2. $\{x+1 = 0\}$ x= x+1; $\{x = 0\}$

3. $\{x + n+1 = \text{sum of } 1..n\}$ x= x + n+1; $\{x = \text{sum of } 1..n\}$

4. $\{x = \text{sum of } 1..n-1\}$ n= n-1; $\{x = \text{sum of } 1..n\}$

5. $\{b = z*x*x^y\}$ z= z*x; $\{b = z*x^y\}$

6. $\{b = z*x*x^{y-1}\}$ y= y-1; $\{b = z*x*x^y\}$

7. $\{0 = a*(2*y)^2 + b*(2*y) + c\}$ y= 2*y; $\{0 = a*y^2 + b*y + c\}$

Take a look at the following use of the assignment statement axiom:

$$\{y = 0\} \quad x= e; \quad \{y = 0\}$$

Any constant could be substituted for 0, and any variable (except x) could be substituted for y. Thus, this Hoare triple indicates that an assignment to x cannot change any other variable! No *side effects* are allowed during evaluation of e. For example, evaluation of e cannot call a function that changes a field of an object that is visible where this assignment statement is, for that would be a side effect.

A form of assignment statement axiom can be developed that caters to side effects, but it is far more complicated. If you want to use the simple assignment statement axiom that we have introduced, you cannot allow side effects.

IV.3.3 Multiple assignment statement

A favorite assignment statement among people in the formal development of programs is the *multiple assignment statement*, which allows several variables to be assigned simultaneously. The first multiple assignment below swaps the values of x and y. The second rotates the values u, v, and w. With the third, if x is 4 initially, upon termination x is 5 and y is 4:

```
x, y= y, x;
u, v, w= v, w, u;
x, y= x+1, x;
```

The multiple assignment is not a Java statement. When developing program, use of the multiple assignment along the way helps understanding and helps reduce errors. Below is the multiple-assignment definition for assignment to two variables. It extends in the obvious way to more variables.

Multiple-assignment statement axiom. For all assertions R,
$\{$e is well-defined and $[v,w\backslash e,f]R\}$ v, w= e, f; $\{R\}$

IV.3.4 Sequencing

We give an inference rule that allows us to conclude:

$$\{Q\} \quad S1; \ S2 \quad \{R\}$$

where S1 and S2 are statements. If we can find an assertion P (say) that satisfies

$$\{Q\} \ S1 \ \{P\} \quad \text{and} \quad \{P\} \ S2 \ \{R\}$$

then we know that execution of S1 begun with Q true will terminate with P true and that subsequent execution of S2 will terminate with R true. Hence, we have the inference rule:

> **Sequencing rule**: Provided $\{Q\}$ S1 $\{P\}$, $\{P\}$ S2 $\{R\}$
> we conclude: $\{Q\}$ S; S2 $\{R\}$

We give an example of the use of the sequencing rule. In fact, we use it and the assignment statement rule to prove that the following sequence swaps the values of x and y:

$$t= x; \ x= y; \ y= t;$$

Moreover, we prove this fact by starting with the postcondition and computing a precondition of the sequence, as follows. Consider postcondition R:

$$R: \ x = X \quad \text{and} \ y = Y$$

where X and Y are names of virtual constants (they cannot be used in the code). First, use the assignment rule to compute precondition P1 in $\{P1\}$ y= Y $\{R\}$:

$$\{P1: \ x = X \quad \text{and} \ t = Y\}$$
$$y= t;$$
$$\{R: \ x = X \quad \text{and} \ y = Y\}$$

Now use P1 as the postcondition for the second statement and compute its precondition P2. Finally, use P2 as the postcondition for the first statement and calculate its precondition:

$$\{Q: \ y = X \quad \text{and} \ t = Y\}$$
$$t= x;$$
$$\{P2: \ y = X \quad \text{and} \ t = Y\}$$
$$x= y;$$
$$\{P1: \ x = X \quad \text{and} \ t = Y\}$$
$$y= t;$$
$$\{R: \ x = X \quad \text{and} \ y = Y\}$$

Now use the sequencing rule to eliminate P1 and P2 and end up with:

$$\{Q: \ y = X \text{ and } t = Y\} \ t= x; \ x= y; \ y= t; \ \{R: \ x = X \text{ and } y = Y\}$$

This Hoare triple tells us that the sequence swaps the values of x and Y.

Note that we *calculated* the precondition from the sequence of statements and the postcondition. The precondition was not given to us; we calculated it. In general, we try to calculate preconditions in this fashion.

IV.3.5 Conditional statements

Consider an if-statement with a pre- and a post-condition:

```
{Q} if (B) S {R}
```

What do we need to know to see that this Hoare triple is true? First, if B is false, then S is not executed, so R must be true in the initial state. Thus, we have the premise: Q and B => R. Second, if B is true, execution of S begun with Q and B true has to make R true, so we have the premise: {Q and B} S {R}. Thus, we end up with this inference rule concerning the if-statement:

if-rule: Provided Q and B => R,   {Q and B} S {R}
we conclude: {Q} if (B) S {R}

You can see that the if-statement rule simply states what any programmer would have to do to understand that the if-statement does its job. There is nothing magic or special about it. In the same way, we have the following inference rule for the if-else statement:

if-else-rule: Provided {Q and B} S1 {R},   {Q and !B} S2 {R}
we conclude: {Q} if (B) S1 else S2 {R}

IV.3.6 The while-loop

We now define the while-loop:

```
{Q} while (B) S {R}
```

in terms of an inference rule. We need to develop some premises from which we can conclude that the above holds. This will require us to use an assertion P, which we call the *invariant* of the loop because it will be true before and after execution of repetend S. To show this, we annotate the loop as follows:

```
{Q}
{P}
while (B)
    {P && B} S {P}
{P && !B}
{R}
```

From this annotation, we can see that {Q} while (B) S {R} holds under the following conditions:

1. Q => P
2. {P && B} S {P}
3. P && !B => R
4. The loop terminates

This leads to the following inference rule:

while-rule: Provided Q => R,   {P and B} S {P},   P and !B => R,
and the loop terminates,
we conclude: {Q} **while** (B) S {R}

The last question to answer is: how do we show that the loop terminates? The only way it could not terminate is if the loop condition never became false, so we need a way to prove that it does.

A *bound function* t for a while-loop is an integer expression in the variables used by the loop that satisfies two properties:

1. Each iteration of the loop decreases t, which we formalize as:

   {P && B} tsave= t; S {t < tsave}

2. If there is another iteration to go, then t is greater than 0:

   P && B => t > 0

Bound function t is an upper bound on the number of iterations still to be performed. Each iteration decreases t by at least 1. Further, if it ever becomes 0 (or less than 0), then, because of point 2 and because P is true before and after each iteration, B is false and the loop terminates. So, we have the fact that:

termination: The loop terminates if there exists a bound function t for it.

At the beginning of this subsection, we showed the annotated loop, with invariant P written in several places, as well as assertion P && ! B. To save writing so many assertions, we abbreviate and annotate the while-loop like this:

```
{ Q }
// invariant: P:  (here we given the invariant)
// bound function: t (here we give the bound function)
while ( B )
    S
{ R }
```

This ends our discussion of the definitions of the basic statements in terms of Hoare triples. In the next section, we investigate developing programs using these definitions.

IV.4   Developing simple programs

One of the important principles is that a program and its proof should be developed hand-in-hand, with the proof ideas leading the way. Further if used properly, one can even *calculate* parts of programs, instead of trying to guess them in an *ad hoc* fashion.

This text is not the place for a full-blown discussion of developing program and proof hand-in-hand, and we limit ourselves to a few examples. In this appendix, we are trying to show some of the thought processes that could be used to solve programming problems. Necessarily, we use as examples programs that are so simple that the methods might not be needed. You may not have thought about *how* you go about writing a program segment; here, you have a chance to think about and study that process to some extent. See Sec. IV.6 for an example in which the methodology really helps.

Finding the maximum

We begin with the problem of storing the maximum of two values in a variable, i.e. we write a program segment s that satisfies the following specification:

$$\{\textbf{true}\} \quad \texttt{S} \quad \{\texttt{R: z = max(x, y)}\}$$

where R names the postcondition.

To solve this problem, we have to know what "maximum" means. One way to define it is to rewrite the postcondition as follows:

$$\texttt{R:} \quad (\texttt{z = x \&\& x} \geq \texttt{y}) \quad || \quad (\texttt{z = y \&\& y} \geq \texttt{x})$$

Now, concentrate on R and ask yourself what statement might truthify it —perhaps not in all cases, but at least in some.

There are two obvious answers: the assignments z= x; and z= y; because, according to R, z will equal x or z will equal y. We investigate using the first assignment. Will it do the job in all required cases? We can see this by *calculating* the precondition $[\texttt{z}\backslash\texttt{x}]\texttt{R}$ of $\{[\texttt{z}\backslash\texttt{x}]\texttt{R}\}$ z= x; $\{\texttt{R}\}$

$$
\begin{aligned}
&\quad [\texttt{z}\backslash\texttt{x}]\texttt{R} \\
&= \quad \text{<Definition of R; perform the substitution>} \\
&\quad (\texttt{x = x \&\& x} \geq \texttt{y}) \quad || \quad (\texttt{x = y \&\& y} \geq \texttt{x}) \\
&= \quad \text{<x = x is true; x = y \&\& y} \geq \texttt{x equals x = y>} \\
&\quad \texttt{x} \geq \texttt{y} \quad || \quad \texttt{x = y} \\
&\qquad \text{<Note that x = y => x} \geq \texttt{y>} \\
&= \texttt{x} \geq \texttt{y}
\end{aligned}
$$

Therefore, the assignment z= x; does the job if and only if x ≥ y. So, we will need an if-else statement:

> **if** (x >= y) z= x;
> **else** ?

where we still have to figure out what to do in the case x < y.

We can then perform the same kind of process with the second assignment, z= y; . However, a mathematician would simply note that, by symmetry, in the case y ≥ x, the assignment z= y; will do. Thus, we end up with the statement:

```
if (x >= y)  z= x;
else  z= y;
```

The astute reader will have noticed that we were not completely formal. And in general, we do not have to be completely formal. Use just enough formality to be convinced that the result is correct, and the harder the problem the more formality is needed!

This example brings out two important points. First, it illustrates that *programming is a goal-oriented activity*. It is the postcondition that is most important at the beginning, not the precondition. The goal, postcondition R, was what we looked at for insight in starting the development.

Second, we were able to *calculate* the if-condition, not guess at it. Of course, in this case, we could have easily guessed the if-condition, but there are situations in which calculation is a far better tool than guessing or intuition, which until now have been the programmers' main tools. In some cases, the methodology we are proposing can lead to programs that you would not have thought of without using the methodology.

Calculating an expression

Consider the following specification for a partially completed multiple assignment statement:

```
{P}  x, k= E, k+1;  {P}
```

where assertion P is:

```
P:  x = sum of squares of  0..k-1
```

Note that the precondition and postcondition are the same, and that k is being incremented. We want to know what expression E to assign to x so that this Hoare triple is true. We discuss the solution of such problems.

Using the multiple assignment statement axiom, we can place another assertion after the precondition:

```
{P} {[x,k\E,k+1]P}  x, k= E, k+1;  {P}
```

Thus, for this to be a true Hoare triple, the following must hold:

```
P  =>  [x,k\E,k+1]P
```

We can calculate E in (at least) two ways: (1) Assume that P holds and massage [x,k \ E, k+1]P into a formula for E, and (2) Massage P until it has the form [x,k \ E, k+1]P. Each method has its own situations where it seems easier. Here, let us try method (2) —the reader should try method (1):

```
        P
   =    <Definition of P>
        x = sum of squares of  0..k-1
   =    <Arrange formula so that it contains "sum of squares of
```

$$0..(k+1)-1">$$
$$x = (\text{sum of squares of } 0..(k+1)-1) - k*k$$
$$= \quad <\text{Rearrange}>$$
$$x + k*k = (\text{sum of squares of } 0..(k+1)-1)$$

The last formula has the desired form, `[x,k\E,k+1]P`, where E is x + k*k. Thus, the Hoare triple can be written as follows:

$$\{P\} \quad x, k= x + k*k, k+1; \quad \{P\}$$

In this case, we wanted to increment k and had to determine what to assign to x so that P would be maintained. We did not guess what to assign to x; we calculated it. We moved the problem away from programming into the realm of logic and arithmetic.

This problem is so simple that perhaps calculation is not necessary to solve it. However, in many cases, such calculation can save the time of repeatedly guessing and testing until one has, by chance, discovered the right expression E. An example of this appears in Sec. IV.6.

IV.5 Developing loops

Chapter 7 discusses the development of a loop:

```
{ Q }
//  invariant: P
//  bound function: t
while ( B )
    S
{ R }
```

in terms of four loopy questions:

1. How does it start? (The initialization should truthify Q.)
2. When does it end? (P && !B should imply R.)
3. How does it make progress? (Each iteration must reduce t.)
4. How does it fix the invariant? (the repetend must satisfy {P && B} S {P}.)

Each of the four loopy questions deals with one of the premises of the while-loop inference rule. Chapter 7 dealt informally with termination rather than use a bound function. So, Chap. 7 was really working with this inference rule. In Chaps. 7 and 8, many loops were developed using the four loopy questions.

Therefore, in this section, we discuss only two issues: (1) how to find invariants and (2) how to develop the repetend of a loop.

IV.5.1 Developing the invariant

Below is the fully annotated while-loop. This annotation shows us that invariant is P true before and after the loop. It is *more general* than Q and R. Thus, in developing the invariant, we seek to generalize either Q or R.

```
{Q}
{invariant: P}
{bound function: t}
while (B)
    {P && B} S {P}
{P && !B}
{R}
```

Usually, but not always, generalizing R is most useful. Here are some ways to generalize R.

Generalize R by replacing an expression by a fresh variable

We used this technique when writing a loop to process a range m..n-1 of integers, where it is assumed that m and n should not be changed. Suppose the postcondition is:

> R: integers m..n-1 have been processed

Then we replace n by a fresh variable k and get the invariant:

> P: integers m..k-1 have been processed

The loop will start with k = m, since initially no integers have been processed, and terminate with k = n. It usually helps (or is even formally necessary, usually to prove termination) to place the conjunct $m \le k \le n$ in the invariant:

> P: $m \le k \le n$ and integers m..k-1 have been processed

If we want to process the integers from highest to lowest, we replace m (instead of n) by a fresh variable and use the invariant:

> P: $m \le k \le n$ and integers h..n-1 have been processed

This is the basis for all loops that process each integer in some range m..n-1, including array algorithms like linear search, selection sort, and insertion sort.

Sometimes, we can determine what variable to use by attempting to initialize variables so that the postcondition is true. An example is in binary search. Initially, array segment b[h..k] is in ascending order, and we want to store an integer in variable i so that:

> R: b[h..i] $\le$ x < b[i+1..k]

Setting i to h-1 truthifies b[h..i] $\le$ x; setting i to k truthifies x < b[i+1..k]. We cannot do both at the same time, so we break the dependence of the formula x < b[i+1..k] on i by replacing expression i+1 by a fresh variable j and end up with this loop invariant:

P: b[h..i] ≤ x < b[j..k]

We could have replaced i instead of i+1 by j and developed the different loop; trying both, once sees later that the alternative we chose is easier to work with. Also, at some point, formally, we will need to bound i and j, and we end up using as the invariant:

P: b[h..i] ≤ x < b[j..k]   and   h-1 ≤ i < j ≤ k+1

Developing the invariant using the technique of replacing an expression by a fresh variable is usually easy, although in some cases it requires practice and experience to be able to see which expression is the better one to change.

Delete a conjunct

The boolean expression X is weaker than, or more general than, the expression X && Y. If X && Y is the desired postcondition, a possible invariant is the more general X (or the more general Y). Here we get the invariant from the postcondition by deleting a conjunct.

Generally, one decides to delete a conjunct by investigating what it takes to truthify the conjuncts of the invariant with simple assignments.

For example, consider a linear search for the index of the first value x in an array segment b[h..k-1]). The postcondition is:

R: x is not in b[h..i-1]   and   (i = k or x = b[i])

We can truthify the first conjunct using i= h;. We can truthify the second conjunct by setting i to k, but then the first conjunct will not necessarily be true. We can delete the second conjunct and use this for the invariant:

P: x is not in b[h..i-1]

Here is another example. Suppose we want to find the largest power of 2 that is at most N, for some N > 0. Here is the postcondition:

R: p is a power of 2   and   p ≤ N   and   N < 2*p

The first and second conjuncts are easy to truthify using p= 1;. The third is harder to truthify, so we delete it and end up with the invariant:

P: p is a power of 2   and   p ≤ N

Here is third example. We want to find the quotient q and remainder r when nonnegative x is divided by nonzero y. The postcondition is this:

R: x = q * y + r   and   0 ≤ r   and   r < y

The first two conjuncts are truthified by q= 0; r= x;. Taking the first two conjuncts as the invariant, we see that the purpose of the loop will be to reduce r until the third conjunct is true —of course, while maintaining invariant P:

P: x = q * y + r   and   0 ≤ r

Dealing with pictures of arrays

Most algorithms that manipulate arrays require loops of some sort, and some people prefer writing the pre- and post-conditions —and hence the invariant— using array pictures. In many cases, the invariant can be seen to be a generalization of both the pre- and the post-condition.

Here is an example. Below, we specify a sorting algorithm:

```
                       h                              k
Precondition:  b  |                 ?                   |
```

```
                       h                              k
Postcondition:  b  |             sorted                |
```

Invariant P is a generalization of the precondition, so P, drawn as a picture, needs a segment labeled "?". P is also a generalization of the postcondition, so it needs a segment labeled "sorted". Thus, we use one of the following two alternatives as the invariant. The first results in a loop that sorts from beginning to end; the second, from end to beginning. (Of course, we have to label the boundary between the two segments.):

```
                      h                              k
invariant P:  b  |     sorted       |       ?        |
```

or

```
                      h                              k
invariant P:  b  |        ?         |     sorted      |
```

This business of developing the invariant as a picture that generalizes both the pre- and the post-condition works quite well. Often it allows one to analyze different algorithms for the same problem —the algorithms being expressed as invariants— without writing a line of code.

Discussion

The three methods of developing an invariant work well in many cases. Sometimes, they are only the start of the development of a full invariant in that a simple but inefficient loop is developed from the invariant. Then, one may have to strengthen the invariant (put more information in it) to remove the inefficiencies. But that topic is beyond the scope of this appendix (although it is a neat , useful idea).

Do not expect the methods discussed above to work in all cases. Sometimes, an additional idea is needed, which is not easily seen. Sometimes, the formal definition of whatever is being manipulated will provide insight into possible invariants.

IV.5.2 Developing the repetend

The repetend of a while-loop has to do two things: make progress toward termination and keep the invariant true. Suppose we look at maintaining the invariant for insight into the development of the repetend. All we can write is:

```
{P  &&  B} skip {P}
```

because **skip** is the simplest way to maintain P, and there is little to suggest doing something else.

Thus, when beginning development of the repetend, we should first see how to make progress toward termination. Suppose making progress is done by incrementing k. The annotated repetend will be:

```
{P and B} S; k= k+1; {P}
```

where statement S is to be determined. Using the assignment statement axiom, insert the precondition of the increment:

```
{P and B} S; {[k\k+1]P} k= k+1; {P}
```

This means that S has to satisfy the specification

```
{P and B} S; {[k\k+1]P}
```

and we can now begin to develop S to satisfy it.

This is top-down programming, or stepwise refinement, at its best. We decide how to make progress; we *calculate* the specification of statement S that is required to maintain the invariant, and we develop S to satisfy its specification.

Here is an example. Suppose invariant P is:

```
P: the squares of h..k-1 have been printed
```

and progress is to be made using k= k+1;. Then S has to satisfy:

```
{the squares of h..k-1 have been printed  and B}
S;
{the squares of h..k have been printed}
```

and S is obviously System.out.println(k*k);.

Suppose the squares are being printed in reverse order, so that progress is made by decreasing h. Then the annotated sequence is:

```
{P and B} S; {[h\h-1]P} h= h-1; {P}
```

so S has to satisfy:

```
{the squares of h..k-1 have been printed  and B}
S;
{the squares of h-1..k-1 have been printed}
```

So, statement S has to print (h-1)*(h-1).

IV.6   A neat example: fusc

Consider a function f defined as follows —e.g. f(13) is 5.

```
f(0) = 0
f(1) = 1
f(2*n)   = f(n)            (for n > 0)
f(2*n+1) = f(n) + f(n+1)   (for n > 0)
```

We want a program segment S that, given N ≥ 0, calculates f(N). One idea would be to assign N to a fresh variable n and then repeatedly decrease n, maintaining some invariant, until n is 0 or 1. The first, naive, invariant would then be:

```
f(N) = f(n)
```

Indeed, if n is even, we can divide n by 2 and the invariant is maintained (since f(2n) = f(n). But if n is odd, there is no way to decrease n and keep this invariant true. The invariant is too simple.

Where do we look for inspiration in developing the invariant? The *only* possible place is the definition of f. Even a postcondition like f(N) = b (meaning b contains the answer) would not help. In Sec. IV.4, in developing a program segment to calculate max(x, y), we also had to turn to the definition of max. Here, it is the same thing: a definition provides the inspiration.

Notice that the right sides of two recursive formulas for f:

```
f(2*n)   = f(n)
f(2*n+1) = f(n) + f(n+1)
```

are linear combinations of f(n) and f(n+1):

```
f(2*n)   = 1*f(n) + 0*f(n+1)
f(2*n+1) = 1*f(n) + 1*f(n+1)
```

and this inspires us to try an invariant in which the righthand side is a (more general) linear combination of f(n) and f(n+1):

```
P: f(N)   = a*f(n) + b*f(n+1)
```

Now, we write the loop, hoping that we can make progress by halving n at each iteration —but we assume we would need two cases, depending on whether n is even or odd. We have skipped all the obvious steps of this development.

```
{N >= 0}
n= N; a= 1; b= 0;
{invariant P: f(N)   =   a*f(n) + b*f(n+1)}
while (n != 0) {
  if (n is even) n, a, b= n/2, E, F;
  else           n, a, b= n/2, G, H;
}
{f(N) = b}
```

where it remains to determine expressions E, F, G, and H. We calculate E and F, leaving G and H to the reader, using the technique given at the end of Sec. IV.4. We assume n is even and greater than 0, so n = 2*k for some k and n/2 = k, and we massage P:

```
        P
    =       <n = 2*k>
        f(N)   =   a*f(2*k) + b*f(2*k + 1)
    =       <Definition of f>
        f(N)   =   a*f(k) + b*(f(k) + f(k+1))
    =       <Rearrange>
        f(N)   =   (a+b)*f(k) + b*f(k+1)
```

This formula has the form [n,a,b \ n/2,a+b,b]P, so we can take E to be a+b and F to be b. Hence, the assignment is n,a,b= n/2,a+b,b; . The assignment to b is not needed. In the same way, we develop the multiple assignment for the else-part and end up with this program:

```
n= N; a= 1; b= 0;
{invariant P: f(N)   =   a*f(n) + b*f(n+1)}
while (n != 0) {
  if (n is even)    n, a= n/2, a+b;
  else              n, b= n/2, a+b;
}
```

As Edsger W. Dijkstra, who first developed this algorithm *in this fashion* in the 1970s and called it fusc, would have said, "Ain't it a beaut?".

Index